JAMES McCLURE

East of Gettysburg

A Gray Shadow Crosses York County, Pa.

YORK DAILY RECORD ■ YORK COUNTY HERITAGE TRUST

World Wide Web:
Part of this work can be accessed at the York Daily Record's Web site, www.ydr.com. For a wealth of information on York County's history and current historical celebrations, events and festivities, see the York County Heritage Trust's Web site, www.yorkheritage.org.

To contact the author:
E-mail jem@ydr.com, or write to James McClure, York Daily Record, P.O. Box 15122, York, Pa. 17405.

To order:
Copies of this work are available through the York County Heritage Trust, 250 E. Market St., York, Pa. 17405, 717-848-1587, www.yorkheritage.org and other York County booksellers. Also, the York Daily Record, P.O. Box 15122, York, Pa. 17405, 717-771-2000, www.ydr.com. James McClure's "Never to be Forgotten," "Nine Months in York Town" and "Almost Forgotten" can be obtained through these outlets. Videos, "Never to be Forgotten" and "Nine Months in York Town," based on the books, are available through these sources.

Copyright ©2003.
James McClure.

ISBN Number 0-9710416-4-4

Library of Congress Control number: 2002117766

McClure, James
East of Gettysburg/A Gray Shadow Crosses York County, Pa. / [Researched and written by James McClure; Edited by Kim Strong; Design, visuals by Ted Sickler]. [York, Pa.]: York Daily Record, [2003].

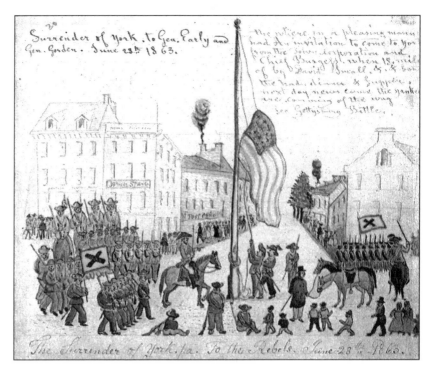

On the cover

Men in Confederate Gen. John B. Gordon's brigade take down the American flag in York's Centre Square on June 28, 1863. Thus began the rebels' two-day occupation of York, an invasion that ended with the recall of Gen. Jubal Early's division to Gettysburg. Lewis Miller, a carpenter who documented York County with his drawings, captures this scene, including children watching the dramatic event.

On the back cover

York's fathers meet the vanguard of more than 6,000 Confederate troops that occupied the borough and sites north of town. The previous day, a committee had traveled to Gen. John B. Gordon's camp, 10 miles west of York in Farmers, to work out the town's surrender. The soldiers carrying picks and shovels, in this Lewis Miller drawing, were part of the pioneer party, assigned to clear road obstructions for the following horde. Some in York believed the soldiers in the lead were coming to dig their graves.

'(Robert E.) Lee looked longingly toward that land lying north of the Potomac, a land of milk and honey, or, as events would demonstrate, a land of apple butter and oven-warm homemade bread.'

— Historian
Wilbur S. Nye

'He (rebel soldiers) would not receive as gospel the dogmas of fanatics, and so he became a "rebel." Being a rebel, he must be punished. Being punished, he resisted. Resisting, he died.'

— Confederate private
Carlton McCarthy

'We would rather give the rascals twice over what we did than have them back! Oh, I could fill sheet after sheet with all their audacious villainies. It is a matter never to be forgotten by us.'

— York resident
Cassandra Small

Contents

Credits and acknowledgments

Author: James McClure
Editor: Kim Strong
Photo/layout coordinator: Ted Sickler
Layout artists: Tracey Bisher Cullen, Samantha K. Harrold, Joanne Althoff
Copy editor: Deborah L. Hummel

Giving due credit

The author thanks the York Daily Record staff members listed above for their tireless work on this project — the fifth most members of this team have worked on.

Also, thanks to York Daily Record Editor and Publisher Dennis Hetzel for his active support of this work. And Buckner News Alliance's officers Philip F. Buckner, David B. Martens and Gail B. Brown for their interest in this and past history projects.

Thanks, too, to York Daily Record editorial assistant Loretta Martin and receptionist Donna Hollinger for helping to prepare the manuscript and York Daily Record librarians Joan McInnis and Nancy Duncan for assisting in research.

Thanks to Messiah College student Joseph McClure for preparing the index and reading the manuscript.

Michael Newsome continues to be a great encouragement on all these works.

Thanks to Della McClure and Joe, Regina and Tony for their forebearance and support.

Much of this work's research came from the York County Heritage Trust's Historical Society Library. Thanks to June Lloyd, Lila Fourhman-Shaull and Nancy Amspacher, all from the Heritage Trust staff, for their assistance and patience. The Heritage Trust has been a helpful partner on his project, as on past coordinated projects. Thanks to James Rudisill and Luther B. Sowers for reviewing the manuscript.

Much appreciation to Thomas Norton, York Newspaper Co., for his assistance.

Points of style:
In accord with the style of the day, the designation "Negro" is used in this work, except in direct quotes where the speaker's or writer's term is referenced. For simplicity, "general" is used for general officers of all ranks.

Reviewers and readers:
The following reviewers provided countless helpful suggestions: June Lloyd and Lila Fourhman-Shaull, York County Heritage Trust.

Photo credits:
York County Heritage Trust, York Daily Record, The Gazette and Daily, Hanover Public Library, Harper's Weekly, U.S. Library of Congress, U.S. National Archives, Jefferson Centennial, Hanover Chamber of Commerce, Pennsylvania State Archives, Historic York, Hanover Area Historical Society, Historical Society of Pennsylvania.

East of
Gettysburg

To the Bergeron
Family,

Greetings to you in
Florida from
hootong Rich — and
very snowy —
York County. I hope this
fuels your interest in
visiting the Petzan
Family!

Happy holidays!

Jace

12/6/03

This scene is from an earlier period but provides an an idea of what the Confederate column saw in heading along West Market Street into the heart of York on June 28, 1863.

Foreword

Farmhouse story indicative of rich tales from York County's past

The farmhouse sits not high on a hill but low in a hollow.

Farmers built many 19th-century houses in York County that way — short on view but close to water sources and shielded from the wind.

The 2 ½-story house does not boast architectural features that would attract the attention of motorists moving today along a paved road that connects with its driveway.

But the house, home to Jacob S. Altland, emerged from obscurity for a moment seven score years ago — a short day that merits a long chapter in York County's story. The farmhouse, aptly located in the village of Farmers, drew dust-covered rebel Gen. John B. Gordon, as he headed with 1,200 or more soldiers toward York.

A meeting at the farmhouse sparked a vitriolic debate in the days surrounding the Confederate Army's campaign of 1863. That invasion ended with a bloody rebel assault on Gettysburg's Cemetery Hill.

One summer night at Altland's, a delegation from the undefended Borough of York handed the town's key to Gen. Gordon.

The controversy started even before the five-man delegation left town to link up with the general from Georgia. And it's a debate that occasionally spurts out to this day. It's a disagreement that is far from resolved but nettling enough to block the view of the county's many contributions to the American Civil War.

The controversy?

Should the town's fathers have surrendered York to the rebels?

• • •

In 1863, Cassandra Small was the 34-year-old daughter of York businessman Philip Small. But the voice in her letters expressed the wonder and worry of a teenager.

Writing to cousin Lissie Latimer at the time of the surrender, she unwittingly framed the debate.

"Another one came to Uncle S. on Saturday and said, 'Well, Sam, all the people around us say you and Philip saved the town so they are going to raise a monument to you as high as the Lutheran steeple,' " she wrote. "Then it is currently reported that we entertained many of the officers, and that Uncle S. had General Early and others there. Such dreadful stories!"

Many Republican-leaning townspeople at that time and some students of the Civil War today believe that the town's fathers were too soft. Gen. Jubal Early, in command of the occupying rebel forces, would not have extracted as much from the town if he had met resistance instead of cooperation. The Confederates were under orders not to harm private property. Early was bluffing, and York's fathers fell for it.

Further, without authority, a self-appointed group of men — York's Committee of Safety — sent an admittedly sparse military guard packing. If the force had stayed, the Codorus Creek could have abetted a defense.

Simply put, if the town had shown any fight and not tracked down the rebels 10 miles out the Gettysburg Pike in Farmers to surrender, it could have preserved its honor.

But the town was virtually unprotected, came the reply. Any opposition would have resulted in destruction or extensive damage to houses and businesses. Rebels were known to fire on towns that resisted. Consider the bombardment of Wrightsville by the same bunch just hours later.

And the brash and unpredictable Gen. Jubal Early, the division commander, burned Thaddeus Stevens' ironworks in Franklin County before his men arrived on York County soil. That speaks to his regard for Robert E. Lee's warning against destruction of Northern property, not that the people in York knew about that order. You don't play poker with a surly general backed by 6,000 well-aimed rifles.

The town's fathers had the hopeless task of defending an undefended town. A deal was necessary to ensure the protection of private property, women and children.

The city fathers simply made a common-sense business decision. Honor was not at stake. York had no real defending force. Under such circumstances, it's better to live than die a hero.

• • •

The controversy would not go away.

Twenty-two years after the rebel visit, David Small's obituary appeared in The Gazette, the newspaper he published. As chief burgess, he was a member of the delegation that met with Gordon. The obituary recognized the "displeasure" Small's visit to Gordon caused but pointed out the occupation left nary a scar.

One hundred years after the invasion, disagreement simmered. A researcher looked for details in a York County library for a piece on the 100th anniversary of the invasion. A query about the surrender drew an angry denial from a librarian. The librarian argued that York did not surrender.

The researcher persisted, finding material on the event. After that, she received an icy reception any time she walked into the library.

York did not do much with that celebration anyway. The county's attention focused on major centennial celebrations in Wrightsville and Hanover, people flushed with honoring the memories of heroic townsfolk and major fighting inside their town borders.

• • •

As this controversy seethed in the background, York has been reveling in its illustrious Revolutionary War past.

The Continental Congress limped into York in late September 1777 and left with a bounce in its step nine months later. During its stay, it adopted the Articles of Confederation, ratified treaties with France and celebrated welcome news that the British had surrendered 6,000 soldiers at Saratoga, N.Y.

The adoption of the Articles and surrender at Saratoga catalyzed an alliance with France. An encouraged Congress left York on June 27 and returned to Philadelphia. The times that tried men's souls had changed to the best of times, and York has celebrated this turnaround ever since.

Eighty-five years later — on June 28 — the Confederates stepped into town, thousands of them. These were the worst of times.

At any minute, Mary C. Fisher said, Early could have given the signal to "unleash the dogs of war in our midst, and give our homes a prey to the invader."

• • •

The problem with controversy is that it often masks accomplishment.

To be sure, York placed itself in a position to attract wrath. As the generations-old saying goes, York County farmers spoke German with a Southern accent.

With strong business and family connections to the South, York's leadership could not muster political support for the Civil War, a bitter conflict that would ultimately end the insidious institution of slavery.

And residents were forewarned an unfettered rebel invasion could flaw their legacy.

"His invasion will destroy your property, will degrade you and your country," Union Gen. William B. Franklin, a native son, wrote in The Gazette before the occupation, "and if allowed to proceed without strenuous resistance, will make you objects of contempt and scorn to your country, and the remainder of the civilized world."

That said — and it's a lot — the people in Wrightsville endured a rebel bombardment and a fire that threatened to burn their town. The people of Hanover were caught in the deadly crossfire of blue and gray horsemen. No one has questioned the fortitude of the people in those boroughs, towns that are located in York County.

The county produced, by one count, more than 6,200 soldiers. And while no final count is available, the number of native sons who died from wounds and disease undoubtedly numbered in the hundreds.

York served as a transportation hub, playing host, often at personal cost, to tens of thousands of soldiers from elsewhere moving to and from battle.

Many county residents did not even take a moment to savor the Yankee victory at Gettysburg. They were too busy gathering food and supplies for the care of the wounded at the battlefield, a short 30 miles away.

York County residents were accustomed to mobilizing in such relief. During the course of the war, volunteers helped nurse more than 14,000 wounded and diseased soldiers back to health at the U.S. military hospital in town.

The four-day rebel visit to the county drained money, food, supplies and horseflesh, critical at harvest time.

These stories of York rising to its feet, rather than buckling to its knees, must be told, too.

• • •

In the past 15 years, York has increasingly recognized its Civil War past. An exhibit at a downtown visitors center now tells of the occupation. A permanent room opening at the York County Heritage Trust's Historical Society Museum culminates the Civil War comeback.

Perhaps this birth of local Civil War interest stems from growing national interest in the war or an increasing professionalism in the York County historical community.

Gerald Austin Robison concluded his 1964 master's thesis on the occupation with a sage observation.

"York had to suffer under the verbal barrage of outsiders, who constantly remind her citizens that it was the largest northern town to be occupied without resistance," he wrote. "How does a town defend itself from such attacks? It does not; it can only hope to live it down through the passage of time and future accomplishments."

Time, indeed, has passed. We're at the 140th anniversary of the occupation and counting. Meanwhile, York County's heroics in World War II demonstrated strength under fire. The York Plan pooled industrial resources to fill large defense contracts. Five hundred and seventy county residents paid the ultimate price, dying for country.

York's connections to the Revolutionary War in the 18th century and its support of World War II in the 20th have squeezed out a debatable surrender in the 19th century.

Today, people even occasionally joke about events from those days in 1863.

In doing so, they join Cassandra Small, who even after the devastation of the rebel visit could laugh with Lissie.

"Aunt Bella said the other evening, she thought it a pity someone shouldn't make an account of all of these funny things, that they would make an interesting book. We can begin to laugh now at it all; a week ago it was certainly too serious."

The realization is growing today in York County that to explore the past — to relish its successes, recognize its failings and occasionally smile about its idiosyncrasies — can be rewarding for its future.

York County's history bears many untold stories. The full story of the Confederate occupation is among its least known and understood.

If these stories are told and retold, forgotten people and landmarks of its past — including a quiet house resting unnoticed in a hollow near Farmers — will finally gain the honor and recognition due to them.

— James McClure

Prelude

'You see, it was getting a little warm down our way.'
— Confederate Gen. William "Extra Billy" Smith

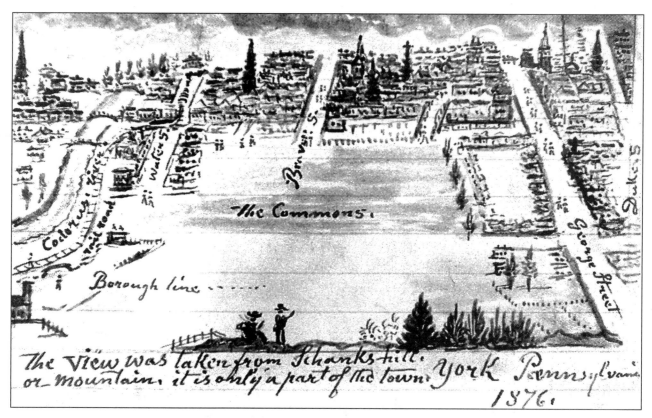

Lewis Miller's drawing shows York looking north from Webb's or Shank's Hill, later called Reservoir Hill. When the Confederates occupied York in June 1863, rebel artillerists planted a battery of cannons on this hill overlooking the town and camped in the U.S. Army General Hospital on Penn Common, 'The Commons' here. When Miller drew this scene in 1876, the hospital had been demolished, and the citizenry used the common for picnics and other gatherings. Since its formation in 1805, the park had held special significance for freedmen as a stopping place after crossing the Mason-Dixon Line to freedom.

'Are we not a fine set of fellows?'

Confederate artillery officer Robert Stiles spurred his horse.

The rebel column was about to trek into York, and the officer did not want to miss the fun when Gen. William "Extra Billy" Smith entered the Pennsylvania town.

Stiles would not be disappointed.

The Yale graduate observed Smith turn to his son, Fred, and issue an order.

"Go back and look up those tooting fellows," the once and future governor of Virginia said, "and tell them first to be sure their drums and horns are all right, and then to come up here to the front and march into town tooting 'Yankee Doodle' in their very best style."

Smith's son and aide complied with most of the order. The band marched toward the head of the column playing "Dixie," as a prelude to "Yankee Doodle."

Thus, this Confederate unit of The Army of Northern Virginia entered York without resistance on a hot day in late June 1863.

The column headed east along the town's West Market Street toward Centre Square, where the road intersected with George Street, a north-south road to Harrisburg and Baltimore.

The 65-year-old general rode alone at the head of the troops, bowing with a hearty smile first to one side and then to the other. It seemed to Stiles that the Virginia lawyer paid particular attention to every pretty girl.

York's residents first appeared astonished, then pleased and cheered as the gallant and grandfatherly Smith and his command reached the town's center. Surrounded by local residents, Smith called for his column to halt and, according to Stiles, organized what amounted to a political meeting in the middle of the street.

The general, whose nickname came from extra government orders garnered with expansion of his mail-coach line, began preaching a rambling sermon from his mount:

"My friends, how do you like this way of coming back into the Union? I hope you like it; I have been in favor of it for a good while. But don't misunderstand us. We are not here with any hostile intent — unless the conduct of your side shall render hostilities unavoidable. You can see for yourselves we are not conducting ourselves like enemies today. We are not burning your houses or butchering your children. On the contrary, we are behaving ourselves like Christian gentlemen, as we are.

"You see, it was getting a little warm down our way. We needed a summer outing and thought we would take it at the North, instead of patronizing the Virginia springs, as we generally do. We are sorry, and apologize that we are not in better guise for a visit of courtesy, but we regret to say our trunks haven't gotten up yet; we were in such a hurry to see you that we could not wait for them. You must really excuse us.

"What we all need, on both sides, is to mingle more with each other, so that we shall learn to know and appreciate each other. Now here's my brigade — I wish you knew them as I do. They are such a hospitable, wholehearted, fascinating lot of gentlemen. Why, just think of it — of course this part of Pennsylvania is ours to-day; we've got it, we hold it, we can destroy it, or do what we please with it. Yet we sincerely and heartily invite you to stay. You are quite welcome to remain here and to make yourselves entirely at home — so long as you behave yourselves pleasantly and agreeably as you are doing now. Are we not a fine set of fellows? You must admit that we are."

Smith's good words flowed even as expletives started floating from the rear of the column.

Gen. Jubal A. Early, the division commander, waded forward in an attempt to discover the gridlock on York's main street. Horsemen, foot soldiers, supply wagons and townspeople slowed Old Jube's forward progress.

"Not a dog, no, not even a sneaking exempt," a fellow officer later wrote, "could have made his way through."

But Jubal Early could grip harder than a bulldog.

Stiles observed Early lean forward in his saddle and catch the preacher by the coat collar. He jerked him back and around, yelling:

"General Smith, what the devil are you about ... stopping the head of this column in this cursed town?"

"Having a little fun, General," came the composed reply, "which is good for all of us, and at the same time teaching these people something that will be good for them and won't do us any harm."

Early's wrath scored its desired effect.

"Suffice it to say the matter was amicably arranged and the brigade and its unique commander moved on," Stiles wrote, "leaving the honest burghers of York wondering what manner of men we were."

This view shows York looking south toward Webb's Hill in 1852. The Harrisburg road, foreground, leads to the center of town where it intersected with the east-west pike, which ran from Lancaster to Gettysburg. Gen. John B. Gordon's brigade, the first Confederate unit, entered from the west, at right, on the pike and headed east toward Wrightsville. Some historians have questioned whether Gen. William 'Extra Billy' Smith's theatrics upon his entry into York happened in the way Maj. Robert Stiles described. Gordon wrote that his brigade entered town first, and Stiles' account is the only source that tells about Smith's speech. But York was the only town of size north of the Mason-Dixon Line that Gen. Jubal Early's division would have entered in such manner, and Smith could have ridden with another brigade. Whether Stiles' recollection is factual, legendary or confused, it illustrates the swagger of the Confederate Army marching across Pennsylvania after routing the Yankees at Fredericksburg and Chancellorsville.

I

America's division touches York County

Feb. 23, 1861 to June 3, 1863

*'Sammy, you go right down to Washington
and fix things. I'll pay the expenses.'*
— A York County resident to Samuel Small

War's thunder heard in North

In late February 1861, York County residents by the scores prepared to salute the man who was about to become the 16th president of the United States, Abraham Lincoln.

The Republican president-elect's extended rail tour started from his Springfield, Ill., home with the destination: The White House, Washington, D.C.

York, a southcentral Pennsylvania town of 8,600 people, secured a scheduled morning visit as the train turned south from Harrisburg.

But on the night before his appearance, as he shook hands in the state capital, Lincoln grappled with a decision.

If he kept his York appointment, he could roll into danger 50 miles farther down the Northern Central Railway tracks. Pinkerton detectives had learned of an assassination plot in Baltimore, a large Southern city whose voters had overwhelmingly sided with Democrat John C. Breckenridge for president.

But if Lincoln arrived in Washington through stealth, some might believe that he lacked courage.

Finally, the decision came.

A two-car train, with Lincoln secretly aboard, headed east toward Philadelphia. Upon his arrival, Lincoln boarded a Philadelphia, Wilmington and Baltimore Railroad car. He pulled into Baltimore in the early morning hours, shuttled to the Baltimore & Ohio line and arrived in the nation's capital at 6 a.m., Saturday, Feb. 23, 1861.

Four hours later in York, Republican leaders, among a crowd of 5,000, waited at the Northern Central station. A band played patriotic music. A four-wheeled carriage — the best the borough could offer — awaited the distinguished guest.

The county scrubbed up well for the chief executive-elect's visit, considering the strong anti-Lincoln sentiment within its borders.

York County voters had supported Lincoln's opponents by a tally of 6,633-5,128 just months earlier. That outcome reinforced the county's reputation as land of the Democrats. The county had backed Democratic-Republicans or Democrats for the presidency in every election in the past 50 years, maybe longer.

The Democratic York Gazette, reflecting the majority view, asserted that county residents should use the ballot to protest potential conflict between the North and South.

A vote for Republican Abraham Lincoln meant a vote for division.

"They (Democrats) are for the Constitution and the Union," the newspaper said, "and will fight sectionalism to the death."

That was the position of the Peace Democrats, derisively called "Copperheads" because of their harmless appearance but potent bite. They called for peace and national unity but shot venom at Lincoln and his desperate efforts to maintain the Union.

In York County, Peace Democrats outnumbered War Democrats, supportive of Lincoln, and Southern Democrats, protective of slavery.

"York was distinctively Northern but not bitterly anti-Southern," A.B. Farquhar, a York businessman, wrote years after the war.

Many in York County believed slavery was wrong in principle, he explained. At the same time, they believed that slavery reckoned better in practice than in theory.

"No matter what his personal disposition might be," he wrote, "slaves were so very expensive that it would be as ridiculous to maltreat them as to maltreat a stable of blooded horses."

Despite such sentiments, the throng strained to see Lincoln as the train pulled into York's Northern Central Railway station from Harrisburg.

Out of the presidential car popped a tall man with whiskers.

Abraham Lincoln, some thought.

No, he was too good-looking.

"Gentlemen," he said, "I am sorry to announce to you that Mr. Lincoln is not in the train. He was called to Washington last night on important business. He was sorry to disappoint you but left this morning in the early train."

Robert Todd Lincoln, the president's son, briefly greeted the crowd as the train headed south, but his gesture did little to soothe the disappointment.

The grumpy crowd scattered, and the empty carriage rattled away from the depot.

"Who will attempt to give the various comments passed upon Mr. Lincoln and his movements?" The Gazette wondered. "Let our readers put their imaginations to work. They cannot fail. Thus ended the grand demonstration in honor of Mr. Lincoln to York."

Important business, indeed, pressed the new president.

The American Union was regressing into disunion.

On April 12, Confederate forces fired on Fort Sumter in Charleston, S.C. — a deliberate act of war.

• • •

York County residents reacted with anxiety toward the rebel capture of Fort Sumter and the president's subsequent call for 75,000 troops.

For several weeks after the first shots of the war roared in Charleston's harbor, crowds besieged York County telegraph offices. People grabbed dailies and extra editions as soon as the newspapers arrived in town.

County residents had worried about war and rumors of war for months.

Earlier in the year, a box arrived at the Jefferson railroad station in southeastern York County. Its shape suggested that it could contain rifles. This perhaps portended some type of uprising in Jefferson. Someone cut a hole in the box, and what he thought he saw — rifles — made their way into the newspapers. The next week, The Spectator in Hanover admitted the story lacked facts.

The real story was this: Two map salesmen thought they would play a trick on the people of Jefferson. They placed the box in someone's care and asked that its contents — two five-foot-long rollers bearing Shearer and Lake county maps — be kept a secret. In a small town, secrecy meant rumors, and the rumors became news in The Spectator.

But now, the reality of the South's uprising had marched into York County's heartland.

Volunteer troops from points east, west and north moved through York on their way to Washington.

Residents flew the Stars and Stripes, and women

worked early and late to make more banners. The flag atop the tallest pole in York — described as 100 feet tall and straight as an arrow — waved above the lumber office of H. Small & Sons. The Worth Infantry, a local military company, and its band stepped to one flag-raising ceremony after another.

"Nothing of the kind was ever seen in York before ... ," The Gazette reported, adding that one of the largest flags in town flew from its office.

The York Republican, its competitor, made the same claim.

• • •

With York County's sons certain to join the fight, community members of all political stripes rallied in support.

A gathering — said to be the largest ever in York — convened at the York County Courthouse on York's East Market Street to raise money for the families of soldiers and to equip the fighting men.

For a moment, many in York County agreed: Now that war had broken out, the men and the military effort deserved full support.

Attorneys John W. Bittinger and John Gibson rose from their courtroom seats to make that point. They deplored civil conflict, but now that the nation was at war with itself, it was time to forget party and rally under the banner for the defense of the government, the best the world had ever known.

Even Peace Democrats, normally strident in their views against war and the sectionalism that it spawned, enthusiastically endorsed remarks that evening. The Gazette counted itself among them. This came as a concession from a newspaper that one time criticized Lincoln for putting forth the notion that all men, even Negroes, were created equally.

A spirit of determination, some observers noted, characterized the meeting.

York County, or at least many of its citizens, had decided to love the warrior, hate the war.

• • •

On April 19, six days after Fort Sumter fell, word buzzed up the tracks to York that Southern sympathizers in Baltimore had fired upon troops from Massachusetts rushing to Washington to protect the nation's capital.

The next day, a Saturday, the news got worse. Sympathizers had torn up the Northern Central Railway tracks north of Baltimore.

That rumor became fact when the telegraph, whose lines followed the railroad, went dead. Men on a train arriving from Ashland, Md., 20 miles south of the Pennsylvania border, confirmed that partisans had ripped away the rails.

The railroad, which ran up and down the county's center, formed a spine for moving supplies and troops from the north and west to Union Army headquarters in Washington. With Virginia joining the Confederacy and the slave state of Maryland undecided, keeping open supply and communications lines to the nation's capital became critical.

Other rail lines from the west — the Baltimore & Ohio Railroad, for example — appeared even more vulnerable to rebel attacks in western Virginia and Maryland. The Northern Central Railway must remain intact.

Meanwhile, distressed people in York with friends or kinsmen visiting Baltimore made plans to bring them

CIVIL WAR COMMENCED!

BOMBARDMENT & SURRENDER OF FORT SUMTER
AFTER 36 HOURS FIGHTING.

A Bloodless Battle.

THE PRESIDENT'S PROCLAMATION.

A CALL FOR 75,000 TROOPS.

EXTRA SESSION OF CONGRESS,
etc., etc., etc.

Our readers were doubtless prepared by the accounts of the preparations going on at New York over a week since, full particulars of which we gave in our last paper, to expect that hostilities might at any moment commence between the Federal and Confederate troops, either at Pensacola or Charleston, but even before we or they anticipated, has the country been involved in civil war by traitors to the government, by opening their batteries upon Fort Sumter in Charleston Harbor, on Friday morning last, at 4 o'clock. We give particulars below:

The following is the telegraphic correspondence which took place between the War Department of the confederate government and Gen. Beauregard, immediately preceding the commencement of the hostilities. The correspondence grew out of a formal notification of the United States government, disclosed in Gen. Beauregard's first dispatch.

Charleston, April 8.

The York County Star and Wrightsville Advertiser presented news about the outbreak of the Civil War with a one-column headline on the second of its four pages in its April 18, 1861, edition. Word of the attack had reached the county five days before. 'News that they were firing on Fort Sumter,' Wrightsville diarist George Stoner Beidler wrote. In those days, newspaper front pages often were devoted to fiction pieces and other timeless material. W. Smith and J. Herr Smith published the York County Star.

home.

"... (O)ur citizens began to realize that the war, which before they had regarded as afar off, had now reached our immediate neighborhood," The Gazette prophesied, "and was likely to call forth our best energies for our own protection and security."

• • •

All day Saturday, people crowded York's Centre Square discussing the latest war news.

They stood in position to hear information coming from all directions. The intersection of two busy roads formed the square: The route running from Lancaster to Gettysburg and the pike from Harrisburg to Baltimore.

Conversation stopped for a moment when Capt. George Hay rode his horse through the square.

The captain, a 51-year-old York furniture maker and undertaker, moved from house to house, ordering local militia members to report to their respective armories. The units would leave that night to an undisclosed site. People massed around the buildings, as the troops gathered their arms and prepared to depart.

At 11 p.m., Hay's York Rifles and the Thomas A. Ziegle-led Worth Infantry, marched to the Northern Central Railway station on North Duke Street. The Worth Infantry Band serenaded the soldiers as they boarded a train bound for Baltimore.

The local home guardsmen learned that their squads would watch over the railroad at points north and south of Parkton, Md., seven miles from the Pennsylvania border. Other squads would patrol the railroad toward Harrisburg.

The following morning — a Sunday — crowds stuck close to the depot to gain news from passing trains.

Residents made certain that sufficient supplies for their hometown soldiers left aboard one train.

On Monday, residents still filled the town's streets, consumed by the topic of war. They made themselves useful, too.

They stocked coffee, bread and cakes for the hungry men of York, who returned from guard duty and marched to the fairgrounds. They would soon call the grassy home of the York Fair near South Queen and East King streets "Camp Delight," contrasting it to "Camp Misery" in Cockeysville.

• • •

By tearing up bridges and telegraph lines, Southern supporters in Baltimore forced the suspension of much Northern business with that port city, long the primary destination for York County products.

The base of the triangular York County rested on the Mason-Dixon Line, and the Susquehanna River separated its northern tip from Harrisburg. The county seat town of York served as an agricultural center, located about 30 miles from Harrisburg to the north and about the same distance from Lancaster across the mile-wide Susquehanna to the east. Gettysburg, about 30 miles to the west, became a county seat after Adams County separated from York County in 1800.

The formidable Susquehanna had helped quell settlement on its west bank until about 1730. The winding ribbon served as an obstacle to trade and transportation to the east after the county's formation in 1749. Once across, an 80-mile trip to Philadelphia lay ahead. Farmers and the county's budding tradesmen preferred doing business in Baltimore, a short 50 miles to the south.

In 1863, agriculture and related businesses put most of the bread on tables in York County homes. In an accounting several years before, more than 25 blacksmiths, 12 tanners and curriers, about eight wagon makers and 14 whip makers operated out of York.

Nine agricultural tool makers, three railroad car shops, five machine shops and seven foundries within York's borders pointed to an emerging industrial base.

Now, with the rail line cut to Baltimore, farmers and businesses adjusted and prepared to ship their products and purchase goods in Philadelphia. Trade with Philadelphia moved along the railroad connecting York with Wrightsville, a borough along the Susquehanna.

A 1 ¼-mile-long wooden covered bridge carried the railroad, wagon path and canal towpaths across the river from Wrightsville to Columbia.

"We deeply regret the severing of the business relations which has so long existed between York and Baltimore," The Gazette said, "but the necessity which has been forced upon us, knows no law, and trade, like water, will always find its level."

• • •

At first, some in York County still did not grasp the seriousness of the war. Or else, they trusted leading York merchants P.A. & S. Small Co. in all matters, large and small.

The words of Small brothers Philip Albright and Samuel made or broke deals in York. P.A.'s dominating personality caused his employees to name him "Boss Philip," while townspeople viewed the philanthropic Samuel as a moral guide in town. His employees referred to him as "Uncle Sammy."

In the early days of the war, Capt. George Hay, an undertaker and furniture maker, provided military leadership in York County. He initially led the York Rifles, a county militia unit, and later became the commander of the 87th Pennsylvania Regiment.

In their mid-60s with vast business interests, the brothers stood at the pinnacle of their power.

Early in the war, a wealthy farmer, particularly disturbed at the war news, stopped at the Small store on the northeast corner of Centre Square and looked up Samuel Small.

Small sat in a private room toward the back of the store.

The farmer laid $100 on the desk.

"Sammy, you go right down to Washington and fix things," he said. "I'll pay the expenses."

'They are expected to report at once'

A day after the York Rifles and Worth Infantry left to guard the railroad, a messenger hustled through the door of Emmanuel Reformed Church in Hanover, about 19 miles from York in southwestern York County.

The messenger requested to interrupt the Rev. William K. Zieber's Sunday sermon for an announcement.

Zieber complied: "If there are any members of the Marion Rifles or the Hanover Infantry present in this audience, they are expected to report at once at their places of rendezvous."

The confusion grew so loud that the preacher could not finish his work.

Soon afterward, fife and drums marked the military procession to the train station, Capt. H. Gates Weiser, Marion Rifles, and Capt. Cyrus Diller, Hanover Infantry, in command.

York County volunteers again had promptly responded to President Lincoln's call for troops.

* * *

One late April evening, word reached Hanover that 200 rowdies and secessionists from Baltimore were marching toward town.

The ringing of bells alerted citizens, who gathered in Center Square carrying all sorts of weapons. A squad of men on horseback rode southeast on the Baltimore Pike to check out the rumor.

Meanwhile, men unlimbered cannons to command Hanover's main streets.

The big guns had a lot of territory to cover. Roads leading to Hanover's square hit most points on the compass. Its crossroads nature helped make it the county's second-largest town, with more than 1,600 residents.

Men from nearby McSherrystown in Adams County lugged three kegs of powder for the big guns. Residents erected barricades at the end of Baltimore Street.

Thirty minutes later, the mounted men returned, quashing the rumor. By then, the report had panicked people in Jackson, Codorus and other nearby townships.

As a newspaper later explained, the rumor commenced when soldiers from Baltimore, bound for the Confederacy, marched toward Westminster, Md., not far below the Mason-Dixon Line.

Town officials considered it prudent to post pickets to guard against any future surprise.

* * *

Wrightsville, the county's third-largest town, welcomed one of many wartime visitors.

A fine large eagle hovered over the river town of about 1,300 people one day in May.

The York County Star and Wrightsville Advertiser conjectured why the national bird visited:

"He came sailing up from the east, doubtless to ascertain whether we were all right on the Eagle question, and seemed, on viewing the large number of flags displayed in all parts of our town, to be satisfied, for on seeing that all was right, he turned in his airy flight, and took his departure for some other locality."

Despite passing this inspection, the town needed one more flag, the newspaper stated. Such a banner, atop a flagpole erected by the town of Wrightsville, should wave in a central location as an official show of unity.

"Let a meeting be called, proper resolutions adopted, and the necessary appropriation be made," The Star urged.

* * *

A town flag would soon tower over York.

One May afternoon, workers raised a 110-foot-tall pine pole with a foot-thick base in Centre Square. The pole stood tall between two market sheds that had resided in the heart of York for years.

The pole raising came at a price. A large truss fell on Dr. John Fisher's head, injuring him severely.

But the ceremony went on.

Judge Robert J. Fisher and the Rev. J.A. Ross of York's Methodist Church addressed the large crowd that had gathered. A beautiful bunting flag was run up the pole as a band played "The Star-Spangled Banner."

Later, men of York substituted a 35-foot-long flag of heavier material, made by a group of women from York.

* * *

American flags soon flapped even higher above York.

Four flags sprouted from spy holes in Christ Lutheran Church's steeple, the tallest of the spires atop York's 15 churches.

John Fissel collected money for the banners and helped place the 7 ½-foot flags in public view.

The banners were visible for miles in all directions.

* * *

The Southern sympathizers' destruction of the Northern Central Railway bridges incensed many county residents.

But their agitation increased when word spread that state officials in Harrisburg were considering retaliatory measures.

A Peach Bottom Township resident responded to a Harrisburg Daily Telegraph story that suggested disabling the Susquehanna and Tidewater Canal, a major transportation artery since the 1840s.

The plan was to tear away the canal's embankment in Wrightsville, the resident wrote.

The canal ran along the west bank of the Susquehanna between Wrightsville and Havre de Grace, Md. There, the river flowed into the navigable Chesapeake Bay. For much of the year, large load-bearing crafts could not navigate the shallow, rocky Susquehanna.

Someone in Harrisburg reasoned that this destruction would stop the flow of badly needed goods from agriculturally rich York County to Baltimore and its secessionists.

The problem with this plan was that it would stop the flow of money northward from Baltimore.

This would destroy commerce in agricultural townships — Peach Bottom, Fawn, Lower Chanceford and Windsor.

The state of Pennsylvania should not stoop so low to an insult from a lawless and deluded mob, the resident wrote.

"Does our honor demand this?" he asked.

* * *

James Gerry, a physician and former U.S. congressman, lived in Shrewsbury, on the pike to Baltimore just north of the Maryland border.

In a letter to his sons in Carlisle, he observed that most people in the stirred-up town of Shrewsbury sided with the Union. Secessionists, mostly those who hailed from Maryland, had left town. Meanwhile, Baltimore residents filled the road all day and most of the night.

"It seems the Baltimoreans are very anxious to leave the city, and it would seem that all are going that can," Gerry wrote to sons E.H. and James.

He urged his sons to come home from Dickinson College, which was experiencing the exodus of many Southern students to their homes.

Gerry provided several bits of wisdom: Pack up books and furniture for the journey home, except what could be sold at a fair price. Do not panic and give those away for little or nothing. Be calm and watch what is said publicly about the national crisis. When it's necessary to give an opinion, do so with conciliation.

Gerry's counsel reflected his own views on the war. The Democrat supported the Union but believed secession could have been prevented if the North had granted the South its constitutional rights. The South should have been more patient, and compromise might have come. The spirit of war won out.

All slave states would secede, he predicted, and the idea of forcefully coercing the South into submission wouldn't work.

He foresaw a long war.

He was right about that.

The war would end with two different nations.

"There will be then, two Confederacies," he predicted, "but before this is fully accomplished, a vast amount of blood may be shed, and treasure wasted, but it must ultimately be settled."

The physician was right about the volume of blood.

But he was wrong about the number of confederacies.

• • •

Communities across York County rallied to raise aid for families of men defending the Union and to plot ways to protect the home front.

The York County Commissioners pledged up to $10,000 for a fund to support families, and borough officials in York and Hanover promised $1,000 each.

Although they lived 25 miles away from the Mason-Dixon Line, men around Newberrytown gathered to form a company of home guards. The actions of the Southern states troubled these residents of northern York County, and the sececcionists cutting the tracks north of Baltimore indicated how close the war had come to their soil.

Those at the meeting, chaired by John Hays, called for every man in the neighborhood to enlist in the militia and have arms and ammunition ready in case the enemy came knocking.

Other companies formed in York.

One unit, with James A. Stahle in command, took the name Ellsworth Zouaves in tribute to a popular Union officer, Ephraim Elmer Ellsworth, who was shot while confiscating a rebel flag in Alexandria, Va.

Zouaves copied the dress of units fighting in French colonial armies, complete with gaudy uniforms, turbans or fezzes — conical, tassled hats. The York unit wore a colorful Zouave uniform of blue pantaloons and jackets with red and white hats adorned with a blue band.

These units earned reputations for their skill in performing military drills, and Stahle's men worked hard on their precision exercises.

• • •

Despite the martial air in the county, people established a pattern they would continue throughout the war. No matter the war news, residents fought to maintain normalcy.

Work on York's new Presbyterian church went on. Plastering the interior started before the war and virtually all that remained was painting the exterior.

That was outside the building. Inside, children were responding to instruction, diligent in completing their Sunday school lessons. Lizzie Boozle garnered recognition for reciting all 107 questions of the Westminster Shorter Catechism without error. A signature on the girl's citation read: Samuel Small.

Col. James A. Stahle led the Ellsworth Zouaves, a colorfully dressed, well-drilled York County unit. Three members adorned in Zouaves attire pose here. The unit later formed part of the 87th Pennsylvania Regiment.

While the church was going up, the old York County Jail, at South George and King streets, was coming down.

The sheriff moved prisoners from the gloomy jail, dating back to the 1750s, after construction of a lockup near the York County Poorhouse and Hospital, northeast of York.

Few would complain. The old jail was no asset, despite a Revolutionary War past that included the detention of British prisoners.

Farmers busily planted corn, with the ground perfect for accepting the seed. Cold, windy weather had slowed buds and flowers but improved May weather turned the county green.

Bumper crops soon would be needed to feed visitors dressed in blue arriving in York and staying, sometimes for weeks.

'All determined to make us comfortable'

Even before its founding in 1749, York County had served as a gateway to German, Scots-Irish and other immigrants heading from the Eastern Seaboard to points south and west.

Immigrants with a final destination of North Carolina could travel along the road from Philadelphia through

Lancaster to Columbia. There, they would cross the Susquehanna River on a ferry — or traverse a bridge after 1814 — and head along the Monocacy Road through York. The traveler then would trek through Hanover to Frederick, Md., cross the Potomac and enter the Shenandoah Valley at Harpers Ferry and continue down the Great Wagon Road to points south.

This access to the South and the port of Baltimore oriented the county in that direction. Many business owners formed partnerships, gained customers and established family ties with counterparts in Southern states. The reverse happened as well, providing an avenue for Southerners and Dixie sentiments to move northward across county soil.

York's access to the South made it a key staging ground for troops, awaiting assignment and then transportation along the Northern Central Railway to Union camps.

Troops bivouacked at the York Fairgrounds, in the southeastern part of York. This gathering spot evolved into Camp Scott, named after the Union Army's top general, Winfield Scott.

Within three weeks of Sumter, the camp accommodated six regiments. Livestock buildings, sheds and other available structures served as barracks, and workers put up other sheds to cover these 6,000 soldiers.

Fences forming a ring for racing came down to make room for drills and maneuvers.

But conditions were not ideal.

Soldiers slept in former cattle stalls and sheds. Roofs on some buildings leaked. An early May snowstorm caused water to puddle in some quarters. Soldiers awoke one morning in a pool of water one-half acre in size.

The people of York quartered some troops, and others found space in the courthouse, churches and vacant buildings until the late-spring sun baked the barracks dry.

These conditions caused colds, fevers and rheumatism. The sick soldiers initially recuperated in private homes, finding soft beds better than lying on damp straw. Residents often welcomed guests from camp — whether ill or healthy — for meals.

Soon, part of the main exhibition building served as a hospital, and 20 soldiers occupied sick beds. Still, an observer from the The York County Star found the town and camp in good order.

"The troops have provisions in plenty," he wrote, "and appear to lead a very pleasant life at present."

• • •

Recruits spent their days in drills at the fairgrounds and on Penn Common. Regiments with bands entertained residents as the soldiers marched several blocks from Camp Scott to the Common.

Penn Common was a large, relatively flat open area in southwest York. The Continental Congress had ordered the erection of makeshift barracks there for soldiers in the American Revolution. Those barracks were long gone, and the land had become a public park upon a grant from heirs of William Penn, founder of Pennsylvania.

Large crowds gathered at the Common to watch the drills. Many neighbors repaid the soldiers for the entertainment by cooking for them.

"Although the novelty of the thing is wearing away," The Gazette reported, "the presence of the large body of

Almost overnight, the York Fairgrounds, southeast of the East King and South Queen streets intersection in York, became Camp Scott, a place for Union volunteers to muster and drill in the war's early months. Regiments of Pennsylvania volunteers started assembling there soon after Fort Sumter fell. Secessionists tore up Northern Central Railway tracks, and the regiments had to backtrack to York rather than proceed to Washington, D.C.

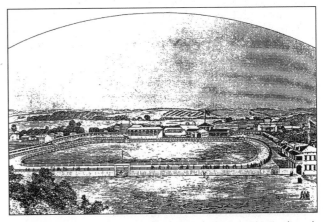

The fairgrounds, operated by the York County Agricultural Society, took on a new look as the home of thousands of troops. The race track was dismantled and buildings converted to accommodate men rather than prize animals.

troops now quartered here is still the source of considerable interest to our citizens and imparts an unaccustomed degree of liveliness to our town."

• • •

Soldiers from Hanover became part of the growing military crowd searching for quarters in York's private dwellings.

Judge Fisher and his wife, Mary, numbered among the generous York residents opening their brick home bordering Market Street.

The Fisher home already bustled. The judge had four children from his first marriage. The widower had married Mary Sophia Cadwell, a teacher in the female division of the York County Academy, in 1853. The couple had two children.

The judge presided over a court that covered York and

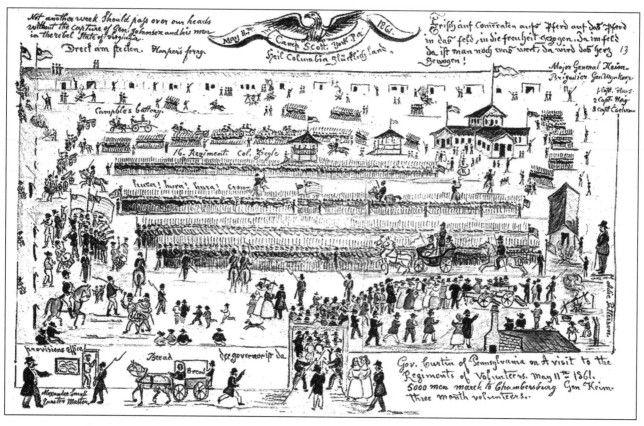

Lewis Miller shows Pennsylvania Gov. Andrew G. Curtin standing in a carriage, right center, to review volunteers. About 5,000 three-month men were prepared to march to Chambersburg in this May 11, 1861, scene. 'Not another week should pass over our heads without the capture of (Confederate) Gen. (Joseph) Johnston and his men in the rebel state of Virginia,' Miller wrote. The artist's observation reflected the thinking in the North that the war would be shortlived.

Adams counties. Mary Fisher had helped form the foundation for soldier relief work in York.

The Hanover men appreciated their quarters. They met in special session at the courthouse, just down East Market Street from the Fisher residence.

M.F. Mulgrew, one of the Hanover men, resolved: "That the Hon. R. J. Fisher and his accomplished lady are entitled to the gratitude and lasting remembrance of every soldier from Hanover for their hospitality at their own house, and their extreme kindness in procuring the best quarters in the county, for the soldiers of York and Adams."

The soldiers asked for the resolution to be sent to newspapers in York and Adams counties.

• • •

The Duquesne Grays, a Pennsylvania regiment, also searched for quarters in York.

No barracks were available to the men so they stayed in the Baptist Church for six weeks.

When the soldiers received orders to depart, they wondered about charges for using the church.

"We baldly do this for our country's sake," a church spokesman replied, declining payment.

The regiment departed and sent back a thank-you — a pulpit Bible that the congregation long cherished.

• • •

Out-of-town newspapers dribbled into the county with accounts of local kindness toward soldiers.

One infantryman from Johnstown wrote about a greeting from women who supplied passing soldiers with buckets of hot coffee, baskets of cakes, crackers and cheese. When the unit reached the fairgrounds, the soldier observed hundreds of women there with pots and kettles cooking for the throng.

"All determined to make us comfortable," he wrote.

Isabel Small, wife of Samuel Small, spearheaded the women's efforts to provide aid to soldiers. The women established an organization to recruit others. The Ladies Soldiers Aid Society had formed.

The women met in a large room set aside at P.A. & S. Small's store. They sorted donated clothing, sewed new clothing and wound bandages. Children helped, too.

Farmers opened great chests brought with them from Germany to equip the women with linen to make dressings for wounds.

Men formed a Committee of Safety, headed by Henry Lanius, with five assigned to canvass different sections of town to learn about the needs of women and children with breadwinners away at war.

• • •

Camp Scott and its hospital provided York County with an early glimpse of the horrors of war. Local newspapers reported the deaths of several soldiers from pneumonia, including a young infantryman from Hanover.

Drills taking place in town squares throughout the county brought wounds and even death.

One of Edward L. Schroeder's comrades cut the Worth Infantry soldier in the back of the head during a bayonet exercise in York's Centre Square.

In the southeastern York County town of Stewartstown, a fellow soldier accidentally blasted Benjamin Ebaugh in the back with his shotgun.

At Camp Scott, a soldier shot a comrade from Pittsburgh in the head after a disagreement.

But the bullet did no harm. It glanced off the Pittsburgh man's head.

. . .

As time passed, military commanders ordered soldiers to stay in camp, tightly controlling passes.

One soldier, identified as George Glass from Johnstown, walked several blocks north from the fairgrounds to a house near the railroad depot.

Glass, with accomplices, entered the residence of a German-speaking man named Steiner. Glass offered an indignity to Steiner's daughter, and the father replied by drawing a pistol and shooting the soldier in the shoulder.

Someone carried the wounded man from the house and deposited him outside nearby railroad car shops. He ended up at the camp hospital.

Such incidents caused the town's leaders to appoint armed local men to guard the town at night. When these local guards saluted, strangers wandering from the main thoroughfares were expected to explain why they were there.

More county men march off to war

York celebrated the first wartime Fourth of July by ringing bells, firing cannons, discharging small arms and igniting a large fireworks display.

The Ellsworth Zouaves, the flashy military unit, provided a demonstration of close-order drills, accompanied by the York Rifles' band and a drum corps.

"Young and old, male and female, were all apparently baptized anew with the fire of patriotism ... ," The York Republican reported.

The fireworks show that evening concluded with the ignition of a large arch, displaying the word "Union," with two large stars on either side.

The town celebrated again later that month.

After their initial railroad detail, members of George Hay's York Rifles, Worth Infantry, Hanover's Marion Rifles and other county units had enlisted for three months. This came in response to Lincoln's 75,000-man call up.

These militiamen marched with other volunteers in The Army of the Potomac, the main Union army in the East.

With their enlistment up in late July, the volunteers returned home to the ringing of bells and the roaring of cannons.

But the celebration turned into tragedy.

A six-pound cannon went off with a rammer still in its barrel, injuring its tenders, Henry Hubly and Moses Bennington. The projectile traveled 400 yards before strik-

York residents enjoyed celebrations. Lewis Miller tells of two on one page: an International Order of Odd Fellows procession of 1850 and the return of three-month volunteers on July 27, 1861. A misfire of a cannon causing the death of a York man marred the 1861 celebration. Many of the three-month volunteers became part of the 87th Pennsylvania, which formed soon after this observation when it became clear that the war could last for months.

This 1861 scene of York's South George Street might have captured the May snowfall that caused flooding at the quarters of Union volunteers staying at Camp Scott. The unpaved South George Street is spotted with snow while the trees are at full leaf. Part of Christ Lutheran Church is seen, left.

ing an elderly onlooker, John Fisher, tearing away his lower jaw. He died about an hour later.

In drawing the scene, Lewis Miller, a York carpenter and artist, could only observe of the crowd, "A confused multitude."

• • •

Since the war's earliest days, many in the North had thought the rebellion would fold within months.

But The Army of Northern Virginia, the mighty Confederate unit in the East, routed Union forces in the First Battle of Bull Run outside Washington, D.C. This rebel victory at the Manassas, Va., field in July portended a long war.

The War Department in Washington organized in earnest for a potentially drawn-out campaign.

Capt. Hay received news of his next assignment. Col. Hay, with his new rank, would head the 87th Regiment, Pennsylvania Volunteer Infantry. His regiment would consist of 10 companies, eight from York County and two from Adams County.

Recruiting began at Camp Scott, the converted fairgrounds in York's southeast end.

Charles Gotwalt answered the call, one of thousands of county residents to step forward.

In camp, the order came for volunteers to form a line. When the names of Gotwalt and other recruits were announced, they ran across a street. An examiner scrutinized each man. If the recruit showed a limp or some other handicap, he was rejected. Otherwise, the volunteer passed his physical and gained a spot of the regimental roster.

In this manner, the numbers soon reached the full complement of 1,000 men, the standard enrollment for regiments, the primary fighting unit for both sides in the Civil War.

Gotwalt was one of the 1,000.

He was 15 years old.

• • •

Abraham Rudisill, a York printer and tailor, had stepped forward to join the York Rifles in the unit's first assignment guarding the Northern Central.

He was accepted, along with a son, and proceeded to the armory, where he set to work making cartridges. But a second son volunteered, taking his place in the unit.

Rudisill accompanied the company to the depot. The band played "Yankee Doodle," the same tune his grandfather marched to in the same town, but a different war — the American Revolution.

All summer, Rudisill tried to be useful, despite rejection by a company of home guards. He even joined a unit as a civilian.

Finally, he concluded he might be deployed as a gunner and put his name forth for an artillery unit forming at Camp Curtin in Harrisburg.

"Feeling an almost irresistible impulse to enter the service of my Country," he wrote the organizing officer, "in defense of those very Stars and Stripes under which my Grandfather, and the Grandfather of my wife fought in the Revolution — a number of my uncles in the War of 1812; and the same noble cause, in defense of which, two of my sons have enlisted in the present War!"

He was sworn in for three years on July 20.

He was 50 years old.

• • •

The 87th Pennsylvania drills in preparation for its initial assignment — guarding Northern Central Railway tracks in northern Maryland. The railroad served as a vital transportation and communication artery between the Northern states and Washington, D.C. York County residents counted on the railroad to move goods to market, and to shuttle friends and family to Baltimore and back. The Army made heavy use of the railroad in the Civil War to move troops and supplies and to transport wounded soldiers to military hospitals.

At 50, Abraham Rudisill initially had trouble gaining a spot in county volunteer units. He eventually caught on with an artillery unit and served until the end of the war.

In September, Hay's regiment received orders to cover familiar turf — guarding the Northern Central Railway in Maryland.

Standing duty one day soon after arriving, a sentinel thought he saw rebel sympathizers on a bridge near Monkton, Md., 12 miles from the Pennsylvania border.

He fired a shot at the culprits.

His shot awoke his squad and another nearby unit. His comrades joined up with the shooter at double-quick pace.

The would-be bridge burner turned out to be a cow whose life was saved when the Yankee's ball missed its mark.

• • •

Regimental life consisted of endless marching drills and military maneuvers. So was telling stories, whether true or half-true.

One story going around involved James Fisher, mustered into service in York as a member of Hay's new command.

In the early days of regimental drills, Fisher came up

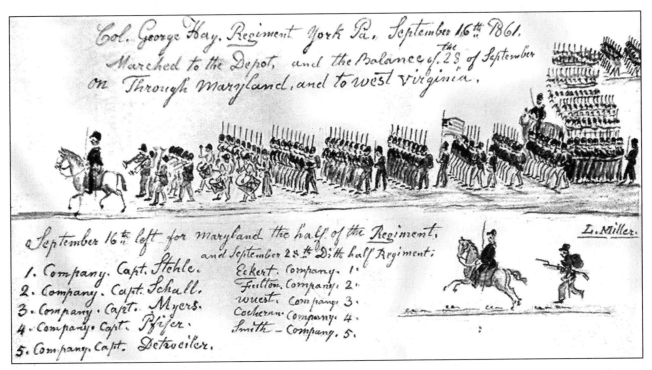

Col. George Hay leads part of the 87th Pennsylvania to the railroad depot on North Duke Street in this Lewis Miller drawing. Five companies of the 1,000-man unit departed York in mid-September 1861, and the other five companies left later that month.

lame. He marched a short distance before twisting his ankle.

"Pass out," came the stern command, an order to take a rest.

Fisher straightened up, marched at double-quick for a distance and back, and then turned a handspring three times, landing in front of his officer.

"You'll do," the officer said with a smile, "a regular athlete, I guess."

• • •

In addition to picket duty and drilling, detachments from the 87th marched on details throughout northern Maryland.

Capt. John Albright and Lt. John McIlvain with 40 men from Company K received orders to interrupt Confederate recruiting in Westminster, Md. Maryland maintained slaves for the first three years of the war but stayed in the Union, a decision that was far from unanimous in the Old Line State.

Upon arrival, Company K discovered recruits drilling inside the town's armory. The detachment rushed through a rear door, surprising the new soldiers, who immediately gave up their arms.

The detachment escorted the captives back to company headquarters.

• • •

Men of the 87th Pennsylvania's Company A made the most of their first Christmas away from York County.

Families from York sent turkey and other Christmas fixings on a train to Camp Melvale in Baltimore County, Md., the company's winter quarters. Some wealthy neighbors to the camp furnished pastry, dried fruits and preserves.

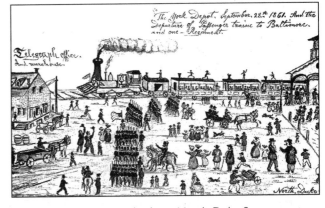

Lewis Miller captures the busy North Duke Street area near the Northern Central Railway depot. Many York residents stuck near the railroad station and telegraph office across the street to hear about war news from afar. The troops marching to the waiting passenger train are part of the 87th Pennsylvania in this September 1861 scene.

This made for a memorable Christmas dinner. A Marylander, reporting back to York, wrote that the men imagined their tin cups holding spring water as flowing bowls filled with drink.

"The recollection of the egg nogs and apple toddies and similar solids drove out of my mind for a moment another treat enjoyed at the barrack — this was some capital singing by about forty members of the company, which I ought to have mentioned in its place," the Marylander wrote.

Perhaps alcohol did make it into the celebration.

The writer allowed that the songs might be "mixed up

in my mind, with other 'mixtures' but I remember it was decidedly musical and pleasant ... ."

• • •

The holidays did not curtail the 87th's main duties.

A company guarding the Northern Central bridge at White Hall, nine miles south of the Mason-Dixon Line, ran off a party of secessionists.

The soldiers discovered the party had drawn four spikes from a rail as it crossed the bridge. This sabotage would have thrown a train into the creek below.

The detail also found straw on the bridge. The rebel sympathizers intended to torch the structure, cutting transportation between Washington, D.C., and the Union states to the north.

• • •

About a thousand horsemen — the 6th New York — rode into York on Christmas Day.

Townspeople greeted them with kindness.

"The citizens had provided a hot dinner of turkeys, meats and the delicacies of the festive season," an officer wrote, "the ladies who provided the dinner serving as waiters on the occasion."

The regiment quartered in the agricultural building at the fairgrounds and at several schools, closed by school board order because of the war.

Soon, the War Department ordered the building of barracks and stables for the New Yorkers on Penn Common to accommodate the visitors. A school on Duke Street served as a hospital, and the Ladies Aid Society helped with care.

'I think the South should be left alone'

In the fall of 1861, members of York's Methodist Episcopal Church found themselves with a vacant pulpit.

The Rev. David Shoaf had discovered a community fractured by the politics behind the war when he rode into York shortly after the bombardment of Fort Sumter.

The outspoken Shoaf, at the helm of the York area's leading Methodist congregation, did not bring peace.

He was a Union man, he said, one who respected the Stars and Stripes.

"But, I think the South should be left alone," he went on, "to do what the people want to do."

Later, he stated his position even more strongly.

"I am against war of any kind," he said, "and I am at a loss to know how any man professing to be a Christian could engage in such a murderous act."

York residents perplexed the preacher, too.

"The people of York are so exceedingly ignorant," he said, "they couldn't tell right from wrong if the two were labeled."

After the preacher asserted that Confederate President Jefferson Davis should be considered as much in power as Abraham Lincoln, people in the congregation voted against him. They withheld their weekly offering.

The Rev. Shoaf got the message. After several comings and goings and pulpit pronouncements, he left the community in late summer.

He would not be missed.

"History proves that the deepest and most desperate

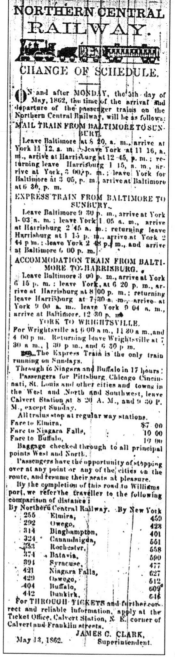

The Northern Central Railway issued weekly schedules that were published in The York Gazette and other local newspapers. The rail schedule changed according to war conditions. This schedule from May 1862 shows that the Civil War benefited the North's burgeoning railroad industry. It touts the advantages of traveling the Northern Central en route to Elmira, Buffalo, and other cities in New York. The railroad had been extended to Williamsport, where the New York connections could be made. Before the extension, travelers reached those cities on longer rides via New York City. The railroad and its employees became a part of community life in the rail corridor. On one occasion in 1862, John Yeakel of York, a conductor on the railroad, received a tip of $50 from people residing along the line from Baltimore to Parkton in Maryland. The residents appreciated the conductor's accommodating spirit toward families, particularly women and children, traveling along the railroad.

revolutions were brooded on by those who made professions of love of country, but who loved the enemies of their country more," someone from the church wrote a York newspaper. "Hence the man, that sympathizes with Jefferson Davis' rebellion, is morally just as much a rebel as the chief of this 'sum of all villainies.' "

• • •

The York Gazette was persistently impatient with presidential policies that split the union. That applied to presidents of both the United States and the Confederacy.

The newspaper denounced Jefferson Davis' insistence in the fall of 1861 that the South would accept no alternative but independence.

The newspaper summarized a Davis address in which he appealed to God on behalf of the rebellion, but the weekly did not consider it worthwhile to run the document.

Davis' bitter pronouncements contained copious misrepresentations.

"Let us hope," the newspaper said, "that 'President' Davis has written his last Message."

• • •

Twelve months after the shelling of Fort Sumter, county residents increasingly chose the Democratic Party's line.

Voters in the spring election in 1862 tagged David Small as York's chief burgess, or mayor, by a margin of 59.

York County had elected Democratic candidates for decades, but certain wards in the Borough of York often backed Republicans.

The Gazette noted that the 51-year-old Small was the second Democratic chief burgess in York in 45 years and credited crossover Republicans with making that so:

"By pursuing the right course ... we hope to secure our recent fellow laborers in the good work of redeeming York Borough, as permanent friends — as fellow soldiers in the grand army which marches under the Democratic flag; which battles now and ever for the Constitution which our fathers bequeathed us as a holy legacy; and which keeps step to the music of the Union."

In gaining the elected seat, David Small added to the roles he filled. He had served as director of the local poorhouse for years and, until the Republicans gained the White House, served as postmaster of York.

But his main job would be most helpful in his new elected position. David Small, chief burgess, was halfway through a 49-year run as owner of The York Gazette.

• • •

German immigrant Lorentz Schmahl had launched the Small family that formed such an integral part of York County's fabric.

Schmahl had come to America in 1743 and settled on a farm in the rolling countryside of central York County carved by the Kreutz, Codorus and Conewago creeks. The Germans favored settlement on this rich farmland in and around the towns of Wrightsville, York and Hanover. Scots-Irish settlers clustered in the hilly southeastern angle of the county, and a band of English Quaker settlements developed across the uneven northern tier.

One Schmahl son, Killian, had seven sons, all of whom became carpenters. George, one of the carpenter sons, started the milling and mercantile business that his own sons grew into P.A. & S. Small.

Another son, Peter, died in 1824, leaving a son, 12-year-old David, under the care of Henry Welsh, a printer, newspaperman and Jeffersonian. Welsh ingrained in David Small's mind his take on the newspaper business.

His newspaper — The York Gazette — existed to promote the Democratic Party, the major party in York County since heavy-handed Federalist actions in the late 1700s converted county residents to anti-Federalists, suspicious of a strong central government. The central government's taxation on whiskey, for example, hit a popular product in the grain-producing county and reminded residents of similar levies in their German hometowns. This tax and others caused the county to shift to the emerging Jeffersonian states' rights view.

The Gazette's function as a Democratic organ helped business because it attracted that party's legal advertising,

Researchers often confuse railroad car manufacturer David E. Small, left, and The York Gazette owner and Chief Burgess David Small, right. Both Smalls were members of the prominent 19th-century York family. Both were active in community life. But the railroad car manufacturer was a Republican and the chief burgess a Democrat.

postmaster positions and other patronage jobs.

In the early years of the Civil War, Oliver Stuck's York Democratic Press joined The Gazette in promoting the party of Jefferson and Jackson. David Frey's York Pennsylvanian and Smyser's and Boyer's York Republican countered these Democrat organs or took positions somewhere in between. In Hanover, The Citizen and Spectator fired solid shots at each other.

"These editors, like all others of the same sort, frequently exchange political cross fires at each other in an editorial way," an observer of York wrote several years earlier, "but we have not heard that there were as yet any bones broken, blood shed, or lives lost in these skirmishes ... ."

After an election, the newspapers generally forgot the bitter barbs, the writer concluded in rose-colored ink.

• • •

The story of the Small family tells of an often-repeated progression in York County.

Many 18th-century immigrants who worked the land begat sons who took a step away from the farms. This generation built the structures in which their 19th-century sons would, in turn, work and worship.

The migration toward town by these sons of farmers did not dilute a heavy German concentration in the county. Those of German heritage owned more than 77 percent of the taxable properties in York in the 1860s and more than 83 percent in Hanover. The York Gazette published a German-language edition for these residents.

Many county Germans were wary of the federal government and viewed the Democratic Party as holding closer to their live-and-let-live ideals. In the 1800s, many county residents preferred to conserve individual rights, states' right and hold down the growth of the central government. They viewed the Republicans as a party that wanted to progressively encroach on these rights.

During the Civil War, county voters increasingly backed Democrats. But businessmen Philip and Samuel Small and other family members leaned to the Republican side. David E. Small, co-owner of railroad car manufacturing shops in York and another kinsman of David Small, the newspaper owner, served as a Republican member of borough council for several terms.

Some years, David E. Small sat on council while

Democrat David Small served as mayor. The two would square off for burgess in one election, with David Small the victor by more than 300 votes.

But the two David Smalls differed in other ways. An industrial accident claimed David E. Small's right arm in 1853. That did not crush his fighting spirit.

"If I can bring down a partridge with my gun," he once said, "I certainly can shoot well enough to go to the defence of my country."

• • •

Unlike his younger relative, David Small, newspaper owner and chief burgess, did not want to fight and eschewed policies that could cause division.

In April 1862, Congress debated freeing Negroes in Washington, D.C. That troubled Small's Gazette.

Pennsylvania bordered states that allowed slavery and boasted a warm climate. Freed slaves would be attracted there, the newspaper fretted.

York County, with 68,200 people including about 1,200 Negroes, would be a destination for freedmen. The county had been a target for Southern freedmen and fugitives since Pennsylvania began gradually freeing its slaves in 1780.

The Gazette reasoned against manumission in the nation's capital:

Suppose 100 Negroes chose York, an estimate believed to be moderate.

If they worked, they would crowd out employment of 100 white men. If they would not work, the people of York would be forced to support them.

They would fill the jail and poorhouse and live off of taxes wrung from York residents.

The Democratic Party was the true friend of the people.

"Its first thought is for the welfare of the great mass of the people," the newspaper contended, "being satisfied to permit the Negroes of the South to remain where they are, well cared for, and are usefully employed."

The Gazette was not alone in giving voice to the Democratic position. Even before Fort Sumter, York's Democratic Press thundered against accommodation of freedmen in York and other Northern counties.

The Press poked at abolitionist Henry Ward Beecher, after 60 freed North Carolina slaves traveled through Maryland:

"We may expect hundreds and thousands of such visitors before long. Let our abolition philanthropists make their arrangements accordingly. Shall the poor negro, unless he be a fugitive slave, be allowed to starve. What says Parson Beecher?"

The same edition further whipped up the case against abolition, "The people, so long blindfolded, will see the guilty demagogues who have used the negro for the destruction of white men. They will mark those who have sung of negro freedom only to destroy the white man's liberty to earn bread for his starving family ... ."

Amid such thinking, Underground Railroad stations, often linked to York County's sizable Quaker population, operated before the war.

Fugitives traveled from house to friendly house, crossing the Susquehanna to Columbia and then proceeding to Canada and other points north.

• • •

Many in Wrightsville connected a series of fires in the summer of 1862 to either Southern sympathizers or Negroes.

York County residents often viewed freedmen with suspicion. Some remembered the "Conspiracy of 1803" in which Negroes and white supporters set a series of barn fires. The arsons erupted after a court verdict against a black woman in the poisoning deaths of two whites.

In 1861, suspicions about the loyalty of Wrightsville's large Negro population had caused the town's leaders to order them to give up guns and ammunition. Several months later, the town's fathers returned the guns, plus $3.50 to one man whose shotgun had been lost.

Now, in 1862, Wrightsville Borough Council ordered armed patrols to guard against arsonists. The fires stopped, as did the nightly patrols.

• • •

A heated discussion with a visiting geography book salesman landed the Rev. Thomas Street in York's lockup one Saturday in early 1862.

York's Presbyterian minister had given the visitor's product an endorsement, soon to his regret.

Street observed the salesman engaged in a heated discussion with Col. Sam Hays, a Union officer recuperating from wounds.

Street detected the salesman's edge and bellied up to the man, who had been spouting Southern sympathies.

"My friend, I'll have to ask you for my recommendation (back)," Street said, "as I cannot endorse anyone who would curse the best government in the world."

Soon, Street and Hays sat in jail, accused of hitting the stranger.

Charles Underwood, proprietor of York's Wheatfield Inn, and Philip Small backed bail for the two inmates.

The next day, Street preached on "The Loyalty of the Citizens," making no reference to the altercation.

Street, indeed, had a combative streak in him.

"It was no doubtful utterance which he made in the name of God for right and liberty and union," someone who knew him said.

Still, his deeply divided church stuck together during his pastorate, which concluded just before the war's end in April 1865.

'Here we have everything that we need'

An assistant U.S. quartermaster visited York in the spring of 1862 to demolish the cavalry barracks on Penn Common.

He determined the sturdy barracks had more value standing than as lumber. He passed on his evaluation to the War Department.

A Union medical official came next, touring the structures to determine if they could serve as a hospital for sick and wounded soldiers. He found the buildings would be just right, with certain alterations. The buildings could accommodate 800 to 1,000 patients with moveable bunks placed every six feet.

The structures could be carved into wards, additional windows cut in and ventilators placed on the roofs. The roofs leaked, so they would be covered with watertight material.

And as each ward was finished, the wounded could be brought in.

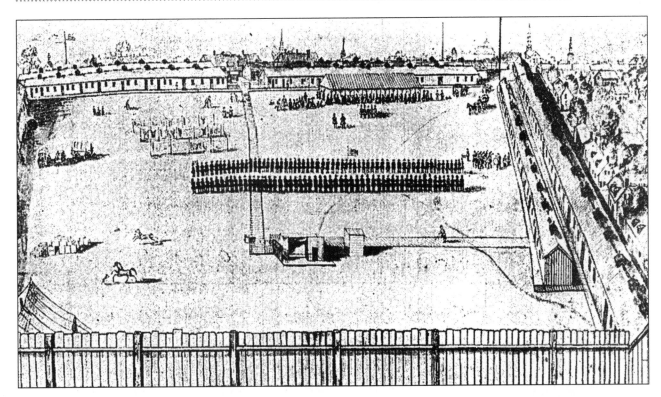

This sketch of the U.S. Army General Hospital on York's Penn Common appeared in a Denver newspaper on the 100th anniversary of the Battle of Gettysburg. Gerould A. Sabin, chief surgeon Henry Palmer's grandson, supplied the drawing and some notes from his grandfather's collection. Palmer left the hospital before the end of the war, for health reasons of his own. John C. Campbell of the 11th Maine is on record as patient No. 1 at the hospital. Suffering from rheumatism, he was admitted with scores of other patients on June 27, 1862. Within 90 days of admitting their first patients, physicians at the hospital had treated 1,606 patients. Of that number, 531 returned to duty, 45 were discharged from the service, 11 died and 114 were transferrred to other hospitals. Hospital physicians were treating 900 patients in early September.

York County would soon play host to a massive U.S. Army General Hospital, a destination for wounded or sick Union soldiers in the East.

• • •

By August, Henry Thiele was preparing York's Juvenile Orchestra to perform for patients who had been filling the military hospital's new wards since late June.

"The merits of the cause and the performers are so well known to this community as to require no extended notice at our hands," The Gazette said. "We hope there will be a full turn out on the occasion."

• • •

Patient William L. Rannells gave the hospital and the Ladies Aid Society — providing nursing care, supplies and comfort — his highest praise.

"The name of York will long be remembered by me," the soldier from the 60th Ohio wrote The Gazette. "Here we have everything that we need to make us comfortable, and there has been nothing left undone by the Medical board of this Hospital that pertains to our welfare ... ."

By early September, chief surgeon Henry Palmer and six other physicians had treated 1,606 patients.

Only 11 patients had died since the hospital opened.

• • •

Even with the wounded coming into town, day-to-day county life remained as event-filled as before the fighting began.

In one week in the summer of 1862, congregants dedi-

William Wagner provided this view in 1830 of the York County Hospital and Poorhouse complex. The almshouse was completed in 1805 and the hospital in 1828. The hospital served wounded Union soldiers when facilities at the Penn Common hospital and Washington Hall overflowed with wounded.

cated a new Evangelical Association church building in Springfield Township, and women at St. John the Baptist Episcopal Church in York held a strawberry festival at the courthouse.

William H. Welsh, longtime York County resident and head of the Pennsylvania Democratic Executive

Committee, presented plans about the upcoming state party convention to sympathetic county newspapers.

W.W. Reed, a local auctioneer, sold 10 shares of York County Bank stock, valued at $30, to another bank.

And a group of young men passed some time at Penn Common by pushing wheelbarrows, while blindfolded, toward a post 100 yards away.

"Many of those who endeavored to touch the post got completely out of the course and wandered about in a circle," The Gazette said, "or passed it at a considerable distance, which afforded much merriment to the numerous lookers on."

• • •

When news reached York that Union soldiers by the hundreds had been wounded in the Second Battle of Bull Run in late August, the Ladies Aid Society promptly assembled to make bandages.

The group spent an entire Sunday working on these dressings for soldiers, taking soft cloth and winding it onto spools. They grew short on material, so they sent out a call to York residents for lint.

"Contributions of linen from those who may not have it in their power to convert it into lint will also be thankfully received," a directive from the U.S. government stated.

Eight surgeons from York County and 11 other members of the medical fraternity boarded a midnight express to Washington, D.C., to treat those wounded at the Bull Run field. The battle covered the same site as the first fight at Manassas, Va., the previous summer.

The doctors soon returned. In the aftermath of the fight, the victorious Confederates controlled the battlefield and all the wounded.

• • •

Soon, all available space in York was devoted to wounded soldiers, including many suffering men whom the Confederates had left behind at Bull Run.

Some patients came from hospitals in Frederick, as northward-moving rebels drove them out of town.

Those able to move stepped to Gettysburg and traveled by rail to York. Orderlies transferred 125 patients to the York County Hospital at the North end of Broad Street in York. That hospital treated indigent county residents and wards from the nearby poorhouse.

One hundred found cots at Washington Hall on South George Street, normally where people gathered for stage performances in York. About 75 squeezed into the Penn Common military hospital.

• • •

In the midst of this, newspapers told of Delphine P. Baker's upcoming free lecture in town.

Many leading men of the nation's capital recommended the speaker, with her topic, "Our Country — Its Wants, and Our Duties."

Gardner and Hemming's Great American Circus was also booked in town. The circus had pleased spectators on a previous visit.

"... (W)e have no doubt that those who see proper (to) attend on this occasion," The Gazette stated, "will be equally well pleased."

The bloody Manassas field was too far away to cancel such events, even if some of those bleeding from wounds sustained in the battle rested in cots around York.

But a rebel thrust farther north would receive a different reaction.

After major battles, the large military hospital on Penn Common, with its numerous wards, could still not handle the thousands of wounded soldiers transported from far-away battlefields. Hospital physicians also treated the wounded in Washington Hall, above, a place for entertainment on South George Street in York, and the York County Hospital, part of the poorhouse complex.

Rebel advance causes scare

The Confederate march toward the Mason-Dixon Line in early September 1862, the campaign that ended in the Battle of Antietam in northern Maryland, worried people in York County.

A large gathering met in the courthouse on a Saturday night, Sept. 6, to consider Pennsylvania Gov. Curtin's call for military companies to defend the state if the Confederate advance could not be stopped.

John Evans, senior member of the York County Bar, chaired the meeting, and Philip Small and Robert Fisher sat as vice presidents.

"On taking his seat, the chairman addressed the meeting in the most stirring and patriotic terms," The Gazette stated, "setting forth the serious character of the pending danger, and the necessity of promptly preparing to meet it."

That week, stores and taverns in York shut down every evening to provide members of the hastily organized home guard an opportunity to drill.

The threat seemed so imminent that some businesses closed in the afternoons, too, and many merchants boxed up their more valuable goods and sent them for safekeeping across the Susquehanna River. Some townspeople sent their families to safer locales.

By mid-week, two cannons and caissons arrived from Harrisburg, along with rifles and ammunition.

• • •

York's borough council called a special meeting at the Laurel Engine Company to respond to the rebel threat.

Council reappointed a Committee of Safety to handle all decisions prompted by a possible rebel invasion. Chief Burgess Small, Robert Fisher, John Evans, W. Latimer Small, Thomas White, Peter McIntyre and Daniel Kraber made up the committee.

This was not the first time that York's fathers appointed a committee to focus on military affairs, and it would not be the last.

About 90 years earlier, a similar group organized county war efforts as Revolutionary War patriots drilled for battle against the British.

That group of town leaders also took the name Committee of Safety.

York sent off a company in July 1775 to aid George Washington's campaign against the British in Boston.

That brisk-stepping company was also a rifle company — the York County Rifle Company.

• • •

A.B. Farquhar, a young York businessman and a relative newcomer to town, rode with a local volunteer cavalry unit toward the Confederate position in northern Maryland. Its mission was to gain information on the rebel movement.

By the time his unit reached Hanover, volunteers unaccustomed to hours in the saddle started dropping out. Attrition took care of his comrades, but Farquhar rode on, confident that he would meet former schoolmates from the South, dressed in gray.

Soon, Confederate pickets slowed him down. He learned that Fitzhugh Lee, nephew of Robert E. Lee and a former acquaintance, commanded a nearby cavalry unit.

He gained directions to Lee's headquarters.

"Is it true," Farquhar asked Lee, "that you are going through York? I am interested because I have some property there."

The cavalryman replied that the Southerners were headed through the Cumberland Valley toward Harrisburg.

The two traded information for several minutes, and Lee provided a password for Farquhar to return through the lines.

Should Farquhar keep the conversation confidential except that the Confederates were not aiming toward York? Farquhar wondered.

"Tell them anything you choose to tell," Lee said, "They will soon know anyway."

Farquhar hurried back to York, grabbed the train to Harrisburg and informed Gov. Curtin of his conversation.

• • •

The ferocity of fighting at the pitched battle between blue and gray at Antietam Creek, near Sharpsburg, Md., did not surprise many in York County. The sound of heavy cannonading reaching the county from that direction on Sept. 17 portended loss of life and limb.

Groups of county residents traveled to the Antietam battlefield in time to see the results of the bloodiest single day of fighting in the war — a day that Union troops stopped the Confederate advance. They rendered some

TO REPEL INVASION!!

The citizens of the several townships are required to assemble at suitable places within their limits, and organize military companies under the act of 1858, to aid each other in repelling invasion of the county. Such organization to consist of the enrollment of 40 men, rank and file, and the election of a captain, and 1st and 2d lieutenants, to enable the companies to procure arms.

By order of the public meeting,
JOHN EVANS, President.
ROBERT J. FISHER,
P. A. SMALL, Vice Presidents.

YORK, Sept. 8, 1862.

Printed at the "Gazette" Office, nearly opposite the Court House, York, Pa.

The northward-bound Confederate Army gave the people of York County a scare in September 1862. This handbill urged county residents to prepare for an invasion. Union troops stopped the Confederate advance in the Battle of Antietam in Maryland. Less than a year later, the Confederates crossed the Mason-Dixon Line and invaded York and other southcentral Pennsylvania counties.

relief for the wounded, including many county soldiers.

The residents returned to York with names of the dead and wounded. People searched the lists, praying that their loved ones would not be on them.

Surgeons E.H. Pentz, Jacob Hay Jr. and W.D. Baily later reached the bloody field to provide medical care.

Meanwhile, locomotives pulling rail cars full of wounded soldiers rushed to York directly from the battlefield, the floors of the cars running with blood.

Orderlies carefully lifted the men from the cars, placed them on stretchers and carried them to the hospital, with well-prepared attendants in tow.

The one-month-old 130th Pennsylvania, with four companies of county residents, sustained heavy casualties fighting in the thick of battle. Twelve county soldiers lost their lives, and at least 35 sustained wounds, including the regiment's lieutenant colonel, Levi Maish.

But Union fighting kept the county safe from a rebel invasion — at least for a season.

• • •

The Yankee check of the rebels at Antietam encouraged Union men of all ranks.

John Miller, serving with the 76th Pennsylvania in South Carolina, wanted to "act guerilla" against the rebel thrust northward.

He wrote his brother, George, in York County that McClellan deployed a sound strategy in allowing Lee's men to move north then entrapping them.

The Confederates, he boasted, learned a lesson.

"... (T)hey will never go back again," he predicted, "for they were too badly licked."

• • •

John Evans found his new position as chairman of the Committee of Safety attracted controversy.

A Philadelphia Inquirer article stated that gunpowder from York was sent to rebel lines. Three wagons loaded with powder and large quantities of salt reportedly passed through Taneytown, Md., toward rebel positions.

The Gazette rushed to Evans' defense, pointing out that the lawyer owned the only gunpowder factory in the county and not a single wheelbarrow load, much less three wagon loads, were stored at any one place.

"Knowing the utter falsity of the powder story," The Gazette stated, "we have no doubt the other part of the paragraph is equally salty."

• • •

About 16 months into the war, county residents regularly read reports of soldiers they knew who died in uniform.

Not all died on the battlefield. Many succumbed to disease in camp or on the march.

News reached York in September that Andrew Hudner, an artillerist, accidentally drowned while crossing a river in Virginia. Hudner left behind a wife and small children, dependent upon him for support.

Such reports dampened volunteerism. Despite the recent rebel threat, voluntary enlistments no longer filled the ranks. In the fall of 1862, the federal government prepared to call out state militia for nine-month periods of service.

A Democratic majority unsympathetic with Lincoln's military policies hampered York County's ability to fill quotas with volunteers.

But York also had shared its resources with thousands of Union troops quartered in the borough. About 2,100 county volunteers were then in the service. The wounded at the military hospital constantly reminded townspeople about the cost of war.

Even with all this sacrifice, The Army of the Potomac was not winning in battle. Lincoln's revelation that the Emancipation Proclamation would become effective Jan. 1, 1863, caused county residents to perceive that the war's goal was to free slaves, not preserve the union.

That concern, plus a part of the proclamation stating that Negroes would serve in the military, reached into Union camps, too.

John Miller of the 76th Pennsylvania, wrote his brother, "...(L)eave me know how recruiting takes in York; if they would know what I know it would go pretty hard to raise one company in York. (I)m afraid the niggar question will raise a rumpus in the army, yet if ever I get back, I'll shoot all the niggars I come across... ."

When more than 2,000 county residents received call-out notifications, 340 reported, and better than 800 found substitutes — men who would take their place for a fee. Sometimes, that payment approached $1,000.

More than 500 failed to report, staying at home or moving from the area.

John Hauser, a 35-year-old farmer from Spring Garden Township was one such resident to receive a call-up notice. He had five days to report to York. There, he would receive transportation to Harrisburg.

"All citizens who have ben drafted are advised to take with them to the rendezvous, if possible, a good, stout woolen blanket," his notice stated. The regular blanket was 84-by-66 inches and weighed 5 pounds.

Some men answering the call claimed exemption because of bad health.

Dr. W.S. Roland and Dr. James M. Shearer kept busy hearing appeals from those seeking to escape duty.

The physicians conducted the hearings at the court-house and then traveled to Lewisberry, in northern York County, and Wrightsville to hear additional appeals for exemptions.

At all sites, large numbers seeking exemption came forward. The physicians approved about 340 exemptions.

Despite this lethargic response, a regiment of county men — Col. Andrew J. Fulton's 166th Pennsylvania — formed for a nine-month hitch in less than a month.

'I am only doing my duty'

By the fall of 1862, Col. George Hay and the 87th Pennsylvania had long ago left behind the familiar duties of guarding the Northern Central.

They marched as part of a western Virginia campaign, winding through the mountains looking for rebel raiders on horseback.

One cold day, the soldiers stepped single file through thick underbrush.

The hammer of a soldier's rifle snagged a branch, and as he fought to disentangle it, the gun discharged. The ball passed through a rolled-up blanket slung across the shoulder of John Q. Colehouse, a Littlestown resident. It lodged in the Adams County man's brain, killing him instantly.

His squad dug a grave with bayonets, wrapped his body in a blanket and buried him on the mountaintop.

A drummer boy tapped out a goodbye, and some fifers played a dirge. The column moved forward, and a few friends lingered to place a stone on the gravesite.

• • •

One day, soldiers from the 87th camped near Beverly, Va. They put up tents near a neat cottage where Mrs. Arnold lived.

She tended to sick and wounded soldiers in a nearby church, converted into a hospital. She also nursed the sick in her own home.

Soldiers from the regiment, guarding the hospital, thanked her for taking care of the sick.

"I am only doing my duty," she said.

They talked about the Second Battle of Bull Run, fought a few days before.

"My brother is an officer on the other side, but I hope he is safe," she said. "He thinks he is right, but I am in favor of the Union."

"Who is your brother?" asked the guard.

"General Jackson," she said, walking into the hospital, "Stonewall Jackson now."

• • •

Federal soldiers in the western Virginia mountains often foraged for their meals. One such collector carried a beehive back to camp with fellow scavengers.

As the weather warmed up that day, so did the bees. Their sting found their mark, and hundreds more followed the soldier as he hastened into camp.

Maj. Charles H. Buehler observed the scene, "The boy didn't seem to know his gun was loaded. Wonder if he could run that fast if the rebels were after him."

• • •

Sgt. B.F. Frick and a group of about 20 men from the 87th guarded a signal station beyond Union lines near

The 87th Pennsylvania called its camp near, New Creek in western Virginia, Camp Jessie.

The 87th Pennsylvania produced a regimental history that combined stories of the unit's actions on the battle-field and in camp. This drawing shows a scavenger returning to camp with a hive, mad bees and all, during a campaign to capture rebel raiders in western Virginia.

Winchester, Va.

One evening in January 1863, a sentry noticed unusual lights in the woods some distance away.

"Mysterion lights," Joe Cook whispered, "what are they?"

A squad accompanied Cook toward the lights, but the soldiers didn't walk far before concluding swamp gas caused the glow.

"I seen it often in the woods and swamps around York," Cook said.

Days later, Cook and others watched the sun set and, looking the other way, observed what appeared to be giants along the eastern horizon.

"A worse sign than the mysterion lights," Cook said, "If the rebels down here are that big, we can never whip 'em."

One of the soldiers raised his arm, and so did one of the giants in the sky.

An atmospheric condition projected the soldiers' shad-ows onto the eastern clouds.

• • •

The band of the 87th did not join their regiment as they walked up and down the hills of western Virginia.

The musicians returned home after their discharge by the War Department. Fewer bands would now accompany each brigade.

All were in good health, The Gazette observed, and the Army experience had improved their musicianship.

No consensus back home

While men were dying or suffering from wounds, many in York County stood toe to toe on the politics fuel-ing the fighting.

Some county residents viewed the Peace Democrat, or Copperhead, position as an insidious force working against the Northern cause.

County Peace Democrats summed up this position with the oft-repeated opinion in The York Gazette, "The Union as it was, the Constitution as it is, and the Negroes where they are."

Such a strong statement inevitably attracted criticism.

Someone in accord with the Lincoln administration wrote in minutes at the Sabbath School, meeting at Sanney's School in southeastern York County, that the Copperheads had tried to ruin the religious group. Their efforts fell short.

"There is still a stubborn feeling among the people on account of their dumb politics ... ," the writer said. "Thanks be to the Lord for the blessing."

• • •

The Gazette underscored the importance of the 1862 fall election.

The Democratic slate opposed the Emancipation Proclamation, Abraham Lincoln's call to free slaves in ter-ritories rebelling against the Union. Every man on the Republican ticket either favored the proclamation by affir-mation or failure to repudiate it.

"The line is drawn!" the newspaper opined. "You must either vote the Democratic ticket or vote to endorse the freeing of the Niggers! You must either be an Abolitionist or a Democrat! Which will you do and which will you be?"

The Gazette backed the Democratic position that each

state should "take care" of its own slaves and free blacks. The Democrats viewed Republicans as advocates of taxation to purchase the slaves of the South and to levy additional taxes to support and school freed slaves.

The forthcoming Proclamation did not resonate in Democratic York County. It often lacked support elsewhere in the North and troubled some top Union Army officers. Many in support of Union forces believed that the reason for war was simply to restore a unified nation, not to end slavery.

When fall voting was tallied, York County fell solidly on the Democratic side.

Voters handed Democratic congressional candidate Adam Glossbrenner a 2,668-vote margin in the county. But the former co-owner of The Gazette fell short in Cumberland and Perry counties by a wide margin to lose the Democratic nomination for the coveted seat by 2,219 votes to Joseph Baily, a veteran state officeholder.

The Gazette, an exuberant Glossbrenner supporter, did not view Baily as an ally of conservative Democrats, "We desire it to be distinctly understood that York is not responsible for the re-election of such a representation — the tools of a corrupt administration ... ."

• • •

In its first edition of 1863, The Gazette harped on Lincoln's newly minted Emancipation Proclamation.

The weight of emancipation was already being felt, the newspaper contended, and Union soldiers were bearing the brunt of it.

The newspaper had received a report that in one chilly night, 12 Union soldiers froze to death when on picket duty near Fredericksburg, Va. They reportedly lacked the proper clothing to guard against a severe winter.

Then came the report that 11 sick and wounded soldiers died from exposure in hospitals near Washington.

Meanwhile, thousands of former slaves were lodged in brick mansions in Washington, rented by the government at great expense. The government fed and clothed them "like princes."

"There are guilty contractors, quartermasters, and higher officials," the newspaper said, "who will have to render a dread account to God and man for the death and sufferings of our brave soldiers."

The newspaper believed Lincoln had recklessly pushed emancipation:

"Controlled as he is by the machinations of the ultra Abolitionists in the Senate and out of it, it became a 'military necessity' in the estimate of the able and distinguished Chief Magistrate and in defiance of the Constitution and regardless of consequences, the proclamation has been published."

• • •

The Gazette critiqued the Negro Brigade Bill, which grew out of Lincoln's emancipation directive. Or perhaps the newspaper focused on the bill's sponsor, Thaddeus Stevens, an anti-slavery Republican congressman who taught school in York as a young man.

The newspaper recounted parts of the bill: The president could arm as many Negroes as he considered necessary for up to five years. Their rations, clothing and pay would be paid at prevailing rates. White or black officers could be in command, but no black officer could exercise authority over white officers or men.

"That's an insult to the darkeys," the newspaper said in an aside.

Then the newspaper turned to Stevens himself, "Old Thad is afraid the Democrats are going to kidnap the president."

The newspaper drew that conclusion from Stevens' closing remarks on the bill. The congressman stated that the Northern Democrats held secret meetings under the guise of the Knights of the Golden Circle, with the view of seizing control of the government and the president.

War not working for Billy Yanks

In late January 1863, Gen. William B. Franklin came home to York, a little more than a month after heading one-third of the Union Army in the disastrous Battle of Fredericksburg.

The Army of the Potomac suffered a devastating loss in fighting in and around that Virginia town.

Franklin lost command of one of the Army's grand divisions. A congressional investigating committee would soon pin the defeat largely on Franklin. Now as the major general visited with old friends in York, he awaited reassignment to a new command.

His name floated around Pennsylvania as a possible Democratic candidate for governor. Franklin had long been a friend and trusted subordinate of former Army of Potomac commander George McClellan.

McClellan was gaining momentum as the Democrat's answer to Abraham Lincoln in the 1864 presidential election. It would be expected that the name of Franklin, a high profile, lifelong Democrat, would be put forth for high office in his home state.

Franklin would gain the full support of The Gazette, "The General's sound Democracy and great popular-

These Nov. 11, 1862, headlines in The York Gazette boast of the Democratic Party's successes, 18 months into the war. Many newspapers of the day promoted political parties. York County was home to several weekly newspapers representing both Republicans and Democrats.

ity and availability commend him in the strongest terms to the Democracy of Pennsylvania, as their standard-bearer in the important contest to be fought in October next in behalf of the cause of Constitutional liberty."

• • •

While William Franklin was battling the Confederates, another son of York County in East Tennessee hoped for a return to health so that he could fight the Yankees.

Confederate Gen. Johnson Kelly Duncan was born and educated in the county. He joined Franklin, Horatio Gates Gibson, Edmund Schriver, Granville Haller and Michael P. Small in the ranks of young county men at the U.S. Military Academy before the war.

Duncan's pre-war Army duties took him to the South, where he later took a civilian position as chief engineer of the Louisiana Board of Public Works.

His wife came from that area, and the military leaders he was closest to sided with the Confederacy. When division came, Duncan joined the Confederate Army.

In East Tennessee, he served as Gen. Braxton Bragg's chief of staff. Then, he contracted typhoid.

The disease took his life in December 1862, in Knoxville, Tenn., far from his native York County home.

• • •

David Small won his first re-election as chief burgess by a 109-vote margin in the March 1863 election.

The vote for burgess and council also gave the Democrats control of the borough.

"And all this, despite the most desperate efforts of our political opponents — despite slander, and charges of disloyalty — despite the opprobrious epithets of 'Copperheads' and traitors ... we have vindicated the cause of the Constitution and Union," The Gazette thundered.

Actually, the Copperhead nickname should be coveted, an article reprinted in The Gazette reasoned.

The Copperhead is a fearless, independent snake that knows its power, and when disturbed, uses it. It never runs except when attacking its foes, and its bite, when aroused, is awful.

The Black Republicans could be likened to a black snake.

"The black snake is a cowardly, hissing, thieving reptile ... ," the newspaper explained.

"He robs birds' nests, visits the barn yard and sucks hens' eggs, and will often be found curled around the legs of a cow sucking her milk, just as Black Republican contractors, jobbers and office holders are now doing with Uncle Sam's cow."

No matter what his party was called, David Small had secured a second term to the most prestigious and responsible public position he would ever hold. As a newspaperman, he was well established, the owner of the noted newspaper of the dominant party in York County.

But the next year would require all of the wisdom he could muster for success in both arenas.

• • •

Despite these views on the war, county residents still loved the warriors. Troops moving south continued to find York a convenient place to bivouac.

One unit — the U.S. Zouave Cadets from Pittsburgh — could not secure space at the fairgrounds. Henry Bayler, a York tanner, quartered the troops in his currying shop. Food for the men came from Sarah Ann Bayler's kitchen, and officers ate at a long table in that room.

'The Negro's Slavery is Abolished, and the Colored population set free,' Lewis Miller wrote beneath his drawing of a gathering celebrating the Emancipation Proclamation. President Lincoln issued an initial proclamation in September 1862, freeing slaves in territories at war with the Union. The proclamation went into effect Jan. 1, 1863. Lewis Miller wrote at the bottom of this drawing, celebrating the Confederate surrender: 'Our gun is pois'd/Our aim is sure/Our wish is good, our End is pure/To virtue we are Sworn allies, and Shoot at folly as it flies.'

Gen. William B. Franklin, a native of York, played key roles in early fighting in Virginia and Maryland and commanded the Left Grand Division of The Army of the Potomac at the Battle of Fredericksburg. He became a scapegoat for the Union defeat there. Before the war, he made a lasting contribution, supervising construction of the U.S. Capitol dome and extension.

The unit left behind a Bible in return for room and board.

Sarah Ann Bayler became known for nursing the wounded but better still for supplying fresh bread from her kitchen to troop trains passing through York.

• • •

A parade of generals commanding the Northern Army contributed to the political confusion in York County and other Yankee states in the spring of 1863.

The latest Union defeat came in Chancellorsville, Va., in early May 1863.

While political consensus in York County was far from

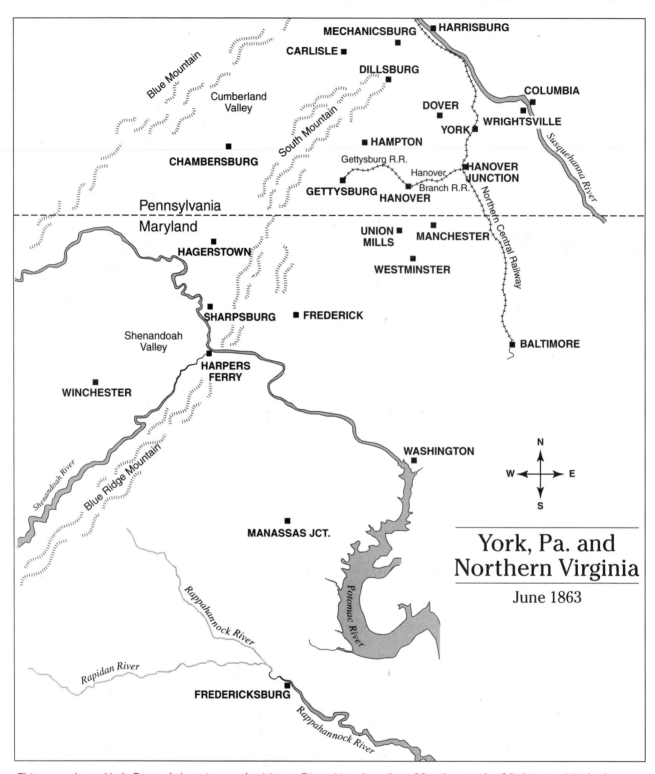

York, Pa. and Northern Virginia

June 1863

This map shows York County's location on the Mason-Dixon Line, less than 50 miles north of Baltimore. Vital telegraph and railroad lines cut through the county, connecting Washington, D.C., with points north. In the campaign of 1863, Confederate troops, starting from the vicinity of Fredericksburg, Va., headed north through the Shenandoah and Cumberland valleys to Pennsylvania. Union troops followed on the east side of the Blue Ridge Mountains. The two sides collided at Gettysburg, Southern forces approaching from the north and Northern forces moving from the south.

clear, Confederate Gen. Robert E. Lee was gaining insight about his next move.

Shuttling between his headquarters near Fredericksburg, Va., to confer with President Davis in the

Confederate capital of Richmond, Lee planned another invasion of the North.

Undaunted that he had been turned away at Antietam Creek in his northward advance the previous summer, Lee

This Harper's Weekly drawing of the York Fairgrounds, converted into Camp Scott, gives a view of the pagentry and optimism of the Civil War's early days. By the late summer of 1861, York County residents and others in the North realized the war would be protracted. By the summer of 1862, York County residents were burying their own dead and caring for the wounded in the military hospital on Penn Common. In the summer of 1863, the ravages of war crossed York County soil.

again looked at the rich cropland of Maryland and south-central Pennsylvania.

Lee weighed several factors, including the fact that his troops could live off of the rich agricultural land north of the Mason-Dixon Line. Virginia would not have to feed his Army, and Old Dominion farmers could harvest their crops without interruption from invading troopers.

Other considerations fed into the invasion decision, as well.

A movement north would distract Gen. Ulysses S. Grant's efforts against beleaguered Confederates at Vicksburg, Miss., and elsewhere in the lower Mississippi Valley. If they stole the march, the Confederates would disrupt Union plans for a summer campaign in Virginia, where the Yankee Army sat after its defeat at Chancellorsville.

Union Gen. Joseph "Fighting Joe" Hooker, Lee's Army of the Potomac counterpart, would be forced to decide whether to protect the nation's capital or follow the Confederates to the North, where the two armies would almost certainly meet in a pitched battle.

If Hooker chose the latter, he would need thousands of soldiers now defending Washington, D.C., weakening the defenses of that city, the heart of the Union war effort.

Politically, by crossing the Susquehanna River to threaten Harrisburg and other Northern cities, Lee's movements might give Democrats in the North leverage to force Lincoln to negotiate a peace settlement with the

David Small signed this oath for a second term as York's chief burgess. The oath stated that Small would 'support the Constitution of the United States, the constitution of the State of Pennsylvania, and further that I will discharge the duties of Chief Burgess of the Borough of York with fidelity during the ensuing year.' Three months later, he would serve as Gen. Jubal Early's primary contact during the Confederate occupation of the borough.

South. If Harrisburg, capital city of a large Northern state, fell into Lee's hands, this signaled that a similar fate could be awaiting other prominent cities above the Mason-Dixon Line.

Further, his men could cut communications and supply

lines between the Midwest and the Eastern Seaboard. If they could interrupt rail and telegraph service on the Northern Central Railway at Hanover Junction, they would hamper communications between Washington and the North.

As for where a battle might be fought, Lee viewed Chambersburg, York or Gettysburg as options.

He preferred Gettysburg, A.L. Long, the general's military secretary, said.

It was nearer to the Potomac River, his base of operations in the North, and he could protect his communications and supply lines in the Shenandoah Valley.

"So, if General Lee remained inactive, both Vicksburg and Richmond would be imperiled," Maj. Charles Marshall, of the general's staff, stated, "whereas, if he were successful north of the Potomac, both would be saved."

• • •

With all these considerations in mind, Lee ordered troops north from Confederate camps around Fredericksburg on June 3, 1863. His plans called for a move up the Shenandoah Valley. He would enter its northern extension, the Cumberland Valley running between South Mountain and Blue Mountain, and march through Carlisle to Harrisburg.

South Mountain, forming the eastern wall of the Cumberland Valley, would be the only barrier of substance between the Confederates and York, 45 miles away.

Actually, that low mountain, the northern part of the Blue Ridge Mountains, would represent but a bump to the approaching gray mass.

"It is stated that a large body of Confederate troops ... passed through Culpepper Courthouse on Monday and proceeded in the direction of Gordonville," The York Gazette said about the initial movement of rebel troops. "No alarm exists in the Federal army concerning those reported movements."

II

A gray cloud blows toward York County

June 4, 1863 to June 27, 1863

'His invasion … will degrade you and your country, and if allowed to proceed without strenuous resistance, will make you objects of contempt and scorn.'
— Union Gen. William B. Franklin

Confederate Army pushes northward

In mid-June 1863, the 87th Pennsylvania stood with Gen. Robert H. Milroy's division in Winchester, Va., braced against The Army of Northern Virginia's threat against Pennsylvania.

The general devoted personal attention to the advancing rebels from a perch in a basket atop a Winchester flagpole.

When the strength of the Confederate advance up the Shenandoah Valley became evident, Milroy devised a plan of retreat, north to Harpers Ferry.

Down from the flagpole after a day in the hot sun, Milroy maneuvered his badly outnumbered troops under the cover of darkness. Soon thereafter, believing that he was surrounded, Milroy personally ordered the 87th to contest soldiers from Gen. Richard Ewell's 2nd Corps at Carter's Woods, outside Winchester.

The men from southcentral Pennsylvania moved into the woods to brawl with battle-savvy Confederates — a far different assignment from guarding a railroad or chasing raiders in the mountains of western Virginia. This was a confrontation with a veteran enemy infantry unit with artillery support, the first time the 87th had been so engaged.

Taking on rugged rebel foot soldiers proved to be more than enough to occupy the 87th. But friendly fire from behind, from the 18th Connecticut, only made things worse.

Milroy raced forward to flag the Connecticut soldiers about redirecting their rifles toward the rebels.

The 87th regrouped, moved ahead and then fell back — way back.

• • •

The Yankee retreat turned into a rout as confused men from Milroy's command scattered under Confederate pressure.

The 87th dissolved into at least three detachments. A group of more than 200, under Maj. Noah Ruhl headed west and then north to Pennsylvania, eventually reaching Bloody Run, a village in Bedford County later called Everett. Regimental commander Col. John Schall's group of about 150 made it to Harper's Ferry with Milroy. Another squad of 50 hoofed it back to York.

The three detachments lost contact. They would not reunite until three weeks later.

Writing from Bedford County, Ruhl reported, "... I am unable to give any account of the losses, in consequence of the regiment being broken up into several detachments, as so far distant as not to have an official report from either detachment."

In time, the men of the 87th would learn about the numbers: The rebels killed 14 men and wounded 26. Nine officers and 190 men fell captive.

Confederate Gen. Jubal A. Early, who commanded a division under Ewell, scooped up the captives and sent them on the long march toward prisons in the South. Then, Early and his division moved North.

Some of the 87th would meet up with Early's men — and guns captured from Milroy's command — again in

Union Gen. Robert H. Milroy commanded the garrison at Winchester, Va., that gave way to the rebel push up the Shenandoah Valley. The Confederates, under Richard S. Ewell's command, routed Milroy's men. The rebels captured hundreds of soldiers under Milroy's command, including men from York County. Those able to get away scattered in an undisciplined retreat.

about two weeks. That time, it would be in their home county of York.

• • •

With the fracture of Union troops at Winchester, no Northern force of any size stood between Dick Ewell's men and Harrisburg. There, the newly formed Department of the Susquehanna desperately fought to recruit, equip and train defensive forces.

"Fighting Joe" Hooker's Army of the Potomac headed north on June 6, about three days' march behind Lee's men.

Rebel infantry units were pacing up the Shenandoah Valley, and Confederate troopers on horseback — the cavalry — screened their movement, plugging the gaps in the mountains. Hooker could only guess about the Confederate Army's movements.

"Old Bald Head" Ewell's men formed the vanguard of the Confederate invasion.

Long a confirmed bachelor, the popular Ewell was recently married. His wedding to a widow, Lizinka Campbell Brown, came during a year-long convalescence from a leg wound — a wound that cost him a leg.

His unit was one of three corps under The Army of Northern Virginia's reorganization. James Longstreet led the 1st Corps and A.P. Hill, the 3rd Corps.

Robert E. Lee restructured his Army after the loss of his trusted lieutenant, Thomas J. "Stonewall" Jackson, to

Gen. Richard S. Ewell, 46, commander of the 2nd Corps and successor to the legendary Thomas J. 'Stonewall' Jackson, headed the vanguard of the Confederate thrust into Pennsylvania. His service as an engineer in Pennsylvania before the war gave him intimate knowledge of the land that lay in his path.

Gen. Jubal A. Early, 46, a cantankerous, often caustic, U.S. Military Academy graduate and Virginia lawyer, headed the rebel infantry division of Richard Ewell's 2nd Corps, that occupied York County in late June 1863. Robert E. Lee called Early 'My bad old man' but valued his tenacity.

Andrew G. Curtin, Pennsylvania's wartime governor, coordinated the defense of Harrisburg and southern Pennsylvania as the Confederates marched north. Pennsylvanians showed their approval of the Centre County Republican's work by re-electing him to a second term in 1863.

friendly fire en route to the smashing May victory at the Battle of Chancellorsville in Virginia. The 39-year-old Jackson died from pneumonia while recovering from bullet wounds that cost him his left arm.

Ewell ended up with most of Jackson's well-oiled command, and Lee ordered those men to lead the invasion onto Northern soil.

Lee split the 20,000-plus man 2nd Corps into three divisions under Early and Gens. Edward Johnson and Robert Rodes. Each division was further divided into brigades. Early's division was organized into four brigades, which were further broken down into 17 regiments.

At the start of the war, 1,000 men would be mustered into regiments. By 1863, casualties and shortages of able-bodied or willing men meant that many regiments were less than half their original size.

Ewell received orders to march to the Susquehanna River and capture Harrisburg, if feasible. His invaders would split in two prongs, one going toward Harrisburg and the other, perhaps as a diversion, heading through the heart of York County toward the Wrightsville bridge, downriver from the state capital.

There, the rebels had orders to burn the 5,620-foot-long bridge and then retrace their steps to York. They would move via Dillsburg, in northwestern York County, to join the main force in Carlisle for the projected assault on Harrisburg.

Hill's corps, the next to march up the Valley, would follow Ewell's southern path toward York and the Susquehanna. Longstreet's men, the last in line, would reinforce Ewell's northern thrust against Harrisburg.

Confederate troops operated under Lee's directive — General Order No. 72 — to avoid destruction of private property. Certain officers could issue requisitions upon Northern authorities or private individuals but would pay market prices for the goods. If refused, supplies could be seized without cash payment, but the victim would be given a receipt, payable by the Confederate government after the South won the war.

Days later, Lee followed up with a reminder, General Order No. 73. "It must be remembered that we make war only upon armed men, and that we cannot take vengeance for the wrongs our people have suffered ... ," Lee wrote.

Lee possibly viewed the directive as a means to maintain discipline, reward the entire Army rather than individual scavengers and to avoid strengthening the enemy's resolve by antagonizing it.

Practically speaking, the Confederates paid for supplies in nearly worthless Confederate money.

The invading rebels kept these orders to themselves. Such secrecy enhanced their ability to wring money and supplies from threatened people in the North.

• • •

When Gen. A.G. Jenkins' cavalrymen crossed the Mason-Dixon Line south of Chambersburg, the horse soldiers became the first rebel unit to do so in the summer campaign of 1863.

Jenkins' men reached Chambersburg late on June 15 and in the early morning on June 16. The rebel raiders collected provisions, paying in Confederate money. But perceiving a mass of blue marching from Harrisburg, a skittish Jenkins returned to the main column with wagons filled with the abundance of Pennsylvania.

The cavalry general revisited Chambersburg on June 23, with Rodes' infantry division following closely behind.

Rodes' and Johnson's divisions would not stay long. They took two different routes toward Carlisle for the projected movement on Harrisburg. Johnson's men stepped along the pike before camping three miles west of Carlisle. Rodes' men marched on Walnut Bottom Road and entered Carlisle on its main east-west street. Ewell, traveling with Rodes' men, set up headquarters in the Carlisle Barracks, then a Union cavalry post.

The third division of Ewell's corps, Jubal Early's men, crossed the Potomac River at Shepherdstown and entered Pennsylvania through Waynesboro in Franklin County. By June 24, he had camped in Greenwood, east of Chambersburg.

There, he made plans to lighten his division's load, retaining only ambulance, medical and ammunition wagons, plus 15 empty wagons for supplies. Officers left behind baggage they could not carry on their horses.

Early and his division — 5,600 foot soldiers, 500 detached cavalrymen, and an artillery battalion numbering as many as 16 cannons with about 400 men to tend to them — could now move east with utmost speed.

They would trek 20 miles a day or more — across Adams and York counties to the Susquehanna.

Pennsylvania and York ponder defense

Abraham Lincoln attempted to counter the Confederate threat with a call for 100,000 volunteers from Pennsylvania, Maryland, Ohio and West Virginia.

The call assigned the Keystone State to raise half of those troops. Gov. Andrew Curtin issued a proclamation on June 12 calling for a corps of Pennsylvania militia to slow or stop the suspected rebel invasion.

The War Department appointed Gen. Darius N. Couch, an able Union commander, to head the Department of the Susquehanna. Couch had resigned command of The Army of the Potomac's 2nd Corps because of differences with "Fighting Joe" Hooker, the commanding general.

An unusual squad stepped forward in response to the governor's call. A Maryland unit, Thomas S. McGowan's Patapsco Guard, traveled to Harrisburg after camping on York's Penn Common.

In York, they met up with the Invalid Corps, veterans from the military hospital. The invalid soldiers, mending from wounds and not fit to join regular units in the field, performed guard duty and other light assignments. But these convalescents joined McGowan's combat unit.

The Invalids marched from the Harrisburg train station, as newspapers pointed out, with many an empty sleeve or with the aid of crutches. Someone observed that they appeared to have some fight left in them.

Couch immediately detached McGowan's unit to Shippensburg to provide cover for repair work on a railroad bridge at nearby Scotland, damaged by Jenkins' raiders. Troops and supplies would pass over the restored bridge to Chambersburg.

After seeing the Invalids, Gen. Joseph Knipe, commanding officer in that area, left the willing but incapable men in Shippensburg.

• • •

As the Invalids headed north for assignment, other military hospital patients moved east, away from any rebel thrust.

"Just now, all the sick soldiers are marching to the depot," young Abram Rudisill wrote his father, Abraham, the Union artillerist from York.

The patients boarding the train enjoyed enough health that they could walk or be moved. Dr. Alexander R. Blair, a surgeon at the hospital, accompanied them to Columbia, at the other end of the bridge from Wrightsville. They found quarters in an Odd Fellows Hall and later a school.

Hospital supplies sat in railroad cars on a siding between Coatesville and Downingtown in Chester County.

Henry Palmer, surgeon in charge of the York hospital, stayed behind with five patients who could not be moved.

The younger Rudisill informed his father about the townspeople's concern over the rebel invasion. Stores were sending their valuables east, out of the invaders' path.

"The Rebels, while I am writing, are reported to be in Gettysburg," he wrote.

Rudisill had picked up some bad facts.

That day, June 16, the vanguard of Ewell's Corps — Jenkins' cavalry — occupied Chambersburg.

• • •

YORK GAZETTE--EXTRA.

YORK, TUESDAY MORNING, June 16, 1863.

An immense Town Meeting was held in the Court House last night, and measures were adopted for the defence of the borough and county against the threatened raid or invasion by Lee's army.— The following Telegrams were received and read to the meeting, viz':

HARRISBURG, June 15, '63. 8 o'clock 35 minutes, P. M.

Mr. H. WELSH :—Another message just received. Mr. Palmer reached Chambersburg a few minutes ago and reports this morning the enemy in large force—cavalry, infantry and artillery—in the vicinity of Greencastle. We may expect great loss of life and devastation of property. Organise every available man.   THOMAS A. SCOTT.

HARRISBURG, 8.45 P. M.

MR. HENRY WELSH :—State news received this P. M. from Chambersburg, says Greencastle operator reports that at 4 o'clock P. M., the rebels in our State with great force. Our pickets driven in and have fallen back between Greencastle and Chambersburg. Rebels occupy Hagerstown in force. It is believed they will occupy Chambersburg to-night. There is no doubt now that they are enroute for the State Capital. Every effort should be made by people to form companies by to-morrow and be prepared to resist them. We hope your people will arouse to the importance of this.   THOMAS A. SCOTT.

As York residents met in a town meeting on June 15, 1863, two telegrams arrived for Henry Welsh, a leading York businessman, from Thomas A. Scott advising the group of the movement of rebel troops north of the Mason-Dixon Line. These were A.G. Jenkins' horsemen, the first Confederates to cross into Pennsylvania in the summer campaign of 1863. Scott, vice president of the Pennsylvania Railroad, was adept at collecting information about Confederate troops movements via a network of scouts and telegraph operators.

News about the Confederate rout of Milroy's men at Winchester, Va., and waves of Confederates moving north rippled toward York.

David Small presided at a June 15 town meeting at the courthouse to thrash out defense of the town and to bolster recruitment of volunteers.

Early in the meeting, those assembled strengthened a 15-member Committee of Safety, granting the power to make arrangements necessary for the protection of the town, county and state.

The committee members represented five wards and would be responsible for recruiting volunteers to form a home guard from those sections.

Two telegrams from officials in Harrisburg kept the assembly up to date about rebel movements: A large enemy force — Jenkins' men — had been spotted near Greencastle, on the Pennsylvania border in Franklin County. It was believed Chambersburg would be occupied that night. Companies of militia must form. Harrisburg would be their target.

"We hope your people will arouse to the importance of this," Thomas A. Scott, vice-president of the Pennsylvania Railroad, telegraphed.

The meeting went on in York.

Gen. William Franklin and Maj. Granville Haller provided counsel to the committee. Couch had placed the officers in charge of military preparations.

"We may, therefore, rest assured that everything that can be done will be done to effectively protect the Borough and county," The Gazette stated.

• • •

James Latimer did not think the Committee of Safety accomplished much.

The 27-year-old York attorney thus informed his brother, Bartow, in a letter written just minutes after the meeting adjourned.

"Nothing definite was done," he wrote, "and it is likely nothing will be done."

Latimer conjectured that at least rebel cavalry would reach York. "It is supposed they will cut the N.C.R. (Northern Central Railway) somewhere, very likely here," he wrote.

When danger became imminent, he would try to convince their mother and sister to leave for Philadelphia. He didn't predict success.

If a company of York County residents formed, he would join its ranks. But if his mother, Sarah, and sister, Jane, stayed in York, he feared that he must stay at home.

• • •

Three days later, Latimer traveled to Harrisburg to gather information from the top about the Confederate threat.

A staunch Republican, Latimer had no problem gaining an audience with an agitated Andrew Curtin. Judging from the governor's nervousness, Latimer conjectured that Lee's entire army was about to cross the Potomac.

Latimer informed his brother about operations under way at Wrightsville to dig entrenchments and rifle pits to protect the bridge. Soldiers guarded the wooden structure day and night with orders to destroy it to stop any Confederate advance.

Granville Haller, in command of a small force from assorted units in York, had orders to obstruct roads and delay the rebels if they headed that way.

"With all this there is not the least excitement here," Latimer wrote. "No one is alarmed. Everyone seems as indifferent as if there were no rebels within a thousand miles."

State and military leaders in Harrisburg were either scared about nothing and making fools of themselves or considerable danger lay ahead.

"Still many people here say it is nothing but a cause-less fight among rail-road men," he wrote.

Latimer couldn't get past York's indifference to the Confederate advance, "Every particle of interest seems to have died out here. And no one seems to think it worth while to inquire where the rebels really are."

• • •

Latimer received correct information about digging operations in Wrightsville.

The borough's council appropriated $50 to acquire rations to feed those sweating with shovels in rifle pits and assigned two councilmen to serve on a committee to carry out the purchase.

Soon thereafter, council received the balance of $23.15. The rations had cost $20.85, and the committee profited by charging $6 for its work.

• • •

William Franklin, still in York, tried to raise applause in Pennsylvania to Curtin's call for volunteers.

The wages of war had drained fighting fervor from the people of York County and elsewhere in southern Pennsylvania. Whatever confidence they had in Lincoln was ebbing. Their priority was to stay put and look for ways to protect their property and loved ones.

Fighting this mindset, Franklin predicted that the Confederate advance was no raid but an invasion. Such a

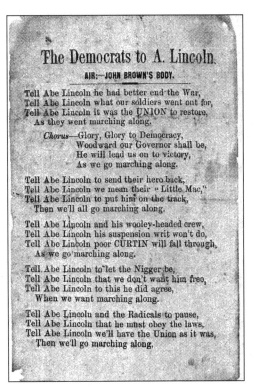

This political song made its rounds in Pennsylvania before the 1863 gubernatorial election. The piece supports Democrat George Woodward against incumbent Republican Gov. Andrew G. Curtin. 'Little Mac' refers to former Army of the Potomac Commander George McClellan, who would run a Democratic campaign against Republican Abraham Lincoln in 1864. York County provided a majority for Woodward and McClellan, both losing candiates, in the fall elections of 1863 and 1864, respectively.

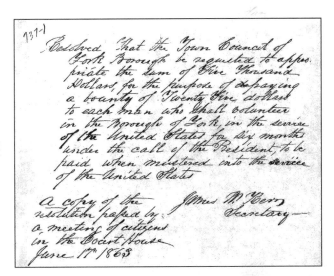

James M. Kerr, York borough secretary, signed this resolution allocating funds to pay a bounty of $25 to six-month volunteers. This emergency resolution offered an incentive for borough residents to volunteer to serve in units to protect southern Pennsylvania against the oncoming Confederate raid in the summer of 1863.

Military and civilian officials in Harrisburg rightly viewed the Susquehanna River as a formidable barrier to the Confederate advance to the east. Still, they supplemented the mile-wide river with earthworks along its course. Here, workers dig trenches near Wrightsville to provide defenders leverage against an anticipated Confederate offensive to capture the bridge spanning the Susquehanna River between York and Lancaster counties.

movement would be devastating to the agricultural base of counties touching on the Mason-Dixon Line for a generation, he argued in an anonymous essay in The York Gazette.

"Even should your crops be neglected, is it not better to lose them while saving your homes from desolation, than to gather them and see the invading horde devour them before your eyes?" he asked.

His essay prophesied several haunting points.

The invaders' main objective would be to cross the Susquehanna River. They would approach the river at several points in heavy columns, living off the land as they marched.

"His invasion will destroy your property, will degrade you and your country," he concluded, "and if allowed to proceed without strenuous resistance, will make you objects of contempt and scorn to your own country, and the remainder of the civilized world."

• • •

Franklin visited Harrisburg to meet with fellow general, Darius Couch.

The state of preparation there did not encourage him.

He also concluded that he should head out of harm's way. Philadelphia would be his destination the next day.

"I agree with you that it would be ruinous to me to be taken here... ," he wrote from York to friend and fellow Union general, William F. "Baldy" Smith.

Franklin had another reason to leave. The Democrats had snuffed out the 40-year-old general's political hopes.

His name had lasted until the eighth ballot for the Democratic nomination for governor. George W. Woodward, Supreme Court justice, had won on the ninth

ballot at the Democratic State Convention.

• • •

York's Committee of Safety asked the York County commissioners to appropriate money to pay volunteers a bounty of $25.

The commissioners threw up a roadblock. The request came from only a committee of the borough. The commissioners would seek the views from people of the entire county about such an expenditure.

"This could not be done in time to be of any service," The Gazette stated.

Later that day, the committee approached York's borough council to allocate $5,000 for bounties. The council unanimously passed the resolution and urged the commissioners to put forth $20,000 for the same purpose.

• • •

People trying to learn the latest on the rebel position filled the streets of Hanover, nearer to the rebel approach than York.

"A thousand and one rumors are circulating in the course of the day of such a conflicting character that it is impossible to give a correct statement of the actual conditions of the affairs," The Spectator reported.

Young men from Hanover, noble men all, had responded to the governor's call to defend Pennsylvania, the newspaper optimistically stated.

"From all parts of our good old Commonwealth," the Republican newspaper observed, "her heroic sons are flocking to her rescue. This is as it should be, and none should stand back from selfish or political motives, as the blow is aimed at us all without distinction."

• • •

Civilians and militiamen put up earthworks near Harrisburg. They built two forts on the west shore of the Susquehanna River to protect Pennsylvania's capital — Fort Washington and Fort Couch.

Workers dug earth at several points along the Susquehanna River.

In Columbia, Harrisburg, Marysville, all in Pennsylvania, and Conowingo in Maryland, militia and an assortment of hired hands moved dirt and mud. Entrenchments to provide cover for riflemen, emplacements for cannons and other defensive measures took shape.

In Peach Bottom, just north of the Maryland border, diggers put up works to defend the ferry running between York and Lancaster counties.

The call had gone out for workers in the Harrisburg area. Notices in local newspapers pledged digging would take place day and night, with work in the dark reserved for men not accustomed to the sun. The hardier men would work during the day.

The Harrisburg notices also called for Negroes, considering their vested interest, to come forth for fortification work. They would be paid $1.25 per day, same as white workers, as long as they would work.

"Turn out then men of all classes and colors, if for nothing more, to the assistance of your country ... ," one notice stated.

A group of Negroes helped dig entrenchments stretching across the pike running between York and Wrightsville on June 18, near the tollgate and gatekeepers' house.

Another group of 100 Negroes built an emplacement for cannons on the Columbia side near Strickler's Run to protect a low dam used to supply the Susquehanna and Tidewater Canal with water and to create a slackwater

Maj. Robert Stiles, a Confederate artillery officer, provided details of the rebel invasion of Pennsylvania in his memoirs, published 40 years later. Stiles, born in Georgia but reared in the North, joined the Confederate Army shortly after his graduation from Yale.

pool.

Mules walked across two towpaths on the 40-foot-wide bridge, pulling canal boats across. Occasionally, when the river level ran high, a strong current drew the boat downstream, sucking mules off a towpath and into the water.

The toll bridge, completed in 1834 at a cost of almost $130,000, replaced another long covered structure knocked down by floating islands of ice two years before. The addition of the towpaths cost another $90,000 in 1840. Railroadmen laid tracks in the mid-1840s when rail service reached Wrightsville, and it became desirable to connect to the vast rail network on the east bank.

Workers built another bastion near Grubbs Ridge, north of town, commanding the bridge. Artillerists would take aim on this valuable and heavily used structure if that's what it would take to stop the Confederate advance.

• • •

Edna Palmer, wife of the York military hospital's surgeon in charge, heard rumors, at her home in Wisconsin, about the rebel threat.

Henry Palmer's most recent letter initially frightened her. She thought it was a notice that he had been injured or killed. When she saw that he had written the letter, she felt comfort. If it had been in someone else's handwriting, she would have rushed to York.

"We are all well, the children talked of Pap half the time. 'When will Pap come again?' " she wrote to her husband.

Before long, Edna Palmer would have her fill of the vast distance separating the family. She and her children would join Palmer in York.

• • •

The town of York had proper warning that a corps of graycoats could be heading their way.

The York Gazette carried a Washington Star story noting Dick Ewell's connections with the county.

"He will probably strike for Gettysburg," the Star conjectured, "and thence to York, for he is personally perfectly familiar with that country, and knows every foot of ground, having in the early days of railroads, surveyed a route for a railroad from the town of Wrightsville ... through York and Adams Counties to Gettysburg."

• • •

People in York County searched for clues in the press about the well-being of troops from the 87th Pennsylvania.

Conflicting reports dribbled back about the bravery of the regiment and other fighting units under Robert Milroy. The Southern press had carried disparaging statements from boastful rebel soldiers that Milroy, a Union major general, would have made a good quartermaster in their Army.

Rob Slaymaker, a member of the 87th who made it back to York, boasted that his regiment had no artillery and little ammunition but still held on for four hours before the entire division dissolved into retreat.

"... (A)s I gather from what he says that he was considerably scared and took very good care of himself, perhaps what he says about their bravery is not very reliable," James Latimer wrote his brother.

Slaymaker had reason to be scared. After spending 24 hours in a rifle pit, he and his captain discovered accidentally that Milroy had left Winchester.

They found their regiment four miles away. Someone had neglected to inform them of the retreat, and they almost found themselves behind rebel lines.

'Yet nothing is being done here'

Within a week of the rout at Winchester, many York businessmen had packed up their valuables and shipped them east.

Bankers moved money to reserves in Philadelphia. Some people in the country made their own deposits, burying their valuables in their back yards.

Those with valuable livestock and horses made arrangements to guard against loss. Some hid them in meadows in the hills or wooded hollows. Others drove them across the long bridge at Wrightsville. Still others

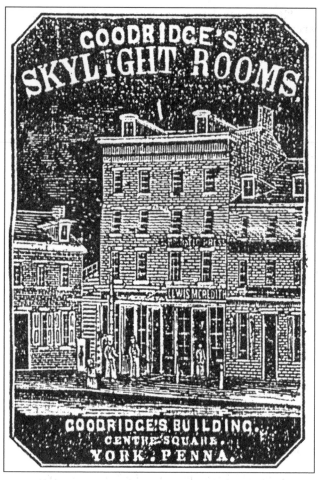

This 1850s advertisement shows William C. Goodridge's Centre Square store in York. Goodridge was believed to be an operator of stations — using his home and store — on the Underground Railroad and would have been a prize catch if he had stayed in town during the Confederate occupation. Many Negroes moved to safety east of the Susquehanna River after hearing that the invading rebels were sending freedmen captured along the way to the South.

William C. Goodridge, son of a slave, operated a variety of businesses in York for decades, including a railroad line running between York and Philadelphia.

secreted them in their homes.

The workhorses — Percherons and Conestogas — had great value to the farmers and provided little help to their captors. But the rebel raiders harvested them anyway to pull wagons or cannons, even if they regretted it later.

The rebels found that the workhorses ate twice as much as the smaller Southern horses and could do only half as much work and sustain half the hardship.

"It was pitiful later to see these great brutes suffer when compelled to dash off at full gallop with a gun," rebel artillerist Robert Stiles wrote, "after pasturing on dry broom sedge and eating ... weevil-eaten corn."

• • •

Long columns of people — white men, women and children, outspoken Republicans fearing retribution, Negro freedmen and fugitive slaves — passed through York from Chambersburg and other points west. Many told of Confederates capturing freedmen and marching them south to slavery.

Some Negroes had wagons, but others headed toward Wrightsville and the safety of the Susquehanna on foot, carrying what they could of their belongings.

Their decision made sense, The York Republican observed.

The Confederates would be pleased to "gobble them up."

As soon as A.G. Jenkins' mounted men crossed into Pennsylvania, they began chasing down Negroes and then sending them — both free and fugitives — south.

"O! How it grated on our hearts to have to sit quietly & look at such brutal deeds — I saw no men among the contrabands — all women and children," Rachel Cormany of Chambersburg wrote in her diary on June 16. "Some of the colored people who were raised here were taken along."

The departure of Negro freedmen in York County to safer locations disrupted the lives of some county residents.

W. Latimer Small and his wife, Mary, lodged with Latimer's parents, Philip and Sarah Small, because all their servants had fled from their house.

• • •

William C. Goodridge, son of a Maryland slave, was undoubtedly among those absent as the Confederates approached.

For more than 30 years, the freedman had operated varied businesses, including an emporium on Centre Square and a railroad line from York to Philadelphia. He would return when the Confederate threat ended.

Goodridge would have been a good catch for the Confederates because of his long-rumored involvement in the Underground Railroad. His railroad cars reportedly served as prime conveyors of fugitives.

• • •

Sixteen-year-old David Sloat, a Wrightsville resident, observed jumpy travelers jamming the road on their way to the Susquehanna River bridge.

It was not unusual to see a wagon piled high with a family's belongings — pots and pails included. A family's cattle and horses followed the crowded wagon, crowned with women and children.

Sloat later fought at Petersburg and around Richmond, but he never saw terror on the battlefield as on the faces of people traversing the road between York and Wrightsville.

• • •

The line of refugees heading east brought conflicting stories about the rebel whereabouts and intentions.

As of noon on Monday, June 22, Granville Haller reported a substantial rebel cavalry at South Mountain, west of Gettysburg. The forces, he said, might come as far east as Gettysburg.

That same day, the news in York was that the rebels

This engraving from Harper's Weekly in 1862 shows Confederate raiders moving Negro freedmen and fugitives to the South. During the Gettysburg campaign in 1863, rebel horsemen repeated their actions, tracking down Negroes in Pennsylvania and escorting them south. After hearing such reports, many Negroes from southern counties in the state headed through York County to the safety of the Susquehanna River's east bank.

had retreated from Gettysburg.

• • •

The Confederates marched two counties away from York, but their deadly presence touched the county.

Lewis M. Drexler, a former resident and lately a dry goods clerk in Harrisburg, worked on entrenchments on the west bank of the river opposite the capital city.

He fell off a ledge and plunged about 80 feet, breaking both legs and his back.

The 25-year-old lived for one painful day before death brought relief.

People in rural parts of the county had an endless appetite for such news. They gathered in central places to exchange information.

Cross Roads, a village in southeastern York County, was one such place. A thousand people assembled when the Confederate scare reached its height.

• • •

On Wednesday, June 24, the day Early's men reached Greenwood, men and women on the streets of York, in the courthouse and in lodges around York still showed little excitement about the gray column pointing toward York.

At least, that was James Latimer's unwavering views about plans to defend the town.

"There is the most extra-ordinary apathy with regard to this invasion," Latimer wrote his brother, Bartow. "If the information we have here is reliable, we may have an attack on Harrisburg in a day or two, and yet nothing is being done here."

The town raised one company of recruits and sent it to Harrisburg to be mustered into service. Latimer put his name down for another company, but not enough men came forward for it to form.

"If men won't go to the defense of their own State, they don't deserve to be called patriots," he wrote Bartow. "I am ashamed of myself and my town."

"That's all I believe. Write me."

Serious business completed, he turned to less pressing matters.

"Whom did Miss Kate Smyser marry?"

• • •

In contrast to Latimer, Sarah Rudisill, wife of Union artillerist Abraham Rudisill, detected considerable worry.

"You have great excitement at York," Abraham responded to a letter from Sarah. "I do not wonder. I am glad you make a statement of public affairs."

The prospect of the rebel invasion affected even the details of his wife's days.

"You had potatoes and meat for dinner. You are going to clean the front room tomorrow if the Rebels don't come," Rudisill wrote. "I suppose then if the Rebels come you will wait awhile. You seem to take it quite cool."

Friday, June 26: Early faces east

Jubal Anderson Early, a 46-year-old Virginian, had earned a reputation for a sharp bite to go along with a loud bark.

Stonewall Jackson had trusted him, although Early was everything Jackson was not — abrasive and sarcastic.

His first name came from the Bible, a character in Cain's line, who is described as the father of all who play the harp and flute. But the only music that came from Early's mouth was irreligious and profane.

Controversy surrounded Old Jube. Lewis Armistead, later a Confederate general, was expelled from the U.S. Military Academy for breaking a mess-hall plate over classmate Early's head. Early had baited him.

The unmarried Early fathered four children from a relationship with Julia McNealey, his housekeeper and mistress. Such an open relationship with someone below his social status was unconventional in its day.

And the wife of one of Early's brigade commanders, Fanny Haralson Gordon, annoyed him. Fanny Gordon often accompanied her husband, John B. Gordon, on campaigns. An officer overheard Early wishing to God that the federals would capture her.

A stooped posture, long, dark beard and black eyes added to his forbidding demeanor.

Early, a lawyer, initially came out against secession but later turned into a vocal backer of a Southern confederation.

Fellow Confederate Gen. Fitz Lee once stated that "when Jubal drew his sword, he threw away the scabbard and was never afterward able to find it."

Such was the man who stood before Republican U.S. Rep. Thaddeus Stevens' ironworks in Caledonia on Friday,

Lt. Col. Elijah V. White, 31, farmed in Virginia before the war. He rose in rank to head a battalion of spirited Virginia horsemen who served as chief scouts for rebel Gen. Jubal Early's division in their invasion of York. White's men gained the name of Comanches for their piercing yell when entering battle.

June 26. These works would be the first target of Early's campaign toward the Susquehanna.

Early ordered the burning of the furnace, sawmill, two forges and a rolling mill. His men hauled off bar iron, destroyed fences and even broke out the windows of the homes of furnace tenders.

The general caused this devastation, in the face of General Order No. 72, to retaliate for similar acts by Union troops in the South and Stevens' vindictive comments in the U.S. House.

Early's pioneer party's handiwork cost Stevens $65,000 and about 200 workers their jobs.

Early contended his order was simply an act of war.

Whatever his reasons, refugees heading east to the Susquehanna undoubtedly alerted York residents and others along the way about the general's capability of issuing orders that could cause fiery devastation.

• • •

Early's division of Dick Ewell's 2nd Corps exited the Cumberland Valley by crossing over South Mountain and passing through Cashtown on this rainy Friday.

Gettysburg, a crossing where about 10 roads came together, lay before it. A federal force reportedly defended this center of Adams County's government, the county seat since Adams broke from York County in 1800.

Ewell's division consisted of four brigades: John B. Gordon's Georgia units, William "Extra Billy" Smith's Virginians, Harry Hays' Louisiana Tigers and Robert F. Hoke's North Carolinians. Col. Isaac E. Avery substituted for the wounded Hoke as commander of the North Carolina brigade.

Early sent Gordon along the main pike connecting Chambersburg and Gettysburg and led the other three brigades along a parallel road through Hilltown and Mummasburg.

Meanwhile, Granville Haller, also in charge of Adams County's defense, made futile preparations to delay the Confederate approach. Hooker's Army of the Potomac was on the march, but five days would pass before the first bluecoats reached Gettysburg.

Haller commanded about 75 horsemen from the Philadelphia City Troop, the same number from Capt. Robert Bell's Adams County cavalry and some civilian scouts. The City Troop, led by Samuel Randall, could trace its roots back to the Revolutionary War.

Just days earlier, these troopers, scouting at Monterrey near Fairfield on South Mountain, had bumped into Confederate pickets. The two sides had exchanged gunfire then were on their way.

Darius Couch, at Department of the Susquehanna headquarters in Harrisburg, also dispatched Col. William Jennings' 26th Pennsylvania Emergency Regiment. Some members of the unit had never fired a gun before duty beckoned.

A company of Hanover-area men and a unit from Pennsylvania College in Gettysburg trudged west to meet the enemy on the road to Chambersburg. Jennings complained to Haller that the mission was suicidal.

"Our regiment marched out the Chambersburg pike to confront the approaching host," Samuel W. Pennypacker, then a private and later governor of Pennsylvania, said.

"The men upon whom this duty was imposed coming from the field, the college and the home, had been in service just four days; not long enough to have acquired a knowledge of the drill, hardly long enough to know their officers."

• • •

Those Gettysburg guardians retreated toward Harrisburg when Lt. Col. Elijah V. White's 35th Battalion, Virginia Cavalry, heading Gordon's column, came along the pike. Before long, White nabbed a large body of the surprised emergency men.

Gordon's column entered Gettysburg and dispatched pickets to the south and east.

Led by Haller, the Philadelphia cavalry, Bell's command and a company of the 26th Pennsylvania chose a route of retreat through Hanover to York.

George W. Sandoe of Bell's Cavalry failed to receive orders to pull back with Gordon's approach, and some rebel pickets surprised him and another trooper.

The rebels shouted for the Yankee troopers to surrender. Sandoe's horse stumbled and fell as he tried to flee. The trooper took a bullet, the first Gettysburg-area casualty in the Confederate campaign.

Meanwhile, Haller telegraphed Couch from Hanover, "Hastened here to collect arms and public property."

Haller explained later that he had sent rifles, cannons and other supplies from Gettysburg to Hanover and rode there to move them out of the rebel path.

The rest of the 26th Pennsylvania scampered toward home, while White's men imbibed drinks from the people of Gettysburg. Before long, White's unit was drunk.

"It was well that the regiment took to its heels so quickly," Early later wrote, "or some of its members might have been hurt, and all would have been captured."

Early dispatched Col. William H. French's 17th Virginia Cavalry, a unit of 250 to 300 men, to pursue the retreating men of the 26th. After the two sides bickered near Hunterstown in Adams County, the men of the 26th continued hoofing it toward Harrisburg.

At Dillsburg, in northern York County, the soldiers ran into A.G. Jenkins' cavalrymen, patrolling south from Carlisle. The two sides drew battle lines, but no skirmishing took place.

Finally, the harassed men of the 26th traveled through Lisburn and New Cumberland to the safety of Harrisburg.

• • •

Back in Gettysburg, Early brought together the town's fathers and demanded supplies: 1,200 pounds of sugar, 600 pounds of coffee, 60 barrels of flour, 1,000 pounds of salt, 7,000 pound of bacon, 1,000 pairs of shoes, 500 hats and 10 barrels of onions.

This requisition came to $6,000 in value. If the town wanted to come forth with money, $5,000 would suffice, Early said.

The demand could not be met, but authorities ordered the opening of businesses for the rebels. The graycoats

Elijah V. White's Comanches troop through Hanover on their way to Hanover Junction. The Confederate battalion raided shops and cut telegraph lines in Hanover before moving by way of Jefferson in southern York County to cut the Northern Central Railway at Hanover Junction.

found shelves mostly bare.

Early did not tarry to squeeze more from the town. He was eager to head east, and the town had no value to him.

The Confederates torched a railroad bridge and about a dozen rail cars after helping themselves to their contents — 2,000 rations. This food had been sent to Gettysburg to fill the bellies of the 26th Pennsylvania.

Instead of standing in line to draw down on these rations, the captives from the 26th found themselves lined up facing Early.

Early presented a speech to his 175 prisoners, before issuing their parole, "You boys ought to be home with your mothers and not out in the fields where it is dangerous and you might get hurt."

He paroled the prisoners who walked toward Carlisle, only to run into Ewell's troops occupying the town three days later. The graycoats ordered the men, who had lost their shoes to the rebels, to line up before paroling them a second time.

Back around Gettysburg, the Confederates camped after a good day's work.

• • •

About 30 miles away in York, businesses closed at 2 p.m. to allow residents to form militia to defend the town. Recruiters opened company rolls, and a crowd gathered at the courthouse.

A telegraph from Haller arrived in the midst of the meeting. The enemy — infantry, cavalry and artillery — had moved on Gettysburg. Citizens should arm themselves, Haller urged. Perhaps the county could be saved.

Another meeting was called that evening. Leaders spoke. Recruiting continued.

These all-day efforts brought the formation of only one company, John Hays in command.

"Rebels in Gettysburg," Haller wired Couch that evening from Hanover. "Ran our cavalry through town; fired on them; no casualties. Horses worn out. Ordered all troops to York ... . Will be in York at midnight. Cavalry, officers and men, did well ... ."

Saturday, June 27: Rebels target Junction

At dawn the next day, Jubal Early's men picked up their eastward trek.

The commanding general, traveling with three brigades and William French's cavalry, started from Mummasburg with plans to pass through Hunterstown toward East Berlin. There, he would enter York County and advance toward York on the roads between East Berlin and Weigelstown on the Carlisle Pike.

From camp two miles east of Gettysburg, Gordon's brigade, with White's horsemen, marched along the parallel pike through New Oxford and Abbottstown into York County.

On the march, Confederate cavalry units generally maneuvered in this manner:

As the columns moved ahead, the cavalrymen traveled well out in front and on both flanks looking for the enemy. The mounted units would order out squads of horsemen to extend scouting duties.

Troopers would regularly race back to the infantry columns to report what lay ahead. Riders then headed past the rear of the column toward Army of Northern Virginia headquarters to report progress. In this campaign, Lee had set up his headquarters near Chambersburg.

These horsemen, thus, played the role of scouts for their division and the entire Army. The cavalry often drew other duties. The horsemen screened movements of their attached infantry units and guarded their flanks during battles. Typically, cavalry did not charge entrenched infantry. Horsemen knew they made a big target.

With each mile covered toward York County, the rebels gained confidence. They faced no resistance, and not even the sound of distant enemy bugles or drums could be heard.

Col. Hamilton C. Jones, 57th North Carolina, remarked that the barns loaded with grain and fields dotted with cattle and horses meant Confederate quartermasters could provide their units with food from York County farms in an orderly fashion.

"The country through which it had marched was largely inhabited by Germans, proverbially phlegmatic," he wrote, "and no sign of excitement was visible among them."

Jones wrote of a land that welcomed and sustained the ancestors of some of his comrades. Many in his regiment and those of other invading rebel units now countermarched the path their ancestors took south several generations earlier. Many of their forebearers from Europe had disembarked their ships at Philadelphia and New Castle,

Dr. William K. Zieber, a Hanover minister, headed Hanover's Committee of Safety. He served as a contact with generals dressed in both blue and gray, whose men overran the town several times in late June and early July 1863.

Del., and passed through York on their way along the Great Wagon Road to the South.

• • •

One brigade walked gingerly along. Hays' Tigers had secured a cache of whiskey in Gettysburg.

"The whole brigade got drunk," Lt. J. Warren Jackson stated, "I never saw such a set in my life."

Some Louisianans with hangovers could not keep up the pace, but sober-minded officers came up with a cure. They threw the stragglers atop a cook wagon loaded with the sharp sides and legs of pots and kettles.

"Those drunk fellows would not ride far," an officer noted, "before they begged most piteously to be taken out and allowed to walk."

• • •

At New Oxford, White's horsemen peeled off in a third parallel column. This cavalry battalion would ride through Hanover, traverse the southwestern part of York County and target Hanover Junction.

There, they would cut telegraph lines and bridges on the Northern Central Railway. If accomplished, their work would disrupt direct communications between the Department of the Susquehanna in Harrisburg and the War Department in Washington, D.C.

The Virginians, a seasoned cavalry unit, had ridden with Stonewall Jackson in many campaigns. The mounted men gained their name from their screeches when attacking, prompting Confederate Gen. Thomas Rosser to call them Comanches.

Their leader, 31-year-old Lige White, farmed in Loudoun County, Va., before the war. Trading his work clothes for a gray uniform, he quickly climbed in rank after demonstrating coolness under fire. His aggressive unit had a reputation for getting the job done.

But the impetuous battalion rode cautiously through enemy territory.

In one village, White stopped a boy and asked for milk. The boy brought some to the colonel, but White asked the boy to take a drink first. He feared someone had laced the drink with poison.

White's unit reached McSherrystown, an Adams County hamlet just west of Hanover at about 10 a.m.

As White's men tried to determine the whereabouts of Granville Haller's force, someone headed toward Hanover with the cry, "The enemy will soon be here."

Many people in Hanover believed the warning and stayed inside.

The Comanches, about 250 strong, moved in a guarded manner into a nearly deserted Hanover. They kept their fingers on the triggers of their rifles and pistols.

A squad of troopers traveled in advance, on the lookout for Union troops. The rest of the battalion observed only townspeople behind shutters on the lookout for them.

The Confederates often paid for supplies requisitioned from Pennsylvania stores in Confederate currency, which held little or no value. Sometimes, the rebels took a step to the worse, if that was possible, paying in counterfeit Confederate currency.

• • •

The Rev. William Zieber of Hanover's Reformed Church stood near the market shed in Center Square.

A rebel at the head of the column rode up, observing people in the square.

"Where do all these people come from?" he asked.

"From the town of Hanover and its immediate vicinity," the minister and head of the borough's Committee of Safety said.

"Are there any Yankee soldiers in town?" the trooper asked. He received no reply.

"So you Yankees are not all in the army, I see," the trooper observed.

"No," Zieber replied, "we are not but we are beginning to find out what the real war is, and I suppose we will soon all join the Union Army."

"The devil you say!" the trooper replied.

• • •

A group of men awaited the troopers in front of the nearby Central Hotel.

White, riding in the middle of the column, moved up to make a brief speech.

His men were fighting for a cause they thought was right, he said, and would do the town no harm.

The Confederates met no resistance, made no demands for goods or money and received no official word of surrender.

• • •

The battalion spent an hour in town, checking out whatever wares still sat on store shelves. Not much had been left behind or at least remained in sight.

One trooper garnered a quart of whiskey after a visit to A.G. Schmidt's drugstore. Other raiders paid for supplies in Confederate money.

An officer sought shoes for his horse at Peter Frank's blacksmith shop on Baltimore Street, setting off an exchange with the proprietor.

Frank said he was closed.

The officer touched his holster.

The blacksmith went to work.

The officer paid $2 in Confederate currency for two shoes.

• • •

Joseph C. Holland operated a shoe store on Baltimore Street. Before the rebels arrived, Holland had moved most of his stock to two less visible locations in town.

The Confederates insisted on entering Holland's store.

A couple of mounted soldiers pointed their pistols his way.

"I don't like that, and you are cowards if you continue it," Holland stated. "If you want to go in my store, I will open it."

A few of the soldiers accepted his offer, entered his shop and ransacked it.

• • •

Men delaying to catch a glimpse of the tattered and dirty Comanches gained a rebel following when they tried to exit.

The troopers fired after the fleeing Hanover men, but their bullets never found their marks.

In one such chase, Confederates overtook a carriage carrying a box bearing 100 watches and jewelry owned by William Broadenhamer. The rebels carried the box under a tree near Mumma's Mill and admired their haul.

A girl in Jefferson, a town of 234 people east of Hanover, produced the only remnant of the jewelry later recovered — a breast pin. A rebel had given her the pendant as payment for a glass of water.

• • •

Hanover telegraph operator Daniel Trone first learned that Elijah White's men controlled the town when he saw a dozen horseman chasing Abdiel Gitt and another man in town.

The pair escaped, but Trone and William Stall, who accompanied him, figured they should hide the telegraph instrument and leave town.

A squad of raiders rode up to the back door of the house where the telegraph operator worked. Trone and Stall quietly left through the open front door. The pair separated, and Trone eventually made his way to Baltimore.

He later learned that the rebels asked about him. A telegraph operator would have been a useful catch for the raiders.

A short time later, he returned and fetched his instrument in a loft where he had left it.

• • •

The rebel troopers did their work with thoroughness — cutting wires and destroying communications. At a prearranged signal, they mounted and scurried toward their destination — Hanover Junction.

The troopers cut off the people of Hanover from the outside world. Confederates seemed to be everywhere. Reports from farmers told of men in gray marching along the York-Gettysburg Pike — Gordon's boys heading toward York.

Hanover's rolling stock — railroad locomotives and cars — had been sent miles away. Telegraph service went out when the Confederates dragged down the wires. No mail or newspapers could be delivered.

The fog of uneasiness settled on the town.

• • •

A letter writer to the Hanover Spectator later reflected the anger that stemmed from White's visit.

Those rebels who did pay in Confederate money knew very well it was worthless, the writer observed. Their transaction amounted to stealing. In fact, the rebels did steal outright in those frequent times when they offered nothing for goods.

The writer had some sharp words for those with Southern sympathies who stuck around town:

"As the carrion crows will collect around their stinking feast, so our sympathizers flocked around these vagrant thieves, to make themselves generally agreeable

White's Comanches enter the village of Jefferson on Saturday, June 27, en route to Hanover Junction, where they worked to disable the Northern Central Railway and cut telegraph communications at that important depot.

and ingratiate themselves into their good graces."

• • •

As White's force moved east, a squad burned bridges on the railroad between Hanover and the Junction, about a dozen miles away.

Other troopers scavenged for horses on the farms along the way and exchanged their jaded mounts for fresh ones.

The number of mounts available in the county served as evidence perpetrators of a scam had worked the area hard. For $1 a year, farmers learned a sign that they were informed would protect their horses. If Confederates approached, they should give the sign, and the rebels would not harm their property.

Farmers also did not easily dispatch their horses because they needed them for the grain harvest. If they sent the horses away, their harvest would be lean. If they kept them for the harvest, they risked losing them to the men in gray.

The main body of Comanches passed through Jefferson, reaching the Junction in the early afternoon.

Hanover Junction gained its name after workers had laid Hanover Branch Railroad tracks in 1852. The 12-mile line connected Hanover with the Northern Central Railway at the Junction, located 10 miles from York to the northeast and the same distance to the Maryland border to the south.

As White's men approached, Conductor John Eckert piloted the last engine at the Junction. It had been left behind as the other rolling stock headed east, just in case the railroad or Union Army needed it.

Warned that the rebels were coming, the conductor figured the train with an attached coach should be on its way.

"Put on steam," Eckert said to the engineer, "and we will hurry away as fast as we can. We need no more pressing orders to leave than the approach of the enemy. They shall not have the train if we can help it."

The Confederates chased the engine but could not catch up.

• • •

White's men made quick work of the telegraph wires, bridges along the railroad, railroad cars and a turntable. They tried without success to torch a large pile of coal.

Blue troops guarded bridges to the north, and White's troopers left them for Col. William French's men to finish off the next day.

A squad found a supply of whiskey on the Fishel farm, north of nearby Seven Valleys. Many troopers drank their fill before an officer dutifully destroyed a large supply of the spirits.

The rebels took clothing and other items from Henry Bott's store in Seven Valleys. One trooper paid with a Confederate dollar, using the oft-repeated line that the note would gain value when the South prevailed.

Union troopers riding by later received a healthier drink from the Fishels.

Rebel work on the railroad kept the farm from shipping milk to Baltimore. So the horsemen in blue lined up to drink a supply that would have otherwise spoiled.

• • •

The rebels did not find many people at home at the Junction and Seven Valleys.

Residents had hastily departed, well ahead of White's advance.

Thirty wagons filled with families and their belongings ended up in Cross Roads, about 15 miles away in southeastern York County.

These refugees would stay there for several days until they were certain that the rebels had cleared the county.

• • •

Late in the afternoon, White's men countermarched to Jefferson, set fire to some rail cars of bark at the railroad station and cracked open barrels of spirits at Rebert's store.

They headed north through Spring Grove to camp for the night on the John Wiest farm, near the village of Nashville.

Their camp sat close to Gordon's headquarters, at Farmers Post Office along the York-Gettysburg Pike in Jackson Township.

Lawyer Thomas E. Cochran provided counsel to York's Committee of Safety. The committee sent out Col. George Hay, its chairman, with a flag of truce. Hay, Chief Burgess David Small and three others surrendered the town to Gen. John B. Gordon the day before the rebels entered York.

'Authorities wish no resistance'

The pace of livestock, horses and their owners passing through York increased Saturday morning.

The drovers related stories about Jubal Early's unimpeded advance and impetuous reputation. Both troubled York residents.

Many who had stuck around delayed no more. Most York businesses never opened that day.

• • •

Early's division marched about 20 miles on Saturday — Gordon along the main pike and the main prong through Hunterstown, New Chester, Hampton and East Berlin in Adams County.

A New York Herald reporter caught up with Early's men on their march. He easily walked in their lines, interviewing men of all ranks.

He came upon a tall, "well-looking" major general who bore himself with dignity and a gentlemanly manner.

The officer wore his brown hat to the right of his head, and he stood tall, not stooped at the moment by chronic arthritis contracted during his stint in the Mexican War.

Old Jube must have been enjoying a good moment.

The correspondent wondered whether he could travel to the rear of Early's column toward the Cumberland Valley.

"I have no time to attend to you just now," Early said in a sharp, but not discourteous, manner. He told the correspondent that no one would obstruct him as he headed west.

On his way, the correspondent ran into some Irishmen from New Orleans.

The Confederates showed confidence, perhaps too much bravado.

"By my sowl, we'll fight till the last man ov us is kilt, and thin, be jabbers, the women will take a hand at it," one Irishman told the correspondent. "You may fight us for all eternity, and then we won't be whipped afthere all."

The Irishmen appeared to like Old Baldhead Ewell but harbored no love for Early They claimed to know several men who would shoot the general as readily as they would a "damned Yankee."

• • •

Gordon's march that day stopped at the house of Jacob S. Altland at Farmers, about 10 miles from York. His men camped in nearby fields. Commanding officers on the march sometimes established headquarters in homes while their men slept in surrounding pastures.

Gordon later wrote of one such house, in which a

German farmer had built his dining room over a spring. One half of the room was floored with limestone and the other half covered with clear and pure spring water.

The cool room brought relief to Gordon — accustomed to riding under the hot sun on dusty pikes — as he sat down for breakfast. He enjoyed a hot Pennsylvania Dutch breakfast, plus the joy of cool milk and cream dipped from large jars standing neck deep in water.

Saturday evening outside York, several farmers provided cattle for a Confederate feast, figuring that the courtesy would bring kinder treatment in return.

The soldiers cooked roast beef in iron pots, pans and skillets. After the meal, two bands played martial music, and the men sang along.

Spirits ran high. The men expected to see the Susquehanna River the next day. But some wondered what Union resistance awaited them.

• • •

Arthur Briggs Farquhar, the enterprising businessman with family and commercial ties to the South, would give them the answer.

Farquhar, born and raised in a Quaker family in Sandy Spring, Md., attended the prestigious Hallowell School in Alexandria, Va.

Decades before, Robert E. Lee had spent time at Hallowell. Farquhar was a classmate of future Confederate officers.

The Marylander arrived in York in 1856 and apprenticed in a machine shop. He married Elizabeth Jessop, daughter of prominent businessman Edward Jessop, in a Quaker wedding in 1860.

Before his marriage, Farquhar had traveled to New York City and gained audiences with A.T. Stewart, William B. Astor, James Gordon Bennett and other men of means to ask the simple question: "How can I make a million dollars?"

Five years later, with a fledgling business to protect and at the beginning of the road to his first million, the 24-year-old would not wait to see what the Confederates would do to York. The contacts he had made representing his company in the South must serve him well.

By now, two weeks after the Battle of Winchester, people viewed the cry of "the rebels are coming" as a sure sign that they were not. But as hours passed on Saturday, the presence of Confederate soldiers only a few miles to the west pressed on the minds of Farquhar, the town's fathers and everyone who had not yet departed York.

Farquhar proposed to the Committee of Safety, meeting in the counting room of P.A. & S. Small's store, that the town could make a better deal in advance. When the enemy soldiers marched into town, they would see how little had been moved across the river.

Thomas E. Cochran, an attorney, saw problems with the concept: Who would go? Could York keep its bargain? Would the Confederates fulfill their end?

Farquhar offered his services as emissary, but the town's fathers did not view the young man's proposal seriously. He said he would go anyway, hitched up his horse and buggy and headed off.

He rode briskly westward on the pike to Gettysburg, intent on asking the Confederates about their plans. He reached their lines near Abbottstown, about 15 miles from York, and met a former school friend from Maryland, Lt. Redik from Georgia.

Gen. John B. Gordon, 31, of Georgia commanded a brigade of Confederates in Jubal Early's division. His men attacked Wrightsville with infantry, artillery and cavalry units, captured the town, but not the prized bridge spanning the Susquehanna River.

When the Confederates invaded York County, A.B. Farquhar, a young businessman, made initial contact with the Confederates. This prompted the Committee of Safety to send a delegation west of town to officially cut a surrender agreement with Gen. John B. Gordon. This drawing captures Farquhar later in life.

"Hello, Farquhar," Redik said, "What are you doing up here among the Yankees?"

Farquhar returned the greeting with a twist, "I came just to find out what you are doing up here among the Yankees. I have some property in York, and I don't want it burned."

The lieutenant escorted Farquhar to meet a courteous Gordon, whom the York man knew through mutual friends.

"What's your business?" Gordon asked.

"General Gordon, unless you have entirely changed from the character you used to have," Farquhar said, "you are neither a horse thief nor a bank robber, and fighting is more in your line than sacking a city."

Gordon asked Farquhar what he proposed.

The general and his men would enter York quietly — without opposition — and make reasonable requisitions. The town's fathers would see that they are honored.

The Georgian said he was glad to save noncombatants from the horrors of war, unlike the actions of Union troops in Virginia.

He signed Farquhar's notes of the conversation, stating that the Confederates would not take private property or molest anyone but would expect necessary supplies.

The signed document would give Farquhar validity with the committee back in York and ease the minds of the terrified women and children, Farquhar told Gordon.

The interview continued.

Gordon asked Farquhar questions about the force guarding York and produced a map of York County that showed the Confederates were well prepared. Gordon knew how many men guarded the town, those in command, troop strength at Harrisburg and key people in town — along with their politics.

This intelligence in rebel hands would not come as a surprise to the people of York. For weeks, reports of mysterious strangers — including a one-armed man dressed in a Union uniform and a religious book salesman — had circulated throughout the county.

In the story about the one-armed man, the visitor had demonstrated skill as a stonecutter, for which he refused

This document, from the papers of David Small, is a portion of the minutes of the Committee of Safety's action at 7:30 p.m. Saturday, June 27, to surrender the town. It reads: 'Resolved that finding our borough to be defenseless, the Committee of Safety request the Cheif Burgess to surrender the town peaceably, trusting that the persons of citizens and private property will be respected.'

payment. As for the urbane and successful Bible agent, word later floated around that he rode near Gordon when the rebel column entered town.

Farquhar had a written deal with Gordon: no property would be destroyed, private businesses would be unharmed if the invaders gained provisions and clothes, and women in town would be respected.

"The slightest indignity offered to any of our ladies would be punished with immediate death," Farquhar learned.

Soon, Farquhar prepared to return to York.

Gordon balked, but the persuasive Farquhar prevailed.

The young man gave his word of honor that he would reveal nothing. In case of resistance, he would return to rebel lines to be hanged as spy.

Farquhar did not obtain passwords to head home through the line. Redik advised him that if anyone tried to stop him, he should just give the horse rein.

The young man rode at a gallop through the last outpost and raced 100 yards down the pike before rebel bullets started flying at him.

• • •

Back in York, Farquhar met Granville Haller, standing with his meager Union force guarding the town.

The town's leaders did not approve of Haller's presence and preparations to defend the town.

"This movement was not appreciated by the Citizens, who, apprehensive that a collision might subject the town to the vengeance of the enemy," Haller later wrote, "believed it would do the inhabitants much injury."

Haller lacked confidence in the report from Farquhar, whom he did not know. The major, a native of York, had served in the U.S. Army for more than two decades and did not know newcomers to town.

Haller and Farquhar went to Smalls' store, where the Committee of Safety persisted in pondering how to defend a town with next to no defenders.

Great numbers of Confederates were headed toward York, Farquhar told the town's fathers. But he could say nothing more.

Cochran, the lawyer, fretted. If the rebels figured out that Farquhar had lacked authorization to make the surrender agreement, they would not honor their end.

To this, Farquhar, joined by some of the Smalls, argued that assigned members of the committee enter Confederate lines to officially arrange the terms.

Those assembled made two decisions: Haller's force would withdraw to the Susquehanna, and a contingent of leading citizens would meet the advancing Confederates to ensure the terms of the surrender agreement were binding.

A civilian committee thus overruled the military command.

"Off toward Wrightsville and Columbia," Haller wired Couch. "The army approach with the Gettysburg force about 4,000. Will respect private property if not resisted, and borough authorities wish no resistance."

• • •

Philip Small, his 34-year-old daughter, Cassandra, and others in his family sat at a table in Small's East Market Street residence enjoying their tea.

Suddenly, music interrupted their quiet time.

Haller's 350-man force had commenced its 12-mile march to the Susquehanna. That inexperienced assortment of soldiers included the detachment of the 87th Pennsylvania that had fled to York after Winchester, the Patapsco Guards including the Invalids, Bell's Cavalry, the Philadelphia City Troop, some militia from York and detachments of the 20th and 26th Pennsylvania Emergency regiments.

"Oh, how do you think we felt — and they, too, for they were leaving us to the mercy of the Rebels," Cassandra Small wrote her cousin, Lissie Latimer, of Wilmington, Del., "but of course it was all right."

• • •

Darius Couch alerted Col. Jacob Frick, in charge of the 27th Pennsylvania Emergency Regiment protecting the bridge in Wrightsville, that Haller was heading his way.

"York has surrendered. Our troops will fall back from there to Wrightsville tonight," Couch wrote. The telegram also ordered reliable men to proceed to the Conowingo Bridge in Maryland, the only other bridge over the Susquehanna River between Wrightsville and the Chesapeake Bay.

Arriving in Wrightsville at 7:30 p.m., Haller discovered the town unprepared for a Confederate assault.

"Wrightsville presented a melancholy spectacle," Haller wrote.

Locomotives, tenders and all forms of rolling stock sat idle near the western portal of the massive bridge, built so canal, rail, wagon and foot traffic could simultaneously cross. A normal practice was to pull railroad cars across the bridge with horses or mules, lest sparks from the stacks set the covered structure ablaze.

But only enough horsepower stood on the west bank to transport normal train traffic, not all available rolling stock from west of the river.

Refugees, wagons and livestock also were lined up. The toll collector caused the logjam in doing a brisk business gathering fares.

Abandoned wagons filled with freight could not be moved. The owners of most horses and mules preferred the safety of the east bank.

The town and surrounding countryside teemed with livestock crying from want of water and feed.

Haller unplugged the jam. He first gained approval from the president of the bridge company, Barton Evans, to waive all tolls. He requisitioned teams from farmers to pull stranded wagons, locomotives and railroad cars across the bridge. Their work done one way, the teams repeatedly re-crossed west and hauled additional loads east.

By morning, the overflow had funneled its way through the bridge. The west bank was clear.

• • •

In York, Haller's grand departure prompted a stampede of sorts. People thought the graycoats had tramped up to York's front door, unaware that it was Haller and his men who had left through the back.

Alexander Frey was among those who panicked. The postmaster finished packing his office but delayed his departure to distribute mail as late as 5 p.m. When Haller retreated, the frightened Frey took no chances.

He ran to the express office, where a horse and wagon, laden with mailbags awaited its teamster. Not finding the driver, Frey hopped up and headed in haste toward Wrightsville.

The wagon's owner came to where it had been parked, learned someone had taken it and took off to recover his property.

He caught up with Frey outside York and demanded the return of his property.

David E. Small and John H. Small happened on the scene in a wagon and agreed to take Frey and the mailbags across the river.

The fastidious Frey was not the last post office official to leave.

He had seen to it that his assistant would stay to close the post office books for the second quarter.

The assistant found it advisable to also depart and joined his boss in Lancaster County after a long walk.

• • •

That evening, David Small, chief burgess; Latimer Small, a town leader and Philip Small's son; George Hay, retired colonel of the 87th Pennsylvania; and Thomas White, a businessman with extensive property holdings, prepared to ride with Farquhar to the Confederate camp.

The hand-picked group included Democrats, Republicans and a military man.

Before the delegates departed at about 8 p.m., some in town discussed whether the large, handsome flag should fly from the high pole in Centre Square.

Some objected, but others maintained that the Confederates should see the colors — a symbol of where the town's allegiance rested. By order of the Committee of Safety, the flag remained atop the pole.

The Committee also resolved: "That, finding our town defenseless, we request the Cheif Burgess to surrender the town peaceably ... ."

After that, the group of five, bearing a white flag of truce, retraced Farquhar's ride from earlier that day.

• • •

The emissaries met Gordon, now at his headquarters at Farmers.

They had tried to raise a force to resist the general's men, but were unable to do so. They asked for protection of the people of York and their property.

Gordon, in turn, reiterated his position: He did not intend to pursue the Union Army's style of warfare. Private property would be respected. Townspeople would not suffer any indignities.

Gen. Early would work out the details for provisions when he was settled into the town.

The committee later maintained that neither party talked about a surrender.

Their business finished, the York officials asked to leave. Gordon again balked, but relented.

'And the war would then be over'

All evening, squads of Confederates dispersed into the countryside to look for new mounts.

A sergeant on Gordon's staff stopped at the Rev. John Roth's house. Two raiders had already procured two of the minister's horses, but left behind Fox, the family's gray mare.

"I want your mare for General Gordon, our commander," he told the family. "The people of Pennsylvania must furnish us horses as well as rations."

A Roth daughter pleaded with the soldiers to spare their horse.

"You will not take the last horse of a clergyman," she said.

If the sergeant took the horse, John Roth pledged he would plead to the general for the return of the mare.

The persistent officer stole the horse and presented her to Gordon.

• • •

That evening, Jubal Early looked for a place to spend the night among the farms 3-4 miles east of East Berlin.

He noted a fine barn sitting in a lush field and figured the farmhouse would be comfortable, with plentiful food. He was disappointed to find a small stone house in a low area, reminding the general of a pigsty.

The Pennsylvania Dutch inhabitant, who spoke no English, was so scared that he could not speak any German either.

• • •

A little farther on, in Big Mount, a large house for Early, with an accommodating porch for his staff, beckoned.

An elderly women came out to a gate along the road and asked in broken English, "Is you gwine to destroy us. Is you gwine to take all dat we've got?"

"No Madam, and to give you the best protection possible," Early replied, "I will stay with you with my staff, and no one shall trouble you."

This appeased the woman, Mrs. Zinn.

"I'm a rale copperhead," she said. "I wish somebody would take old Abe Lincoln by de head and cut his troat off."

Col. Jubal Early's Virginia unit fights at the Battle of Bull Run in the summer of 1861. He was promoted to general after that battle. He commanded units in most campaigns in Virginia, Maryland and Pennsylvania until just weeks before the Confederate surrender.

• • •

The general rode several miles to the pike to meet with Gordon about entering York the next morning.

Early found his subordinate resting on a feather bed in Altland's house.

"I have come to give you directions how you should enter York tomorrow, and you must waken up," Early said in greeting.

"I am glad you have come," Gordon replied, "for I have been visited by a delegation from York and have agreed to take possession of the town without destroying property."

"I could not have given you better instructions," Early said.

The two talked about what their men would face.

If no Union force greeted the Confederates in York, Gordon's orders were to proceed to Wrightsville and secure the bridge on both ends.

Lee had ordered the burning of the bridge, but the easy-going caused Early to conclude that he could get across the river, take Harrisburg and maybe even capture Philadelphia.

• • •

When Early returned to Big Mount, he found the widow Zinn had reserved supper for him.

Sitting with the woman and her teenage daughter, he enjoyed a fare of 15 to 20 Pennsylvania German dishes, particularly the fresh vegetables.

The dinner conversation touched on several topics.

"Well, is Stonewall Jackson dead, sure enough?" the woman asked.

"Unfortunately, madam, he is dead."

Some of the Yankees believed he wasn't dead, the woman said. As Early later wrote, the woman related "some of em said he was dead as h-n sh-t."

The daughter did not blush, and Early conjectured she was accustomed to the earthy language.

By this time, some of the invaders had concluded that they preferred the gentile manners of Southern women to the coarse mouths of women north of the Mason-Dixon Line.

• • •

Early slept for seven hours in a clean bed that night but still made time for some ambitious thinking.

"For I firmly believed that the Confederate army would win; that we would soon dictate terms of peace in Philadelphia and New York and the war would then be over," he wrote.

Meanwhile, Early's host fretted to a member of his staff about the cost of war.

Mrs. Zinn took a dim view of the value of money in wartime.

"I wonder if dey are gwine to have good money once more again," she said, "de money dey've got now aint fit to wipe de b—k s-de on."

• • •

The York delegation returned home at 1:30 a.m., warning the town that an immense army would march down its streets later that day. They would become prisoners of war.

Any resistance would be madness, the delegates said, and the town would be laid in ashes.

"We felt so relieved," Cassandra Small wrote, "that all was settled."

III

Confederates march down York County's main streets

Sunday, June 28, 1863

Front of The Court House in York Pa, built 1839.

'Humiliated! Disgraced!
Men who don't often weep, wept then.'
— York resident Cassandra M. Small

Rebels enter York without resistance

It was 10 a.m. Sunday.

Church bells beckoned York residents to worship, and townspeople, dressed in their best, were ready to respond.

But the bells could not muffle a cry spreading from the town's west end toward its east.

"They are coming."

The Confederates arrived in dribbles before waves of graycoats washed into York.

Pickets first appeared in front of residences and businesses along Market Street and other major roads. They paced their posts to maintain order in town. This included restraining their comrades, keeping them away from private property, particularly taverns.

These sentries were part of Col. Clement A. Evans' regiment — the 31st Georgia — assigned as the provost guard.

Then, the first brigade emerged from the dust cloud kicked up along the York-Gettysburg Pike. John B. Gordon's men. They marched in three columns, the center down Market Street.

Bands blared, regimental flags waved, touting various designs and colors.

"Oh, Lissie, what did we feel like?" Cassandra Morris Small wrote her cousin. "Humiliated! Disgraced! Men who don't often weep, wept then."

• • •

Some residents thought the officers would lead their troops into town, mounted on spirited horses with spotless uniforms.

After all, these men had marched with the famed Stonewall Jackson.

Instead, those in the lead — the footsore pioneer party — bore shovels, spades and pickaxes, carried like guns.

These ragged and grimy men held the thankless job of clearing obstructions and widening roads for the thousands of soldiers who would follow. They kicked up the limestone dust from the pikes that then covered their butternut and gray uniforms — and the horde behind them — with a fine gray powder. Even more than their pathfinding work, the pioneers sometimes pulled details to bury dead Yankees and horses.

"Oh, my heavenly father, protect us," one lady said, "they are coming to dig our graves."

The invaders glanced curiously from side to side, equally astonished. Here they were, often shirtless and shoeless in worn pants, eyed by women adorned in fashionable finery and the men in their Sunday go-to-meeting clothes.

• • •

Gordon's brigade of more than 1,200 men halted in Centre Square. Much to the dismay of townspeople, his sweating men plopped down wherever they could — on porches, curbs and sidewalks.

The large American flag flew atop the tall pole in the heart of York, the seat of justice located in the center of the county.

Moments earlier, before the Confederates had interrupted, one last debate had taken place about whether to fly the flag.

John Evans, the veteran attorney, begged his fellow townsmen to take down the flag.

"Is it possible I have lived to this day to see the flag torn down and trampled in the dirt?" he wondered.

Others took his side.

The banner was atop the straight pole, placed on the

To York residents, the parade of rebels passing along York's streets was a line with no end. Here, the town's fathers stand in a row to meet the mounted Confederate officers as they move from West Market Street into the town's square. The sidewalks are crowded with people on their way to church, including the German Reformed church, whose steeple is shown, top center.

The American flag is pulled down from the 110-foot pole on York's Centre Square. The invading Confederates then carried off the 35-foot-long by 18-foot-wide banner, made by the women of York. The presence of the flag caused some in York to argue, after the rebels left, that the town did not surrender. Lewis Miller, who captured this scene, asserts the surrender in two places.

very site that the beleaguered Continental Congress adopted the Articles of Confederation 86 years before during
the American Revolution.

The Articles loosely bound the 13 Colonies into a
nation. That Gordon's men were fighting to unbind the
nation, operating under a separate confederation with a
different flag, was not lost on the people of York. They
had been schooled since infancy about the sacrifices made
by America's founders in the 45-by-45-foot York County
Court House in the dead center of that square.

Latimer Small, Philip Small's son, ended the debate.

"Let them take the flag, and I will replace it," he proclaimed.

Now the rebels, seeing the Stars and Stripes still atop
the pole, pulled down the banner and took off with it.
A.B. Farquhar, always around the action, begged the
rebels not to put up their own flag. Gordon complied, for
the moment, allowing that he might later decide otherwise.

Farquhar urged the Confederates to camp at the hospital on Penn Common.

The rebels would not burn buildings that provided
shelter, and the hospital buildings sat so near private residences that the Confederates would refrain from destroying them.

Or so it was hoped.

• • •

Earlier, Charles Morris had placed his hat on his
head, ready for church at St. Paul's Evangelical English
Lutheran.

"Charles, where are you going?" his wife, Cassandra
Small Morris, asked.

"To church," he answered calmly.

Morris met with seven other congregants for worship
in a full Sunday service, despite the Confederate presence.

St. Paul's minister, the Rev. William M. Baum, was a
Unionist. In recent weeks, he had been drilling with other
residents of York, carrying a wooden gun.

Another congregant that day, a man named Major
Emmitt, was the son of a commissary major in the War of
1812. His father's rank was transferred by inheritance to
his son.

• • •

The minister stood in the pulpit of another York
church when a messenger approached.

The Confederates had arrived.

"The reverend man folded his arms upon the pulpit,
bowed his head upon them, and wept," Mrs. L. M.
Hartman wrote.

The congregation proceeded to the church steps just
as the Confederates marched by playing "Dixie."

The people followed them to the square.

• • •

Gordon's brigade did not stop long in York, stepping
east on Market Street to allow soldiers following in the
gray column room to enter town.

The Georgians marched for two miles, before halting
to rest near a 125-year-old stone building, later the York
Valley Inn. The troops prepared to make their way toward
Wrightsville and its coveted bridge, about 10 miles due
east on the pike.

Bystanders noticed that several rebel wagons and
cannons bore U.S. insignias. Knapsacks carried the markings of the 87th Pennsylvania Volunteers, taken from the

Four generals stood at the helm of Confederate units occupying York. Coincidentally, all four general officers prac-ticed law before the war: brigade commanders Harry T. Hays, left; William 'Extra Billy' Smith, right; John B. Gordon; and division commander Jubal Early. Smith's and Hays' brigades camped north of York near Small-owned mills.

local unit at Winchester. Seeing the 87th's signs on the
backs of the invaders would have disturbed many townspeople, some still unaware of how their sons fared in the
rebel assault at the Virginia town.

Two of Early's brigades — Hays' Louisiana Tigers
and Hoke's North Carolinians — also carried new rifles
and other small arms picked up after Milroy's rapid departure from Winchester.

As his men marched, Gordon rode up to the front of
Philip Small's East Market Street home.

He felt self-conscious about his dust-covered uniform. An opportunity to change uniforms evaporated when
the supply trains parked in Franklin County three days
before.

A Friday rain had settled the dust when the division
marched near Gettysburg. The rain had created mud. Now,
the rainy weather had turned into gloomy, overcast days,
further adding to the rebels' gray.

"... I lost sight of the fact that this turnpike powder
was no respecter of persons, but that it enveloped all alike
— officers as well as privates," Gordon wrote.

He spotted a group of women on the porch —
Cassandra Small and other women of the household —
and paused to address them.

They cried in alarm, but he reassured them:

"Ladies, I have a word to say. I supposed you think
me a pretty rough looking man, but when I am shaved and
dressed, my wife considers me a very good looking fellow."

He promised them that his men would bring no harm,
unlike the Yankee conduct in the South. In fact, he would
have the head of any of his men who insulted a woman,
disturbed a private residence or destroyed private property.

"You need not have any fear of us, whilst we are in
your midst," he said. "You are just as safe as though we
were a thousand miles away. That is all I have to say."

He bowed, turned his horse and headed east with his
men.

• • •

The 31-year-old Georgia lawyer did not take the
name of his wife lightly.

Gordon had left Fanny and their two sons in
Richmond. She did not accompany her husband this campaign as she had in the past.

Fanny Haralson Gordon was helpful to the general
when she did come along. Fighting in the sunken road at

Antietam, Gen. Gordon sustained five wounds. A bullet hole in his cap kept him from drowning in his own blood.

One bullet struck him in the face, passing through his left cheek and out through the jaw, just missing his jugular. He would carry that prominent scar for the rest of his life.

When his wife first saw him in a field hospital, his face bore a black hue, and both eyes had nearly swelled shut. She suppressed a scream and went to work nursing her husband through a long convalescence.

With his wife now in the South, all Gordon could do was write endearing letters.

"God only knows how I love you," he wrote during the campaign. "Honor, reputation, money, ease and comfort could all now be gladly parted with if it purchase for me, the constant presence of my Fanny."

In his travels in Pennsylvania, Gordon showed a revived sense in the presence of God, who had spared him thus far.

"My confidence ... is pretty strong. I trust in Him," he wrote Fanny. "Pray that I may trust Him more and pray with faith."

Gordon was prepared for his death and encouraged his wife to be ready as well.

"My life is in the hands of a wise and good God," he wrote. "If He takes it, it is all right."

• • •

As Gordon headed along East Market Street, a girl perhaps 12 years in age, ran up to the general's horse and handed him a bouquet of flowers.

Examining the bunch, he observed a note, in fine handwriting, with numbers and positions of Union troops in Wrightsville.

"I carefully read and reread this strange note," Gordon wrote. "It bore no signature and contained no assurance of sympathy for the Southern cause, but it was so terse and explicit in its terms as to compel my confidence."

• • •

The women in York might have had nothing to fear, but farmers did not share in the same promise. Those failing to move their horses risked losing them.

As Gordon's men rested along the road to Wrightsville, a stolen mount bearing one of Elijah White's troopers gave out. The man searched for a remount to replace that horse and finally stole one from a stable.

He started riding up the pike when a fellow trooper gave him some disconcerting news.

He recognized the horse from 10 years back when he had taken some Virginia horses to Lancaster for sale. She was an old mare even then. That's why the owner did not take her across the river ahead of the rebels.

The horseless trooper removed his bridle and saddle and carried them to camp, where someone finally provided him with a mount, probably also purloined.

• • •

George Latimer, a member of the prominent York family, marched with Gordon's men. Cassandra Small knew Latimer had entered town but did not see him. If she had, she would not have spoken to him.

The Latimers and Smalls, two great York names, had a long history of family and business connections. Sarah Small, Cassandra Small's mother and Philip Small's wife, had been a Latimer.

The name of W. Latimer Small, son of P.A. and Sarah Latimer Small, reflects the marriage of two of York's prominent families — the Latimers and the Smalls. The 32-year-old Latimer Small contributed to the decision to surrender the town and then to boldly keep the flag flying as the rebels entered York. He vowed to replace the flag, if the rebels carried it away.

Fanny Gordon often accompanied her husband, Gen. John B. Gordon, on campaigns. She helped nurse him back to health after he sustained severe wounds at Antietam in 1862 but did not accompany him during the campaign into Pennsylvania — and York County — a year later.

James W. Latimer, the young York lawyer, and brother, Bartow Latimer, were devoted Republicans and Unionists.

Their cousins, Georgia natives George and Thomas Latimer, later moved north, but did not give up their secessionist views. Some York people believed George had to leave the county because of these sentiments. He joined Thomas in Baltimore, and the brothers enlisted in the Confederate Army.

The war had split yet another family.

During the march through York, George Latimer did run into some of his Copperhead friends and shook their hands, Cassandra Small wrote. Latimer begged them not to tell her they had seen him, but they couldn't resist.

Small respected Latimer, despite his enemy uniform, more than Copperhead ladies of York who quietly — or maybe not so secretly — harbored sympathy for the Confederates.

Some ladies waved handkerchiefs and red streamers. Others pestered the invaders for buttons, to keep as mementos. Some went out to visit the rebels at the military hospital.

"There will be a dividing line drawn here," Small informed Lissie. The actions of these ladies would be long remembered.

Small contended the Confederates held friendly York County residents in contempt:

"The Rebels, themselves, spoke of them to some of our townsmen and said had they dared they would have put bullets through the hearts of those persons who welcomed and waved to them — that 'friends in an enemy's country are worse than traitors.' "

• • •

Cassandra Small did not name those in York who waved to the Confederates, but James Latimer, writing to Bartow, revealed the sympathizers.

Women fluttered handkerchiefs from the Tremont House and Washington House, from Pete Ahl's and Dr. Charles M. Nes' houses. Miss Chapman, Nett Welsh Wickes and a few others standing on Democrat Henry Welsh's porch asked rebel officers for buttons.

Twenty-seven-year-old York lawyer James Latimer, left, wrote his younger brother, Bartow, right, about events before, during and after the Confederate occupation. James Latimer, a staunch Republican and later a York County judge, took a dim view of the actions by borough authorities to surrender the town. Glenalvin Goodridge, son of former slave William C. Goodridge, produced this daguerrotype of James Latimer at his studio in York.

Thirty-four-year-old Cassandra Morris Small's correspondence with her cousin, Lissie, provided a glimpse into the frayed emotions of York's people. As a daughter of town leader Philip Small, she had a close vantage point to events surrounding the occupation. She lived at the northwest corner of East Market and North Duke streets, giving her a view of passing troops dressed in butternut and gray.

The word came later that Jubal Early had dined with a York man, "old Barry," on Sunday, and several Confederates had stayed at Dr. Nes' house most of the time.

Rebel officers said they could get information on anything and anybody they wanted, from supporters in York. Early knew the identities of the strong Union families.

"One copperhead," Latimer informed his brother, "hearing a Union man asked by an officer for a Map of York Co., which was, of course, refused, volunteered to take him to his house and give him a map."

• • •

Gordon's men marched east quietly, under strict discipline, for what seemed like hours.

Of course, Cassandra Small wrote, York's people did not insult them or fire at them.

No one waved the colors in their faces, as happened when Northern soldiers marched through Southern towns.

• • •

James Latimer kept his family out of sight and his parlor shutters closed as the rebels trudged by. In fact, he talked to only one of the occupying soldiers.

His solitude was an exception. Most of the town turned out to gawk. Some men talked freely with the invaders. For the most part, women stayed at home. They tried to contain their children, but some youngsters mingled with the invaders.

"I thought the conduct of the people in crowding out to see them was disgraceful," Latimer wrote.

Even Philip Small, who should have known better, allowed Cassandra and others to stand on their porch, he wrote.

• • •

Some loyal Unionists pitied their bushed and famished invaders.

Sarah Ann Bayler, maker of so much fresh bread for Union troops, saw some ragged rebels resting in front of her house.

She detected their youth, just boys far from home. She took them some food, which they gratefully accepted.

'I am sure you can find it hoarded up'

Maj. Gen. Jubal Early brought a bit of a celebrity to the people of York County.

Near Davidsburg, northwest of York, people sat on a fence, along Canal Road, watching the troops pass Sunday morning.

Early spotted John B. May holding a York newspaper. He asked the man for it, and May readily handed it over.

Civil War officers regularly read local and city newspapers to keep themselves informed of enemy and allied troop movements and the nature of the territory in which they were occupying.

"This is just what I wanted," he said.

He read as he rode.

• • •

If Old Jube was trying to understand the people of York, many borough residents entertained the same curiosity about him.

Coatinental Square looking eastward & southward

This pre-Civil War photograph shows York's Centre Square, looking southeast, before the flagpole was erected between the market sheds. The corner of P.A. & S. Small's four-story building is seen at left. The steeple of the York County Courthouse towers farther down East Market Street. Christ Lutheran Church sits along South George Street, right. The six-story Hartman building, middle, the tallest building in town, is on the southeast corner of Centre Square.

Early, riding with Hoke's brigade, moved through Weigelstown on the Carlisle Pike into town.

Smith's Virginia brigade and Hays' Tigers headed toward camp north of town, near the Small-owned Loucks and Codorus mills. These mills sat along the Codorus Creek and the Northern Central Railway, which followed the waterway.

The invaders positioned a battery on Diehl's Hill, near where the creek cut through a ridge north of York. The cannons pointed toward York, along the Codorus below.

In York's square, residents observed that the stooped Early wore a faded gray suit that showed the soiled effects of weeks of continuous marching along dusty roads. His beard needed a trim, and his broad-brimmed hat showed wear.

The high-ranking general reminded one resident of a plain, country farmer. His manner was brusque and off hand, but his darting dark eyes took in the abundant town.

• • •

Two market sheds, sitting east-west in Centre Square, supplied Early with easy proof of York's might as a regional agricultural center.

These two 100-foot by 40-foot sheds resembled canal boats turned upside down. Sloping red tin roofs covered the sheds. Market-goers enjoyed a brick floor in the eastern shed. The base of the other shed covered a shallow cellar that served as police headquarters and lockup.

Butchers operated out of stalls on Wednesday and Saturday as did vendors of ginger cakes, pretzels, candy and fruit.

Before sunup on market days, farmers from miles around spread their produce on the curbs of the square's four blocks.

But before this Sunday, the vendors had packed up their wares before the Confederates could pick them clean.

• • •

Early went to David Small's house, a short distance from Centre Square on South George Street. He left his staff outside and shared some refreshments with the chief burgess.

Soon enough, he arrived at the reason for his call. He must have $100,000.

The greenbacks had value, unlike Confederate money, and Early had thousands of men to provide for.

The town could not produce that amount, Small informed him. The banks had sent it all away.

"What, in such a rich country as this, these people must have laid by immense sums," the general argued. "I am sure you can find it hoarded up in the farmers' canvas bags and housewives' stockings."

"But these hard-working people," Small replied, "have not earned their money to give it to you."

Henry Barratt's illustration shows the bustling scene on market day. Farmers brought goods to market twice a week — on Wednesdays and Saturdays. Jubal Early, observing such prosperity in and around York, incorrectly believed the town would fulfill his $100,000 requisition.

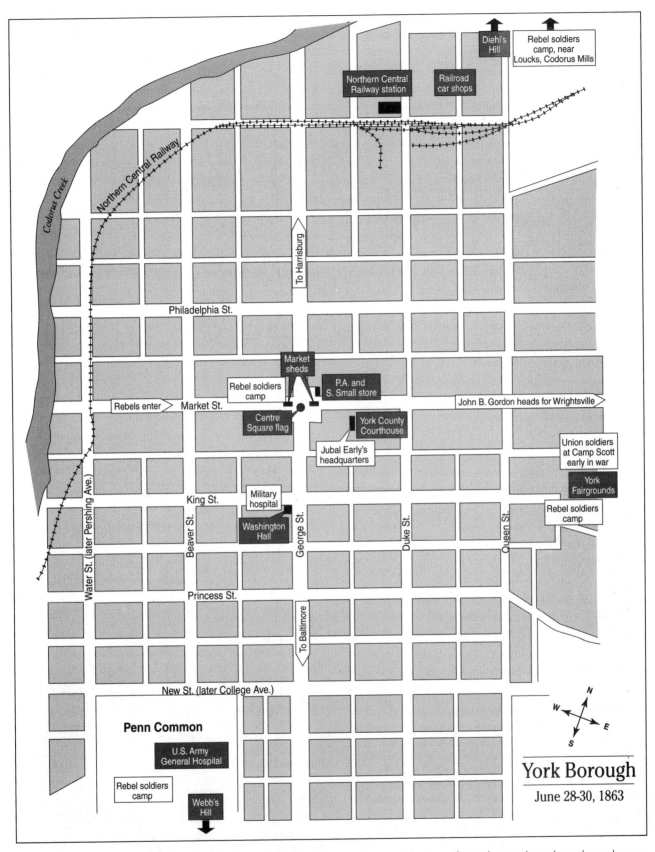

Diehl's Hill

Rebel soldiers camp, near Loucks, Codorus Mills

Northern Central Railway station

Railroad car shops

Northern Central Railway

Codorus Creek

To Harrisburg

Philadelphia St.

Market sheds

Rebel soldiers camp

P.A. and S. Small store

Rebels enter | Market St.

John B. Gordon heads for Wrightsville

Centre Square flag

York County Courthouse

Jubal Early's headquarters

Union soldiers at Camp Scott early in war

York Fairgrounds

Rebel soldiers camp

Military hospital

King St.

Washington Hall

Beaver St.

George St.

Duke St.

Queen St.

Water St. (later Pershing Ave.)

Princess St.

To Baltimore

New St. (later College Ave.)

N
W   E
S

Penn Common

U.S. Army General Hospital

Rebel soldiers camp

Webb's Hill

York Borough
June 28-30, 1863

This map shows York under siege by the Confederates. Cannons covered the town from the north and south, and more than 6,000 soldiers camped in and around York. 'No one but those who were eye witnesses to the occupation of York can have any conception of the extent of the anxiety of our people during those two days' occupation ...,' Martin L. Van Baman later observed. Van Baman was 16 at the time of the invasion.

Early countered that he must — and would — have the money. He called for a meeting at the courthouse to take up the matter further.

As the pair talked in Small's parlor, a clatter came from the sidewalk outside.

A nervous Early immediately peered through the window blinds, for he thought someone was attempting to enter the house and take him prisoner.

A soldier had caused the racket by dropping his rifle.

With fears allayed, he left to make his headquarters in the courthouse.

• • •

Soldiers from Hoke's brigade, led by Col. Isaac E. Avery, camped at the York Fairgrounds and in the hospital on Penn Common. They made Henry Palmer and the five patients under his care prisoners of war.

A Confederate major told Palmer to remove his coat and epaulettes.

"Never," the surgeon replied, "except when ordered by a superior officer."

The major did not persist.

• • •

Palmer had directed a supply of rifles to be broken before the rebels arrived.

But the rebels missed a wagon full of muskets that remained in town.

Some men, lacking aid from scarce horses, rolled the wagon down a hill to an outhouse, out of rebel sight.

• • •

Some of Hoke's soldiers did not move any farther than Centre Square. The North Carolinians camped in the two market sheds.

Artillerists set up a battery on Webb's Hill, south of York. The big guns pointed north.

The town was now commanded by cannons on hills to the south and north, a battery in town, and another battery moving with Gordon — perhaps 16 artillery pieces with hundreds of soldiers attached to man them. York was chockfull of foot soldiers, mounted riflemen, couriers, ambulance wagons and empty wagons to collect the wealth of what the area had to offer.

More than 6,000 soldiers were positioned in and around the town of 8,600 residents.

Confederate presence felt in countryside

Congregations worshiped in the hinterlands of York County, with one eye toward the church windows.

Turnout was particularly high at the Sabbath School at Sanney's School in southeastern York County.

Reports of Confederate movements across the county caused grim faces.

The congregation spent time reading, singing and praying. Brother McKindles preached about the unsearchable riches of Jesus and his precious promises.

Outside, animals, wagons and people, fleeing the rebels, lined the road.

"The Lord save us and our country from destruction," someone wrote in the Sabbath school minutes. "The present time seems to be a dark hour indeed. Oh, that it may be near the breaking of day when joy and gladness shall again lighten our homes."

• • •

Later in the day, residents on picket duty yelled in alarm when what appeared to be hundreds of rebel troops approached along the Brogue road, not far from Sanney's School.

Without establishing their identity, the flustered sentries fired upon the soldiers and then scurried away in fear, alarming residents for miles around.

"The fright is said to have been almost beyond description," The York Pennsylvanian reported.

People and their animals ran around in wild confusion. Many residents cut the harnesses from horses hitched to wagons and fled on bareback. Families ran to hiding places in the hills.

Several hours passed before it became known that the sentries had shot at friendly troops dressed in blue.

The threat passed, and it took some doing for the families to find their animals.

• • •

Daniel Roland was away at war, leaving his wife, Ellen, to fend for herself and their five children.

The family lived in a remote wooded area, more than a mile from Emigsville, a village north of York along the Northern Central Railway.

Ellen Roland figured her family was safer in Emigsville from foragers and potentially drunken rebels.

On her way to town with her children, she ran into a band of about 20 graycoats.

"Where's your husband? Why are you leaving home? Do you know we will burn down your home sooner, if it were unoccupied than if you lived there?" they asked her. The invaders often used the threat of firing homes but never intentionally did so during their occupation.

They let her go, and she walked through rebel lines to the safety of friends in town.

• • •

Riding about five miles from York, in Weigelstown, Early had dispatched 200 troopers from Col. William French's cavalry to move north of York to destroy Northern Central Railway bridges, including a large structure where the railroad crossed the Conewago Creek.

French's raiders found George H. Wolf, proprietor of a store in Mount Wolf, packing shoes, boots, hats and other goods for transport across the Susquehanna.

The rebel raiders confiscated these items and paid for them in Confederate currency.

They proceeded on their main mission in cutting telegraph lines, small bridges and the larger structures over the Conewago, north of Mount Wolf.

They conscripted a farmer as a guide to the bridges, which they promptly set afire with coal oil.

The Confederates did their work without opposition. Command in Harrisburg had assigned a battalion of the 20th Pennsylvania Emergency Regiment to guard railroad bridges north and south of York as well as the line running to Wrightsville. This unit crossed the Susquehanna on flatboats after learning about the Confederate approach.

Later, French's men took care of bridges that White's troopers did not destroy on the railroad south of town toward Hanover Junction. The troopers would have taken satisfaction in knowing that they caused $150,000 damage to the railroad.

Front of The Court-House in York Pa., built 1839.

Gen. Jubal Early used the York County Courthouse as his headquarters during his division's visit to York. Early operated out of the sheriff's office in the East Market Street courthouse, finished in 1839. It replaced the county's Centre Square brick courthouse, erected in 1756, home of the Continental Congress when it visited York County for nine months in 1777-78. The county used the East Market Street courthouse for less than 60 years. It was demolished to make way for its multi-domed successor, which occupied the site after 1900.

• • •

Anna Meisenhelder maintained a reputation as a stubborn Conewago Township farm woman.

She wouldn't smoke a pipe, as other women did, because she thought it was harmful to her health.

But one of the horses on her farm showed an even sharper stubborn streak.

French's men, on their way to destroy the Conewago bridges, dismounted at the farm that she and her husband, David, worked. After eating a bite, one of the rebels attempted to make off on a farm horse. When the rider attempted to jump a fence, the horse stopped. The would-be thief kept going.

The workhorse ran back to the safety of the stable.

No other man in gray sought out the horse.

• • •

Many in York County fought to keep their horses, but they did their best to accommodate their visitors with the hope that their property would be spared.

"The people all treated us very kindly ... ," one soldier wrote, "though I think that their kindness was more through fear than anything else."

Another graycoat commented in a letter about the "Dutch people in York Co. turning out with water and milk and bread and butter and 'apple-butter' for the 'rugged rebels.' "

He believed them naive, noting that residents "gener-

Brothers Philip Albright Small, left, and Samuel Small had much to lose if the rebels burned York. Their holdings included a large store, mills and warehouses. As it turned out, the rebels protected the mills, probably figuring that the invading soldiers would need flour if their visit north of the Mason-Dixon Line became a permanent stay.

ally seemed not to know exactly what to expect, and I don't think would have been at all astonished if every building had been set on fire by us as we reached it, nor would a great many have been surprised if we had concluded the business by massacring the women and children."

• • •

Jittery people on the east bank of the Susquehanna sought safety against a possible Confederate crossing.

John and Rachel Denney felt particularly vulnerable. They lived in the "Furnace House," a residence for families working the Henry Clay Furnace, about two miles above Columbia in Lancaster County. The Denneys believed the Confederates would target their property because it provided pig iron to mills for the production of arms.

At dusk, Rachel and her two children headed to her brother-in-law's house in Christiana, to the east.

Positioned in the bed of a cart loaded with straw, they shared the road with fellow travelers, all heading away from the Confederates. "It was a weird and dreary night," Rachel recalled.

They heard stories about a rebel invasion all along the way. By then, she was prepared for the worst that war could bring.

• • •

Not far from York County's northern border, mounted Confederates occupied Mechanicsburg in Cumberland County. These men, part of 2nd Corps Commander Dick Ewell's Northern thrust, probed Harrisburg, nine miles to the east.

These troopers — A.G. Jenkins' men — kept in contact with Gens. Ewell and Robert E. Rodes, occupying Carlisle about 10 miles to the west.

The cavalrymen had ridden toward Carlisle Saturday morning and had met a deputation with a flag of truce. Their unguarded town would offer no resistance, they said. A cavalry attack could cause women and children to panic.

Jenkins' troopers had marched guardedly into Carlisle, reached the square and demanded food for 1,500 men and forage for their horses. Residents had scurried to meet their requests. These provisions were just the start of rebel requisitions fulfilled in Carlisle. Ewell's men collected $50,000 in medical supplies and food to feed Rodes' and Johnson's men with a surplus to send back to Virginia.

The next day, as Early's men entered York causing

the cancellation of church services, Ewell declared a day of rest and an observance of the Sabbath for his troops.

The corps commander and his staff attended services at the former Union cavalry barracks, corps chaplain Tucker Lacy presiding. Other soldiers worshipped with their units or at Carlisle's churches.

A committee of pastors visited Ewell to inquire if he minded if they offered their usual prayer for Abraham Lincoln.

"Certainly not," Ewell replied, "Pray for him. I'm sure he needs it."

Later that day, Ewell ordered a flag-raising observance at the post. His men pulled up a new banner, made by women in Richmond, showing a red field and blue cross — the Stars and Bars.

The Confederate Congress had recently adopted the Stars and Bars as the official rebel banner. The former flag resembled the Union standard, easily confused on the battlefield.

• • •

Sunday morning, a squad of Jenkins' men crossed Yellow Breeches Creek at Williams Grove and headed toward Dillsburg, several miles south of Mechanicsburg, in York County.

At that time, horses and wagons filled Dillsburg. Refugees from Maryland and Chambersburg jammed the town through a notch in South Mountain, giving easy access to York County and the Susquehanna River.

The people of Dillsburg had heard so many rumors about the approach and withdrawal of the Confederate raiders that Jenkins' men almost caught them off guard.

Seizing the moment, Dillsburg resident Lee Welty rode out to meet the troopers.

The rebel commander asked about a flag positioned high on the mountain.

A unit of federals, Welty claimed, had dug in around that mountain. If the rebels rode into Dillsburg, they would face a large enemy force.

"The devil you say," the officer said.

The Confederates believed the story and rode off in a different direction.

This gave some of the refugees time to point their horses down the road to Dover and cut across toward Lewisberry and the river, where they crossed the Middletown Ferry to safety.

• • •

Back in York, Alfred Jessop's experiences typified those of many county residents that day.

Standing on Webb's Hill that morning, he and A.B. Farquhar, his brother-in-law, had watched the first gray column enter town.

By the time they made their way the couple of miles to Centre Square, Gordon's men were pulling down the flag.

That accomplished, Jessop observed the rebels tug down the flag outside Morris Drug Co., just east of the square. He eyed Gordon as he rode to Philip Small's house, a bit farther east, to make his speech to the ladies.

Jessop returned home to Springwood, south of York, and observed a visit from a squad of gray horsemen.

As they talked with Edward and Mary Jessop — Alfred's parents — his brother, Charles, went outside. The horsemen quickly accosted Charles, dressed in a Union uniform. The soldier produced papers that showed that the

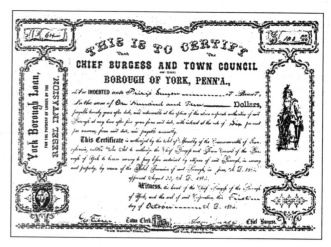

This document, printed on the press of David Small's York Gazette, certified payment to Philip Smyser for money given to satisfy Gen. Jubal Early's demand for $100,000. York borough assumed the debt for the money, food and supplies provided by townspeople and later levied a special tax on property owners to cover the liability. David Small, chief burgess, signed the certificate.

rebels had captured him and released him on parole. The soldiers left him alone, not interested in re-arresting a paroled soldier.

The horsemen spotted a tree near the farmhouse, bearing the finest crop of cherries Jessop ever saw it produce.

"... (T)he Capt. asked father if they could have some and he told them to help themselves, that they could get all they could eat without dismounting, & that is what they did," Jessop wrote.

Their stomachs assuaged by the fruit, the rebels asked to swap horses. All had been moved across the Susquehanna, except one fine-looking horse that had a bad case of the heaves.

Jessop welcomed them to check out the horse, but they believed him and rode off without inspecting the mount.

Stern Early demands hefty requisitions

The columned York County Courthouse on East Market Street, the seat of county power, stood as an apt and inviting headquarters for the imposing Jubal Early. The deserted courthouse was not usually open for business on Sunday, even less so now that the enemy camped in the row offices.

The division commander, settling into the sheriff's office, now knew that he could have his way with his hosts. He ordered his aides to write down two requisitions.

The first, under Capt. William M. Thornton's name, focused on food: 165 barrels of flour or 28,000 pounds of baked bread; 3,500 pounds of sugar; 1,650 pounds of coffee; 300 gallons of molasses; 1,200 pounds of salt; 32,000 pounds of fresh beef or 21,000 pounds of bacon or pork.

In the second, chief quartermaster Maj. C.E.

Snodgrass called for clothing to aid the soldiers in their long marches: 2,000 pairs of shoes or boots, 1,000 pairs of socks and 1,000 felt hats.

Snodgrass concluded his list with a demand that would cause residents to gasp: $100,000.

Twenty-four years earlier, county residents had paid that much to construct the beautiful courthouse that the rebels now enjoyed.

• • •

At 2 p.m., Early ordered the tolling of the courthouse bell, the customary way to call a meeting.

David Small and a mixture of town officials and curious residents crowded into the courtroom. Judge Robert Fisher was there, too, watching as Early took the chair behind the bench.

"I have taken possession of your town," Early began, "by authority of the Confederate government."

The town was safe, he said. Private property would be protected. Guards stood watch over public buildings. Taverns were closed. But his men needed food and clothing.

Early wanted his yet unlisted requisitions filled at once. If the town did not comply, his soldiers would enter stores and houses to seize the items.

After the reading of the demands, David Small stood to object and repeated what he had told Early privately.

Most of the goods and bank holdings had been sent east ahead of the invasion.

A couple of members of the Committee of Safety echoed Small's remarks.

Early persisted.

"Then I shall have to take the hats from your heads, and shoes from your feet, and the coats from your backs," he said, "for I must have them, and I must have some money too."

The general abruptly left the room.

• • •

Community leaders huddled in the courtroom to figure the next step. They appointed collectors, and these men fanned out. Two men worked each of the town's five wards. Certificates would be given for the donated supplies and money.

The food requisition called for delivery to the market houses in Centre Square by 4 p.m. The people of York had only a couple of hours to fulfill the demands.

Still, Jubal Early kept up the pressure. After his brusque departure from the courthouse meeting, he ordered Maj. Snodgrass to get a progress report from David Small:

"Sir, General Early directs me to ascertain whether or not the requisition by me will be filled," Snodgrass wrote David Small.

• • •

Philip Small was one of the leaders collecting Early's claims. He stepped up to the door of James Latimer's house. Small, one of the town's richest men, had given all the money in his house. He argued that Latimer should do the same.

The lawyer had $200 but parted with only $100.

He would regret his generosity.

Others gave less in proportion, he learned, and some refused to give a cent.

Some residents came forth with $5. Others paid more. P.A. & S. Small provided $2,502. One resident —

Maj. Granville Haller, a York native and U.S. Military Academy graduate, assumed field command of largely untested units cobbled together to slow the Confederate advance across the southern tier of Pennsylvania. Facing overwhelming enemy forces, Haller's command spent most of its time in retreat.

Catherine Snyder — put up $1,000.

• • •

Philip Small faced financial ruin if the rebel torch were applied to his company's mills and other holdings. His concern showed.

"... (I)n fact, I think he was quite demented for a while," James Latimer wrote Bartow.

A report that the Confederates had torn down one of his mills didn't help Small's disposition.

The businessman appealed to Early, who checked and rechecked the report. If the mill had been damaged, Early's orders called for immediate execution of the perpetrators.

The Confederates operated under another terse order: Insult or injury offered to a female would be punished with death.

The report of damage to the mill proved false.

• • •

Small's worry translated into P.A. & S. Small singlehandedly complying with Early's requisition for groceries and flour, which represented about three days' rations for his men.

The Confederates paid the Smalls in Confederate currency, and the business sent about $1,200 south to Richmond to care for prisoners of war from York County.

About 35 hatters, shoemakers and clothing stores supplied other parts of the requisition, with the understanding that the borough would assume the debt. The borough also would repay money donated by banks and private citizens.

"... (E)very effort was made to fill the requisition," David Small's York Gazette reported. The Gazette placed the cost of money and goods collected in York at $36,000.

When notified of the collection, Early believed that the townspeople had done their best to supply the required articles. They had met the food, hat and sock demands and delivered most of the shoes — 1,200 to 1,500 pairs — including shoes that had been in the shop for repair.

The soldiers immediately received the badly needed clothing. They treasured their newfound stores of sugar, molasses, coffee and salt — scarce items in the South.

Early was not as pleased with the town's contributions toward the $100,000. The amount added up to $28,600.

Supply officers used some of the money to purchase cattle. The farmers were less vocal in parting with their livestock when handed greenbacks compared to Confederate money.

The rest of the money went to J.L. Corley, The Army of Northern Virginia's chief quartermaster, the officer in charge of all purchasing for Lee's Army.

Early would remind York's leaders of his displeasure with their efforts to satisfy his demand for money numerous times in the next 24 hours.

• • •

Philip Small's son, Samuel, rode north between two Confederate soldiers in the vanguard of a wagon train.

He proceeded with the enemy to the mill to pick up flour. The rebels were looking to make bread at a large bakery at the military hospital.

Along the way, Small talked tough with his rebel escort. He was a Black Republican, a strong Unionist, and he hoped the Yankees would fight until every rebel was taken or surrendered.

The Confederates respected this plain talk, disliking those who pretended to be friendly.

In a short time, Small returned to York with loaded wagons.

"Oh, my! oh, my!" Cassandra Small wrote to her cousin, after observing her brother leave and return, "who would have thought we could have lived through it. Mother doesn't think she could again."

That evening in and around York, the invaders ate their fill of hot bread and roasted beef.

'The dogs of war in our midst'

All Sunday, a sentry paced in front of the door of Mary C. Fisher's East Market Street house.

The judge's wife asked why the house was guarded.

"I must obey orders," came the reply.

She offered him food and water.

"I thank you madam, we are not allowed to accept anything," the guard said. The town was silent, Fisher observed, except for the march of troops in front of her house, plus the sound of the guard's tread.

She later discovered that the sentinel stood guard against Dr. W. S. Roland's escape. The physician, guest of the Fishers, served as an Army surgeon and, thus, was a prisoner of war.

Fisher viewed the rebel troops as well behaved. The taverns were closed, and soldiers were forbidden to enter houses. But people in town feared an outbreak at any time.

"We knew not how soon might come a signal to unleash the dogs of war in our midst, and give our homes a prey to the invader," Fisher wrote. The watch continued until the town filled the requisitions for meat and flour.

Then, the sentinels departed for a warm meal.

• • •

Few visitors from the South were encumbered with a shirt. That resulted in fewer inches of fabric for the best friends of the rebels — fleas, lice and their kin — to lodge.

" ... (T)here was quite a busy time among them," The Republican noted, "in gently crushing the parasitical vermin that infested their persons and clothing."

Their good manners, nonetheless, came through.

"Still, they were no doubt, the real Southern chivalry," the newspaper said, "and every one 'As mild a mannered man/As ever scuttled ship or cut a throat.' "

• • •

Sunday afternoon, Mary Wilson, a friend of Cassandra Small, recognized a number of her Baltimore beaux.

Members of a Negro militia unit rallied to extend trenches in Wrightsville, as the Confederates advanced toward the town. They stayed in the rifle pits to fight, and one soldier lost his life in the battle. Here, Lewis Miller shows a well-equipped Negro soldier ready for service. York County produced scores of Negro soldiers serving in the United States Colored Troops, organized after the Emancipation Proclamation on Jan. 1, 1863.

But she turned her back on all of them.

• • •

No soldier could enter any York store without a pass from the commanding general himself. They paid in nearly worthless Confederate money — including totally worthless counterfeit rebel notes — and Union greenbacks.

The rebels did not approach one jewelry store.

The proprietor had placed a placard in the window: "Small Pox within."

The invaders particularly sought out stockings — socks.

Some men went barefoot, and others wore shoe soles strapped to their feet.

Cassandra Small observed that no two dressed alike.

Some soldiers rode around adorned with high silk hats, sometimes two to a horse. Others dressed in colorful coats and trousers, leaving behind their tattered gray uniforms.

But the Southerners were well behaved, for the most part. They allowed residents to roam freely around town, though requiring passes to leave town.

Residents became inmates, and the town served as their gigantic prison.

Sunday evening in Wrightsville

While York residents coped with the Confederate presence, the people in Wrightsville braced for the inevitable rebel advance. The only question was how many soldiers would march their way.

Enjoying lunch 10 miles away, Gordon would provide the answer: a brigade. The general set the size of his unit at 1,200. He may have marched with as many as 1,800. Commanders sometimes minimized the size of their units — and inflated the strength of their opponents.

Gordon ate lunch at "The Cedars" on the north side

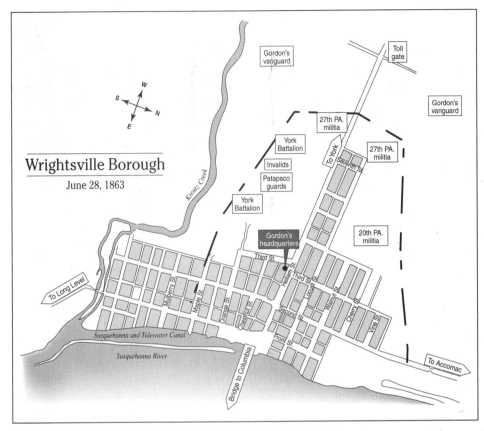

Wrightsville Borough

June 28, 1863

Gordon's vanguard

Toll gate

Gordon's vanguard

27th PA. militia

York Battalion

27th PA. militia

Invalids

Patapsco guards

20th PA. militia

York Battalion

Gordon's headquarters

Third St.

To Long Level

To York

Seventh St.

Hellam St.

Third St.

Locust St.

Walnut St.

Cherry St.

Vine St.

Mulberry St.

Maple St.

Orange St.

Chestnut St.

Second St.

Front St.

Kreutz Creek

Susquehanna and Tidewater Canal

Susquehanna River

Bridge to Columbia

To Accomac

This map shows the horse-shoe-shaped defensive line protecting Wrightsville. Union soldiers stood in recently dug ditches along this defensive line in an attempt to slow or stop the rebel advance and to protect the bridge across the Susquehanna River. After the Confederates deployed their artillery and ordered flanking movements to the north and south, Yankee commanders concluded that further defense was pointless and directed a withdrawal across the bridge. 'We pitched into them and after a brisk little battle of about a half hour duration, routed them,' William D. Lyon, an Alabama soldier marching under John B. Gordon, later wrote.

of the pike to Wrightsville, a couple of miles east of York. Daniel Smyser, owner of the large home, had died the year before, but his wife and two relatives served a generous dinner to the general.

Gordon headed toward Wrightsville after asking Mrs. Smyser to report any property loss to him.

The Georgian must have known his men.

Eighteen-year-old Albert Smyser, a son, discovered that his horse was gone and brought that detail to Gordon.

The general gave an order to an aide, and Smyser reclaimed the horse.

• • •

Gordon paused on a high ridge outside of Wrightsville at about 5:30 p.m. The note handed him in the bouquet of flowers in York indicated that he could see the federal positions from this point.

A look through his field glasses revealed the accuracy of the note, which he now surmised was written by a woman.

He saw a blue line of soldiers guarding the approach to town along an intervening ridge, stretching across the pike. A deep ravine, created by Kreutz Creek, ran toward the river south of the bridge.

"Not an inaccurate detail in that note could be discovered," he wrote.

He concluded part of the note made particular sense: Send a body of men down the ravine to outflank the Union troops and reach the bridge first. At the same time, he decided to test the north flank of the enemy, too.

• • •

Granville Haller and Jacob Frick guided defensive preparations to about 5:30 p.m. — the time that pickets reported the advance of Gordon's forces.

Earlier on Sunday, the two commanders sought to

strengthen and extend Wrightsville's defenses. Entrenchment tools supplied by Columbia hardware stores and the railroad company helped. During the night, four companies from Columbia, 175 men including a company of Negro troops, marched across the bridge to add to the defense.

As the digging continued that day, three companies from Columbia returned to their homes. Frick's men and the company of Negro soldiers did the dirty work, particularly on trenches extending from both sides of the turnpike, west of Wrightsville. The digging continued until the Confederates appeared. At that point, the men put down their shovels and shouldered their rifles.

Haller and Frick directed other defensive measures.

Workers pointed two cannons in Columbia toward the bridge, in case the Confederates overran the Union defense.

All day, Wrightsville resident Samuel H. Mann directed men in town as they barricaded the streets and the pike in Wrightsville with lumber.

Closer to the bridge, hopper cars loaded with iron ore stretched at right angles to the structure to slow any mass attack on the bridge.

Wrightsville's churches canceled full Sunday morning services. Some held morning prayer meetings, and all canceled Sunday school.

Women in town fed the sweating men and soldiers.

• • •

Gen. Darius Couch's directive to forces in Wrightsville was to protect the bridge.

Commanders in Wrightsville knew that their mile-long line, manned by an estimated 1,100 to 1,400 troops, stood too thin to fend off an infantry attack. They estimated the enemy force at 2,500, about twice Gordon's count.

This drawing shows the crowded east bank of the Susquehanna River in Columbia, looking west toward Wrightsville and York County. The Baltimore and Susquehanna Railroad Station accommodates a crowd, center. Confederate Gen. Jubal Early planned to mount his men on the abundant horses on the east bank and attack Lancaster, Harrisburg and other Pennsylvania cities. The blazing bridge, top, foiled his plans.

Haller and Frick knew that their trenches were particularly susceptible to artillery fire. Two high ridges, to the north and south, stopped at the river near Wrightsville. If artillery were placed on these heights, they would command the Union defensive positions.

The horseshoe-shaped blue line consisted of a hodgepodge of units: About 650 men from Frick's 27th Pennsylvania including the volunteer Negro company that had helped dig the trenches; about 240 members of the Invalid Company from the military hospital in York with the Patapsco Guards; members of the 87th Pennsylvania and assorted militia from York; and 200 militia in three companies of the 20th Pennsylvania Emergency Regiment under Lt. Col. William H. Sickles.

A detachment of the 27th and about 50 tired militiamen from the 26th Pennsylvania — with Haller since duty against Jubal Early in Gettysburg — stood guard on the west bridgehead.

Earlier, the Patapsco Guards barely escaped the rebel advance up the Cumberland Valley to Shippensburg. As other state volunteer units pulled back from Chambersburg to escape the oncoming assault, commander Thomas S. McGowan had messaged his superior, Gen. Joseph Knipe, "Have you any instructions for me?"

The next day, the unit finally drew its orders: Clear out.

The unit made it back to York County, where they gamely awaited Gordon's assault.

Bell's Cavalry patrolled the countryside and heights outside town to determine the enemy numbers. They would be the first to see the approaching enemy.

Randall's Philadelphia City Troop patrolled inside Wrightsville's borough limits, making certain all soldiers manned defensive positions and helping with communications between units.

Of all these units, only the Invalids and Bell's Cavalry had "seen the elephant" — had been shot at in combat. The Invalids drew the toughest assignment, manning the line as it sloped toward Kreutz Creek.

They would fire on any flanking movement down the creek's ravine.

• • •

At the bridge, Robert Crane of Columbia led a team of 19 carpenters working to separate the roof and sides of one span and to weaken that span's arches and supports.

They drilled holes and inserted powder charges in the arches then attached fuses.

They chose the fourth span from the west bank — the fourth of 28 spans making up the wooden structure.

After any retreat by Union soldiers, workers would explode the charges, and the span would fall into the river. The bridge sat 15 feet above high water, and a missing span of perhaps 200 feet would impede any advance, or so it was planned.

"When you find it necessary to withdraw the main body of Colonel Frick's command from Wrightsville," Gen. Couch ordered from Harrisburg, "leave a proper number on the other side to destroy the bridge and use your own discretion in the destruction. Keep them open as long as possible."

The 1 ¼-mile bridge was a formidable structure built to accommodate great stress, including, as it turned out, exploding mines rocking one of its spans.

• • •

Gordon's troops advanced slowly on the town at about 6 p.m., rising from fields of grain to pepper those in the trenches.

Then, the attackers unlimbered four cannons from W.A. Tanner's Courtney (Virginia) battery, including two captured from Union artillerists at Winchester.

James Kerr Smith, a Hellam Street resident, counted 40 shots, both solid shot and exploding shell.

Jubal Early later wrote that the Union defenders started running on the third shot, suggesting a shorter bombardment.

Whatever the number, one of the shells found its mark, decapitating a Negro soldier in the trenches. The rebel artillerists increased their range and shot started falling in town. Some shells dropped into the river.

Others barely missed civilians. Amanda Beaverson, crossing a street with her two children, escaped the explosion of a nearby shell without injuries. Jacob Freet brought her to the safety of a cellar.

Another shell struck the Presbyterian Church and bounced along Locust Street before coming to rest in Freet's house.

The Ferry House, called the "Big Brick Hotel," sustained damage when one exploding shot damaged the first floor. Another shell entered the second floor but did not explode. Someone wished that the second floor shell had detonated. Prohibitionists — Sons of Temperance — and Know Nothings — an unpopular political organization in those parts — met on that floor. Later, residents gathered such unexploded shells from around town.

One shell crashed near Fourth and Hellam streets, and a fragment entered James Kerr Smith's house and ended up in a wall.

Residents and defenders escaped the balls from the guns of rushing Confederate infantry, although a captain in Frick's regiment sustained a leg wound. He hid in Joshua Isaac's residence until the rebels left town. He died from the wound.

• • •

The bombardment brought the desired result. The artillery rattled Wrightsville's defenders.

"But our evil genius, Gordon's Brigade, with Cavalry and Artillery, again presented itself, and while getting into its position and reconnoitering our lines, quite a number of shots were exchanged, and sufficient members of their force were displayed to show the hopelessness of a defense of Wrightsville ... ," Granville Haller wrote.

Haller and Frick studied a dispatch from a scout saying that three brigades of enemy infantry and one regiment of cavalry had Wrightsville in their sights. The numbers came in high. Gordon commanded a brigade, and the size of White's cavalry battalion fell far short of a regiment.

Frick's men fought without artillery support and could not withstand an enemy of that reported size with cavalry, infantry and cannons. Frick saw flanking movements from the rebels along the Hellam Hills to the north and the Kreutz Creek ravine to the south.

Knowing that the rebels would maneuver into striking distance and then rush with abandon, Frick ordered a general retreat across the bridge. He later wrote with satisfaction that his men had held off the enemy for 75 minutes.

In ordering the retreat, he brushed aside Haller's suggestion to destroy the bridge, forcing the Union men to stay and fight.

Haller later explained that he was skeptical that soldiers never exposed to an attack could retreat in order and that a plan had been put forth to ford the river above Wrightsville if the enemy cut off their retreat across the bridge.

As the federals fell back, rebel soldiers with 20 hot weather miles on their legs that day gave chase.

"... (T)he enemy beat him running," Early stated.

For the most part, the Union retreated in orderly fashion. The men of the veteran Invalid Corps were the most adept, returning fire as they hobbled toward the bridge.

All Union infantry made it across except Sickles and 19 of his men, who surrendered to the oncoming Confederates — a move Frick considered unnecessary if the unit had obeyed his orders.

Worse, two companies of Sickles' unit hastened safely across the bridge and kept going through Columbia to Lancaster, causing alarm by spreading stories about the rebel horde.

Bell's Cavalry rushed into town from its scouting duties, met rebel resistance and retreated. One trooper, whose horse was shot from under him, hid in a house until the enemy left. The rebels captured another horseman.

The remainder of Bell's troopers made it safely across the mile-wide river downstream.

• • •

Samuel Kauffelt saw the Union defense dissolve soon after Tanner's battery began its work.

Knowing that a defended town would be subjected to the whims of the military invaders, he nailed a piece of white cloth onto a wooden pole and attached it to the chimney of his Hellam Street address.

His flag of truce suggested to passing rebels that he intended no fight.

• • •

Maj. Charles McLean Knox, of Couch's staff, positioned himself on the bridge to view the Confederates descending the hill toward the structure. Haller, in the vanguard of the retreat was nowhere in sight. He was in Columbia, organizing the defense of that town.

With the rebels about to overtake the bridge, Knox issued the order to blast the weakened bridge span. Frick gave his blessing.

It was 7:30 p.m., about 90 minutes since the fight had begun. John Denney, John Lockard, Jacob Rich and Jacob Miller set off the powder charges. The blasts rocked the structure, but the span did not fall, retaining enough strength to carry the charging Confederates across.

Frick, commanding the rear of the retreat, observed that the rebel onslaught would not be deterred. He ordered his men to set fire to the bridge. Its middle section, previously soaked in kerosene and crude oil, easily ignited. The fire immediately spread in both directions.

The vanguard of the Confederate column crossed about halfway before the flames beat them back.

Union soldiers joined Columbia residents on the east side in battling the blazing structure. They hacked away at the bridge with axes, hoping to eliminate fuel for the flames.

The flames consumed the bridge, but firemen with

This sketch shows the Susquehanna River bridge burning from the middle toward each end. Union defenders ignited the 40-foot-wide bridge after an attempt to drop a span into the river failed. The possibility of damaging or destroying the bridge to stop the Confederate advance had been pondered for months. A letter from the Lancaster Committee of Safety raised the prospect of making the bridges at Columbia-Wrightsville and Conowingo in northern Maryland impassable when the Confederates threatened the North in September 1862. The best means of defense open to those east of the Susquehanna was to make its 'broad waters impassable to our foe,' the Lancaster officials stated. Columbia's chief burgess replied that the state had accepted responsibility if the military was forced to destroy the bridge to prevent it from falling into the hands of the rebels.

their equipment, soldiers and civilians kept the flames from spreading to the town. Only one building burned.

Confederates on the west end — the Wrightsville side — tried to control the fire, initially interested in continuing their advance. They fought with blankets and called for buckets. All had been carried across prior to their visit, they were told.

Soon, the fire blew toward town, and the invaders fought the flames with a different mission: to save the town. At that point, pails appeared.

Gordon wrote about the mysteriously appearing buckets:

"But when the burning bridge fired the lumber yards on the river's banks, and the burning lumber fired the town, buckets and tubs and pans innumerable came from their hiding places, until it seemed that, had the whole of Lee's army been present, I could have armed them with these implements to fight the rapidly spreading flames."

Rebel soldiers and Wrightsville residents fought the flames side by side. Gordon's men, a well-coordinated unit, went into an unprecedented formation.

"... (T)he only chance to arrest the progress of the flames was to form my men around the burning district, with the flank resting on the river's edge, and pass rapidly from hand to hand the pails of water," Gordon wrote.

The fire raged toward one particularly attractive house on the main pike, but the soldiers rallied to beat back the blaze. This was the home of Wrightsville's Mayor James F. Magee and his daughter, Mary Jane Rewalt.

Before the blaze was extinguished, it claimed three houses and G.W. Harris' foundry; Henry Kauffelt's planing mill; and Kauffelt's and Lanius' lumber yard.

Immediate estimates of the property damage ranged from $16,000 to $21,000.

Casualties sustained by soldiers came in light. One graycoat was wounded. Two Union soldiers died, and nine were wounded. Frick applauded the fight of the Negro soldiers.

"After working industriously in the rifle-pits all day, when the fight commenced they took their guns and stood up to their work bravely," he wrote.

• • •

People in Harrisburg, more than 30 miles up river, observed the glow from the blazing bridge in the darkening sky.

Those viewing the eastern horizon in Hanover, about 30 miles west, thought York was burning.

This view shows that Wrightville, even 30 years after the war, was still a small town. The Confederates approached from the west, right, bombarded the town and then made it to the bridge too late. The successor bridge to the structure burned by Union soldiers is seen at bottom, center. It sits on the same piers. Hellam Street, the main street in town, heavily blockaded with lumber and iron ore cars, runs toward the bridge. The body of water adjacent to the Susquehanna River, left, is the Susquehanna and Tidewater Canal.

Observers remarked how the massive arches holding up each span remained stationary as the timbers around them burned. The river reflected the fiery skeletons.

"Some of the timbers as they fell into the stream seemed to form themselves into rafts, which floated down like infernal ferry boats of the region of Dante ... ," The York Gazette reported.

• • •

As the attack on Wrightsville was raging, A.G. Jenkins' rebel troopers returned to Dillsburg and entered the now-quiet town, where they acquired clothing, food and other needed items from the stores. They freely spread around their Confederate dollars.

A squad rode up South Mountain to remove the flag used to divert them earlier that day, and others set up camp on the Lerew farm south of town.

To the southeast, they observed the glow on the horizon from the burning bridge and pointed to their successes. Their fellow soldiers had torched property, they said, and maybe even the town of York.

Whatever was burning, they boasted, marked the handiwork of the Confederates. And the Union Army was not to be found.

• • •

In Lancaster, a correspondent provided The New York Times with a story on the encounter at Wrightsville and the burning of the bridge that was "worth a million."

"The firmament is illuminated by it even at this distance," he wrote.

The wide river did not represent a sufficient buffer to calm the people of Lancaster.

"The excitement here now amounts to a panic," he wrote. "Everything is leaving."

Trainmen moved the rolling stock of the Northern Central and Hanover Branch railroads even farther east.

• • •

Back in Wrightsville, Mary Jane Rewalt sought out Gordon amid the turmoil and thanked him for saving her house.

How long would he be in Wrightsville? she asked.

Informed that the Confederates would be leaving the next day, she invited the general and some of his men to breakfast.

The young woman, wife of an Army surgeon Luther L. Rewalt, was staying in her father's home with her husband off to war.

Gordon pledged to Mayor Magee that his men would cause no more damage. Magee invited Gordon to use his house as a headquarters and lodge there for the night. The Georgian accepted.

Gordon's men bivouacked on the Detweiler farm near Kreutz Creek, the stream offering an ample water source for the men, sweating from the summer heat and the blazing bridge.

• • •

With the bridge gone, some rebel soldiers attempted to cross the river by walking on the breast of the low dam downriver from the burning bridge.

The dam's causeway was too narrow for cannons, and the men in gray observed big guns mounted on the east bank pointed in their direction. They gave up.

The river's depth at that point eliminated the possibility of wading across. Even if they could find a ford to do so, the artillerists would have problems dragging their cannons across. An attack on the opposite shore without artillery support presented a problem.

But these men testing the dam reached farther east than any other Confederate troops.

• • •

Jubal Early headed toward Wrightsville Sunday evening, observing the smoke from the burning bridge soon after leaving York.

By the time he reached his destination, the bridge was destroyed — and so were his grand plans. By now, he had hoped to cross the bridge, mount his men on the abundant horses on the east bank, march to Lancaster and then move to the rear of Harrisburg.

He would have grabbed a big prize — the capital of the North's second-largest state. Camp Curtin, a major recruiting and training center, operated there. Republicans Andrew Curtin and Abraham Lincoln strongly supported each other. If Curtin were pushed from Harrisburg, that would undermine Lincoln as well. Harrisburg stood as the primary link in Northern east-west communications and represented a vital north-south transportation connection.

Early conferred with Gordon, ordering him to march

back the next morning. Dick Ewell's order called for them to move to Dillsburg to join the corps commander's projected assault on Harrisburg. Perhaps what couldn't be done from the rear could be executed head on.

Early returned to York that night.

The day had been an eventful one for the Virginian. Without loss of men and supplies, he had marched into the largest Northern town the Confederates would occupy. He came within minutes of controlling a major crossing that would have led him to the backside of a major Northern capital city.

His own plans foiled, he nevertheless had executed Ewell's orders to destroy the bridge.

Early, under orders to burn the bridge, had fought hard to save it. Frick's men, with initial orders to protect the bridge, had struck the match that ignited it.

• • •

Jubal Early's busy Sabbath amounted to a day of rest compared to events west and south of York that day.

Fighting Joe Hooker asked to be relieved of command of The Army of the Potomac after a dispute with the War Department. Hooker's superiors in Washington took him up on it, and Hooker joined the likes of deposed commanders George McClellan, John Pope and Ambrose Burnside.

Pennsylvanian George G. Meade, Hooker's replacement, learned that the last of the northbound Confederate troops had passed through Hagerstown. This signaled to him that Lee's entire army was marching somewhere north of the Mason-Dixon Line.

At his headquarters in Frederick, Meade sifted through reports and looked toward the east where he could relieve pressure on Harrisburg and guard against any rebel movement on Washington.

"I propose to move this army to-morrow in the direction of York," he wrote the War Department.

Jeb Stuart, the top Confederate cavalry general, commanded a long column of gray-clad cavalry pacing toward Pennsylvania. He learned that the Union Army was north of the Potomac, chasing the Confederates. That much he knew. He did not know that his comrades were spread out from Chambersburg to the banks of the Susquehanna, about 75 miles.

And Robert E. Lee gained confirmation from actor-turned-spy James Harrison that the entire Union Army was sniffing out his trail, north of the Potomac. One successful westward thrust toward the Shenandoah and Cumberland valleys, and Meade's army would sever Lee's supply and communications line to the South.

As Sunday turned into Monday, Lee shifted his thinking. Instead of concentrating to the west, his forces must come together at Cashtown or Gettysburg, east of South Mountain.

That movement would force Meade's men to also respond by staking a position between Washington and Baltimore, to the east, alleviating Yankee pressure on his supply line.

"Tomorrow, gentlemen, we will not move to Harrisburg as we expected," Lee would conclude on Monday after digesting Harrison's report, "but will go over to Gettysburg and see what General Meade is after."

IV

York County deals with rebel visit

Monday, June 29, 1863

'But we do not war upon women and children.'
— Confederate Gen. Jubal A. Early

Early shakes down York

Robert J. Fisher served as judge over court in York and Adams counties. He exchanged words and wit with Confederate Gen. Jubal Early, who threatened to burn the York County Courthouse.

Jubal Early must have mulled methods to collect the remaining $71,400 due from York residents during his overnight stay at Metzel's Hotel, down the block from the courthouse.

He embarked on a plan to progressively raise tension in an already tense town to break loose any remaining Northern greenbacks.

In the morning, he summoned Robert Fisher to his headquarters for a lawyer-to-lawyer talk.

"I want all the keys to the Court House," Early told the judge.

When Fisher asked why, Early responded that he would burn the county's records. Fisher reminded the general of his pledge not to destroy private property.

It would be in retaliation for a similar act Union troops perpetrated on the courthouse in Fairfax, Va., Early said.

"Two wrongs would not make a right," Fisher argued.

The judge begged the general not to torch the records. But Fisher had prepared for this moment.

Before the rebels arrived, Fisher had ordered the records in the Register of Wills and Recorder of Deeds offices to be carried to the courthouse basement. There, the deed documents went in one corner and the will records in another, hidden by straw and large pieces of paper.

Early gave in, but put forth one more question.

Was any property left in York County that would be contraband of war and used for federal military purposes?

Fisher offered only one thing: Cigars made from York County tobacco.

Early, a confirmed Virginian, was wary of the quality of Northern cigars.

He declined Fisher's offer.

• • •

Early spent the morning touring the camps of the three gray brigades around York. At one point, old Jube ran an errand for his superior, Richard Ewell.

Benjamin S. Ewell, Gen. Ewell's brother, was a colonel in the Confederate Army. During the war, his wife, Julia McIlvaine Ewell, resided in York, her hometown.

After entering Pennsylvania, Ewell had warned Lizzie, Benjamin and Julia's daughter, via letter that he would be close to her kinsmen in York.

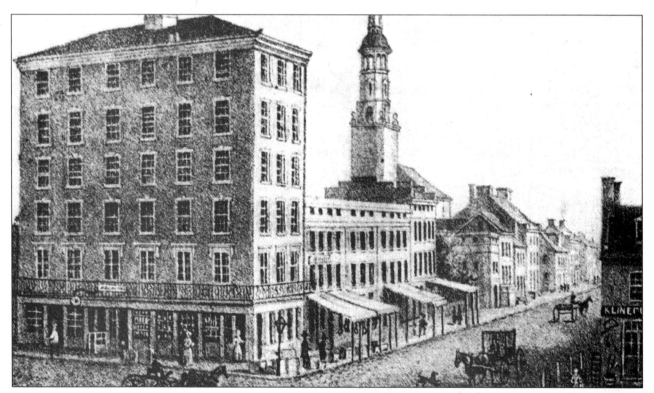

The Hartman Building on the southeast corner of Centre Square, York's tallest building, helped add to the prosperous appearance of the borough. Even as he rode out of town Tuesday morning, Gen. Jubal Early remained convinced that York's residents could have forked over more than the $28,600 delivered in response to his requisition. Wagons move on South George Street, right, the road to Baltimore.

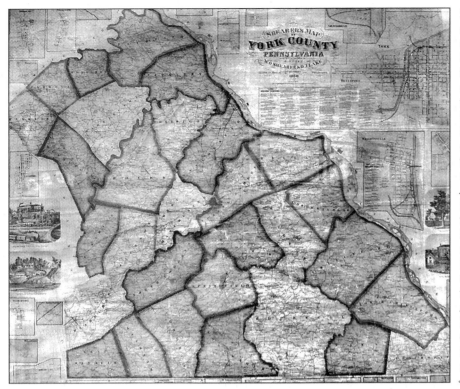

Shearer's map of York County, dated 1860, shows York, the dark spot in the middle of the triangular-shaped county. Confederate forces moved from west, left, to east, before Union men stalled their advance by burning the bridge across the Susquehanna River, running along the county's eastern border. Jubal Early's men took parallel paths across the middle of the county to York. Gen. John B. Gordon's brigade then followed the pike, barely visible on this map, from York toward the bridge in Wrightsville. Gordon's men countermarched to York on Monday, June 29, and the entire division marched west to concentrate at Gettysburg, in adjoining Adams County, the next day. The Mason-Dixon Line defines the county's southern border and Harrisburg, the state capital, sits near the county's northern tip.

"The people look as sour as vinegar," he wrote, "and, I have no doubt, would gladly send us all to kingdom come if they could."

He continued writing in good humor.

"I will let your relations off tolerably easy on your account — probably not taking more than a few forks and spoons and trifles of that sort — no houseburning or anything like that," he kidded.

Ewell's spirits might have been good, but the McIlvaine family was not in a good mood when Early came to visit. His stay was short.

Mary McIlvaine, Julia's sister, left the house because she had no desire to speak to the commander of the occupying force.

After Early left, Mary washed the chair he sat on with soap and water.

• • •

Word was going around York that the mills of P.A. and S. Small had been sacked and grain and flour thrown into their raceways.

The raceways funnelled water from the Codorus Creek to the mills. If these water channels were clogged, the millstones would not turn, and the mills would shut down.

Samuel Small, Philip Small's son, brought this concern to Early, who denied that it had happened and urged him to see for himself.

Small hesitated about riding several miles through an area occupied by hostile troops.

"You must go, but I will give you a pass," Early said, and directed an aide to draft a letter for safe passage.

Early also offered Small a horse, but the young man wanted to take his own, concealed in a stable behind the Morris drugstore on East Market Street.

Small made the journey and found the mills safe.

He received several offers to exchange horses along the way, but Early's pass meant he could reject them. He gained safe passage to the mill and back.

Gordon finds bravery in Wrightsville

The potential of a rebel crossing Monday morning concerned Col. Jacob Frick and Maj. Granville Haller, who had led the defense of Wrightsville the previous day.

From Columbia, they peered across the foggy Susquehanna. They could see the sturdy stone piers stretching across the river with no load. These bridge supports were all that remained of the bridge, other than the smoldering wood bobbing around the piers.

All the boats and rafts along that part of the Susquehanna had been floated to the east bank. But the Confederates had shown skill elsewhere in improvising river crossings. One time, Jeb Stuart's cavalrymen had made a bridge from wood recovered after dismantling a warehouse in Virginia. And Wrightsville was known for its lumber yards.

A hastily built bridge across a river the width of the Susquehanna was not likely, but the Union officers gazed to see if any makeshift rafts floated their way.

For most of the day, Frick and Haller explored Columbia to determine defensive positions in case the Confederates would try to cross. They ordered the digging of more rifle pits and the strengthening of defenses near fords in the river.

Late in the afternoon, they learned that the Confederates had moved west.

• • •

Mary Jane Rewalt, the mayor's daughter and John B. Gordon's hostess, enchanted the general. She warmly provided breakfast for Gordon and a handful of his officers.

The Georgian had not slept well that night.

After lights went out, the canopy hanging over Gordon's bed fell, covering the general. For a moment, he thought his enchanting hostess had set a trap for him.

Gordon wiggled free, lit a lamp and discovered the innocent source of his concern.

Over breakfast, the lawyer in Gordon probed whether his hostess held Southern sympathies, perhaps thinking that she might have written the note among the flowers.

She firmly stated her conviction in a room full of convinced Southerners and high-ranking Confederates: "General Gordon, I fully comprehend you, and it is due to myself that I candidly tell you that I am a Union woman. I cannot afford to be misunderstood, nor to have you misinterpret this simple courtesy. You and your soldiers last night saved my home from burning, and I was unwilling that you should go away without receiving some token of my appreciation. I must tell you, however, that, with my assent and approval, my husband is a soldier in the Union army, and my constant prayer to Heaven is that our cause may triumph and the Union be saved."

No Confederate, Gordon wrote, left that room without respect or admiration for the brave Mary Jane Rewalt.

• • •

Gordon's quartermaster unit set forth a series of demands for goods from stores in Wrightsville. While in the home of one town leader, the quartermaster examined a manual for the Independent Order of Odd Fellows. The fraternal organization met in a building at Front and Locust streets.

The officer asked if the town had a lodge.

Morgan L. Bahn, a businessman present at the time, questioned the officer about whether he was a lodge member. The officer indicated that he had been in the past. They traveled to the lodge room, where the American flag was raised on both sides of the Noble Grand's seat.

"Do all Lodge rooms have this flag?" he asked.

"Is it not beautiful?" Bahn answered.

The officer indicated that it was.

"Brother, I cannot understand," Bahn said.

"What, pray?" the officer asked.

"You know in our ritual we teach this beautiful sentiment: 'You cannot become an Odd Fellow in spirit and in truth unless you are grateful to your Creator, faithful to your Country, and fraternal to your fellow man.' "

The officer replied, "Brother, just now we do not look at all things alike."

In leaving, the officer told two soldiers, "Stay here, do not let anyone enter the building while we stop in this town."

• • •

Gordon's men operated under Robert E. Lee's Order No. 72 — the prohibition against plundering. Or so Gordon believed.

Gordon would soon become defensive about press reports that the Confederates set fire to Wrightsville. He had resolved to leave no ruin in the wake of his march through the bucolic Pennsylvania countryside.

The general later listed two exceptions to Lee's order. Finding his men short of firewood, he acquiesced to a request to take the top rail on nearby fences. The next morning, most of the rails were gone. Each man had taken the top rail so the fences gradually disappeared from top

VOL. XII—NO. 3670.

THE REBEL INVASION.

Approach of the Rebels to Harrisburgh.

Their Advance Near the Fortifications.

Some Shelling During Yesterday Afternoon.

Burning of the Bridge Near Columbia by Our Forces.

A SKIRMISH AT WRIGHTSVILLE.

Two Rebel Cavalry Companies Defeated Below York.

Rapid Organization of Troops at Harrisburgh.

NO GENERAL ENGAGEMENT.

TELEGRAMS FROM HARRISBURGH.
Special Dispatch to the New-York Times.
HARRISBURGH, Sunday, June 28.

Our forces have slowly retired, and are now in and around the fortifications of Harrisburgh. The enemy is advancing slowly, and in all probability will soon commence an attack. Gen. SMITH has made proper disposition of his troops.

Throughout the day men have been coming to the defence of the city, in response to the Governor's proclamation. Among the number are a great many contrabands. They were all furnished with guns and ammunition, and sent across the Susquehanna.

Capt. BRISBANE, Chief of Cavalry, who was on a reconnoisance this afternoon, reports the rebel scouts to have been within three miles of our pickets.

The reports from the direction of York are very conflicting. An extra train was run to Philadelphia at 12, noon.

This New York Times article, published on Monday, June 29, came from dispatches sent from Harrisburg. The headlines summarize the previous day's events with accuracy, except for the report of the defeat of two rebel cavalry companies below York. Col. Elijah V. White's Comanches chose not to attack Yankee troops guarding railroad bridges near Hanover Junction, hardly a Union victory. The Times' story admits that reports from the direction of York, locked in a rebel stranglehold, were conflicting. It also tells of 'contrabands' responding to the call to defend Harrisburg. Authorities provided these fugitive slaves with guns, sending them to fortifications opposite Harrisburg on the west shore of the Susquehanna.

to bottom.

"It was a case of adherence to the letter and neglect of the spirit," Gordon wrote, "but there was no alternative except good-naturedly to admit that my men had gotten the better of me that time."

The other exception was the conscription of horses. One Pennsylvania Dutchman, a German-speaker who knew only a little English, was so put out about the loss of his horse that he took his case to Gordon. No argument would shake the man's determination to get his mare back.

Finally, in exasperation the man made a comparison that showed his love for his horse. "I've been married, sir, t'ree times," he said, "and I vood not geef dot mare for all does voomans."

Gordon did not find the argument convincing, but the man was so distressed that he returned his horse.

• • •

Maj. Robert Stiles, the artillerist assigned to Early's division, observed little plundering by the invading Confederates, except once or twice soldiers broke branches full of fruit from cherry trees.

The men followed Lee's directives so carefully that some Pennsylvanians admitted to Stiles that if compelled to play host to either Union or Confederate soldiers, they would choose the latter.

This observation did not apply to quartermasters, particularly of artillery units, who were avowed horse thieves — a practice that continued unabated wherever Confederate forces moved in southern Pennsylvania.

Sometimes rebel quartermasters paid with generally worthless Confederate money, and according to Stiles, the owners sometimes took it as "better than nothing — how much better it would be difficult to say."

Horse owners went to great lengths to conceal their animals from the rebels, including hiding them in their houses. The savvy Confederates had seen all the tricks and usually found their prey.

Residents, needing horses to tend to their farms, gave up much, but the rebels came away with big horses of little value.

"They seemed to pine for the slow draft and full feed of their Pennsylvania homes," Stiles wrote.

While the rebels admired the lush Pennsylvania farmland and large barns, they did not completely give up their love of all things Southern.

The German families lived in Yankee style, one soldier wrote. Wife and daughters did all the work.

"It makes me more than ever devoted to our Southern institutions & customs," he wrote.

• • •

David Sloat, the Wrightsville youth, found Gordon's Confederates more pleasant than their reputation.

He and his father took David's grandmother, an invalid, to an uncle's house at Canadochly, southwest of Wrightsville. En route, they came across 11 mounted rebels. They stopped and talked, and both groups went their ways without incident.

Ten-year-old John Holtzinger viewed both men in blue and gray as engaging.

Before the rebel visit, the Wrightsville boy carried water to a squad of Union soldiers dumping iron ore on the railroad tracks running to York.

The soldiers rewarded him with a horse. The boy's grandfather, having no need for a mount, gave it to an older boy, Tempest Wilson.

After the Confederates ran off the federals, the boys mingled freely with the men in gray.

Holtzinger made many friends with the rebels, and their consideration of Wrightsville residents impressed the boy.

• • •

Although the Southerners did not disturb people or property during their occupation of Wrightsville — save for fence posts and livestock — they caused immense destruction on their countermarch west.

After spending the morning on the banks of the Susquehanna, Elijah White's Comanches burned bridges — 14 in all — on the railroad that paralleled the path of the march back to York.

Gordon overlooked or chose not to destroy a public work that aided the Union war effort, the Susquehanna and Tidewater Canal.

Cutting the canal or destroying the dam spanning the Susquehanna below the bridge piers would have severely

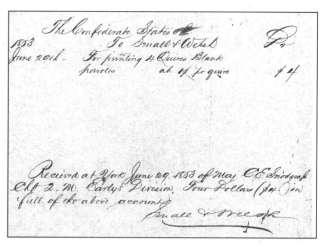

The Confederates did some business with local firms during their short stay in York. This paperwork shows that C.E. Snodgrass, from Gen. Jubal Early's staff, requested Small and Welsh to print 100 — four quires — blank parole forms to be issued to captured Union soldiers. The printer received $4 for the work. Small and Welsh also owned and printed The York Gazette.

impeded freight service to Harrisburg and Baltimore.

• • •

After the Confederates left, word spread throughout Wrightsville about Ella Lloyd's brave statements to Gordon.

As the story goes, the Wrightsville teacher served a meal to Gordon during the occupation. She provided the Southerners with the best from the pantry and her most tart-tongued views about their cause.

She expressed her views as she served each course.

Gordon was so moved that he drafted a poem at the table.

"We thank you for your brandied peaches," the verse concluded, "But do abhor your Union speeches."

• • •

Samuel and Eliza Smith were among those in Wrightsville who had crossed the river before the Confederates arrived.

When they returned, they found two surprises in the house they rented from the Harris family on Locust Street.

First, it had been struck by one of the Confederate shells.

The second was a more welcome addition.

Their son, Silas, a Union soldier had carried a pocket testament with him, given to him by his parents. He was wounded in the South and had died in a Confederate hospital.

Silas' testament now rested on a table in one of the rooms in their house.

No message was attached to it. A soldier had simply returned it.

Rebels sleeping in the house the previous night did no damage. Nothing was missing.

• • •

Gordon's men reached York at about 4 p.m. Someone counted that they traveled with 12 ambulance wagons, bearing U.S. markings.

They marched through town and camped along the

Carlisle Pike, ready to complete Ewell's order to meet him in Dillsburg for the assault on Harrisburg.

Their ambulances burst with men, who were hitching an easy ride.

• • •

The 20th Pennsylvania's Lt. Col. William H. Sickles had a more difficult ride back to York.

Gordon paroled the commander after his capture during the defense of Wrightsville Sunday.

Sickles rode an overcrowded handcar on what was left of the railroad between Wrightsville and York on Monday.

He fell under the car, fracturing one of his legs.

'Our services have not been called for'

William J. Seymour, aide and brother-in-law of Gen. Johnson Kelly Duncan, the late Confederate general from York County, marched with the Louisiana Tigers brigade. He traveled from camp near Loucks Mills into York Monday afternoon, finding some of the buildings imposing, yet tasteful.

Disappointed that the stores were closed so he could not purchase badly needed clothing, he looked up a major from Early's staff, acting as provost marshal. The major, named Hale, helped him get into a large store through a back door, where he bought a bottle of old cognac and some other items.

The proprietor, a Baltimore woman, appeared happy to be in the midst of the Confederate troops and willingly accepted rebel money. In general, Seymour found residents held to the Copperhead position and opposed to the war.

"Not much faith to be placed in their professions," Seymour wrote in his diary, "they are a mean, selfish, sordid people, who would profess to do anything to save their money & property."

• • •

The Louisiana Tigers could hardly tag other people as selfish.

The unit earned a reputation as fierce fighters, causing Confederate high command to overlook the Tigers' propensity to plunder. That is, except for one time during the winter when Hays and Early got into it. The Tigers demonstrated a bent toward thievery that even Early considered excessive.

Their recklessness spawned a reputation that preceded them on the march. In Gettysburg, a frightened woman begged a Tiger to help himself to her property but spare her household.

"She was," the soldier said later, "the worst scared woman I had ever seen."

Along the march, another Tiger entered the residence of a woman who was alone. She inquired about his regiment. When informed, she fainted.

The soldier rushed to her side. At that point, the woman's husband arrived and demanded an explanation as to why the two were together on the floor.

The soldier quickly related their conversation.

That explained it, the husband replied.

The Louisiana unit worked hard to maintain their rep-

The invading Confederates freely passed around practically worthless Confederate States of America currency. This $2 bill was passed in York County.

utation.

As the Tigers crossed the Mason-Dixon Line, the Louisianans told gawking Pennsylvanians that that they had eaten the "last mule we had and had come over to get some beef and bacon."

When Hays' and Hoke's brigades walked along roads around York, soldiers overheard a child say, "Why Papa, I thought the Rebs had horns. Where are they?"

Some soldiers turned toward the child, pointed their bayonets that way and exclaimed, "Here are our horns."

• • •

Sometimes, attempts to appease the Tigers backfired.

An elderly proprietor of a clothing store in York told a Louisiana soldier that he had no shirts. When offered gold instead of Confederate notes, he managed to locate some of the requested clothing.

The pleased recipient of the new shirts went back to camp and identified the seller. A group of Tigers hastened to the store and brushed aside the proprietor after he refused to do business. They searched his shop and found clothing plus a supply of aged whiskey and other fine spirits.

The proprietor objected to their taking the liquor, too, but they pushed him out of his store, locked the door and enjoyed their newfound cache. The Tigers' state of mind and body made them oblivious to the large crowd drawn to the disturbance.

This could have been the same group of Tigers who gained notoriety around campfires in York for getting drunk and engaging in "a general family fight" that resulted in severe injuries to an officer and the disciplining of several soldiers.

• • •

Seymour intended to look up the sisters of Johnson Kelly Duncan — Henrietta DeHart Yocum and Margaret Beitzel — who lived in York.

He called on one of the sisters and received a "frigid" reception. As he rode up to the house, the husband bolted out of the back door. His wife received Seymour.

"After I had remained for some time, the old man's curiosity got the better of his fears," Seymour wrote, "and he returned, and was hugely relieved and rejoiced at finding that my visit was not for a hostile purpose."

• • •

James Gall of the U.S. Sanitary Commission steamed toward York on the Northern Central Railroad to check out the needs of the Union soldiers expected to be massing in that area.

Harry Hays' Louisiana units were among the troops camping around Small's Codorus Mill, along the Codorus Creek, north of York. The mill was one of several in the York area owned by major grain exporter P.A. & S. Small.

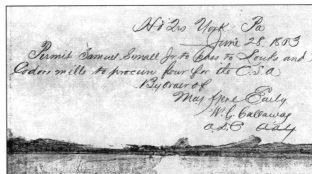

The Confederates issued this pass to Samuel Small, son of Philip Small, to acquire flour from Codorus and Loucks mills.

This P.A. & S. Small advertisement ran in an 1863 York directory. The York firm shipped thousands of bushels of corn to Ireland during the famine in the 1840s and later exported 90,000 barrels a year to Brazil. The firm also became involved in ironmaking, establishing large furnaces in Ashland, Md., north of Baltimore. After the war, P.A. & S. Small's interests resulted in one-sixth of the freight shipped over the Northern Central Railway.

Early in the war, the U.S. government had formed the Sanitary Commission to combat diseases — dysentery, diarrhea, typhoid and malaria — caused by unhealthy conditions in camp and on the march.

The train carried Gall as far as Parkton in northern Maryland. Then he started walking toward York at 9 a.m. Sunday. He reached town later that day, walking unimpeded through rebel lines.

The inspector made the most of his freedom to walk around the occupied town.

Monday afternoon, he hung about Confederate camps in York and those of the Louisiana and Virginians north of town.

"Their dress was a wretched mixture of all cuts and color," he reported. Many dressed in blue pants, probably extras that Milroy had left behind in Winchester.

Each soldier traveled light, typically bearing a worn wool blanket, slung from his shoulder, and a cartridge box. Such equipment weighed 12 to 15 pounds. Gall observed that this light load helped the rebels march faster and longer than the better-equipped Union men.

The federals compared favorably the more Gall walked around town. The rebels marched in an irregular and careless manner, and their weapons were rusty.

The Louisiana brigade had drawn its supply wagons into a "sort of straggling hollow square." The soldiers stacked their weapons in its center along company lines.

Only a few officers had tents. The men cooked a supper of well-salted, fried beef, received from the York requisition, and wheat griddlecakes raised with soda and water. The men lacked coffee or sugar.

The men divided themselves into squads or messes of five to six men, each carrying cooking utensils on their marches.

"The men expressed themselves perfectly satisfied with this kind of food," Gall reported, "and said they greatly preferred the bread prepared in this fashion to the crackers issued the Union soldier. I question if their bread is as healthy and nourishing as the army biscuit."

• • •

The ever-curious Gall asked a rebel soldier how he fared without a tent.

"First rate," came the reply. "In the first place, I wouldn't tote one. In the second place, I feel just as well, if not better, without it."

The weather that day, like the previous day, was overcast and dreary.

What did the soldier do when it rained?

Gall's report captured the soldier's reply: " 'Wall,' said he, 'me and this other man has a gum blanket atween us; when it rains we spread one of our woolen blankets on the ground to lie on, then we spread the other woolen blanket over us, and the gum blanket over that, and the rain can't reach us.' "

The inspector concluded that this was how most of the Confederate Army slept, except for a few top officers.

"Everything that will trammel or impede the movement of the army is discarded, no matter what the consequences may be to the men," Gall wrote.

York Bank, left, York's oldest, sent away its assets for safekeeping before the Confederate Army reached York. In gathering its money for shipment, the bank found $7,576 in damaged $1 and $2 notes. Officials destroyed the bills because they were too unwieldy to send off. The rebels found US. currency scarce in tight-fisted York, and their stiffest threats brought only one quarter of what they were seeking. The National House, an early York hotel, stands at right.

Gall talked to a Confederate officer who saw no problem with sleeping under the stars without a tent. The Army, the officer contended, was in its best condition ever.

But Gall counted the lack of tents as a detriment.

The Confederates seemed to be in good shape, Gall admitted. But he assigned that to the past winter when they had shelter, and the weaker men had died or had been discharged. Those left were stronger and less susceptible to disease.

Further, the weather had been good, the infantrymen had faced little opposition and had been relatively well fed in a fertile land.

The Confederate officer voiced reservations about Union soldiers he had met along the march.

"They are too well fed, too well clothed, and have far too much to carry," he told Gall.

Gall didn't buy the first two points, but he thought the officer had a point about all that Union soldiers carried.

At Chancellorsville in early May, the common soldier carried rations to last eight days, 60 rounds of ammunition, a rifle, a wool blanket, rubber blanket, overcoat, extra shirt, drawers, socks and a tent. He estimated the weight at 60 pounds.

"Think of men, (and boys, too) staggering along under such a load," he wrote, "at the rate of fifteen to twenty miles a day."

• • •

Residents of York found they, too, could walk from place to place in town. They walked because, as far as any of the locals knew, only three horses remained in town.

Samuel Small's horse, under protection from Jubal Early, was one. A second horse was well fed in a back kitchen and another found secret quarters in someone's cellar.

In fact, it was commonly believed that only three horses stayed behind between York and Wrightsville, and those were 30 years old.

• • •

Jubal Early provided a pass for Dr. E. H. Pentz to move around in York to see his patients.

The pass stated that neither man nor horse should be bothered.

Pentz appreciated the pass, but the dispensation to keep his horse safe was unnecessary. His mount grazed somewhere in Lancaster County.

The horses, some noted later, seemed eager to trot down the pike toward safety across the river in Columbia — as impatient as their owners and others to escape whatever the invaders would bring their way.

• • •

The banks did a thorough a job of removing their assets before the rebels could help themselves to the cash.

It had not come easily. The York County Bank held thousands in $1 and $2 notes. The bulk of the bills meant transportation challenges. The bank located a large carpetbag that could accommodate the pile of money, and it effectively kept the notes together on its trip to Philadelphia.

Charles Weiser Jr. of Weiser Sons & Carl accompanied his bank's assets to Easton. He arrived after the bank closed, and the hotel safes overflowed with valuables.

He took the booty to his hotel room where he spent a long, fretful night.

Residents had claimed their silverware and valuables from the banks, except for one container too heavy to transport. The Confederates overlooked the box, tucked away inside one of the banks.

When opened after the rebels left, bankers found that it held thousands in government bonds and a considerable amount of gold and silver coins.

• • •

The Confederates visited the office of Fred Scott, supervisor of the Northern Central Railway shops.

They took the Stars and Stripes that he displayed there but did not discover valuable tools and oil that had been left behind. Scott had hidden the supplies in a pile of cinders and a recently dug sewer trench.

The rebels later returned his flag in good shape.

• • •

Early kept his horses in the stables at the Wheatfield Inn, across the street from his courthouse headquarters.

Soldiers lighting matches and smoking in the stable caused the hostler, John Armpriester, to fret about a possible fire.

One soldier treated Mrs. Charles Underwood, the proprietor's wife, with disrespect. He told her that she could spit on them, but she could not shoot them.

"No lady would do that," she replied.

A short time later, an officer knocked at her door.

He had heard that one of his soldiers had insulted her.

"No," she replied, "I considered the source it came from."

If you want, the officer said, you can ask for his life.

"Oh no," she said, "his life would mean naught to me."

The rebels removed the horses from the Underwood stable and placed a guard around the property.

• • •

Maria Underwood, the proprietor's daughter, and other girls of the inn wore small American flags in their belts while serving meals.

One soldier admired the flag and related his story: He was there because the rebel government forced him to serve. He could not desert because his wife and babies were in the South.

• • •

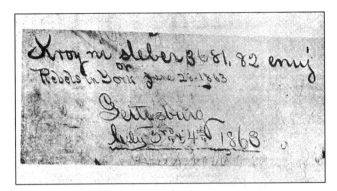

Confederate troops invading York searched the Morris Drug Co. on East Market Street for medical supplies. Tradition states that Geoffrey Yost, longtime proprietor, inscribed 'Rebels in York, June 28, 1863/Gettysburg, July 3rd and 4th, 1863' forward and backward on a wall in a third-floor storage room. The drug manufacturer and seller operated from 1823 to 1961.

John Hay, a York resident, walked to the rear of the courthouse when he saw a photograph on the ground.

It was an image of Stonewall Jackson.

A Confederate soldier had carried the picture to town and had accidentally dropped it.

Hay kept the souvenir of the rebel visit.

• • •

Confederates searched the East Market Street drugstore and pharmaceutical lab of Morris Drug Co.

Their mission was to find drugs that would help the sick and wounded rebels.

Charles A. Morris, Geoffrey Yost and others connected with the noted York pharmaceutical house had hidden the drugs, only to break them out within days to treat the Union wounded at Gettysburg.

Someone, possibly Yost, later wrote on the building's third-floor wall: "Rebels in York June 28, 1863/ Gettysburg July 3rd and 4th, 1863."

• • •

Col. Hamilton C. Jones had ample opportunity to observe the town's residents, who tended to gaze on the Confederates "with something like stupefication."

Jones commanded the 57th North Carolina, a regiment in Hoke's brigade that camped in town.

When the Confederates entered, the town's residents gave up any idea of going to church. The women went home, and the men "hobnobbed" with the men in gray, who showed few signs of bitterness about the occupation.

Civilians and officers drank together and talked about the war. Union men who stayed behind freely expressed their opinions, and Jones thought many in town did not support Lincoln or the war.

The number of men, of fighting age, who lounged around town amazed the Confederates.

An officer approached a group of such men.

"What are you doing here?" he asked, "Why are you not in the service?"

"Oh no, we are not needed yet," one joked, "our services have not been called for."

York's Northern Central Railway station, in this 1852 drawing, was the scene of many events during the Civil War. It was the primary point for soldiers to arrive and depart. Trains arriving in the North Duke Street station brought war news. Abraham Lincoln's funeral train stopped briefly at the station on its trip from Washington, D.C., to Springfield, Ill. Sitting in this depot on Monday, June 29, 1863, Confederate Gen. Jubal Early was making another round of demands for money from the residents of York when a messenger rode up with orders from Gen. Robert E. Lee to concentrate to the west. The railroad line from Baltimore reached York in 1838, 25 years before the rebel visit.

General seeks money still due

The return of Gordon's brigade Monday afternoon renewed Cassandra Small's fears about the invaders' intentions toward her family and town.

The burning of the bridge thwarted Early's plans.

Now what would the general do?

After tea, Small's family bolted the doors and closed the shutters.

"But all was quiet — no disturbance at all ... ," she wrote to Lissie.

• • •

The Rev. John Roth kept good his pledge to talk to Jubal Early about the return of his mare. He located the division commander, who referred him to Gordon.

"Since you tell me you are a minister," Early said, "you may get back your family horse."

Roth later ran into Gordon, now back in town.

"I have heard that you are a Mennonite minister," Gordon told Roth. "When this news came to me before I entered York, I turned your white mare over to my adjutant, and he must give the horse to you."

The minister thanked Gordon but was concerned that both he and his horse would be captured on the way back.

Gordon ordered his adjutant to accompany the minister home, where the family invited the escort to a large meal as a thank you for returning its prized mare.

• • •

The minister was not the only resident from the county to complain about the loss of animal power. One man groused to a rebel captain about the confiscation of his mules.

"How many did you lose?" the officer asked.

"Two," the farmer answered.

"Two mules! What an example of the patriotism of these Northern heroes," the captain said. "I have staked everything on this issue, houses, lands, Negroes, money, everything I have in this world, and you complain of two mules."

With that off his chest, the captain advised the farmer to take his complaint directly to Early.

The farmer complied and got his mules back.

• • •

Dealing with such complaints did not distract Early from persisting in demands for the remainder of the greenbacks owed him Monday afternoon. He concocted another strategy for straining more money from York residents.

"I have determined to burn the shops," Early told David Small.

Small walked with Early down North Duke toward York's extensive railroad car manufacturing and maintenance shops — shops with enviable records of producing more than 1,000 cars some years.

David E. Small's and Charles Billmeyer's company, one of three shops sitting near the railroad station, spread out over a five-acre site. It included a planing mill, lumber yard and parts warehouse and employed 700 people at times. Pfleiger, Hess and Nevin and the Northern Central Railway operated the other shops.

"These shops are built of wood," Small argued. Fire them and the risk was high that the flames would spread to the entire town. The general had promised not to harm the town.

"Then call out your fire department to protect the

homes and other buildings," Early replied.

• • •

By now, more than 30 hours into the occupation, Jubal Early had grown to like David Small.

"I was very favorably impresses with his conduct in every way, while there was nothing at all in it inconsistent with his position and duty as a citizen who adhered to the side in which his state was enlisted," he wrote years later. "He recognized the situation and complied with my requisitions in such a spirit as relieved me from the necessity of enforcing them by any harsh measures, and rendered it a pleasure to me to protect the citizens of York from any depredations."

Despite his regard for Small and his privately held opinion that torching the shops, indeed, could ignite the town, Early sounded so convincing that word traveled quickly up and down York's streets to brace for the worst.

In the neighborhood of the shops, residents filled tubs, buckets and any container that they could find with water. They lugged their furniture outside.

By this time, a group of leading townsmen followed the general and chief burgess toward the railroad shops. Behind them, a delegation of boys and men tagged along. As they passed, weeping women and bawling children begged the general to save their property — to refrain from burning the railroad car factories.

All day, the town had been filled with rumors. Word spilled from one resident to another that soldiers in gray had rebelled and stood poised to sack the town. According to another rumor, the Confederates had hatched a plan to cut the wooden and iron pipes bringing water into town from a reservoir fed by springs in the hills to the south. No water would be available to douse the flames from the Confederate torches.

A.B. Farquhar walked with the dignitaries trying to keep up with the general, but he claimed to be privy to information that Early would not risk the town by burning the shops.

He either did not share this information with the town's fathers, or they did not believe him.

• • •

Jubal Early convinced Mollie Cox about his fiery intentions.

She was a student at the York County Academy, stranded in York because she could not travel to her Maryland home.

Mrs. Charles Underwood called Mollie and her own girls into a room at the Wheatfield Inn, where the student was staying.

She gave them each a sheet and instructions: Spread the sheet on the floor, and pack necessary clothing in the event that they would have to leave town.

The girls laughed at the prospect of marching out of town with a pack on their backs but prepared to follow Mrs. U.

An image of Ruth with her mother-in-law Naomi came to Mollie's mind: "Whither thou goest I will go and where though lodgest I will lodge."

The biblical characters made the journey from Moab to Bethlehem. As it turned out, the girls did not have to follow Mrs. U. from York.

• • •

Earlier that day, the general had ordered a squad to burn railroad cars at the depot, cars made for government

Address of Gen. Early to the People of York.

York, Pa., June 30th, 1863.

To the Citizens of York:

I have abstained from burning the rail-road buildings and car shops in your town, because after examination I am satisfied the safety of the town would be endangered; and, acting in the spirit of humanity which has ever characterized my government and its military authorities, I do not desire to involve the innocent in the same punishment with the guilty. Had I applied the torch without regard to consequences, I would have pursued a course that would have been fully vindicated as an act of just retaliation for the many authorized acts of barbarity perpetrated by your own army upon our soil. But we do not war upon women and children, and I trust the treatment you have met with at the hands of my soldiers will open your eyes to the monstrous iniquity of the war waged by your government upon the people of the Confederate States, and that you will make an effort to shake off the revolting tyranny under which it is apparent to all you are yourselves groaning.

J. A. EARLY,
Maj. Gen'l C. S. A.

Confederate Gen. Jubal Early issued this handbill, shortly before leaving York, touting his magnanimity in not burning the town. Some people in York saw the address as an attempt to undermine the authority of the U.S. government. The handbill came out of the print shop of The York Gazette. Handbills, also called broadsides, were widely used for immediate communication in York and other towns that lacked daily newspapers. The York Daily, the county's first daily newspaper, began publication in 1870.

service.

The troops spared several cars filled with lumber marked for the Presbyterian church. The captain of the squad was a member of that denomination and had vowed long before that he would never burn church property.

Their actions increased anxiety among the town's leaders about what Early might do to the shops. Would he use the excuse that they manufactured cars for the U.S. government? Remember what he did to Thaddeus Stevens' furnace? The rebels had destroyed railroad switches, tracks, bridges and now cars. What was next?

Seated in the railroad depot — surrounded by unopened boxes of goods and reportedly energized by some snorts of Mount Vernon whiskey — Early made another snatch for the greenbacks.

He reiterated the simple message: If he received the balance of the $100,000, his men would not burn the factories or the depot.

Northern Central Railway Supt. James Hopkins, whose office the men occupied, argued with Early about his demands and received vitriol in return.

"General," Small argued, "I would do so very willingly, but the fact is I have raised all the money I could raise in town, and a good deal of it has been contributed in small sums. I don't know any man in town that has more than $1."

At that point, a nervous Philip Small played a card he had been holding since the rebels entered town.

Desist from burning the factories, he said, and he would give a $50,000 note drawn on a Philadelphia bank, payable however the war played out.

Early did not have a chance to respond. Just then, a courier speeded down North Duke Street to the depot on a lathered horse.

• • •

Elliot Johnson, from Dick Ewell's staff, had entered town only moments before.

Dr. S. J. Rouse saw the dispatch bearer gallop up on a calico horse. He asked for the general's headquarters and was directed to the courthouse.

Riding to the seat of justice, he met John D. Daniel, Early's aide, who pointed him to the railroad where the lawyer-general had convened court with the town's leaders. Moments later, Johnson found Early and handed him a message.

Early stepped aside, read the note and returned to the York leaders. He would consider Philip Small's proposition that night.

Then, he told David Small privately that he would not torch the buildings because he believed it would endanger the town.

• • •

The messenger's note concerned Jubal Early, an outwardly untroubled man. Walking with Small, he retraced his footsteps on North Duke Street and retired to his headquarters.

Ewell's dispatch included an order from Robert E. Lee, indicating that the Union Army had crossed the Potomac and marched north of Frederick. It called for a concentration of all divisions of The Army of Northern Virginia west of South Mountain in Franklin County.

Early immediately sent out word to his brigade commanders that the division would retrace its steps early the next morning.

He would not tell the people of York his intentions. At that moment, many of his own men believed their next move would be on Harrisburg — or further east.

"The boys are a jovial set of fellows," a rebel soldier wrote that day. "Confident of being able to take Philadelphia."

The people of York remained in turmoil.

The messenger had rushed into town on a lathered steed. Gordon's brigade had countermarched through town. Regiments showed restlessness, gathering supplies and making other preparation to break camp. Wagons loaded with requisitioned supplies moved out the Carlisle Road.

What would be Early's parting shot?

Rebs prepare for westward march

Monday night, the lawyer in Early took one last opportunity to make a closing argument to the people of York and all Northerners.

The York Gazette's press printed an address explaining why he would not burn railroad buildings and car shops: Such an act would endanger the town. If he had started the fire without concern for its aftermath, he would have been justified. The Union Army had done just that in the South.

"But we do not war upon women and children ... ," he wrote.

He hoped the occupation would give the North a taste of the "monstrous iniquity" of the war wrought by the United States government.

A.G. Jenkins' mounted men, known for their lack of discipline, raided Dillsburg and other towns in northern York County. Jenkins, a 33-year-old Harvard-educated lawyer, served as the advance guard for Gen. Richard Ewell's 2nd Corps, the rebel unit that led the invasion into Pennsylvania. Jenkins sported a long beard, popular among cavalrymen. The beards often masked the youth of the officer behind the hair.

• • •

James Gall's observations squared with Early's account: The general kept his men from destroying private property in the city.

But the Sanitary Commission agent wrote that Early did not prevent his soldiers from taking horses and mules from farmers.

"The rebel cavalry, as a general thing, are splendidly mounted," Gall wrote, "better, I think, than the Union cavalry, and their free and easy manner of procuring horses explains it."

• • •

Assessing Early's address several days later, The Republican reflected the growing view in town that Early was anything but noble:

The Confederates had fleeced York County's people with its requisition, sacked houses, stolen horses and even taken earrings from women.

On top of that, Early had appealed to the people to rise up against the U.S. government.

All Early had accomplished with this pillaging was to convince county people that it is better to live in liberty under a free government than to be robbed by traitors who just want to destroy government and subvert the law.

• • •

Dick Ewell, accompanying Robert Rodes' division in Carlisle since Saturday, also broke camp after a comfortable three-day stay in the well-stocked town. Carlisle housed a federal barracks and other government buildings, along with federal stores of whiskey.

Lee's orders to countermarch disappointed generals

Jeb Stuart's mounted men, on their way north to meet up with Robert E. Lee's infantry forces, captured a long Union wagon train near Rockville, Md. The 125-wagon train, loaded with supplies for the Union troops moving toward Gettysburg, proved to be a liability, limiting the number of miles Stuart's column could ride in a day. Stuart and his wagon train eventually joined Lee on the second day of fighting at Gettysburg on July 2.

and privates. On Tuesday, Rodes' division had planned to march on Harrisburg.

During a skirmish at Oyster's Point, a crossroads about midway between Mechanicsburg and the Susquehanna River, a scouting party sneaked to the Susquehanna on Monday.

Jenkins, members of Ewell's staff and an escort of 60 troopers rode through Shiremanstown to the area of Slate Hill.

There, the officers viewed Harrisburg and its fortifications through their field glasses before riding back to Carlisle to give their assessment that a Confederate assault would succeed.

Gen. Isaac Trimble, accompanying Ewell's 2nd Corps, vowed he could take Harrisburg with a brigade.

But the message from Lee that was relayed to York arrived. The Confederates must concentrate.

The disappointed rebels had reached the northernmost point of this raid — or any raid.

Early becomes a wanted man

As Lee urgently directed his corps to concentrate, Union commanders used forced marches to overtake Lee's thrust into Pennsylvania.

The farther George Meade moved from Washington,

the more difficulty he had in finding ways to communicate with the War Department. Elijah White's assignment at Hanover Junction and that of other mounted Confederate raiders had been to cut telegraph wires and disturb rail transportation. They did their work well.

On Monday, Meade sent a courier with vital communications to Army command in Washington. The rider, starting north of Frederick, Md., would have to find a telegraph station still transmitting in Hanover Junction or some other point along the Northern Central Railway.

The courier enjoyed a fine meal at the home of John B. Gallatin, a storekeeper in Marburg, a hamlet outside Hanover in Manheim Township. He sought a guide, but Gallatin refused at the urging of his wife, concerned about his return alone.

Now near midnight Monday, the east-bound courier had come to a fork in the road near Green Ridge, in a remote area of Codorus Township in southern York County. He headed toward a farmhouse to gain directions and perhaps some grain for his horse.

George Bair, living in Green Ridge, became frightened when the mounted courier called on him.

Bair, a German who did not understand English, thought the horseman was one of the invading Confederates, perhaps one of White's men.

When the courier knocked on the farmhouse door, Bair's wife opened a window on the second floor and sounded a horn to alert neighbors.

The stranger told her that if she did not stop the

NEW YORK HERALD.

NEW YORK, TUESDAY, JUNE 30, 1863.—TRIPLE SHEET.   PRICE THREE CENT

E THREATENED ATTACK ON HARRISBURG.

on of the Capital of Pennsylvania---The Approaches to the City from the West.

THE INVASION.

Advance of the Rebels Upon Harrisburg and Washington.

Skirmish Near Oyster Point and Maysville, in Front of the Harrisburg Defences.

Operations of the Rebels at Wrightsville.

The Destruction of the Bridge at Columbia.

Withdrawal of the Rebels from Wrightsville to York.

A Contribution of Money and Supplies Levied on the Citizens of York.

The Main Body of the Rebel Army Moving on Gettysburg.

Work Commenced on the Defences of Philadelphia.

The New York Herald reported on the Confederate threat to Harrisburg, the burning of the Wrightsville bridge and other developments from the rebel occupation of York County in its Tuesday, June 30, edition. This map focuses on the rebel advance toward the west bank of the Susquehanna River opposite Harrisburg. The availability of the telegraph enabled correspondents to send news about the withdrawal of the rebels from Wrightsville to York and other events in time for Tuesday publication.

alarm, he would shoot her. Mrs. Bair either did not understand or ignored the demand, and the stranger threatened to burn her house.

Meanwhile, George Bair loaded his gun, aimed it at the stranger and squeezed the trigger. The shot killed the stranger instantly, his pistol dropping to the ground beside him.

The distressed gunman realized his mistake — the horseman was a Union courier, not a rebel — and surrendered to military authorities.

The courier's body, buried in the nearby Stone Church Cemetery, carried a dispatch from Meade stating, "I send this by courier with the hope and expectation that it will reach you safely."

Meade was trying to inform his superior, Henry W. Halleck, about his new plans for movement:

His Army would track down Lee by moving toward Gettysburg instead of eastward toward York, keeping his men between Lee and Washington. If Lee fronted Harrisburg, Darius Couch's men must delay the enemy until Meade's men could fall upon the rebel rear.

• • •

Monday night in York, the streets teemed with activity as thousands of soldiers and teamsters and wagons prepared to retrace their steps.

Sentries from Hoke's brigade positioned in town withdrew from the hotels and taverns joining the rest of their regiment in the march out the Carlisle Road.

Meanwhile, Early unknowingly was a wanted man.

A Union cavalry division under the command of Gen. Judson Kilpatrick was moving north to sniff out Early's trail. The main body of Confederate cavalry, under the command of Jeb Stuart, also was in an urgent search for the Confederate general.

Kilpatrick, nicknamed "Kill-Cavalry" for his reckless direction of his men and horses, camped at Littlestown, about seven miles south of Hanover on the Pennsylvania border.

Two other Union cavalry divisions were riding north that day. David Gregg's men headed toward Westminster, Md. John Buford's troopers moved toward Emmittsburg, Md.

The columned York County Courthouse, left, survived Jubal Early's threats to burn it to the ground. It remained standing until the late 1800s, when it was demolished to make way for a new courthouse covering its footprint. Lewis Miller drew this scene of York, looking south.

Buford would reach Gettysburg first.

Kilpatrick and his two brigade commanders, Elon J. Farnsworth and George Armstrong Custer would be delayed in their quest for Early. Events the next day in Hanover would dictate that.

Jeb Stuart's three brigades of 4,000-4,500 men spent the night in Union Mills, Md., not far from Littlestown.

Earlier, Lee had directed Stuart, known as the "eyes and ears" of the Confederate Army, to "feel the right of Ewell's troops" and forage for supplies for the rest of the Army. This meant that Stuart would supply intelligence and Union troop positions to Lee or other commanders.

Ewell's right was Early's division, and Stuart did not know where to find it. York was his best bet.

"...York, Pa. was designated as the point in the vicinity of which he was to expect to hear from Early, and as the possible (if not probable) point of concentration of the army," Stuart aide H.B. McClellan later wrote.

Stuart had been out of touch with Lee's command for 72 hours. A rain-swollen Potomac had slowed his march. The saddle-deep water forced the troopers to carry artillery shells and powder bags across the wide river by hand. The current tugged the waders downstream, and it was difficult to keep on the path of the ford in the dark night.

"No more difficult achievement," one of the riders later wrote, "was accomplished by the cavalry during the war."

Finally across, Stuart's command cut supply and communication lines between George Meade and Washington, D.C. The raiders damaged the Chesapeake and Ohio Canal and captured a dozen canal boats.

Stuart's men resumed their march north and pounced upon a Union wagon train near Rockville, Md. The wagons stretched out more than eight miles. The wagon farthest from Stuart's men reached within 3-4 miles of Washington, D.C.

Stuart paroled 400 men but kept 900 mules and 125 cumbersome supply wagons headed for Union forces and their coveted contents — oats, whiskey, bacon, hams and sugar. The wagons also carried forage — feed for his horses and the horses of the main body of Confederates and grain that he could deny the Yankees. Stuart could not bring himself to leave the booty in the middle of the road, especially when his orders called for him to gather supplies.

The cavalry general considered a raid on Washington, but feared such a night attack without the element of surprise.

Stuart's ride in the vicinity had caused a panic in Washington. People in the city had worked to erect barricades across streets. Militia and government employees guarded the obstructions.

Ewell's right was north, and Stuart headed that way, the long wagon train in tow.

• • •

In York, Early was spending a quiet evening in his hotel room at Metzel's, oblivious that horsemen in both blue and gray wanted to make contact.

As it turned out on Tuesday, neither Kilpatrick nor Stuart connected with Jubal Early. But on the streets of Hanover, the two generals got to know each other intimately.

V

Confederates leave York County doubting its future

Tuesday, June 30, 1863

'I may take too gloomy a view of affairs,
but things seem at their worst.'
— York lawyer James W. Latimer

Rebels turn toward the west

Most of Jubal Early's men cleared town early Tuesday morning.

Stragglers and deserters lounged around town as late as Tuesday night. Some tarried for a reason. They would desert and remain in the North.

These deserters traded places with a number of recruits in York County who joined Confederate forces during the occupation.

With the squeaks and groans of wagons outside, The York Gazette published Tuesday, undeterred by the disturbance of the past few days.

The writer of the invasion story, probably David Small, finished the piece at dawn as the last rebels — a few pickets and scouts — passed through town.

Sensing the surrender of York would not be popular now that the Confederates were gone, the writer concluded with a mixture of justification for the past and prayer for the future:

"But the people submitted with becoming resignation to imperious necessity. What shall yet be our fate or the fate of our beloved country must be developed by the future. God grant us a happy deliverance."

• • •

John B. Gordon's graycoats gained a head start on the rest of Jubal Early's division of the 2nd Corps by moving out the Carlisle Pike the night before. Hoke's men joined them.

The last soldiers, the brigades positioned north of town, marched through York at 4 a.m. Their bands saluted farewell by playing loudly.

Lige White's Virginians rode on the York-Gettysburg Pike to scout for Northern troops. The infantrymen marched out the Carlisle Pike, headed west at Weigelstown and stopped for a rest near Davidsburg.

Early left with the rearguard at about 7 a.m. and followed the marchers to Davidsburg, a farming community along an old road that led to Shippensburg. The commanding officer, his staff and Gens. Smith and Hays stopped at William Julius' hotel for their midday meal.

The staff ate quietly in one room, several reading their Bibles. They anticipated a battle soon, perhaps even the next day.

After paying for 20 meals with four Confederate $5 bills, Early stepped outside and proceeded along the road toward East Berlin.

Soon, he heard the sound of cannons from the south and reasoned that the battle had begun between the main forces.

He did not figure that the booming came from Jeb Stuart's horse artillery and that Judson Kilpatrick's column was riding smack in the way of Early's rendezvous with Stuart's cavalry.

• • •

Resuming the all-day march, Early camped Tuesday night about 3 miles east of Heidlersburg in Adams County. The only incident that day came near East Berlin, where White's cavalry advance brushed against a squad of federal horsemen.

William Seymour of the Louisiana brigade recorded the distance marched that day: "We left York at daylight passing through the town of Berlin & camped at dark. Distance 22 miles."

Early rode to Dick Ewell's Heidlersburg headquarters. There, the corps commander received a messenger with a note from Robert E. Lee ordering a change of plans. The projected point of concentration had moved. Ewell's men would meet the rest of the gray forces east of South Mountain in either Cashtown, at the foot of South Mountain, or Gettysburg, the crossroads farther east of Cashtown.

That evening, A.P. Hill's men camped at Cashtown, and Longstreet's Corps rested west of the mountain in Chambersburg.

Ewell ordered Early's and Rodes' divisions to march on parallel roads and, depending on intelligence gathered along the way, improvise from there.

With the prospect of another long march and a fight the next day, Early's men settled in for the night.

Had the people of York known the condition of many soldiers in gray, they would have given a rare chuckle and smile. Many in Early's footsore division rubbed their toes. The ill-fitting shoes filched from York had torn up their feet.

'The spirit of the chase'

Hanover residents crowded the streets to herald Judson Kilpatrick, George Armstrong Custer and the men of the 3rd Cavalry Division, The Army of the Potomac. The famished Yankees rode into town on Frederick Street from Littlestown at 8 a.m.

It had been a trying three days for news-starved Hanover residents. Ever since White had stopped in town, they had been isolated — no train, no mail, no telegraph, no regular outside newspaper.

The sight of blue uniforms — albeit grimy blue uniforms worn by saddle-weary troopers — encouraged Hanover's citizenry.

After meeting with Kilpatrick, 26, and his brigade commanders Custer, 23, and Elon J. Farnsworth, 25, in Jacob Wirt's Frederick Street home, the Rev. William Zieber knew the town must provide aid.

"These soldiers are our friends and protectors," Hanover's Committee of Safety head told a crowd on Wirt's front steps. "They are tired and hungry. The best thing we can do is feed them."

Hanover residents promptly produced coffee, milk, bread and meat. They fed still-mounted cavalrymen along Frederick Street and into Center Square. Some girls, standing in front of the Lutheran parsonage on Frederick Street, serenaded the waiting soldiers with songs to stir national pride.

By about 9 a.m., Kilpatrick and his division's first brigade — Custer's men consisting of the 1st and 7th Michigan plus two batteries — moved northward through the Pidgeon Hills on the road toward Abbottstown. They rode to find Early, presumably still in York.

Farnsworth's brigade inched up the road to receive the bountiful meal. At 10 a.m., Farnsworth's 1st Vermont and 1st West Virginia had passed toward Abbottstown, and the men of the 5th New York gobbled their meals.

The 18th Pennsylvania — Farnsworth's fourth regiment — moved toward the center of town, ever closer to the food. As the rear guard, Lt. Col. William Brinton's Pennsylvanians watched the brigade's supply and ambulance wagons, all separating them from the New York unit.

The town had fed about 3,500 hungry men in the two brigades in two hours.

• • •

That morning, Jeb Stuart ate a full meal at the William Shriver home in Union Mills, Md., 14 miles southeast from Hanover. For dessert, he and other officers entered into a joyous round of "Join the Cavalry" around the Shriver piano.

"Our only regret," Mrs. Shriver later wrote, "was that our entertainment was so inadequate for the occasion, but they made us feel as though it was elegant."

Thirty-year-old Jeb Stuart, plume in his hat, enjoyed a reputation for playing hard and working hard, often at the same time. This boosted his standing as a master cavalryman but also promoted him as a target of controversy.

In a past raid, he monitored a federal telegraph wire before playfully tapping out a telegram to the U.S. quartermaster general. He complained about particularly poor quality of mule flesh. The federal mules would not move quickly with the wagons he captured.

"J.E.B. Stuart," he signed off.

Finding Confederate infantrymen without reinforcements on another occasion, Stuart lashed tree branches to the halters of his horsemen. This maneuver kicked up a cloud of dust, convincing Union officers that they should not attack that weak position.

"I realize that if we oppose force to force we cannot win, for their resources are greater than ours," he once wrote. "We must make up in quality what we lack in numbers. We must substitute esprit for numbers. Therefore, I strive to inculcate in my men the spirit of the chase."

• • •

Thomas Herbert Shriver, Stuart's host's 17-year-old son, led the column north on a direct road to Hanover, trying to avoid Littlestown and the federal troopers known to be riding there.

Gen. Fitz Lee, commanding one of the three brigades forming the rebel column, had obtained a reliable map from a sympathetic resident detailing Kilpatrick's movements.

Stuart accompanied Col. John R. Chambliss' men in the vanguard of the invading column. Chambliss commanded W.H.F. "Rooney" Lee's brigade. Rooney Lee, Robert E. Lee's son, was at his home near Richmond recuperating from a wound received at Brandy Station, Va., in early June.

Gen. Wade Hampton's brigade rode in the rear, guarding the 125 captured wagons. Fitz Lee's column guarded the column's left flank in case the Union troopers in Littlestown headed east.

As the vanguard of Stuart's troopers neared Hanover, Chambliss saw the end of an unsuspecting blue column — the 18th Pennsylvania — on Frederick Street in the Pennville area, stretching from Plum Creek to the Hanover boundary.

Elon J. Farnsworth

George A. Custer

Judson Kilpatrick

Gen. Judson Kilpatrick, division commander, led the Union column into Hanover. Two recently promoted generals, Elon J. Farnsworth and George Armstrong Custer, reported to Kilpatrick as leaders of brigades. About 3,500 blue-clad horsemen fell under Kilpatrick's command. All three Union generals were in their 20s.

Gen. Jeb Stuart, head of the Confederate cavalry, and his men ate breakfast at the William Shriver residence in Union Mills, Md., just south of the Mason-Dixon Line. The main rebel column rode along a secondary road before entering Hanover along the Westminster Road. The initial clash of the Battle of Hanover occurred around the intersection of the Westminster Road and Frederick Street, the road to Littlestown.

Stuart later wrote that the blue-clad troopers were plugging the gap in the Pidgeon Hills that he intended to take to join Lee. The Union cavalrymen arrived there first, but Stuart would not wait for the passage to clear. He would push the blue line out of his way.

Chambliss ordered the 13th Virginia forward. Stuart called for Lt. Col. William Henry Fitzhugh Payne's 2nd North Carolina to charge, too. The attacking force, taking the Westminster Road, slammed into the 18th Pennsylvania, cutting the unit in two.

The Battle of Hanover had begun.

• • •

The Confederate charge pushed part of the surprised

18th Pennsylvania, now in its first large-scale fight, into the center of town. The gray charge pushed the blue horsemen through and around the 60-foot market shed and out the other side of Center Square, across the railroad tracks toward Abbottstown.

The other part of the 18th fled west and regrouped in McSherrystown.

"Owing to the suddenness of the attack, the (18th Pennsylvania) regiment was thrown into some confusion and forced back upon the main column, throwing that also into confusion, and for a few moments the enemy evidently had a decided advantage," Col. Nathaniel Richmond of the 1st West Virginia wrote.

The charge spun the town into turmoil. At first, many thought the booming of the Confederate cannons, supporting the rebel charge, saluted the Union men.

Soon — very soon — the citizenry realized that a gray column was barreling through town, with the Yankees fleeing its advance.

Louis Boudrye, chaplain of the 5th New York, observed the growing terror, especially in the women and children who had been ladling food for his regiment along congested streets.

Maj. John Hammond of the 5th New York yelled for civilians to clear the streets.

"Please go to (your) homes and into (your) cellars," he said, riding along Frederick Street. "In a few minutes there will be (more) fighting in your streets."

The 5th New York and scattered troopers from the 18th Pennsylvania reformed on the nearby public common and countercharged.

Men, women and children of Hanover mixed with men in blue and gray battling saber to saber on main and side streets. Runaway supply and ambulance wagons and galloping pack animals added to the melee.

The counter by the reformed New York and Pennsylvania regiments initially pushed the attacking 13th Virginia and 2nd North Carolina back along Frederick Street.

Farnsworth and his 1st West Virginia and 1st Vermont troopers soon added to the bluecoat numbers.

The young general had heard the skirmish from the New Baltimore crossroads on the Abbottstown Road, a mile north of town. Farnsworth bolted into town and led another countercharge that pushed the gray horsemen farther backward. Close combat took place along Frederick Street and Westminster Road.

The Union troopers met added resistance from the 9th and 10th Virginia regiments. Still, the Union Army had regained the town. Stuart's men took to the heights south and east of town. Hampton, with the wagons, was far behind, and Fitz Lee's men had not yet arrived.

Stuart did not enter the battle with his full force. But neither did the Yankees, with Farnsworth and Custer north of town and Kilpatrick even farther north in Abbottstown.

• • •

Seeing the fighting, William Zieber hurried to his York Street house and herded his family into one room, closed the shutters and bolted the front door.

Before leaving, he gave his family a certain sequence of knocks to identify him on his return. Back on the street, he immediately met up with Dr. George W. Hinkle.

"Doctor, our services are needed; there are wounded soldiers up there. Will you go with me and render them

Fitz Lee Wade Hampton John R. Chambliss

Jeb Stuart

Jeb Stuart commanded more than 4,000 men in the Battle of Hanover. Brigadier Gens. Wade Hampton and Fitz Lee reported to Stuart as did Col. John R. Chambliss, heading W.H.F. 'Rooney' Lee's brigade. Hampton, 46, one of the South's richest planters, was the oldest brigade commander from either side at the Battle of Hanover.

assistance?" he asked.

They walked to Frederick Street and moved three or four dead soldiers from the road onto sidewalks. Just then, Gen. George Custer's brigade came racing down Abbottstown Road into town.

Blue and gray clashed in front of Zieber and Hinkle.

"The doctor and myself, like other citizens who remained on the streets during the fight, had lost all consciousness of danger and whenever we saw our (Union) troops gaining any advantage over the enemy, we applauded them," Zieber later wrote.

• • •

Early in the fight, Stuart threw out two cannons from his horse artillery on a high field south of town to support his mounted men. Opposing guns now arrived on the other side of town.

Lt. Alexander Pennington Jr. and Lt. Samuel Elder — part of the 2nd and 4th U.S. Artillery, respectively — positioned their batteries on a rise known as Bunker Hill, northwest of town.

A fight of more than an hour commenced with the guns from each side targeting the enemy, shot flying over the town. The booming of the guns, deafening in Hanover, could be heard on the streets of York.

The barrage stopped about mid-afternoon, and the town largely escaped damage. No civilians sustained

The market shed dominates this scene of Hanover's Center Square, where roads heading in all major compass points met. Fighting took place in and around the shed. Some horsemen riding through the shed thought they were crossing a bridge. A jail below street level gave rushing horsemen the impression that the shed crossed a waterway or gully.

injuries. But some shot came close to townspeople.

One shell penetrated an upstairs balcony door of the Henry Winebrenner residence on Frederick Street. It shattered a bureau, burrowed through the floor and struck a brick wall in a sitting room.

The shell did not explode. Winebrenner picked it up and threw it in the yard.

• • •

Lt. Col. Payne, a 33-year-old Virginia lawyer temporarily assigned to head the 2nd North Carolina — captured Abram Folger of the 5th New York in town, and he and his orderly walked Folger south toward rebel lines.

Folger spotted a rifle on the road, picked it up and fired at Payne's horse. As the horse struggled in pain, it fell toward some uncovered vats from Winebrenner's Tannery located close to Frederick Street. Payne ended up in one of the vats, filled with tanning liquid. The orderly tried to fire on Folger, but his pistol jammed. Payne's aide considered jumping a fence but surrendered instead.

Folger had fired his last shot at Payne's horse, but the orderly did not know that. He gave up his gun, and Folger ordered him to help Payne out of the vat.

The liquid stained Payne's face, hair and gray uniform, with its velvet facing and white gauntlet gloves, Folger wrote. The colonel presented quite a sight.

Folger marched Payne and the orderly behind Yankee lines, Payne's appearance providing some comic relief.

At least, that was one story going around about Payne's capture, improbable as it sounded. Three other Union soldiers either took or gained credit for this prized prisoner.

This view looks from Center Square in Hanover northward toward Abbottstown. In their initial thrust, rebel troopers pushed Yankee horsemen along this street. The Union troopers regrouped and countercharged, eventually regaining the town.

For his part, Payne said he fell in the vat trying to avoid capture.

• • •

Stuart, mounted on his mare, Virginia, barely escaped a similar fate.

As Farnsworth's men charged the North Carolina and Virginia regiments, Stuart, his staff and couriers attempted to buck up the fleeing gray horsemen along Frederick Street.

"Rally them, Blackford," Stuart yelled to aide William Blackford.

The party left the road and entered a field to fire their pistols on Farnsworth's racing men charging along the road.

In an instant, a flanking unit of about 25 Union troopers came upon Stuart's party. The rebels heard the order to halt but spurred their thoroughbreds forward. Tall grass covered the field, so the officers did not see a gully — Plum Creek — until a couple of strides from its edge.

Blackford's horse, Magic, jumped at least 6 feet from the edge of the creek, estimated up to 15 feet across and 3-4 feet deep.

"Stuart and myself were riding side by side, and as soon as Magic rose I turned my head to see how Virginia had done it," Blackford wrote, "and I shall never forget the glimpse I then saw of this beautiful animal away up in mid-air over the chasm and Stuart's fine figure sitting erect and firm in the saddle."

Stuart's horse landed on her feet with the general still aboard. Blackford contended his horse, goaded with a sharp kick of his spurs, landed six or seven feet beyond the far bank. Others in Stuart's party tried to make the leap and did not finish. They landed in the shallow creek, then scrambled to the safe side.

The Union troopers did not try the hurdle.

"The ludicrousness of the situation, notwithstanding the peril, was the source of much merriment at the expense of these unfortunate ones," H.B. McClellan, another Stuart aide, wrote.

• • •

When Stuart found Chambliss' command, he was greeted with a happy yell. The rumor had passed through the ranks that the general had been captured.

The close call did not dampen Stuart's sense of humor. Sometime later, he passed near a cherry tree bearing rebel cherry-pickers. Union soldiers, seeing the easy enemy targets sitting in the tree, fired in their direction.

The exposed cavalrymen jumped to the ground.

"What's the matter, boys?" Stuart roared. "Those cherries sour?"

Meanwhile, a second close encounter followed Blackford's first brush with the Yankees. He cooled down Magic by walking him around the base of a hill when he heard a horseman approaching.

A glance backward informed Blackford that the hoofbeats came from a Union trooper's horse. The trooper raced ahead with saber drawn, looking to run him through. Blackford mounted Magic, put his left spur into the horse and the horse and trooper swerved to the right.

The action caused Blackford's left arm to lift from his side, and the bluecoat's saber thrust went between Blackford's body and arm. Blackford escaped, and the Union trooper moved toward his cheering companions. They thought he had sliced Blackford, and the bluecoat did nothing to discourage that thinking.

"I would have given anything if I could only have had half a minute's notice of his coming, for I don't think there would have been then anything for them to cheer," Blackford wrote. "... I could only show my feelings upon

Confederate Gen. Jeb Stuart, atop his mount, Virginia, hurdles Plum Creek to avoid capture by a squad of Yankee soldiers during the Battle of Hanover. William Blackford, riding with Stuart, later wrote that he would never forget the incident — the thoroughbred gliding across the gully with Stuart sitting firmly in the saddle.

the subject by shaking my fist at them as I moved slowly on to the battery on our hill."

• • •

Kilpatrick, at the head of the column, had reached Abbottstown, about six miles from Hanover, and had just received a message from his commander, Gen. Alfred Pleasonton. Stuart might attack him, Pleasonton warned.

The sound of fighting from Hanover dated that warning. At first, the rattling of muskets from the rear sounded like the cracking of horses' hooves on stones.

"But as we listened, the boom of a cannon was plainly heard, and then the General mounted his horse in haste and rode back to Hanover, it is said, in twenty minutes," Samuel L. Gillespie, a Yankee bugler, wrote. "Several of our horses were injured in trying to keep up with him as the column opened ranks to let us pass."

Kilpatrick rode back at top speed, leaving the road and cutting across fields to shorten his course. He galloped into town, dismounting his sweating horse. He quickly sized up the battle, reformed the units and spoke to his men:

"Boys, look at me. I am General Kilpatrick. I want you to know me, and where I go I want you to follow. Stuart is making a call on us, and we are going to whip him."

Kilpatrick established headquarters in the Central Hotel. His horse later died from exhaustion and gained a

An artist captures Union Gen. Judson Kilpatrick riding furiously to join the fight against Jeb Stuart's rebel cavalrymen at Hanover. Riding ahead of the federal column, Kilpatrick had reached Abbottstown on the pike connecting York and Gettysburg when he learned his men were locked in battle to the south.

Union troopers seized Confederate Lt. Col. William H. Payne during the Battle of Hanover. Accounts of his capture differ widely, but the apprehension of an officer of such rank was considered a prize. Payne's capture actually benefited the rebels because he exaggerated the Confederate strength well-positioned in the hills south and southeast of Hanover.

Gen. George Armstrong Custer, left, is photographed with his commanding officer, Gen. Alfred Pleasonton. Pleasonton commanded three recently re-organized Union cavalry divisions in the Gettysburg campaign. Gen. Judson Kilpatrick's division fought Jeb Stuart's Confederate troopers in Hanover. David M. Gregg's division chased Stuart as the Confederate column headed from Hanover to Carlisle through the heart of York County. The third division under Pleasonton, John Buford's horsemen, attempted to slow rebel infantrymen advancing east toward Gettysburg on the first day of the battle.

permanent resting spot on high ground — Hanover's Bunker Hill. Hanover residents burned the carcasses of other horses killed that day.

The countermarch to Hanover brought other casualties.

The 2nd U.S. Artillery lost a man and two horses on the road to Abbottstown when an ammunition chest on one caisson exploded near George Wertz's farm. A shifting load set off some powder on the hasty trip back to Hanover.

• • •

In town, Kilpatrick added to his staff.

A 12-year-old bugler named Smith survived the fight, although his horse was shot out from under him. Kilpatrick adopted him as an aide, inseparable thereafter whether in battle or on the march.

Kilpatrick soon met with the stained and tired Payne.

The Confederates had 12,000 troopers on the hill, Payne told Kilpatrick and Custer. He tripled the actual number to discourage the Union from attacking his comrades.

At one point, the division commander surveyed the town from horseback.

"Dead horses were lying along the streets and upon the sidewalks, where the battle had raged, with here and there a gray coat and then a blue, sleeping their last sleep together in the dust," Gillespie, the bugler, wrote.

• • •

Seeing the Confederates on the heights in the afternoon, Custer and his men did not wait to see what the Confederates would do next. He planned a maneuver to dislodge the Confederate left.

He led a unit of 600 soldiers across a pasture, sometimes crawling on hands and knees to within 300 yards of Fitz Lee's men, who were manning their artillery. Custer's men, acting on a signal, rose and fired their brand new seven-shot Spencer repeating rifles at soldiers and horses

Two Union batteries unlimber on Bunker Hill, overlooking the main streets of Hanover after countermarching from a position along the Abbottstown Road. The Union cannons dueled with Confederate artillery units positioned on the ridges to the south and southeast of Hanover during the Battle of Hanover. The cannon fire did little damage to buildings in the borough or the soldiers manning the Yankee and rebel lines. Most blue and gray casualties occurred in fighting on Hanover's streets.

around the cannons.

Fearing loss of the big guns, Fitz Lee called for reinforcements, and Custer answered with another barrage. Custer could not take the hill, but Stuart's artillery could not chase him away.

He constituted a threat to the Confederate left until rebel troopers left town.

• • •

Custer, a newly appointed brigadier general, did not look the part of a leader grizzled troopers would want to follow. In fact, apart from the 46-year-old Hampton, the division and brigade leaders on both sides were in their 20s or had just tipped 30.

Custer dressed in a velveteen jacket with five gold loops on each sleeve, a dark blue sailor's shirt with red tie and a soft Confederate's hat. His long hair fell in curls to his shoulders. One of George Meade's officers later claimed he looked like a "circus rider gone mad!"

But his leadership that day brought applause.

"It was here that the brigade first saw Custer," James H. Kidd, 6th Michigan, said. "As the men of the 6th ... were deploying forward across the railroad into a wheat field beyond, I heard a voice new to me, directly in the rear of the portion of the line where I was, giving directions for the movement in clear resonant tones, and in a calm, and confident manner, at once resolute and reassuring."

Men in blue, gray dig in

As the hours passed into the late afternoon, the two sides stood face to face. The Union reinforced its position in Hanover and toward the Pidgeon Hills to the north and west, while the Confederates held good ground on the hills to the south and east.

Citizens and soldiers barricaded the main streets through town — York, Baltimore and Frederick — with boxes, wagons, barrels, bar iron and fence rails and anything else on hand to stop an enemy charge.

Dead horses lay in the streets. Broken sabers, carbines and cartridge boxes littered the roads. Townspeople helped carry the dead and wounded into homes, where physicians went to work.

• • •

The casualties wore uniforms of both gray and blue. A bullet struck Isaac Peale, a rebel trooper, in the chest in Center Square fighting. Then a Yankee bullet hit his horse. Peale struck his head on the street when the horse collapsed.

"Have the Yankees got me?" he asked William Zieber.

"No matter where you are, you are in the hands of friends," the pastor told the dying man.

By the time Jeb Stuart's column had reached Hanover, even the general considered a 125-wagon train captured near Rockville, Md., a detriment. But Stuart's cavalry kept the slow-moving wagons in tow as the horsemen rode through York County on their search for Robert E. Lee's troops. Here, teamsters park the train on a farm near Hanover. This maneuver would have enabled the rebels to burn the wagons if Union soldiers had threatened their capture.

Are you a surgeon? the soldier asked.

Zieber answered that he was a preacher.

"Pray for me," Peale said. "My wound is serious. I am suffering extreme pain."

The minister prayed as the soldier requested.

As Zieber and Dr. William Bange tried to make the wounded trooper comfortable, a squad of 10 graycoats dashed toward them.

"What are you doing with that man?" an officer, brandishing a sword, asked.

"We are trying to aid a wounded man, and we will take care of him," Zieber responded.

"Thank you, sir," the officer said, as he mounted his horse and rode away.

Earlier, John Hoffacker, riding with the 18th Pennsylvania was killed in the first charge. He died only a few miles from his West Manheim Township home.

A wounded Union soldier was taken to the home of young Lydia Wertz on Ridge Avenue. The terrified girl was home alone with the bleeding soldier.

One woman, handing out food just seconds before, observed a Union trooper riding toward her. She looked the man in the face as he drew near, acting as if he wanted some cake and pie. Just then, the trooper wheeled around and dropped from his horse, having taken a bullet from a rebel trooper.

Townspeople repeatedly witnessed these grim scenes.

"God bless the ladies of our town," The Hanover Citizen later commented, "and forbid that their nerves ever again be shocked by the roar of cannon, the clashing to steel, or the ghastly visage of murdered men."

• • •

Lewis J. Conrad, a local resident, had been inspecting a construction job in McSherrystown that morning. He learned Union cavalrymen had been sighted moving toward Hanover and rode east to get a look at them.

He stood near the Winebrenner residence on Frederick Street when he heard shooting in the direction of Westminster Road. He saw Union soldiers dash south toward the sound. Soon, balls from enemy guns rattled along the top of the nearby Forney barn.

Next, he observed a cannon shell enter the Winebrenner residence. In the thick of the fighting, he ducked into a cellar in the home of David Diehl on Frederick Street. During a lull, he made his way toward his Carlisle Street home.

Conrad crossed the square, noticing five or six dead horses. He safely made his way home and crawled through a trap door onto the roof of his house. There, he could see the gray and blue troop movements. The gray lined the hills to the south and east near the cemetery. Union soldiers took positions along Bunker Hill to the north and west. The men in blue sometimes crept forward toward the rebel position.

The cannons from both sides threw shot across the town, one shell whizzing 20 feet over Conrad's head.

"Presently, a shell passed within six feet of my head," Conrad recalled, "and I concluded to leave the roof, and I quickly climbed through the trap door."

• • •

Brothers Samuel and John Forney, working in a cornfield on their farm near Frederick Street, looked up after hearing yells and shrieks coming from the Westminster Road. This was Chambliss' initial charge. The rebel troopers discharged their rifles as they approached the 18th Pennsylvania.

The brothers hastened their unhitched horses across the field to the safety of McSherrystown.

When they returned home later that day, three Union men and one Confederate soldier rested in their house. The rebel soldier had sustained a critical wound — a ball passed through his chest. Before he died, he handed a New Testament to the Forney boys' sister.

"Take this book and send it to my home," he said. "That address will reach my sister. She gave me this book when I left home two years ago, and she asked me to keep it and bring it back again when the cruel war shall have ended. It has ended now for me."

The Union soldiers later were carried to one of the makeshift hospitals, the Pleasant Hill Hotel on Baltimore Street. Before long, local and military physicians treated wounded men at Eckert's Concert Hall, Center Square; Marion Hall, Foundry Alley; Albright's Hall, Broadway, and other locations.

• • •

As the face-off continued, both sides looked around for the missing in the ranks. According to a later count, the Union incurred more casualties — 19 killed, 73 wounded and 123 missing. Confederates sustained nine killed, 50 wounded and 58 missing.

Judson Kilpatrick kept his commanding officer, Alfred Pleasonton, informed at several points during the battle. One message apprised Pleasanton of the casualties.

"My loss is trifling. I have gone into camp in Hanover. ...We have plenty of forage, the men are in good spirits, and we don't fear Stuart's whole cavalry," Kilpatrick wrote.

After the battle, he evaluated his division's losses differently and put the casualty count at 183.

"Owing to the nature of the attack," he wrote, "our loss was greater than that of the rebels."

• • •

By now, Wade Hampton had brought the slow-moving train up and parked the wagons on the farms of Samuel Keller and Henry Gotwald. The teamsters positioned the wagons in a tight square to be burned, if discovered by the enemy.

By this time, many Confederate troopers considered the wagons an impediment.

"We were just opposite Gettysburg, and if we could have made our way direct, the fifteen miles of distance to that place would have passed that day, and we could have effected a junction with General Lee the day before the battle began," William Blackford, Stuart's adjutant, later wrote. "It was here the wagon train began to interfere with our movements, and if General Stuart could only have known what we do now, it would have been burned."

Stuart shared the same sentiments.

"Our wagon train was now a subject of serious embarrassment ... ," Stuart later wrote.

• • •

Jeb Stuart did not want a prolonged clash with the enemy or to take Hanover — the Union guns on Bunker Hill easily commanded the low-lying town.

His position on the high ground, extending from the Keller farm near Pennville and crossing Frederick Street to the Mount Olivet Cemetery, gave him a path toward his primary goal — York and Jubal Early.

He studied his options. That afternoon, he received a newspaper, probably The York Gazette published that morning, telling of Early's occupation and departure from York. But the newspaper did not say where the tight-lipped Early was heading on his westward march.

Stuart was in a quandary. Unwittingly, he was in the middle of The Army of the Potomac. An equal number of blue-clad infantrymen were to his north and west as were coming up from the south.

Specifically, he couldn't stay there because he feared Gen. Henry Slocum's Union infantry corps was heading his way from the south. But he could not move anywhere fast. He could only march 25 miles on a good day with the wagons, rather than the 40 miles his cavalry column normally traveled. Yet his men had worked hard to capture the wagons, and his orders stipulated that he should gather supplies.

He didn't know that another Yankee cavalry division, under Gen. David Gregg's command, was also in pursuit from Maryland. If he had, he might have taken some satisfaction in knowing that he was tying up two enemy divisions — Gregg's and Kilpatrick's — leaving only John Buford's cavalrymen to determine the whereabouts of Robert E. Lee's army.

Stuart couldn't get to Lee, moving over South Mountain toward Cashtown, about 20 miles to the west. Not that he knew Lee's location.

But he did know that the Union cavalry and untold infantry troops were on the move to his left, west of his location.

For his part, Lee was frustrated, attempting to concentrate his forces and feel out the enemy without his chief scout, Jeb Stuart.

Stuart decided his best option was to head east to pick up Early's trail near York. To do so, he would wait until dusk, then retrace the steps Lige White's horsemen took three days earlier — move through Jefferson across the southern part of York County.

'Things look blue'

York residents found themselves terribly isolated that Tuesday.

The Confederate Army was positioned to the west, and the bridge at Wrightsville smoldered in its watery grave. Telegraph lines and railroad bridges were down north and south. The gloomy, wet weather, the humiliating presence of the enemy and the halt of local commerce all cast a gloom over York.

The extent of the damage inflicted by the rebels was not immediately clear. It was raining so hard for much of the day that few ventured forth.

• • •

That morning, James Latimer hoped to get a letter detailing the occupation to his brother via a boat or ferry moving between Wrightsville and Columbia.

"We have been cut off from the World for two days (it seems like as many weeks)," he wrote to his brother in the morning, "and I hope communication will be resumed soon."

Their mother and sister had stayed through the occupation.

"I regretted very much afterwards that I had not sent them off," he wrote, "as of course there was all the time danger of the officers losing control of their men."

People from the country had begun to trickle into town.

They told how the Confederates had plundered their farms, particularly the Louisiana Tigers.

"Horses and mules taken, houses broken open and everything the thieves fancied, stolen," he wrote.

• • •

As Latimer was writing Bart, Cassandra Small was hurriedly sharing her sentiments with Lissie Latimer in a letter. The woman learned about the rebel departure after her mother awoke her Tuesday morning.

"Oh, what a happy people!" she wrote her cousin. "How thankful we should be that our lives and property are spared."

Her family rejoiced that they didn't leave as the Confederate threat deepened and stayed through the occupation.

"Oh, Lissie, you can't form any idea of our situation, but thanks be to our Heavenly Father, they have all left us this morning," she wrote.

Still, the woman feared a rebel return.

"In case they (Union forces) are defeated, all will come rushing back pell-mell on us," she wrote, "Oh, how fearful we still are... ."

While his sister was writing, Latimer Small left York to view damage in Wrightsville.

The rumor going around York suggested that the rebels destroyed a considerable part of the river town. Lat Small found the report to be greatly exaggerated.

• • •

Others in York feared the return of the rebels if the Confederates triumphed in the much-anticipated battle west of York.

Military authorities impressed all black men who could be found to erect defensive works near town.

They completed their work Wednesday morning.

"The enforcing of the conscription caused great excitement among the dusky portion of our population," The Republican reported, "who did not exactly comprehend the nature of the affair."

• • •

Jere Carl, a York resident and one of the collectors of Early's requisition, wrote his sister that day about the town's isolation.

They knew nothing about what was happening outside York since noon Saturday.

"I don't want to see any more confederation armies never but must say while here treated us well and if they never come back will call them gentlemen," he wrote. "They are a hard looking set but the blood is there."

Carl said he would visit Columbia the next day to mail the letter.

• • •

As the hours passed on Tuesday, James Latimer grew increasingly eager for news from the outside.

He traveled to Wrightsville, saw what was left of the bridge and boarded a ferry to cross the river to Columbia.

He found only one Union regiment and battery there. He guessed that the Union forces had concentrated in Harrisburg to guard against a river crossing.

"Things look blue," he wrote Bart.

Whether Lee's men took Harrisburg or were delayed, the nearby York would be in line for regular rebel visits.

Once across the river, Philadelphia would be open to the Confederates.

"I may take too gloomy a view of affairs," he wrote, "but things seem at their worst."

He advised his brother to write him back, on two sheets if necessary. He could show one, which did not reflect the severity of their situation, to their mother and sister. The other would be for him alone.

"At all events, I wish very much Ma & Sister were away from York, tho' I would not let them know I fear anything, for the world," he wrote. "However, no place seems safe."

Stuart rides toward Dover

In Hanover at dark, Fitz Lee's men took over the wagon train from Wade Hampton's brigade and moved toward Jefferson. Chambliss disengaged, and Hampton followed him from the field. As the rebel horsemen rode, they foraged through the southern York County countryside.

Several troopers rode toward the George Dubs farm near Dubs Union Church. Mrs. Dubs, home alone, led the family's most valuable horse, a black stallion, into a vaulted cellar and shut up the house in advance of their arrival. The rebels went for two workhorses in the Dubs' barn, but Mrs. Dubs raised a protest.

Dr. W.F. Brinkman was not as fortunate in escaping the rebel net.

Four troopers surrounded him as he took a black gelding and bay mare into hiding in the Jefferson area.

The rebels grabbed the gelding but left behind the mare.

Samuel Flicking lost a horse, saddle, bridle and some hay to the rebels, but the real loss came when the rebels freed 80 mules to graze in his oat field.

In Jefferson, William T. Crist, operator of a store on the town square, learned the rebels were not choosy. They took a variety of goods: 12 hats, six caps, 22 pairs of boots and shoes, 300 yards of calico, 40 yards of muslin, six silk handkerchiefs, five table oil cloths, six pairs of traces, five pounds of tobacco, 200 cigars and several other items.

Daniel Shue lost out in both Confederate raids: White's men took a mare, and Stuart's troopers took oats, hay and let their horses graze in an oatfield.

"They came into and about the house in large numbers," he later wrote, "and acted in boisterous manner."

The rebels probably didn't know — or didn't care considering their weariness — that the people of Jefferson

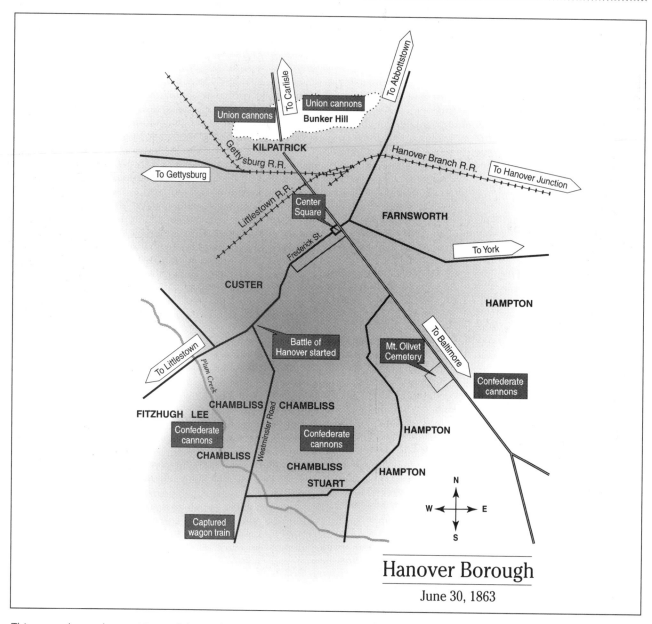

Hanover Borough

June 30, 1863

This map shows the positions of the Yankee and Confederate cavalry brigades in the afternoon of June 30. The Yankees, under Gen. Judson Kilpatrick, occupied the town and the high ground north and northwest of town, blocking Confederate Jeb Stuart's men, in position to the south and southwest of town, from riding through Hanover to Abbottstown to meet up with Jubal Early's infantry division. Early's men had departed from York early on June 30 and marched from Weigelstown to East Berlin before stopping near Heidlersburg in Adams County that night. Stuart, riding north, would probably have intersected with Early's column, marching west, sometime that day. His men would have been ready to fight on the first day at Gettysburg on July 1. Stuart finally caught up with Robert E. Lee in the afternoon of July 2, the second day of fighting at Gettysburg. Union resistance at the Battle of Hanover, thus, delayed Stuart from rejoining Lee by about two days.

and the surrounding township of Codorus were a sympathetic bunch. Their presidential vote in 1861 went 349 for the Democrats and only 22 for Lincoln.

Codorus produced only 12 enlistments for Union ranks in the first 18 months of the war. Lower Chanceford, with a similar population, sent 42 men to war.

The famished troopers needed food.

They unloaded some wagons laden with goods for market and raided Albert Kraft's and Jacob Rebert's stores.

The invaders even scooped honey from some hives.

• • •

Stuart, his men, 125 wagons, hundreds of captured horses and 400 prisoners collected along the way plodded through Jefferson until late at night.

The people of Jefferson thought the parade would never stop. First, it took up to three hours for the column to pass through town. And stragglers and foraging parties followed after that.

Stuart, fearing Union troopers on his trail, unlimbered

Union Gen. Judson Kilpatrick used the Central Hotel on Hanover's square as his headquarters during the cavalry battle in this southwestern York County town of 1,630. This square was the scene of deadly fighting between Kilpatrick's troopers and Jeb Stuart's Confederate cavalry. Hanover trailed only York in size among boroughs in York County.

cannon on the hills around Jefferson. He posted guards around town.

• • •

At John Zeigler's farmhouse and tavern near Hanover Junction, Stuart conferred with his brigade commanders.

Now aware of David Gregg's approach from the south and east, the commanders decided the long column should point north. Stuart's men headed up Panther Hill, past Ziegler's Church and on through York New Salem. By morning, he reached Dover after a ride of more than 25 miles.

"Whole regiments slept in the saddle, their faithful animals keeping the road unguided. In some instances, they fell from their horses, overcome with physical fatigue and sleeplessness," Stuart wrote.

The lack of forage and water made the tired mules pulling the wagons even more cantankerous. When the rebels forced their prisoners to take the reins, those unmotivated drivers guided the wagons.

Sometimes, the entire column stopped when a driver fell asleep, and his team stopped in their tracks. The column stretched so far that Stuart asked an aide, John Esten Cooke, to wait at York New Salem to direct the wagon train to Dover. Guards, posted at hotels in the town operat-

ed by Francis Gipe and Simon Givens, prevented troops from becoming drunk.

The line of horsemen in the early morning hours stretched between Dover and York New Salem, a distance of about 10 miles.

The troopers crossed the York-Gettysburg Pike and the East Berlin Road, intersecting the paths taken by White's horsemen and Early's foot soldiers earlier that day. At the pike, Fitz Lee learned that Early had been in York but had retraced his steps. The best intelligence available suggested a concentration of rebel forces near Shippensburg.

Even generals slept that night.

Near dawn, Wade Hampton dismounted, found a haystack, curled up in his cape and fell asleep.

• • •

At least Stuart's men did not feel pressure any longer from Kilpatrick.

Kilpatrick set up camp for the night and belatedly sent only small detachment of troopers after Stuart. By keeping the main body together, he followed orders to stay in touch with Army headquarters in Taneytown.

He rightly feared riding northward toward East Berlin in pursuit of Stuart. Rebel infantry — Early's men

As soldiers in blue and gray battle, Lewis Miller shows
Gen. Judson Kilpatrick conversing with a resident near
Hanover. Miller shows a man named 'Rudyseal' standing
on a fence. 'I am an old Jackson union man,' Rudyseal
said. 'Come to my house and take some wine. You do me
a favor. Let us stand up for the government and all bear
against the rebel.'

— had been spotted there.

His cavalry had fought well. The Hanover battle provided another example of Union cavalrymen, long pushed around by the Confederate horsemen, holding their own. The first in a series of clashes began when Union troopers had surprised Stuart's men at Brandy Station on June 9. Now, on the last day of the month, Stuart's men could not throw blue cavalry out of their way.

Stuart's men occupied two Union cavalry divisions, but Kilpatrick's unit had kept Stuart from joining Lee before fighting began at Gettysburg.

And by tying up Stuart, he kept the graycoats from brushing against Buford. Dismounted men from Buford's 1st Cavalry Division slowed the rebel advance sufficiently on the Battle of Gettysburg's first day that Union infantry reinforcements gained good ground — Cemetery Ridge and Hill — to fight the battle.

Kilpatrick's men had earned the praise bestowed in their commander's battle report, even with certain embellishments: "For a moment, and a moment only, victory hung uncertain. For the first time, our troops had met the foes in close contact; but they were on their own free soil; fair hands, regardless of the dangerous strife, waved them on, and bright, tearful eyes looked pleadingly out from every window. The brave Farnsworth made one great effort, and the day was won. The foe turned and fled. He

had for the first and last time polluted with his presence the loyal town of Hanover."

Still Stuart's men could ride.

If the Union cavalry detachments ever caught up with Stuart's brigades, the soldiers from the South never observed them.

• • •

As Stuart searched to find Early on the Confederate right, Lee's infantry had effectively concentrated.

Lee's force of about 75,000 men camped in a 30-mile bow north of Gettysburg from Heidlersburg to Chambersburg.

The Union lines of about 93,500 men rested in roughly the same arc south of Gettysburg, but the blue corps generally faced a farther march to Gettysburg. Gen. John Sedgwick's corps, for one, camped 35 miles away in Manchester, Md.

Even lacking the information Jeb Stuart would have provided, Lee's campfires burned closer to each other and nearer to Gettysburg, the place where the two sides would meet the next day — Wednesday, July 1.

VI

Men in gray pay 'very dear for their fun'

Wednesday, July 1, 1863 to Tuesday, July 14, 1863

'*All good citizens, while they deplore the
humiliation of the occupation . . . are grateful for our
fortunate escape from the horrors of war.*'
— Minutes, Sabbath School meeting at Sanney's School

York struggles to recover

About 200 of the paroled men from Maryland, Hanover and others whom Jeb Stuart collected along his route walked from Dover toward York on Wednesday, July 1.

Word of their approach excited residents. Requests went out to send provisions for them to the market houses on Centre Square.

Almost immediately, the best food York could muster appeared.

The parolees' presence Wednesday afternoon signaled that the Confederates had left the county.

"It was the first certainty we had of it," Cassandra Small wrote to her cousin, Lissie Latimer. "Oh what a happy people!"

Flags appeared on windowsills and doors.

• • •

After that, York showed renewed signs of life.

Citizens ran a flag from the military hospital up the Centre Square pole to replace the one the invaders had confiscated. Farmers started returning with their livestock and horses from the east bank of the Susquehanna even before the outcome of the battle to the west was decided.

Others traveled to the battlefield area with the conflict still raging.

Workers cleaned the military hospital to usable fashion after the untidy rebels had left it in disarray. The rebels had destroyed pictures that previously brightened the walls of the wards.

The market houses, where some of the invaders slept, crawled with lice and other bugs.

Someone paid a man to clean them. He sprayed down the structures with a hose, expunging the town of any lasting residue from the dusty visitors.

• • •

A scouting party of 20 troopers, detached from Kilpatrick's division, rode into town Thursday afternoon. The presence of soldiers dressed in blue reassured people, and the news that The Army of the Potomac had massed at Gettysburg added to the good feelings.

The soldiers enjoyed a substantial meal in one of the market houses.

As the horsemen ate, a sentinel warned them about a potential enemy approaching from the west. The troopers mounted instantly, forming a line with saber and carbine.

They sat tall in their saddles, poised to race down York's West Market Street. But an officer assigned to probe the threat returned to the squad with an explanation. It was a farmer driving a loaded hay wagon pulled by six horses, kicking up considerable dust.

The troopers dismounted with a laugh and resumed their meal.

Ewell's corps moves to battle

Jubal Early's and Richard Rodes' divisions carried out Dick Ewell's orders to head south or west toward the

Pennsylvanian George G. Meade, 47, a Union corps commander, gained command of The Army of the Potomac just days before the decisive Battle of Gettysburg. He was another in a parade of generals to head the Army and held the position through the war's end, although President Abraham Lincoln elevated Ulysses S. Grant as his superior in 1864.

Gen. Robert E. Lee, 56, commanded The Army of Northern Virginia in its campaign north of the Mason-Dixon Line in the summer of 1863. His Army's loss at the Battle of Gettysburg is viewed as the 'High Water Mark of the Confederacy.'

suspected enemy, as conditions dictated. They marched south on separate roads Wednesday morning, awaiting further orders.

A short distance past Heidlersburg, Early received the definitive order. Forget Cashtown to the west; march south to Gettysburg.

The order came after Gen. John Buford's dismounted Yankees, later reinforced by Gen. John F. Reynolds' 1st Corps, clashed with rebel infantry, west of Gettysburg. Gens. Henry Heth and Dorsey Pender, heading divisions of Gen. A.P. Hill's corps, represented the rebel vanguard along Cashtown Road.

Both George Meade and Robert E. Lee seemed reluctant to engage at that location at that moment, but unit after unit from each side deployed until the skirmish turned into a pitched battle.

Reaching the eastern part of the field at about 3 p.m., Early's men smashed into the Union right, ran the Yankees through town and pushed them up the high ground commanding the town.

• • •

As the men in gray fought their way toward Gettysburg, John B. Gordon spotted a Union general lying among a group of dead Yankees. At least, this was the story he wrote and lectured about years later. The Georgian dismounted and offered the officer, Francis C. Barlow, water from his canteen.

Barlow suffered from severe wounds, and Gordon did not think he would survive. Before Gordon's men conveyed the general to a shady spot in the rear, Barlow made a request: If Gordon lived to the end of the war and should meet his wife, please say that her husband was thinking of her in his last moments.

"He wished me to assure her that he died doing his duty at the front, that he was willing to give his life for his country, and that his deepest regret was that he must die without looking upon her face again," Gordon wrote.

Under flag of truce later that day, Gordon offered Arabella Barlow, who had accompanied the general on the campaign, safe passage through Confederate lines to see

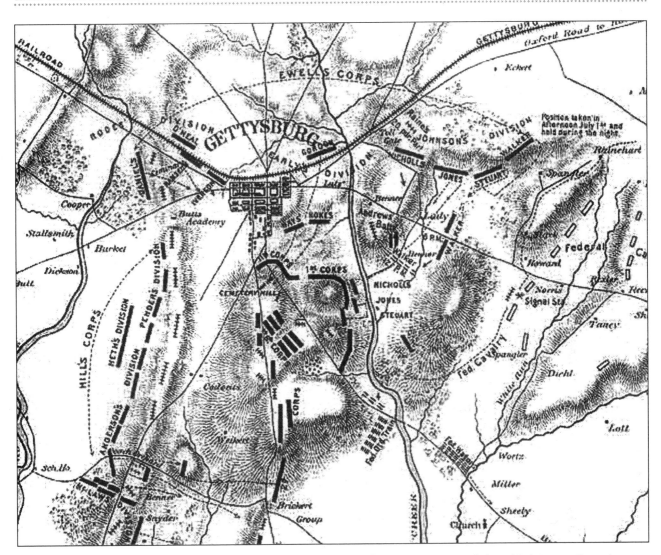

An Army of Northern Virginia topographer's map shows troop positions on the second day of fighting at Gettysburg. Gen. Jubal Early's division, now back from York County and heavily engaged in fighting, is positioned in and around the town of Gettysburg. Harry Hays' Louisiana Tigers and Robert Hoke's North Carolinians face strong Union positions on Cemetery Hill. John B. Gordon's Georgians are along the Gettysburg Railroad, not far from the York-Gettysburg Pike and the road to Hanover. According to one recently published account which differed from Early's own numbers, Early's division sustained the following casualties — dead, wounded and missing soldiers — by brigade: Gordon, 30 percent of 1,813 men; Hoke, 33 percent of 1,244; Hays, 26 percent of 1,295; William 'Extra Billy' Smith, 26 percent of 806.

her husband.

Gordon did not think again about Barlow, other than figuring he was among the dead.

• • •

Ewell's three divisions manned the Confederate left for three bloody days at Culp's Hill, Cemetery Hill and in and around Gettysburg. Early's men fought against the rounded part of the fishhook-shaped Union line.

Many a man died with York County beef in their bellies and bread in their knapsacks in uphill fighting against well-positioned Union soldiers, particularly on the second and third days of battle.

Hays' and Hoke's brigades took the crest of Cemetery Hill on the evening of the second day but could not hold the rise, southeast of Gettysburg. The units needed reinforcements and help did not come.

According to Early's accounting soon after the battle, total casualties from his division numbered 1,180 out of about 5,600 infantrymen. That broke down to 154 killed, 799 wounded and 227 missing. One-third of Hoke's brigade, the unit that occupied the public buildings around York, sustained casualties. Col. Isaac E. Avery, the brigade's commander, was the division's highest-ranking casualty, sustaining mortal wounds on Cemetery Hill.

The argumentative Early later contended that the Battle of Gettysburg was a draw, that the Confederates left the field to an enemy in a superior position because of shortages of ammunition and food.

"That position fought the battle for him," he wrote.

'Democrats have seen all they wish of rebels'

Jeb Stuart rode through northwestern York County, 25 miles away when fighting at Gettysburg began. The gray cavalry column reached Dover after its overnight march from Hanover early Wednesday morning.

Dover's residents had seen rebel horsemen a couple of days before. Scouts from A.G. Jenkins' unit had ridden into Dover as Dick Ewell's men edged from Carlisle toward Harrisburg.

The next day, as Early moved toward York, some of his men raided Dover and obtained items from the town's stores.

Now on Wednesday morning, Wade Hampton lightened the column's load by paroling about 400 men collected along the way. Hampton took a room in Dr. John Ahl's office, on Dover's square, to carry out his business.

Some of these paroled men enjoyed the feast in the York market sheds later that day. The troopers fed their horses by placing hay, gleaned from nearby barns, in the gutter of Carlisle Road, the length of the village.

At about 8 a.m., Stuart directed those at Jacob Fries' Upper Hotel to serve breakfast to his staff and brigade commanders. The officers, comporting themselves with dignity, talked about their long ride while devouring a big meal. In an adjoining room, surgeons worked on those suffering from saber cuts and other wounds sustained on Hanover's streets.

Stuart paid the proprietor in greenbacks rather than Confederate money.

Meanwhile, squads went into the surrounding countryside gathering new mounts and often leaving their jaded horses behind. Resident Emanuel Daron observed that the rebels paid for their store purchases in Yankee currency but merely helped themselves to horses and harnesses. They took his buggy worth $100 and a harness valued at $25.

The invaders seized a saddle from young Rosa Leese. The girl's father appealed to the raiders that the saddle was special, and the invaders returned it.

George Lecrone had just moved one of prominent citizen Englehart Melchinger's horses to a lumber camp outside Dover. The rebel horsemen spotted him heading out of town with another buckskin. A trooper, waving a pistol, chased down Lecrone and ordered him off the horse.

Lecrone told him the horse would be no good for the soldier's purposes. The rebel again barked at him to dismount. Lecrone believed it in his best interest to follow orders.

Guards stood watch around the hotels to prevent soldiers from venturing inside to get into their supplies of whiskey.

The guard was unnecessary. With the enemy in the area, whiskey and other spirits found a new home in an unlikely place — the cellar of the town's United Brethren church.

• • •

The Confederate soldiers fended for their breakfasts.

Some rebels halted at Mary Ann Weaver's farm, north of Dover, to grub for some breakfast.

They confiscated hams from her and ordered them cooked.

For six hours, the woman prepared the meat and griddle cakes for the passing soldiers.

Some of the famished rebels burned their fingers, grabbing the cakes out of the hot pan as they cooked.

• • •

Ready to resume the march, Stuart released three guides, who had led the column from Hanover to Dover.

They enlisted local men to guide them through Dillsburg to Carlisle, about 12 miles to Dillsburg's northwest.

Stuart ordered the column onward — toward Carlisle — where he hoped to meet up with Ewell's men. In doing this, he opted not to follow Early, who reportedly was heading west toward Shippensburg, the likely concentration point for Lee's men. Carlisle, closer to Harrisburg, would put Stuart in the vanguard of any assault on the capital city.

The column headed toward Dillsburg on the long march toward Carlisle. The general sent out two aides, A.R. Venable and later Henry Lee, to contact Early or any other Confederate commander.

As Stuart headed northwest, he could not hear the big guns booming in Gettysburg, where fighting had begun.

• • •

The Confederates were scarcely out of Dover before people started telling their stories about the visit.

One story went around about an old woman who protected her prize horse by smearing cow dung all over the animal. The invading rebels saw the animal, laughed and rode off.

Someone found a complete rebel uniform, rifle and other items near a bridge crossing Fox Run. People conjectured a rebel soldier located some civilian clothes and deserted.

The Confederates had threatened to kill anyone named "Lincoln," according to another story. The rumor was that two families in Dover had boys with that name, and they headed out of town toward East Berlin. Some troopers caught a girl on the street, and she proposed pointing out where the boys named Lincoln lived.

The rebels reportedly said they felt sorry for any boys so named. If anyone should be punished, they said, it should be the parents.

• • •

Stuart traveled toward Dillsburg in two columns.

One headed straight through the road crossing at Rossville, and the other headed west toward Wellsville and then north. Squads of horsemen combed the surrounding countryside for food and horses or rifled through stores in villages along the way to take what they could.

At one point, the column halted for a rest at the Moore farm in Warrington Township. A squad rode up nearby Round Top and found horses hidden on the mountainside. By the time the column left the county, they herded or rode about 1,000 often-clumsy draft horses collected along the way.

Squads of roving Union horsemen kept their distance from the main columns but converged on rebel riders straying to fill their pockets.

In Rossville, Sgt. John M. Griffith of the 87th Pennsylvania, dressed as a civilian, had returned home to recover from a wound sustained at Winchester. The rebels ordered him to accompany them, and he rode to Gettysburg.

· · ·

The columns came together near Dillsburg and passed through the town.

Some troopers halted, scavenging for supplies from the stores and robbing the post office of money and stamps. Most of the column exited York County near Dillsburg and finally reached Carlisle by evening.

Stuart found the town occupied by about 3,000 stubborn Union troops under the command of William F. "Baldy" Smith. The troops had slipped in from Harrisburg soon after Ewell's men departed toward Gettysburg.

Although he had only a few regiments of Union infantry and cavalry and limited artillery, Smith refused to surrender the town.

By now, Stuart's men and their horses were spent and badly needed food and forage in town.

"Here some of our men were busy in a search for rations," rebel officer R.L.T. Beale wrote, "but most of them ... lay on the road with bridles in hand, some on rocks, and others on the wet earth, slumbering soundly."

Stuart saw a man climb a fence, put one leg over, find his balance and drift off to sleep. Stuart, hoping to convince Smith and civilians in Carlisle to surrender, ordered Fitz Lee to bombard the town. Lee's men lobbed more than 130 shells into Carlisle.

"And now began a general flight of the inhabitants into the country and cellars and behind anything strong enough to afford hope of protection," a townsman wrote, "a stream of women and children and ... people on foot, with outcries and terrified countenances."

The shelling caused minimal damage, killed one Union soldier and wounded about 12 others.

As the rebel cannons boomed, Andrew Venable and Henry Lee returned with information about Robert E. Lee's whereabouts. Stuart had moved his men to Carlisle, thinking that The Army of Northern Virginia would move on Harrisburg. Lee's message beckoned him to Gettysburg, 27 miles to the south, where the rebels had pushed around George Meade's men on the first day. Stuart's men were needed for the second day, looming in the morning.

Stuart set fire to the Union cavalry barracks, a lumber yard and the local gas works and started the long ride toward Gettysburg at about 1 a.m., on Thursday, July 2.

"This night march was the most severe I ever experienced," rebel officer John Esten Cooke said. "The long succession of sleepless nights had protracted the strongest, and General Stuart and his staff moving without escort, passed over mile after mile asleep in the saddle."

Stuart dismounted at dawn and slept against a tree. He awoke two hours later, mounted his horse and headed to Lee.

The wagon train never made it to Carlisle. When the head of Stuart's column finally pointed south, the train left camp near Dillsburg and also headed toward Gettysburg. When the tail of the wagon train crossed York County's boundary, the last of the invaders passed from county soil except for occasional scouting parties and stragglers.

"Fortunately, even the Democrats of York County have seen all they wish of rebels — a column of whom can be smelled as far as a slave-ship," a Union officer later wrote.

Hampton's men, the guardians of the wagon train, turned over the 125 wagons to Lee's quartermaster several

Gen. George Sykes, top, assumed command of the 5th Corps after its commander, George Meade, became the top general of The Army of the Potomac. His men trooped through southwestern York County on a forced march that brought them to the battlefield at Gettysburg on the second day of fighting. One of Sykes' regiments — the 20th Maine under Col. Joshua Lawrence Chamberlain, bottom — arrived just in time to play a pivotal role in the defense of Little Round Top.

miles north of the battle. They would be put to good use soon enough, helping to carry the wounded south after completion of the battle now under way.

'Something to remember our Johnny by'

At the same time that Stuart headed out of northwestern York County, a Union infantry corps gathered in its southwest corner. People of Hanover killed 19 cows to feed the blue-clad 5th Corps.

On Tuesday, as troopers battled on Hanover's streets, Gen. George Sykes' Corps marched 23 miles before camping for the night in Union Mills, Md. Now, as the first day's battle raged at Gettysburg, the tired corps moved into Hanover by late afternoon and prepared to camp for the night in fields southwest of the town.

"... (T)he ... fires had hardly blackened the coffee-dippers, and the hardtack hardly been hammered into working order by the bayonet-shanks, when everything was stopped short by whispers of disaster away on the left," Col. Joshua Lawrence Chamberlain, commander of the 20th Maine, wrote.

Sykes sat at the dinner table in the Henry Sell home on Frederick Street when a messenger rode up on a lathered mount.

George Meade, recently promoted from his top 5th Corps post to commander of The Army of the Potomac, ordered the troops onward. A night march lay ahead. The two Union corps that had fought an overwhelming Confederate force in the first day at Gettysburg needed help.

Bugles sounded, the men formed columns and marched west on the road between Hanover and Gettysburg, their meals still cooking over the campfires.

They would reach Gettysburg the next morning — the battle's second day — after a rest in Bonneauville.

The men would long remember the eerie night march, complete with moonlight, shadows and cheering towns-

This illustration shows the conversation between a soldier and a Hanover resident about the Confederate horseman — a member of Jeb Stuart's cavalry — buried under the roses. The resident performed the deed in return for a similar act of kindness shown to his son, a Union soldier who died in the South.

folk. The crowning point came when the rumor moved along the weary column that George Washington had been spotted riding a white horse on the battlefield at Gettysburg.

"Let no one smile at me," Chamberlain later said. "I half believed it myself."

The 5th Corps' perseverance — 26 miles in one day — paid off. Chamberlain's 20th Maine would be widely credited for its timely and tenacious defense against rebel assaults on Little Round Top fighting on the second day.

• • •

When Sykes' troops marched near Hanover, the bodies of dead soldiers and the bloated carcasses of horses still lay in the road.

Townspeople caring for the wounded troopers had not yet dealt with all the dead and debris from the previous day's cavalry clash.

One man in blue, George F. Williams, waited to help himself to water from a pump near the road. Williams spotted a fresh grave among some rosebushes.

"Whose grave is that?" Williams asked an elderly man standing nearby.

"A Johnnie," he replied. "One that got killed in a fight the horsemen had here yesterday."

Williams wondered about the grave's location.

The elderly man told of his own son, named Johnny, killed near Richmond.

The man received a letter from a woman who had buried Johnny's body in a garden.

"So when I saw that poor Johnnie a-layin' out thar, all dead and bloody in the dust of the road, I sed I'd bury him. And the gals, they sed, 'Yes, father, bury him among the rose-trees.' That's why I did it stranger," the man explained.

"It must be some consolation to remember what you have done for the man whose body lies there under the bushes," Williams said.

"Yes, stranger; that 'ere grave ain't much ... but it will be something to remember our Johnny by."

Williams moved along, his eyes full of tears.

• • •

A.H. Byington, a New York Tribune correspondent, reached Hanover on Wednesday. The town appeared disorderly after the big cavalry fight.

People stayed close to their homes. Telegraph wires, Byington's main interest, curled around poles.

Byington located Daniel Trone, the telegraph operator, and asked him where his battery was.

"At home under the bed," he said. "The wires are all cut, and there is no use trying to telegraph."

Byington would have none of that. He paid men to go out on a handcar to fix the wires. Someone fetched the telegraph instrument from under Trone's bed, and Hanover made contact with Baltimore. Trone promised Byington rights to the wire for two days.

Byington headed to the battlefield and ran into Union Gen. O.O. Howard. He learned about the first day's battle and the death of Union 1st Corps Commander John Reynolds. He sent off an assistant to Hanover to deliver the story for transmission.

Trone successfully transmitted Byington's work.

• • •

As it turned out, Stuart had made a sound decision Tuesday night to move his column north toward Dover instead of heading east to York.

David Gregg's cavalry division of about 3,000 troopers had marched from Manchester, Md., through southern York County to Hanover Junction.

The blue column reached there Wednesday shortly after Stuart's men had cleared Panther Valley Road. Gregg found telegraph communications still out at the Junction, thanks to the Comanches.

• • •

The lack of clarity about the rebel position led to a series of orders from Meade's Taneytown, Md., headquarters. The first told Gregg to head south to Baltimore, a second to countermarch toward York and a third informed him of the concentration of troops at Gettysburg.

His final orders: Proceed to Gettysburg. This took Gregg through Jefferson, where some of his men took badly needed mounts and left town singing, "Dear father, will you meet us? We will meet in the promised land."

They rode into Hanover at midnight Wednesday and the early morning hours of Thursday.

Even at that hour, the town came out for the Union troopers. Residents supplied hearty provisions, possibly some of the leftovers Sykes' men had left behind. The horsemen plopped down on the street for a three-hour rest.

A messenger from Gettysburg awakened the horsemen.

"... (S)oon afterward we heard the booming of cannon and the rattle of musketry from the battle of Gettysburg," Gregg later wrote. His men rode to fight in the second day's battle, joined in McSherrystown by a tall, armed farmer on horseback, whose name was never recorded.

On the third day of fighting, Gregg finally ran into Stuart. His men helped keep the graycoats from harassing Union lines from behind, as James Longstreet's corps, under Gen. George Pickett's direction, unsuccessfully assaulted Cemetery Ridge from the west.

County responds to battle's aftermath

People in the corners of York County heard the sounds of guns — the big ones — booming from the west, from Gettysburg.

Emaline Smeigh was one of them. The 14-year-old farm girl lived in Brownton in southeastern York County.

The Confederate presence had interrupted her fami-

Pennsylvanian David Gregg's 3,000 troopers reached Hanover at about midnight Wednesday, July 1, and early the next morning. The horsemen enjoyed a warm welcome, a hearty meal and then rested on the street. They departed before daybreak to join in fighting on the second day of the Battle of Gettysburg.

FRIDAY, JUNE 22, 1906

YORK'S ONLY LYNCHING OCCURRED JUNE 30, '63

UNKNOWN NEGRO RIDDLED BY WARRINGTON FARMERS

WAS CONFEDERATE CAMP-FOLLOWER

Grangers Feared He Might Steal Horses—Well-Known Men Arrested and Jailed—Grand Jury Ignored Bill, Judge Discharged Prisoners

What is said to have been York county's only lynching occurred on the old state road, in Warrington township, about one-half mile northwest of Emig's mill, when, on June 30, 1863, an unknown negro, who was probably a body servant of some Confederate officer, was shot to death by a party of five prominent residents of the district on what, in the west, would be called "general principles."

As a result of the killing six men were charged with murder, some of them being jailed in this city; but a grand jury ignored the bill, and all the accused were discharged by General Fisher. At least one of the participants is still living, and the descendants of others are well and favorably known throughout the city and county. Incidentally, the account of the lynching was suppressed by the only newspaper published in this city at the time, and this is the first time that the story has been published.

A newspaper tells the story years after the fact about the shooting of a Negro, probably left behind by the invading Confederates in late June and early July 1863. Local residents pushed for the prosecution of a group of their neighbors who shot the servant, but the case never went to trial. Newspapers of the day covered the event, and this article revisited the incident.

ly's life the past few days. Her father, Jonathan Smeigh, hid horses in the nearby woods, just in case the rebels came down the Peach Bottom Road.

Days earlier, Emaline had witnessed the reflection in the sky from the burning of the Wrightsville bridge.

Near York, 16-year-old Martin L. Van Baman wandered along the Codorus to swimming holes, Laurel Rocks and Indian Steps. There, he and his friends heard the booming of cannons and the rattle of muskets.

Alfred Jessop, A.B. Farquhar's friend who witnessed the Confederate entry into York just days earlier, mounted Webb's Hill and peered to the west for any signs of the battle. But nothing could be seen from his vantage point.

Residents of Hanover could also hear the sound of big guns and small arms. And some people contended that they could follow the flight of shells in the night sky.

"The ground was fairly shaken by the concussion," The Hanover Spectator reported, "and the whole country for miles around was filled with the terrible sounds of warlike strife."

Lewis Miller captures the fighting on the third day of the Battle of Gettysburg. Miller wrote under his drawing: 'Fight on Soldiers fight. The battle you Shall win; Renew it boldly nor lay thine Armor down, Our work will not be down (done), till we obtain the field.' It is not known whether Miller witnessed Pickett's Charge, but some York residents did go to the field while the battle was raging.

• • •

Some farmers in Warrington Township learned about the presence of a Negro man unknown in those parts of northern York County. He was probably a servant of a Confederate officer riding with Stuart, left behind after the raiders passed through.

On the march and in camp, Negroes often accompanied Confederate soldiers. They worked as teamsters, personal servants or cooks.

Someone had spotted the visitor with the rebels atop a horse stolen from George Emig.

"Well Jim, did you get that horse?" a rebel soldier asked him.

Yes, the rider said, and he's a good one, too.

A couple of days later, the Warrington man who had overheard that conversation advised the visitor, still hanging around the area, that he should leave. The visitor, now a suspected horse thief, stayed, and Jeremiah Spahr, Henry Spahr, Levi Reiver, Lewis Spahr, William R. Smith and Lewis Reater found him.

Jeremiah Spahr, of the 87th Pennsylvania, leveled a gun at the visitor and shot him.

After a coroner's inquest, residents John E. Wells and David Cadwalader pushed for the six to be arrested.

The men were released on bail. A grand jury later dismissed the charges.

• • •

Henry Harris and another young man visited Philip Small's home Wednesday evening.

They were the first outsiders to make it to York by rail since the occupation. The pair traveled in handcars. When they came to a damaged portion of track, they would walk until they could find another car.

• • •

By Friday after the occupation, people in York County were feeling less isolated, even with a raging battle to the west.

A stage regularly ran from York to Wrightsville, and a steam ferry shuttled across the Susquehanna to Columbia to pick up mail and newspapers.

No one had spotted rebels in York since Tuesday. By now, people were aware that the thousands of horses and troopers making up Stuart's cavalry came within four or five miles of town Tuesday night and Wednesday morning.

Still, York had been spared.

The booming of cannons from the Gettysburg field reminded county residents that the rebels could return. Unfortunately for many people, the sound of the big guns did not tell how the Yankee defenders were faring.

The people of York braced for a rebel return. Businesses remained closed and not much happened in town.

James Latimer, the young York lawyer, tried all day to find a wagon and horses to head toward Gettysburg to gain information, but no one would take him.

• • •

Abraham Rudisill did not have to guess the results of

the battle. The Yankees held their position in this fight to the death.

Rudisill helped man a battery on Culp's Hill, trying to fend off Ewell's men attacking the Union right all three days of the battle. "Extra Billy" Smith's men, detached to Gen. Edward Johnson's unit, formed part of the gray assault on the hill where Rudisill fought.

On Friday evening, after Pickett's unsuccessful charge, on the Union center, Rudisill paused near his gun to write in his diary. The outcome of the battle was still in doubt, even after the Yankees repelled Pickett's massive assault.

"Soon firing gradually ceased more or less and now while I write at the side of our cannon No. 1, there is comparatively a great calm," he wrote. "Perhaps the Rebels are charging or falling back. We will see; but the storm may rage again ere long. Lord Keep Us. Praise the Lord for his goodness. I see men reading the Testament. Just in front of me the cannons are booming; now and then a shell passes here; sometimes cutting the limbs of trees."

• • •

Though news about the Union success on the third day rapidly spread through the county Friday night, people knew that Lee's men remained in position.

Latimer Small, Philip Small's son, was one who brought back word that the Union lines had held. He ventured to Gettysburg on Thursday and Friday, even as the fighting took place. He returned to York to explain developments in the battle.

Small prepared to return Saturday with aid for the wounded. Early that morning, he headed to the field with five women from York and a well-supplied wagon, among the first to respond to the dire needs of the wounded.

York would send scores more relief wagons to Gettysburg.

• • •

With the disappointment of the recent rebel occupation, the two armies still facing off at the field and the devastating loss of life in Gettysburg, the Fourth of July passed without celebration in York.

Some boys exploded firecrackers and fired pistols, but most of the citizenry looked to the west. The rebels remained only 30 miles away.

Randall's City Troop and Bell's Cavalry, scouting throughout the county, brought in 100 stray mules and horses. Some of the animals must have run away from Stuart's herd on his ride through the county. They grazed at the fairgrounds, available for their owners to pick up.

Some time that morning, several respected citizens arrived from Gettysburg with additional reports of the devastation. Word of the carnage washed over York in waves.

Chief Burgess David Small presided at a hurriedly called town meeting at the courthouse to put forth plans to gather supplies for the wounded.

Ten people were assigned to spread word about the dire condition of the wounded.

In two-and-one-half hours, townspeople carried enough supplies to the Centre Square market sheds and courthouse to fill 40 wagons.

Several nurses volunteered to accompany the wagons loaded with bread, cakes, hams, preserved fruits, clothing, blankets, bandages and other hospital supplies. After the wagon train left, York residents continued dropping off

To the Patriotic and Humane Citizens of the Borough and neighborhood of York.

A Town Meeting was held this morning, July 4, to adopt measures to forward supplies to our gallant and suffering soldiers who were wounded in the recent terrible battles at Gettysburg. The call has already been nobly responded to, and large quantities of supplies are now on the way, but the good work must not stop here. You are therefore requested to send bread, cakes, boiled hams and shoulders, preserved fruits, wines, liquors, and such other articles as you may have, even if in small quantities, to the Auditor's office, in the COURT HOUSE, THIS EVENING AND TO-MORROW, where they will be received by the Committee in charge.

As great difficulty may arise for want of transportation, persons having horses and wagons are earnestly entreated to have them in front of the Court House, this evening or to-morrow morning, or report them to the Committee.

The Committee appointed at the Town Meeting, consists of

E. G. SMYSER,	P. A. SMALL,
PETER BENTZ,	E. C. BENDER,
JOSEPH SMYSER,	PETER M'INTYRE,
J. R. DAVIS,	GEO. H. MAISH,
D. D. DOUDEL,	HENRY KRABER.

DAVID SMALL, Chief Burgess.

York, July 4th, 1863.

This handbill went out after an initial load of food and supplies had been sent from York for relief of the wounded after the battle at Gettysburg. The notice named committee members who would receive the large quantities of supplies anticipated from the community. York County residents offered wagons to transport the goods, but movement of the badly needed supplies had to wait for horsepower. Eventually, horses and mules arrived from the east bank of the Susquehanna, and York County came through with scores of wagons full of supplies.

goods at the courthouse in great quantities.

"So much for the citizens of our patriotic borough," The York Gazette said in its July 7 edition, "so much slandered and maligned by the lying abolition press of Philadelphia and elsewhere."

• • •

While the wagons with aid for the wounded rumbled from York toward Gettysburg, Robert E. Lee sent his own long trains away from the field toward the Potomac.

Hundreds of wagons — filled with wounded soldiers, booty gleaned from the invasion and military equipment — rolled through passes in the South Mountain toward the Potomac.

Union Gen. Hermann Haupt supervised the construction of this temporary Northern Central Railway bridge over the Codorus Creek between Hanover Junction and Seven Valleys on July 4, 1863. Confederate cavalry destroyed the bridge during the rebel occupation of York County days earlier. The completion of the bridge meant that the wounded from the Battle of Gettysburg could be carried northward along the railroad to hospitals in York and elsewhere in the North.

After darkness fell, gray infantry units started leaving the field. First, Hill's men departed, then Longstreet's 1st Corps. Richard Ewell's men manned the rear.

The rebel army was in full retreat toward the west and south, straining to reach the Potomac. The Confederates no longer posed a threat to York County, and other points east of Gettysburg, at least for the summer of 1863.

When news of Lee's retreat reached James Kendig and other York County residents, flags again appeared.

Kendig's wife and two friends had raised money to make a large flag after the attack on Fort Sumter. Kendig erected a tall pole outside his East Market Street house.

Kendig figured it was time again to raise his patriotic banner.

But this was no time for parades in York. The wounded needed relief, the people felt the loss of horses and supplies to the Confederates and the wisdom of the surrender to the rebels divided people. The depth of that division was just now beginning to emerge.

• • •

On Saturday, Abraham Rudisill scrawled his impressions. He noted the previous night and that day had been quiet. It was becoming apparent that the Confederates would not again attack.

"Praise the good Lord for the great deliverance and victory He has given our troops, though undeserving and unworthy as we are," he wrote in his diary.

But the boom of big guns the day before had made its mark.

"Such a cannonading as took place on both sides was scarce ever witnessed in similar circumstances in the annals of warfare," he wrote.

And the bloodshed was horrible. A horse had limped past, guts hanging out on both sides.

"And I heard the poor horse actually uttering a shriek or clear voice of agony," he wrote.

He stood by the side of a dying soldier, who drank from his canteen just before his death. The soldier's entrails protruded from his belly, the handiwork of a shell fragment.

An officer approached Rudisill's battery and asked if he and his mates had maintained that position the past three days.

"We did hold the hill all the time was our reply," Rudisill wrote.

• • •

Gen. Hermann Haupt, chief of military railroads for the federal government, spent the Fourth of July weekend mending damaged tracks and bridges outside of Gettysburg.

Haupt had earned an impeccable reputation for repairing railroads rapidly.

Mary C. Fisher arrived at field hospitals in Gettysburg soon after the battle ended. The seasoned nurse, accustomed to seeing the wounded transported to the U.S. Army General Hospital in York, later related the terrible condition of the wounded in Gettysburg in a Philadelphia newspaper. '... (B)ut vivid as those scenes were, they paled into insignificance in the presence of the actual battle ground ...,' she wrote. Fisher, seen above in the living room of her East Market Street home, gained wide recognition after details of her work among wounded soldiers ran in The Philadelphia Times 20 years after the war ended, right.

His work in fixing a span near Washington, D.C., had caught Abraham Lincoln's eye.

"That man Haupt has built a bridge ... about 400 feet long and nearly 100 feet high, over which loaded trains are running every hour, and, upon my word, gentlemen, there is nothing in it but beanpoles and cornstalks," Lincoln marveled in 1862.

Now in York County, Haupt moved with urgency. Railroads would be needed to transport the wounded from the battlefield to York's military hospital and other infirmaries along the Eastern Seaboard.

Repair work on the Northern Central Railway at Hanover Junction and the Hanover Branch and Gettysburg Railroad was at the top of Haupt's list. The 25-mile Hanover Branch and its extension to Gettysburg represented a direct link to move the wounded from the field.

Haupt's report from Hanover Junction to Army headquarters in Washington Saturday told of a good morning's work on the Northern Central Railway: "Our men rebuilt entirely the bridge at this junction, three spans of about 40 feet, this morning."

Later that day, his telegraph from New Oxford, between York and Gettysburg, told of more progress.

VOL. VI.—NO. 44.

Annals of the War

CHAPTERS OF UNWRITTEN HISTORY

A WEEK ON GETTYSBURG FIELD

What a Good Samaritan Saw During the Days Following the Battle.

TWENTY THOUSAND PATIENTS

Food for the Starving and Reviving Cordials for the Lips of the Dying.

MANY PATHETIC INCIDENTS

Strong Men in Dire Need and Mere Lads Hungry for the Mother's Care.

BY MRS. MARY CADWELL FISHER.

It was impossible for one who lived in the sections of the country remote from the seat of war to realize the meaning of life in the Border States in that time that tried the souls of all men and wrung with anguish the hearts of the devoted women both North and South. Unprotected by military force, with no natural barrier between the seceding and the loyal States, the exaggerated rumors and the constant suspense were appalling in the early days of the deadly struggle. But soon familiarized to the life we became indifferent to danger, and with the advent of the summer campaign sent away our plate and valuables and calmly awaited whatever might come to us in the fortunes of war. We devoted ourselves to preparing supplies for the Sanitary Corps and to hospital work, which alike filled our hearts with compassion and our hands with labor. Situated but a few miles from the border, the sick and wounded were often sent to us directly from the field, giving most forcible impressions of the revolting results of every battle; but vivid as those scenes were, they paled

"We have been at work on a large bridge near this town, which is considerably damaged. It will require two hours to-morrow to finish it, when we will proceed to Gettysburg."

• • •

Weekend rain drenched roads and fields causing the cancellation of the Sabbath School at Sanney's School.

Word had made it back to this remote part of southeastern York County that thousands had lost their lives in Gettysburg, and the rebels had robbed York of $100,000 in money and supplies.

Someone noted in the Sunday school minutes that the rebels were on the run.

"We think they have paid very dear for their fun," the writer said. "... We think they will not come back again to Pennsylvania."

County residents help tend to the wounded

Mary C. Fisher, the volunteer nurse at York's military hospital, was among the scores of York County people who provided aid in Gettysburg.

The judge's wife departed York at about 3 p.m. Saturday, riding in the train of loaded wagons. Two other women and her oldest son accompanied her.

Before she left, York resident Jeremiah S. Black, U.S. attorney general under former President James Buchanan, offered her several dozen bottles of imported liquor. Fisher added a quantity of fine whiskey from a York County distillery to this cache.

The train traveled the longer route to Hanover to avoid the York-Gettysburg Pike. Straggling bluecoats, who might have a hunger or thirst for some of the cargo, occupied the pike.

The wagons paused in Hanover, and part of the train proceeded through New Oxford late in the night of July 4. About 30 wagons from the York train stayed in Hanover and started rolling sometime after Fisher's wagon had departed. Some of the wagons came to a stop when a Union officer under Gen. Judson Kilpatrick ordered them to be unloaded. They were needed to transport wounded officers.

Just then, a distinguished gentleman arrived on the scene. He identified himself as Gen. O.O. Howard's chief corps chaplain and asserted that suffering soldiers in field hospitals needed the most attention. His view won.

The train pressed westward, moving to a barn filled with hundreds of the wounded.

"In all that ghastly array of human misery, between three and four hundred men, there was not one whole individual," Fisher wrote. "Everyone had lost either an arm or a leg, and in some cases both were gone. One poor wretch had both legs and his right arm torn off by a shell, and one had lost both arms and one leg."

Fisher was a seasoned hospital nurse, accustomed to seeing troops arrive on rail cars to the hospital in York, cars dripping with blood from running wounds.

But what she saw when she reached the battlefield gave her a new view of human suffering:

"No imagination could paint the picture in that wood. I instinctively recoiled from the sight. Grouped beneath the trees we saw about five hundred men, who had hastily been removed beyond fighting limits. They were lying upon the bare ground, some of them literally half buried in mud. There was no shelter. Wounded chilled, starving and racked with pain, how they welcomed us as we carried food and reviving cordial."

• • •

Fisher stayed at the field for 11 days, treating scores of wounded soldiers, men in both blue and gray.

Moving from makeshift hospitals in barns, houses and churches, she rationed Jeremiah Black's liquor.

"My stock, like the 'widow's cruse of oil,' held out in a marvelous manner," she wrote, "and the surgeons often told me that Judge Black's brandy bottle saved more lives than their instruments and medicine combined."

The relief workers initially identified soldiers without severe wounds, fed and clothed them and provided whiskey as a stimulant. Then, those recovering soldiers could help the nurses tend to the others.

One sunny evening, the nurse ran across a case that stuck with her. She nursed one youth, who had run away from his Rhode Island home to serve as a drummer boy. The boy was in a section of a hospital designated for hopeless cases. Fisher asked the boy what she could do for him.

"Oh, I want my mother!"

Fisher took him in her arms and tried to comfort him.

"I am so tired," he said, laying his head against the nurse, appearing to sleep.

Suddenly, he opened his eyes.

"Kiss me, lady, before I die!" he said.

"Clinging still closer to the stranger who could but faintly represent the fond mother's tenderness he so eagerly craved, he dropped his heavy lids and slept away his brief life as peacefully as a child goes to sleep in its mother's arms," Fisher wrote.

A newspaper applauded Fisher's acts of mercy, "She had the consolation that, through her devoted efforts, she helped to save the lives of a number of men and comforted hundreds of them in their deep distress."

• • •

With the battle still raging, A.B. Farquhar rode toward Gettysburg to seek service with the hospital corps.

He used the passwords gained from his earlier visits to move through Confederate lines.

On the battle's second day, he entered the Union lines, and the provost guard arrested him. Someone had spotted him coming from the rebel position.

Fortunately, a soldier who knew Farquhar observed his situation and vouched for the York man's reputation.

He told the arresting officer that Farquhar was not a spy.

"Then you had better see General Kilpatrick mighty quick. He is just about fifty yards away," the officer said. "You run for him and I will follow."

He jumped from his buggy and ran toward Judson Kilpatrick, the officer following.

Farquhar told the general he was there to help care for the wounded.

"If you are an imposter," Kilpatrick said, "you are more dangerous than Jeff Davis."

He released Farquhar, and the young man joined his medical corps.

Farquhar made certain he was useful.

That night, Kilpatrick laid down for some rest, and Farquhar laid his head across Kilpatrick's knees.

"What in the ____ are you doing?" Kilpatrick asked.

Farquhar explained that no one would wake him if a need arose, but Kilpatrick's aides were certain to rouse the general.

A short time later, the Louisiana Tigers made an attack, and Farquhar was stirred into service.

Union officers took his horse and buggy to transport the wounded, the last time Farquhar ever saw them.

• • •

The numbers of wounded were so great and the medical resources so limited that Farquhar could do little except supply water and make soldiers a bit more comfortable.

For a moment, he seized command.

Some troopers rode up to collect hay for their horses from a barn loft. Their actions caused dust to float down on the wounded below.

Farquhar ordered them to stop, and they followed his directive.

• • •

Word about Farquhar's arrest quickly found its way back to York. By the time James Latimer heard the rumors on Friday, they contained different facts from the story Farquhar told.

Kilpatrick placed Farquhar in irons after he had gained a pass from the general to come to York from the cavalry's camp near East Berlin.

Some Union men observed him heading toward Confederate lines. That's when they arrested him.

"I don't know what they did with him," Latimer wrote.

• • •

After his hospital stint in Gettysburg, Farquhar rode into York expecting to share in the joy that the rebel threat had been turned back.

He picked up that people were jeering at him.

"Then I learned that after the news of Lee's defeat had reached town," Farquhar wrote, "the pinchbeck patriots had crawled out of their holes and decided that our Committee, instead of saving the town, had sold it to the Confederates and that I, as the man who had opened the negotiations, was something near to being a traitor! I shall never forget those days, being pointed out as 'the man who had sold York' to the Rebels, instead of one of those who had saved it."

Then and there, Farquhar decided to make his case to the highest patriot in the land — Abraham Lincoln.

He traveled to Washington and learned that Lincoln would go to the War Department at an appointed time. He waited outside the door of the White House for the chief executive to appear.

The president was punctual.

"Well, sonny, what are you after?" Lincoln asked.

As they walked, Farquhar explained the whole story.

Lincoln, saying little, took Farquhar before Secretary of War Edwin M. Stanton.

"Stanton, I have captured the young chap who sold York, Pennsylvania, to the Rebels," he said. "What are we going to do with him?"

Farquhar thought Lincoln was making a serious query.

Stanton answered just as gravely, "I think we ought to promote him."

The secretary explained that Farquhar's action had probably saved millions in property damage at a small cost.

Lincoln praised Farquhar for being of service and admonished him not to worry about what people said about him.

Farquhar's best service, the president contended, would be to enlist in the Army. The York man explained that he had a family, a business and could provide more service at home than in the field. He had paid a substitute and could help in medical service, as he did in Gettysburg.

"Being married is no excuse," Lincoln said, "but you, maybe, are contributing your mite, and that is all any of us can do."

In parting, Father Abraham gave Farquhar the absolution the young man sought, "You can go home and tell them what I have said to you; tell them that you have my thanks and the thanks of the Government."

News of the meeting preceded his arrival in York. People in York cordially received him, he wrote.

'We belonged to the rest of the world again'

James Latimer finally found transportation to Gettysburg.

Strangely, he did not see much upon his arrival on Sunday after the battle. The dead had been buried and the wounded removed before he got there, he wrote Bart.

Latimer surveyed part of the field to understand the battle lines and viewed evidence of severe fighting.

Others from York County also searched for horses and carriages to travel to the field, sometimes just to rubberneck.

• • •

On Monday, food and supplies continued to pour into York. Farmers joined in by furnishing badly needed wagons to transport items for the wounded suffering in barns, churches and private homes around Gettysburg.

"Many an oven was heated on the Sabbath that never knew fire before on that day," The York Republican stated, "and it felt that the noble work of charity and mercy was no infraction of holy time."

Some wagons from York delivered supplies to the wounded from a Pennsylvania regiment. The surgeon in charge thanked the people of York with tears in his eyes. The soft, fresh bread revived many of the wounded. Up to that point, hard crackers had been their fare.

Those with enough strength gave York County residents three hearty cheers.

• • •

Lancaster County's John Denney guided the cart bearing his wife, Rachel, and their two children back home from Christiana, a week after they departed with Gordon's men heading their way.

Riding up river from Columbia toward home, John Denney pointed to the river. The mile-long bridge was now but a line of bare piers. The remains — blackened and yet smoldering timber — pierced the surface of the water.

"We had to burn it," the husband said without

elaboration.

Rachel Denny later learned that her husband performed important duties in defending the bridge, setting the powder charges in the unsuccessful effort to drop the span.

• • •

The Patriot Daughters of Lancaster finally arrived in Wrightsville after a long delay waiting for the ferry to take them across the Susquehanna, swollen by recent rains.

The east bank, one of the relief workers wrote, resembled Gold Rush-era California, with its motley assortment of men, wagons and horses. The women had to wait overnight in Columbia. The ferry captain would not put nurses ahead of those waiting all day to return to the west bank.

But now in Wrightsville, they saw evidence of the skirmish and Confederate occupation. They viewed a house destroyed by fire near the bridge, many dwellings damaged by cannon shot and hastily dug rifle pits. On the way to York, the countryside appeared to be untouched, even the fence rails.

The group reached York that day and met friends returning from Gettysburg. The women learned that tin cups, washbasins and other tinware would greatly aid their nursing work.

Though they had become aware that controversy surrounded the York Committee of Safety's decision not to contest the rebels, they found the town supportive and ready to assist.

A stranger named Alfred Gartman provided them with a fine dinner, which the women would relish in their long days of tending to the wounded.

Those arduous duties started the next day when they reached the field.

• • •

Seven days after the last rebel headed west to Gettysburg, no other soldiers dressed in gray had been spotted.

The elation was evident over the beating the rebels had taken on the field and their hurried getaway, trying to beat Meade's men to the Potomac.

"We are glad that they are fully occupied elsewhere," The Gazette stated, "by our gallant army under Gen. Meade."

• • •

Surgeon Henry Palmer, on his way to Gettysburg with Jubal Early's men, had escaped from Confederate custody before reaching the field. He journeyed back to York, where he prepared the military hospital for massive casualties.

"RR communications open," he wrote the medical director of The Army of the Potomac a week after the Confederates had departed. "Hospital ready for 500 wounded immediately. Shall be ready for more in three days. Will go to Gettysburg on first train. Can you detail any assistant surgeons for this place?"

Most patients, earlier evacuated to safer quarters in Columbia under the care of Alexander Blair, had returned to the hospital.

Palmer found transportation to Gettysburg to provide medical care and assess the devastation.

He returned to York with full knowledge of the medical challenges that lay ahead.

"Just returned from field," he wrote to his superiors

Dr. Henry Palmer headed the U.S. Army General Hospital in York for more than two years. He stayed behind with patients who could not be moved. The invading Confederates arrested him, and he escaped from their custody and returned to York to head the treatment of hundreds of Union soldiers wounded in the Battle of Gettysburg.

on July 11.

"8,100 wounded. Will need more assistants."

• • •

Cassandra Small, Philip Small's daughter, heard that the military hospital would receive 1,110 wounded from Gettysburg, as soon as transportation could be obtained.

Well, despite this, York and its residents had been mercifully spared, she wrote Lissie.

"We would rather give the rascals twice over what we did than have them back!" she wrote. "Oh, I could fill sheet after sheet with all their audacious villainies. It is a matter never to be forgotten by us."

• • •

A week after the Confederates departed and just days after Haupt worked his engineering miracles, the first train pulled into York.

The town had gained a much-desired connection with the outside world, although the wounded filled most of the cars.

"Only think," Cassandra Small wrote Lissie, "this is the first day for nearly two weeks that we have heard the whistle of an engine! When the engine came in we began to feel as though we belonged to the rest of the world again."

• • •

Still, those traveling on rail through York County faced obstacles.

Medical officials struggled to efficiently move the wounded from Gettysburg to hospitals in York and Baltimore. The government took over the Hanover Branch and Gettysburg Railroad for uses it deemed appropriate.

In a report, Edward P. Vollum, U.S. Army medical inspector, reviewed transportation problems faced in the days after the battle.

The first temporary bridges put up were too unstable except for the lightest of engines. Rising water from the heavy rains after the battle carried some away. Breaks in the telegraph lines slowed communication.

Then, the Conewago Creek bridge on the Northern Central between York and Harrisburg gave way, diverting trains for five days.

When the trains were successful in moving the wounded, aid was readily available. At Hanover Junction, the Christian Commission provided food and refreshments.

In Baltimore, a group of benevolent societies distributed food. The U.S. Army Commissary Department arranged to feed the wounded in Harrisburg.

• • •

Vollum passed through Hanover on his way to Gettysburg. One week after the cavalry battle, the medical inspector found about 150 wounded Union troopers there,

This view shows Hanover after the June 30 cavalry battle on its streets. The crossroads community played host to a Union cavalry division and a Yankee infantry corps, both heading toward the battlefield in Gettysburg, the day after blue and gray horsemen clashed. Counts of injured and wounded from the cavalry fight vary, but one authoritative count places Union casualties at 19 killed, 73 wounded and 123 missing. Confederates sustained nine killed, 50 wounded and 58 missing.

mostly from Kilpatrick's command. The wounded rested comfortably in a school and in quarters around town.

"The inhabitants had furnished them with bunks, bedding, dressings, utensils, and food in sufficient quantity," Vollum said in his report, "the people in each street furnishing food, delicacies, nurses ... two days at a time."

• • •

York bustled with visiting friends and families of wounded soldiers trying to find transportation to Gettysburg.

Livery horses were in short supply thanks to the Confederate sweep. Farmers needed horses and mules for the harvest season.

When train service started, passengers could ride toward Gettysburg in gondola or freight cars. Once there, they faced scarcities of food and accommodations.

Sleeping in the open or on the floor of a bar room represented a small price for those aiding their loved ones. But for the many who traveled to the field as a curiosity, that inconvenience seemed greater, The Gazette noted.

Return transportation on trains filled with the wounded was much more difficult.

Occasionally, the lucky passenger could gain standing-room-only status for the trip to Hanover Junction and then north on the Northern Central.

• • •

Samuel Wehring, former chief of York's police, successfully made the trip west.

He went to help clear the field still littered with items discarded or lost in battle. As he picked up firearms from the field, a gun accidentally discharged, killing him.

Wehring's body was returned to York, and interment took place the next day at Prospect Hill Cemetery, north of the borough.

A large number of family members, friends and members of the Humane Lodge of Odd Fellows attended his burial.

David Small's The York Gazette published its first defense of the decision by chief burgess David Small and other town fathers to surrender to the Confederates. That defense appeared above the news of the Union Army's triumph in the Battle of Gettysburg. 'This invasion will prove a terrible experiment to the rebels,' the newspaper accurately reported. But the article went on to speculate the Confederate Army could be captured and destroyed. The war wore on for almost two years after the pivotal Gettysburg conflict.

Debate commences over York surrender

David Small accurately predicted that the surrender of the town would attract criticism.

In its edition on July 7, The Gazette responded to criticism about the surrender and its reporting of the occupation the previous week.

"The slanderers of York, who seem to regret that our beautiful borough was not laid in ashes by General Early (and we regret to say that a few such wretches reside in our midst) still persist in their misrepresentations," The Gazette said.

The newspaper attempted to debunk one rumor: Reports that the railroad gave a large amount of money to save its property were incorrect. The Confederates secured about $36,000 in money and supplies.

"All good citizens, while they deplore the humiliation of the occupation of the town by the enemy," The Gazette said, "are grateful for our fortunate escape from the horrors of war."

The Gazette clearly outlined its defense as well as the

case for those authorities behind the surrender: "The people, conscious of their defenceless condition, submitted to imperious necessity and, in saving their lives and property, did what humanity and common sense dictated."

• • •

David Small, the newspaperman, deflected the all-out written assault on his role as chief burgess. The Philadelphia Inquirer picked up a New York Tribune dispatch, which Small construed as containing charges that he failed his duties.

The report must have been delivered to the Tribune by one of the "cowardly and lying Black Republicans," who fled York and never slowed until he reached New York, The Gazette said.

Small believed he had earned the approval of York's citizens by his untiring efforts to protect them during the occupation.

"The prevalence of this opinion may be unpleasant to the weak-kneed Refugees," The Gazette stated, "but they will find this feeling has grown so universal that 'falsehood cannot shake it, nor perfidy steal it away.' "

• • •

The Evening Bulletin in Philadelphia reported that it was not the Unionists who had fled York, leaving helpless women and children behind.

"The town of York, which is infested with Copperheads and cowards," the Philadelphia newspaper said, "was almost deserted by them."

The town's authorities, under requisition, had contributed heavily to the rebel army. Those who had run away should be called upon some day to settle the town's debt, the newspaper said.

The Age in Philadelphia, operated by two of Small's former business partners, tried to set The Bulletin straight about who actually skedaddled: Nine out of every 10 citizens who fled were abolitionists.

"The Democratic Chief Justice, David Small, Esq., remained faithfully at his post," the newspaper stated, "and by his unwearied exertions saved from destruction the property of the very Jacobins who fled from town... ."

• • •

Even The Republican, a supporter of Lincoln's policies, found it necessary, at least at one point, to defend the decision to surrender without resistance.

The gallant Union Army had avenged the humiliation of the Confederate occupation and prevented a possible second occupation, the newspaper said.

Those carping elsewhere, who left York for safety, should organize relief for the wounded instead of visiting the battlefield empty-handed to fulfill some "vain curiosity."

• • •

In its July 14 edition — two weeks after the Confederate occupation — The Gazette kept up its defense of the decision to surrender the town. The newspaper ran extracts from the Chambersburg Valley Spirit and the Carlisle American Democrat that detailed the devastation exacted on those towns and, by comparison, how York avoided such pillage.

York escaped because of the borough authorities' and Committee of Safety's prudent management of the rebel forces, the newspaper contended.

The Gazette pointed to Carlisle as a particularly interesting example. The town refused to surrender to demands

from Gen. Fitz Lee, so Jeb Stuart's men shelled the town and set fire to the Army barracks.

Even the town of Gettysburg came under attack from The New York Times, which The Gazette called another rabid abolitionist journal.

A Times correspondent contended that the people of Gettysburg were so "sordidly mean and unpatriotic" as to feed the belief that they were indifferent to which side won or lost. The men ran away, leaving their women and children to the mercy of the invaders. On their return, they looked first to collect for damages from the Army rather than care for the wounded.

The Gazette indicated that nearly every house in Gettysburg served as a hospital. The people of Gettysburg deserved thanks and sympathy, not reproach and slander.

" ... York is not the only place that has been ruthlessly assailed by the party," The Gazette stated, "which has brought all the troubles upon our suffering and bleeding country."

• • •

The Gazette touted its "Roll of Dishonor," a list of 80 citizens who fled from York after learning about the Confederate approach.

But the newspaper did not publish the list, holding it under advisement.

The Gazette was not impressed with the actions of some on the list who had returned.

"... (W)e may have occasion to refer to it hereafter," the newspaper observed.

• • •

James W. Latimer was among those who disagreed with the town's fathers' decision to surrender the borough.

The delegation went to meet the rebels along the pike, but the report from their visit was that they made no formal surrender, Latimer wrote his brother, Bart. Still, if Early's demands for goods and money had been refused, no damage would have occurred, Latimer conjectured.

"I do not believe such large requisitions would have been made," he wrote, "had not the Boro' Authorities behaved so sheepishly in regard to the surrender."

Latimer believed the rebel visit would teach the Copperheads a lesson. Dover, the Codoruses and other Copperhead townships sustained the heaviest loss of horse flesh.

Reports trickled into town that some people disclosed information to the rebels — where their neighbors concealed horses and other valuables. The rebels respected those who did not hide their status as Union men.

Some residents were duped into paying to join the K.G.C. — Knights of the Golden Circle — and learned signs they supposed would save their property, he noted.

The signs puzzled the rebels, who ignored them and helped themselves to the property. The befuddled K.G.C. men went to York after the rebels cleared out with the claim:

"Here, we want our dollar back, we showed the ticket, and made the signs, but it did no good. They struck it out of our hands, and said we don't care for that now, and made us give whatever they wanted."

• • •

As leading businessmen in town, Philip and Samuel Small attracted either scorn or praise from their fellow county residents. Some country folk blamed the Smalls for making the war to begin with. Thus, they could pay for it.

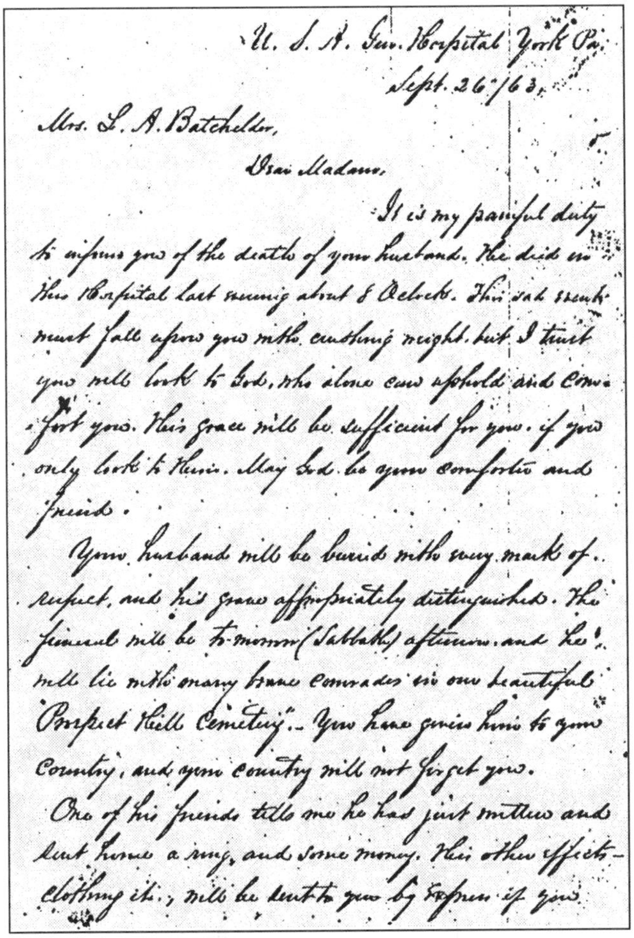

U. S. A. Gen. Hospital York Pa.
Sept. 26th/63.

Mrs. L. A. Batchelder,

Dear Madam,

It is my painful duty to inform you of the death of your husband. He died in this Hospital last evening about 8 Oclock. This sad event must fall upon you with crushing weight, but I trust you will look to God, who alone can uphold and comfort you. His grace will be sufficient for you, if you only look to Him. May God be your comforter and friend.

Your husband will be buried with every mark of respect, and his grave appropriately distinguished. The funeral will be to-morrow (Sabbath) afternoon, and he will lie with many brave comrades in our beautiful "Prospect Hill Cemetery". You have given him to your Country, and your country will not forget you.

One of his friends tells me he had just written and sent home a ring, and some money. His other effects - clothing etc., will be sent to you by Express if you

A chaplain at York's millitary hospital wrote to the wife of William Batchelor about the death of her husband. Batchelor, serving with the 16th Maine, was wounded at Gettysburg and fought to regain his health for almost three months before succumbing. 'It is my painful duty to inform you of the death of your husband,' the letter began. 'He died in the hospital last evening about 8 o'clock.' The chaplain urged Mrs. Batchelor to look to God, 'His grace will be sufficient for you, if you only look to Him. May God be your comforter and friend.'

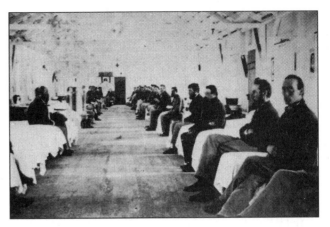

The U.S. Army General Hospital in York became a major site for treatment because of its proximity to Virginia, where many Civil War battles took place, and its location on a major rail line. At the same time, it was positioned in the North, off the paths typically taken by the Confederate Army. However, the Confederates took over the hospital during the Gettysburg campaign. When they left, York volunteers launched a major cleanup effort. They had to work quickly. After the battle, hundreds of Union soldiers were treated there. Here, convalescents pose in one of the hospital wards.

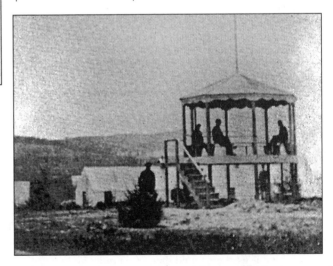

This gazebo aided the recovery of the wounded taken to the Penn Common hospital in York.

Others believed the Smalls helped avert the damage visited on Carlisle and other towns.

"Well, Sam," one resident told Samuel Small, "all the people around us say you and Philip saved the town so they are going to raise a monument to you as high as the Lutheran steeple."

• • •

Writing to Lissie a week after the Confederates departed, Cassandra Small defended the town's fathers' actions: If the town had been surrendered, it would not have been a disgrace.

But no surrender was requested. The Committee of Safety's delegation traveled to Gordon's camp on behalf of the women and children.

If the rebels meant harm, the committee would have bought time for women and children to flee. But the invaders meant no harm.

"How do you come," the delegation asked.

"Peacefully if unresisted, but if resisted, your town shall be laid to ashes," came the response.

"Oh, how well it was that we had such thoughtful men," Cassandra wrote, "what a panic we would have been in! The first we would have known of their approach would have been shells in our midst."

Small gave appropriate credit to those who saved York from destruction at the hands of the rebels. Her own father, Philip Small, was among that prudent group.

"It was plain as daylight that an Almighty Power saved us and that our Safety Committee was the instrument in his hands," she wrote.

The Confederates viewed York as their potential headquarters, Small said. That was why the town was spared.

"The battle was to be here and that was the reason they guarded our warehouses and mills so well," she wrote.

• • •

The debate in the newspapers continued for weeks — in fact, years.

David Small took time from defending his actions to go on the offensive in his newspaper's Sept. 1 edition. The newspaper's target was Robert Todd Lincoln, Abraham Lincoln's oldest son. Small reminded his readers that 30-year-old Bob Lincoln, a stout, athletic man, was spending his summer in the White Mountains rather than on the battlefield.

"Why don't Robert try his hand with a musket?" the newspaper wondered.

Either Lincoln is a hypocrite who does not believe the war is just as he professes, Small argued, or he is too selfish to make the sacrifice he demands of other parents.

Half-worn pantaloons become acceptable

Shortly after rail service returned, the Union started filling the military hospital and emergency tents dotting the hospital's grounds.

York residents knew some of the wounded.

Simon J. Arnold, formerly of York, was treated for a leg wound. He was taken prisoner by the rebels, but the Confederates left him behind.

The Gazette made certain that his friends in town were aware that he was expected to recover.

Meanwhile, Henry Palmer prepared for a thousand wounded Yankees but declined to accept wounded Confederates.

The surgeon, Cassandra Small contended, would resign rather than treat rebel wounded, at least that's what he said.

But military officials at the field sent about 25 wounded rebel soldiers from a North Carolina regiment to York and quartered them in Washington Hall, the entertainment hall that took overflow patients.

Hospital workers found these men quiet and respectful.

Palmer continued his work, nonetheless.

• • •

Five surgeons set up a military hospital on a train car at York's Duke Street station, drawing rations from the military hospital several blocks away.

The reconstructed bridge over the Conewago Creek went out, prohibiting the train from proceeding north.

These makeshift quarters brought more comfort than conditions in Gettysburg. The Union soldiers' stay was brief, but three died and were buried in York.

• • •

Surgeons in York used great care in preserving the limbs of the wounded.

Amputation was a common way of dealing with bullet wounds. The .58 caliber Minie ball, a heavy, conical-shaped bullet, caused large wounds and typically shattered bones.

The nature of the wound and heavy casualties caused military surgeons to opt for the faster amputation than the delicate task of removing a bullet.

At one point, York received about 75 men with bullet-inflicted compound thigh fractures — a condition that often led to amputation.

Using such radical surgery only when necessary, most recovered completely, retaining their legs and scars from their wounds.

• • •

Three weeks after the battle, Edward P. Vollum reported success in moving thousands of wounded Union and Confederate soldiers from the battlefield.

Trains had carried 7,608 Union wounded and 3,817 Confederates to hospitals elsewhere. Most passed through Hanover on the railroad to Hanover Junction.

Henry Palmer got his wish. Confederate wounded generally went elsewhere, and about 625 Union wounded had ended up in York's hospital to date.

Vollum praised the benevolent organizations that had come forward, noting that the battle caused the greatest amount of human suffering since the nation's founding. The response was the greatest ever.

But he granted no praise to the railroad men:

"The railroad companies, who got the only profit of the battle, and who had the greatest opportunities for ameliorating the sufferings of the wounded, alone stood aloof and rendered no aid."

Railroad agents only showed interest in counting the numbers transported so they could bill the government.

"There was no water, or vessels to contain it, no lanterns, no straw — absolutely nothing but the bare cars," Vollum fumed, "filthy from the business of transporting freight and cattle."

• • •

A month after the battle, Palmer and other hospital physicians had treated 1,000 patients, with another 400 reported to be on their way.

For the first time, residents in the York area could not fulfill the hospital demands for medical supplies, clothing and even delicacies — jams, jellies and wine — for the patients.

The Ladies Aid Society put out a call for help from "abroad."

"Half-worn pantaloons are also very acceptable," The Gazette reported.

• • •

Palmer saved many soldiers from death, but he was not successful with his own 5-year-old daughter, Kittie, who died after a lingering illness of three weeks.

"Edna (Palmer's wife) had previously communicated to you her condition," Palmer wrote to his parents, "and we had anxiously hoped to see her again restored to health, but an All Wise Providence has ordered otherwise."

Kittie was growing increasingly ladylike and well-mannered, more in the character of an adult than of a child, Palmer wrote.

She was strong even in pain.

"... Papa do cure my headache for it makes me feel cross, and I don't like to be cross," Kittie had told her father.

The Palmers buried their daughter in York with the expectation that they would move her body to Janesville, Wis., when they returned to that town.

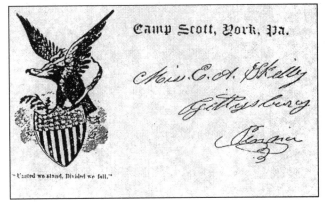

Johnston H. Skelley, a soldier in the 87th Pennsylvania, wrote his mother, Mrs. E.A. Skelley, from Camp Scott in York, early in the war. Two years later, Skelley died in a Winchester, Va., hospital. His fiance, Jennie Wade, was the only civilian victim of the Battle of Gettysburg. She died days before Skelley died from wounds sustained in the Battle of Winchester.

'I think six months will close the war'

The battlefield at Gettysburg was no place for ladies, according to those who visited it.

Stories were going around about the unburied and half-buried and the smell of bloated human and animal flesh.

Some strong, hearty women had been committed to rest in bed since their return from Gettysburg.

"We think it is caused by the terrible smell," Cassandra Small wrote.

Heads stuck out of the ground, dismembered feet and arms lay here and there.

Cassandra Small Morris, aunt of the letter writer and active in volunteer efforts in York to aid the sick and wounded since the war's earliest days, was among the bedridden.

She sat up in a large chair all night, never getting into her bedclothes. She looked miserable, never smiling.

• • •

The restoration of rail service meant distressed York residents, who had the means, could get away from it all.

Annie Weiser, for one, believed she was injured from all the excitement.

She planned to head to the Catskills in New York, if the Northern Central Railway bridge was open to Harrisburg.

• • •

The occupation drove a stake between families — even neighbors — who had been longtime friends.

One neighbor of Philip Small entertained Southern officers, and the neighbor's sister was among those waving her handkerchief at the passing soldiers.

She waved, that is, until a clergyman challenged her.

"If you have no respect for yourself," he said, "have some for the people you live among."

Despite their hospitality, a rebel officer walked through the neighbor's office, into his back yard and approached his stable. There, he helped himself to a horse.

Now, Philip Small's family and the neighbor no longer spoke.

• • •

Some in Baltimore could not in good conscience travel northward to York.

Union authorities controlling the city insisted travelers take an oath to the United States.

A friend of the Smalls, who had Southern allegiances, would not do so.

That was just as well, Cassandra Small wrote, because many would not call on her, although real Southerners are more bearable than professed Northerners who masked their allegiance to the South.

• • •

During the five days that the bridge over Conewago

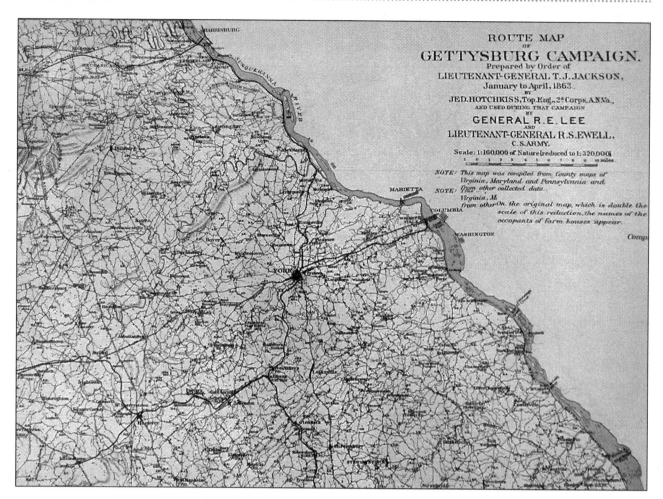

Early in 1863, Gen. Thomas J. 'Stonewall' Jackson ordered Jedediah Hotchkiss, his trusted topographical engineer, to draft a map of southern Pennsylvania. This section of the map covers York County. The darkest lines trace the route of the railroads. The Northern Central Railway extends toward York, bottom, and the Hanover Branch Railroad extends west from the Northern Central at Hanover Junction. The focal point of the Confederate invasion of York County — the bridge between Wrightsville and Columbia — is seen east of York crossing the Susquehanna River. The map also shows ferries crossing the river. Hotchkiss notes on the map that the original large map gives the names of the occupants of the farmhouses. The engineer notes on this map that he used county maps from Pennsylvania and other states. He probably referred to Shearer's map of 1860, pictured on Page 73.

Creek was out, some passengers found a way to continue on their trips.

The hastily built bridge, replacing the structure burned by the Confederates, had given way under the weight of a stock train.

Part of the train ended up in the creek. Three men had been injured, and many animals had been killed.

For the next several days, trains could only go as far as the bridge abutments. But passengers walked across what was left of the bridge to board a train on the other side.

• • •

The twisted rumor made the rounds that President Lincoln's soldiers from the North invaded the county rather than rebel soldiers from the South.

One who heard the report was a woman in Muddy Creek Forks, southeast of York.

Samuel A.W. McPherson, a Lower Chanceford Township native, wrote his sister, Catherine, from his mil-itary post in Harrisburg, "... I hear the leading copperheads is telling the dum Dutch that it was not the rebels, it was Lincoln's hirelings."

McPherson could foresee the war's end.

"I think six months will close the war, if they keep on as they have been doing," he said. "I think Lee will never try the Old Keystone state again."

McPherson had just returned from guarding a railroad car bearing sugar on the Lebanon Valley Railroad near Harrisburg. Someone had broken open the car and hauled off six barrels of the sweet stuff.

His sister had written him about all the soldiers from their neighborhood sent to Camp Curtin in Harrisburg. McPherson had run into these acquaintances. It seemed like home, he wrote, to see so many friends around the Union camp.

He was impressed that one neighbor — a man named McKinley — was in camp.

When such a man is serving his country, his motivation was clear.

"... (I)t was not money nor fear of draft," he wrote, "but love of country."

• • •

George Bair was back in his Codorus Township home.

He went before military authorities in Frederick for his mistaken killing of the Union courier bearing Meade's dispatches.

The authorities exonerated him from all blame in the shooting.

Soldiers experience mixed fortunes

As Confederates were invading the North, nearly 200 soldiers from the 87th Pennsylvania captured at Winchester marched south under guard to Richmond.

There, the rebels divided the prisoners. The commissioned officers went to Libby Prison. The rest ended up at Belle Island on the James River.

Charles E. Gotwalt was one of those county natives on Belle Island. He had argued his way into the war when he was 15 years old and had just turned 17 earlier in 1863.

But at least he would gain parole in a month. Other captives would fight to survive in the unhealthy prison for months. Soon after the prisoners arrived on the island, a Confederate guard asked for the Yankees from York.

About a dozen soldiers responded.

The Confederate Army had visited York, the guard advised, and the battle at Gettysburg had ended in a draw. The rebels were marching toward Philadelphia and New York. With the capture of those cities, the war would be over.

"I'll bet it's a lie," Sgt. Albert Ford stated, "for all their drawn battles are victories for us."

The guard pointed his gun at the sergeant. But seeing no other guards nearby, he did not shoot.

• • •

Cpl. Johnston H. Skelley died in mid-July from wounds sustained in fighting near Winchester.

Skelley, serving in Company C of the 87th Pennsylvania, took a bullet as his regiment fought Dick Ewell's advance in the Shenandoah Valley toward Pennsylvania. The Gettysburg soldier never learned of the death of his fiance, Jennie, just days earlier.

Jennie Wade was baking bread at her sister's residence on Baltimore Street, squarely between the volleys

This illustration from Harper's Weekly shows the Louisiana Tigers attacking a Union battery on Cemetery Hill. The Louisiana Brigade, one of four such units back from their invasion of York County, sustained heavy casualties in its attack against a foe holding higher ground south of Gettysburg.

John B. Gordon's brigade had the first duty of guarding the rear Confederate wagons, similar to the train in this Harper's Weekly engraving, as it left the field at Gettysburg. The long Confederate wagon trains, filled with wounded men, supplies and captured goods, headed with dispatch to the Potomac. The swollen river impaired crossing, but Robert E. Lee's Army had forded the waterway to the safety of Virginia by mid-July.

of sharpshooters dressed in blue and gray fighting in Gettysburg. It was the third day of the battle — July 3 — and the bread was badly needed to feed the soldiers.

That morning, a bullet found its way through a door into the kitchen, striking the 20-year-old in the back. She died instantly.

• • •

Sgt. David Alva Barnett, a York County soldier dressed in blue, had been on the heels of the Confederates since the rebels retreated from the field at Gettysburg on July 4.

It rained all day that Fourth of July, and Barnett was with a group of soldiers positioned about 100 yards from some rebel sharpshooters "who kept picking at every head they could see."

"So we were obliged to lay rather close to the ground, then was comfortable," he wrote from Virginia several weeks later to his cousin, Robert J. Barnett.

David Barnett's 99th Pennsylvania pursued the retreating rebels to within three miles of the Potomac. There, the men found tough opposition from a dug-in enemy. If the Union forces had attacked, the result would have been Gettysburg in reverse.

"Then those great experienced fireside generals would have changed their tune from 'crush Lee's army' to 'drive it from the state,' " wrote the soldier who would die from a wound in November. "They must learn that to crush such an army is no child's play."

• • •

John B. Gordon's brigade drew the dangerous assignment of initially guarding the rear of the Confederate retreat to the Potomac.

It was fitting that the brigade that reached the far-

thest point east — to the shores of the Susquehanna — now represented the eastern-most point of the Confederate Army as it left the battlefield.

At 2 a.m. Sunday, July 5, the Georgians began their protective work. Union skirmishers caught up with the retreating rebels at Fairfield in western Adams County. Gordon detached a regiment, which effectively checked the enemy, allowing the retreating army to gain in its race to cross the Potomac.

Most of Jubal Early's battered division forded the rain-swollen Potomac the night of July 13 and the early morning of July 14 at Williamsport, Md., water up to the soldiers' armpits.

"To the giants in the army, the passage was comparatively easy, but the short-legged soldiers were a source of anxiety to the officers and of constant amusement to their long-legged comrades," Gordon wrote. "With their knapsacks high up on their shoulders, their cartridge boxes above the knapsacks, and their guns lifted still higher to keep them dry, these little heroes of the army battled with the current from shore to shore."

Some put the best face on the high-water crossing, appreciating the much-needed bath, "The first we have had, boys, for weeks, and General Lee knows we need it."

Thus ended the South's three-week invasion of the North.

• • •

Alabaman William D. Lyon, who marched in Gen. John B. Gordon's brigade, was among the fortunate Confederates who stood on the shore of the Susquehanna River in Wrightsville and made it back safely to the south bank of the Potomac.

On July 18, he wrote a letter to his brother, George,

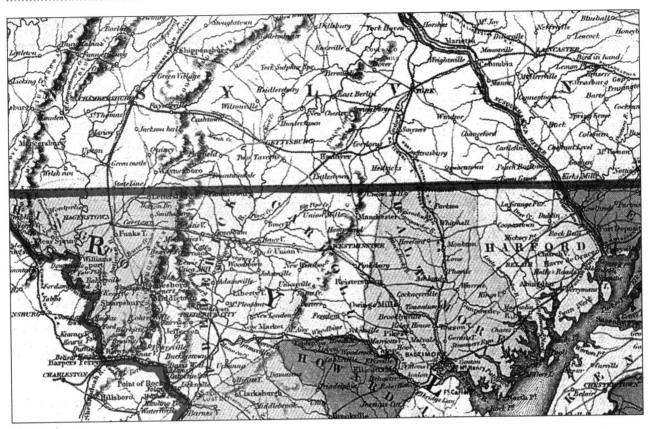

This portion of Johnson's Map of Delaware and Maryland captures the approximate area north of the Mason-Dixon Line covered by the Confederate campaign of 1863. The most intense rebel raiding took place in the area from McConnellsburg to the west; through York County to the Susquehanna River, east; Carlisle, north; and Mason-Dixon Line, south. Confederates also marched through much of northern Maryland, from the Potomac River, west, to Carroll County, east. This map does not completely show McConnellsburg to the west and Carlisle to the north.

illustrating the arc of emotion felt by Lee's men who marched to Pennsylvania's breadbasket expecting victory and then retraced their steps to the South in defeat.

"Separated from the main army, and on to save if possible the bridge which crosses the Susquehanna River between Columbia and Wrightsville. I never enjoyed myself more than I did on that march," he wrote.

"We passed through the most beautiful and highly cultivated country that I ever saw. It was literally a land of plenty. The people, who were all Dutch, were very much frightened of our appearance, and full expected to be the victims of the most horrible atrocities."

Lyon then wrote about defeat at Gettysburg, highlighting the significance of an army accurately understanding topography: "The battle of Gettysburg was by far the most bloody and obstructive battle that Gen Lee's army was ever engaged in. The Yankees had every advantage and were forced to act on the defensive. Gen Lee made a great mistake in storming the heights. It is said that he acted upon what he considered reliable information of the topography of the hills, but which was really unreliable."

• • •

Back in York, a large flag again waved in Centre Square by mid-July, replacing the banner borrowed from the military hospital.

W. Latimer Small kept good on his promise, made as the rebels neared York, that he would supply another flag in case the Confederates carried away the town's banner.

"The flag is of bunting and is far handsomer and more graceful," The Gazette stated, "than the old merino one that formerly flaunted from the same staff."

VII

York County battles
until war ends

July 15, 1863 to April 21, 1865

*'This day . . . shall be remembered as the beginning of
increased Union and Loyalty and Fidelity to the truth.'*
— The Rev. Henry E. Niles, York

'Your children want to hear you'

Abraham Lincoln's train chugged northward on the Northern Central Railway and pulled into the station at Hanover Junction. There, the president changed trains on the last leg of his trip to Gettysburg for a dedication address for Union soldiers at the national cemetery the next day, Nov. 19, 1863.

He was scheduled to meet Andrew Curtin, but the Pennsylvania governor's southbound train did not arrive in time. Lincoln headed west on the Hanover Branch and Gettysburg Railroad for a trip of about 12 miles to Hanover and then another jaunt of 14 miles to Gettysburg.

Lincoln passed the stations in Jefferson and other hamlets, retracing the path taken by thousands of injured soldiers carried on the line from the Gettysburg battlefield only four months before.

At Hanover, Lincoln's train paused on a siding to allow passage of an eastbound train. There, railroad President A.W. Eichelberger and a large crowd welcomed him.

"Father Abraham," M.J. Alleman, pastor of St. Matthew Lutheran Church called out, "your children want to hear you."

That comment brought forth the president.

The Hanover Spectator reported a Lincoln quip, "Well, you have seen me, and according to general experience, you have seen less than you expected to see."

The presidential train continued along the Gettysburg Railroad toward its destination. Lincoln arrived in the small borough about 5 p.m.

• • •

After the president gave his brief address in Gettysburg the next day — brief compared to Edward Everett's preceding two-hour speech — he moved toward a group of wounded Union soldiers, transported with their band from the military hospital in York.

A one-armed captain with the York group had sobbed during the president's address. Someone wrote that "his manly frame shook with no manly emotion ... . He lifted his still streaming eyes to heaven and in low and solemn tones exclaimed, 'God Almighty bless Abraham Lincoln.' "

Addressing the group's chaplain, Lincoln stated, "The men upon their crutches were orators; their very appearance spoke louder than tongues."

• • •

A 15-year-old soprano performed a solo as part of a church choir that day.

For Louisa Vandersloot's good work, she received a handshake and later a fatherly kiss from the tall, bearded gentleman who uttered such simple, profound words at the cemetery.

Before she met Abraham Lincoln, the girl viewed him as unattractive. After looking into his kind and sympathetic eyes, she considered him "pleasing to look upon."

"When Lincoln talked, he said something," Louisa Vandersloot Smith of Hanover said years later.

The size of Lincoln's hand made a lasting impression on "Aunty" Smith, as she was commonly called.

Her tiny hand seemed lost in it.

Abraham Lincoln passed through Hanover Junction on Nov. 18, 1863, to Gettysburg to make his famous address and returned again the next evening after his speech. That much is known. A long-simmering controversy is whether the tall man with the stovepipe hat, center background, is the president. Some believe the figure is A.W. Eichelberger, president of the Hanover Branch Railroad, left.

• • •

After a program at Gettysburg Presbyterian Church, Lincoln and his entourage departed from the station between 7 and 8 p.m. At Hanover Junction, he waited several hours for a train to carry him to another connection in Baltimore and then home to Washington.

Lincoln did not join much in the conversation during the wait with the small party of military and political dignitaries accompanying him.

"Resting on his elbow on the arm of his chair," an observer wrote, "he leaned his head on his hand, listened and smiled at the quaint sayings of those around him, but joined sparingly in their conversation."

Lincoln arrived in Washington after 1 a.m. Soon thereafter, his physician diagnosed Lincoln as suffering from a mild case of smallpox.

• • •

The York Gazette published a couple of reports on President Abraham Lincoln's speech, which became known as the Gettysburg Address.

It ran a brief dispatch on the address from The Age.

"Mr. Lincoln made a joke or two ... ," the newspaper quipped.

The Democrat newspaper from Philadelphia concluded its report with the statement: "With the groans of the wounded still resounding in the air — the corpses of the slain still unburied — the bereaved still clad in the emblems of mourning, and their tears still flowing — these men meet to laugh and joke and electioneer."

The Gazette's own report was more charitable than

P.S. Weaver, a Hanover photographer, captured this scene of the exhumation of the bodies of Union soldiers. Samuel Weaver, holding a book in the foreground, oversaw the exhumation from the German Reformed Church cemetery. The bodies were reinterred in the new national cemetery in Gettysburg. President Abraham Lincoln helped dedicate the cemetery in delivering the Gettysburg Address on Nov. 19, 1863.

The Age.

The York newspaper observed that the president appropriately performed the dedication.

• • •

Residents and businesses in York flew their flags at half staff on the day of Lincoln's speech. Gov. Curtin had asked for such a show of respect throughout Pennsylvania.

The next week, York residents responded to a call from Lincoln for a national observance of Thanksgiving.

Stores and other businesses closed, and churches opened their doors for special services.

Such a day was not new for York County residents. Eighty-six years before, the Continental Congress, meeting in York, had issued a proclamation from York setting aside a national day of Thanksgiving and Praise.

This first of seven such days during the American Revolution came in response to news about another decisive event in an American war. Continental troops had accepted the British surrender at Saratoga, N.Y., in October 1777, considered the turning point of the American Revolution.

'Abolitionists ... produce their inevitable fruits'

That November, Andrew Curtin was giving speeches of his own.

In the general election, the Republican beat George W. Woodward, the Democratic nominee for governor who had edged out Gen. William B. Franklin earlier in the year. Voters in Pennsylvania thereby signaled their accord with Curtin's actions in the face of the Confederate invasion.

But York County voters went against this Republican trend. The county solidly backed Woodward over Curtin by a majority of 2,559 votes.

Pennsylvanians in Richmond's Libby Prison held their own straw poll for governor. The prisoners backed Curtin 95-18.

"... (I)t makes my heart throb with joy to know that Handy Andy (Curtin) is still the peoples choice, this is none of the best places to receive good news but then a word of encouragement is very acceptable just about this time," prisoner Charles P. Stroman of York County wrote to a friend.

• • •

Several months later, The York Gazette railed against

Massachusetts Sen. Charles Sumner.

First, the abolitionist lawmaker presented to Congress a petition from blacks in Philadelphia asking for the right to vote. The Constitution left the power to vote within the jurisdiction of the states, the newspaper contended.

During the same winter week in early 1864, the Republican senator referred to the case of a Negro military officer who had been ejected from street cars for refusing to take one of the cars specially prepared for Negroes and forcing himself into a car filled with white men and women.

The newspaper predicted that the railroad would be compelled to carry a mixture of white and black people in their cars to recognize the dignity of the Negroes.

"It become more evident every day," The Gazette stated, "that the Abolitionists are determined to force on the people complete Negro equality."

To underscore this theme, The Gazette ran another story that edition telling of the wife of a Chester County soldier who eloped with a Negro. She took with her money sent home on occasion by her husband, who was away in the field.

"The teachings of the Abolitionists are beginning to produce their inevitable fruits," the newspaper reported.

• • •

Many in York viewed the spring election of 1864 as a referendum on the decision by David Small and other town officials to surrender to the Confederates.

When election workers counted the tallies in late March, Small bettered his Republican opponent by 206 votes, a nearly 100-vote gain in his victory margin over the previous spring.

Other Democratic candidates fared well, too.

The Gazette observed that, since the rebel invasion, The Republican has been "uttering its foul abuse against our Borough Authorities, falsely charging them with dishonorably surrendering the Borough to the enemy, while the leaders of the Abolition faction have written far and wide to the city papers repeating the foul slanders."

By their votes, York's people have shown their appreciation to the authorities for affording protection, while the abolition leaguers ran away. They deserted their homes, leaving them to the mercy of the enemy.

"They (the voters) have signally rebuked these slanderers of our people ... ," The Gazette commented.

'We would warn those fungi of humanity'

Another voice entered the York County political stage when the U.S. Army General Hospital began publishing The Cartridge Box in March 1864.

The newspaper strove to promote the interests of the sick and wounded soldiers at the military hospital, cheer them to recovery, and relieve the monotony of hospital life.

One edition of the weekly newspaper urged readers to supply books for the hospital library and to establish a reading room.

As for its name, the newspaper provided a ready explanation: "We would rather fight until the last man is slain than yield to southern tyranny: and though we are at present temporarily unfit to take the field and hurl the contents of our trusty cartridge boxes against armed rebellion, yet we will endeavor to make a vigorous use of this cartridge-box, and arm it with such missiles as the God of nature has given us for the benefit of such rebels that are too cowardly to fight ... ."

• • •

The Cartridge Box aimed its guns at the Copperheads, who failed to back Curtin for governor in the previous fall's election.

After the Yankees took the South, they would return home to clean out those who have "slimed over some portions of the fair soil of our Commonwealth."

The soldiers will go snake hunting to clean out the "vile reptiles" from the state.

"We would warn those fungi of humanity," the newspaper warned, "to beware of the blue coat and brass button in the approaching Presidential campaign."

Despite such vitriolic comments, the newspaper refrained from profanity on its pages. In fact, The Cartridge Box reflected a movement within the hospital to discourage profanity, perhaps in deference to women volunteers.

"We the undersigned of the U.S.A. Hospital, York, Pa., 6th ward, 1st room, believe that the habit of using either intoxicating liquors, or profane language is a great sin against our Creator and degrading to ourselves. Resolved, that we will do all in our power to suppress these evils," the newspaper reported.

If any of those signing struck his name from the list, he was required to pay $1.

• • •

The hospital sponsored other entertainment to lessen the tedium of recovery. Patients organized a literary society to meet each Thursday.

A notice in the Cartridge Box said J. M. Johnston, hospital steward, would speak at a March 10 meeting after which those gathered would debate the question: "Resolved, that we are indebted more to man than woman for our character as a nation."

In time, the hospital became a miniature town complete with a school. A Yale-educated teacher came aboard to teach a full curriculum, complete with an optional course of German.

The hospital complex included a post office, printing press, cabinet and carpenter shop, tin shop, bake house, wash house, kitchen and "dead house" or morgue. The camp had "water hydrants" for fires and a sewage system. Workers built a fountain in a flower garden, and the hospital band played in an elevated pavilion surrounded by bushes and plants.

At dinner, 800 patients could eat together, more than resided in many towns in the surrounding county. A track with small cars to convey food ran down the center of the mess table fueled by pulleys, a much-admired convenience for the diners.

• • •

Food remained in abundant supply at York's markets in the spring of 1864, despite demands to feed scores of hospital patients and the fact that scores of countians manned the battlefield instead of the cornfield.

Choice cuts of beef, lamb, mutton, pork and veal were selling at 15 cents per pound and ordinary cuts at 10 to 12 cents.

Butter was priced at 40 cents per pound, dipping to 35 cents on some days. Chickens went for 75 to 80 cents per pair.

The fish markets were well-supplied, although at a premium price. Shad was selling for 50 cents to $1 per pair.

Talk around town dealt with inflated wartime prices — so high as to put many items out of the reach of many families.

But some establishments in town sought business from soldiers in the hospital and those regularly passing through town.

"Is it possible that any soldier can be so foolish as to leave the city without a supply of Halloway's Ointment & Pills?" one business advertised. "Whoever does so will deeply regret it. These medicines are the only certain cure for Bowel complaints, Fevers, Sores and Scurvy."

The cost: only 25 cents for each box or pot.

This drawing shows soldiers from the 87th Pennsylvania 'working on the rail-road' near Petersburg, Va. The soldiers from York and Adams counties were among the Union men who destroyed the Weldon Railroad, a vital supply link to the besieged town of Petersburg, south of Richmond.

'The Johnnies are peppering my dinner'

Soldiers from the 87th Pennsylvania with the rest of the 6th Corps established quarters for the winter of 1863-64 near Brandy Station, Va. The men received a large number of boxes from folks back home in York and Adams counties containing good things to eat. The treats were viewed as highly acceptable Christmas gifts.

Soon afterward, the wives and families of some of the officers came to camp for a winter stay.

"To see ladies here does us all good," one soldier said in a letter home. "The hard every-day life of the army is hostile to the cultivation of refinement of manners. Their presence softens the nature of the soldier, who has been separated so long from home and all its endearments."

• • •

When the weather warmed, the brutal campaigns of 1864 heated up.

This campaign season, most units of The Army of Northern Virginia would not venture north of the Potomac. They stayed at home and attempted to deflate the ever-increasing Union pressure on Richmond.

Cold Harbor was one such battle.

The 87th Pennsylvania bounded over the Confederate works in June. The regiment was one of the first to make it through the rebel line near this strategic crossroads. The York County soldiers captured many North Carolinians from Hoke's Brigade — one of the rebel units that had invaded York the year before.

The 87th sustained losses at Cold Harbor as well.

War stories about these bloody days emerged — and perhaps grew — over the years.

As soldiers lay behind breastworks, according to one story, a tired federal rested on the ground with his squad. A dream agitated him. Unaware of his dangerous position, he raised himself above the breastworks.

A ball from a rebel rifle struck him, and he fell.

"Boys, I'm shot," he said.

"You are dreaming," a fellow soldier said.

"I was dreaming, but am I not hurt? What means this stinging pain in my breast?"

He appeared to drift off to sleep.

The next morning, his comrades found him dead. The ball had passed through his heart.

Avoidable misfortune struck the 87th at Cold Harbor, as well.

Aaron Stahl of the 87th was cooking his dinner one evening at Cold Harbor. As the story was later told, a Confederate rifle ball slammed into the earth near him.

"Hello, the Johnnies are peppering my dinner," he told his mess mates.

"Get down behind the works or they will pepper you," a sergeant said.

"They can't hit me," came the reply as a rifle ball slammed into his thigh.

He dropped to the ground, kicking over the skillet.

"Save my meat!" he exclaimed. "Save my meat."

• • •

After Cold Harbor, the 87th Pennsylvania moved to Petersburg. There, they took part in initial movements that would result in a siege of the town, 20 miles south of Richmond. Union troops would blockade the railroad center from mid-June until just days before the war's end.

Christian List of the 87th, soldiering around Petersburg, moved through some dense underbrush as he and other skirmishers felt out the position of the enemy.

It was growing dark, and List could see only a short distance ahead. He wasn't far in front of his own skirmish line when someone said, "Hello! Yank come with us."

The rebels led him away as a prisoner.

List's fellow skirmishers moved back a bit to wait it out until the morning light would show them where the enemy waited.

Battle lines often proved hard to sort out. This time, a Confederate soldier wandered toward Yankee lines. Armed with canteens filled with water for himself and his fellow rebels, the graycoat became lost on his way back to rebel lines.

He approached the 87th, its men lying in trenches.

The Pennsylvanians spotted the number of the rebel's unit on his hat.

"What regiment is that," the rebel called out.

"The 8th Georgia," came the reply.

"All right, thought yo' uns were Yanks," the reb said, as he climbed into the Union trenches.

"We want you and your canteens, Johnnie," said a

Yankee.

"And you are Yanks, be gad," said the newest Union prisoner.

• • •

The rebels captured about 75 soldiers from the 87th Pennsylvania at Petersburg and marched them toward prisoner-of-war camps in the South. As they walked toward Danville, Va., an elderly woman took a basket of cherries to the Southern guards.

"Grandmother," James Oren of the 87th asked, "will you give me a few cherries?"

"No, I won't," she responded, "you Northern people have no business roaming over our country."

"We are not much interested in this kind of roaming," the Yankee replied.

• • •

The soldiers arrived in Danville in time to celebrate the Fourth of July, 1864, in large tobacco barns. There, they were well-fed, but it was the last good meal for many of them for months — and the last change of clothing, too.

Capt. Henry Morningstar, a Hanover native and a company commander, was in captivity for 21 months. He wore the same clothes the entire time.

Five days after Independence Day, they arrived at Andersonville in Georgia, the largest of the Confederate prisons with about 33,000 prisoners that summer. The prisoners lived under wretched conditions, digging for roots to furnish firewood to cook occasional rations provided by the Confederates. Many starved to death there or died from scurvy or chronic diarrhea.

Henry Shultz, Edward Rudy, Joseph Hummel, William Ramsay, Henry C. Welker, Jeremiah Flinn, Franklin Seip, William S. Stewart, George Bollinger, John Everhart, David G. Myers, Eli Farrar, Frederick Brecht and other soldiers from the 87th died at the Georgia prison.

At one point, a Confederate inspector surveyed the camp and reported to the prison commandant, "This beats anything I ever saw or heard of; it is indeed a hell on earth."

Capt. Henry Wirz, in charge of the prison, dismissed the inspector's report. He would later be hanged for murder for his command of the camp.

• • •

Lt. W.H.H. Welsh of the 87th Pennsylvania, captured at the Battle of Winchester in June 1863, was among a group of prisoners who managed to escape Camp Sorghum near Columbia, S.C.

The Northerners handed a guard $1,800 in Confederate bills as they walked from imprisonment. The guard discovered that he had netted only $400 wrapped around a wad of brown paper. The jilted guard and his companions fired after the escapees, who dropped as if hit and then made their escape in the darkness.

The next day they covered themselves with leaves until night again came.

They worked their way north for the next month, eating fruit, raw pumpkins and occasionally gaining aid from slaves.

At one point, the rebels captured Welsh and his companions, but the lieutenant managed another escape.

Later, Welsh headed north with a group of Confederate deserters.

A squad of Confederate cavalry attacked the group,

Lt. W.H.H. Welsh of the 87th Pennsylvania escaped a Southern prison and worked his way north toward Union lines. At one point, he and other escapees built a log hideout before continuing their adventure. He eventually found safety in Tennessee. His story was uncommon. Many men from York County died in Southern prisoner-of-war camps.

but Welsh again escaped with two others, a Yankee captain from New Jersey and a Confederate deserter named Tinsley.

The trio finally met up with friendly forces near Chattanooga, Tenn.

Welsh took Tinsley home to York, and the Southerner returned to his plantation after the war ended.

Jubal Early stirs up York County, again

Jubal Early was at it again, moving through northern Maryland in early July, 1864. This summer, his target was Washington, D.C. Badly outnumbered Union troops under Gen. Lewis Wallace fought to slow Early's advance until reinforcements could arrive to man fortifications around the nation's capital.

Early's and Wallace's troops engaged at Monocacy Creek near Frederick, Md. Early got the better of it and moved on to the outskirts of Washington by July 11. But Union forces, including men of the 87th Pennsylvania shuttled northward from Petersburg, tied up Early for a day at Monocacy.

Southern forces did not have enough muscle left to raid Washington. Defenses filled with reinforcements as Early stood watching. That day's delay at Monocacy foiled Early's plans.

Early believed his raid was successful, nonetheless.

"Major," Old Jube told one of his officers, "we haven't taken Washington, but we've scared Abe Lincoln like hell."

Fighting at Monocacy proved to be expensive for the 87th. The fighting force sustained heavy casualties — 74 men killed, wounded or missing in action.

• • •

Early's movement on Washington spelled trouble for William B. Franklin.

The general, again between assignments after commands in Louisiana and East Texas, headed by rail to Philadelphia.

Maj. Harry Gilmour, leading a squad of Early's cavalry, raided the Gunpowder River area north of Baltimore, destroying bridges and disrupting telegraph service.

Gilmour's troopers intercepted Franklin's train and gained a prize — a Union major general.

"I was prepossessed from the first in his favor by his blunt, though polite and gentlemanly bearing," Gilmour wrote.

The major did not get to know Franklin well.

On the first night of captivity, the general waited until his drunken guards fell asleep and slipped into the woods.

He hid the next day among blackberry bushes, attempting to fend off mosquitoes and the sun.

He moved again the next night before fatigue and hunger caused him to conclude that he would stop at the first house he found. He came across two farmers who guided him to a house — the dwelling of a Union sympathizer.

A Union cavalry escort returned Franklin to the safety of Baltimore.

Gilmour, meanwhile, had come across his sleeping guards and correctly conjectured Franklin was gone.

"Right glad am I that my pious friends were not there to hear me," Gilmour wrote, "when I found that Franklin had indeed escaped."

• • •

Early's raid north of the Potomac River refreshed still-raw memories of the rebel invasion from the previous summer.

A steady stream of refugees, with horses, cattle and belongings, passed through York on their way to safety eastward. As the numbers of refugees increased, York's bankers and storekeepers sought to ensure the safety of their valuables, dumping them into boxes to move east.

Locomotives and cars from the Hanover and Gettysburg railroads reached town, out of Early's path if he turned north.

Home guards formed after a meeting at the courthouse in York. Recruiting efforts raised five units.

• • •

Business in York came to a standstill as residents waited for Early's next move.

The stores were empty, and banks operated with empty vaults. The Confederates had cut the Northern Central Railway, so no trains could arrive from Baltimore.

"The weather, too, being very warm, added to the general physical and mental languer produced by the entire prostration of business," The Gazette stated.

• • •

When it became clear that Union forces in Maryland would tie up Early's men, a cool breeze blew through York. Refugees passed westward again. Businesses reopened.

Friends and relatives in York County mourned the heavy losses in the ranks of the 87th Pennsylvania. Flags through York flew at half staff. Some traveled to Frederick and Baltimore to check on the wounded. The less severely

York County residents anxiously looked toward the west when a unit of Confederate cavalry raided Chambersburg on July 30, 1864. Gen. John McCausland burned the town, in part as a payback for similar action by Yankee forces in the Shenandoah Valley. 'I am alone responsible,' Gen. Jubal Early later said, 'as the officers engaged were executing my orders.' After observing Early in action, some in York felt vindication for surrendering their town the previous summer.

wounded returned home.

Soon, residents erected a flagpole on South Water Street.

Annie Zimmerman and other women in York presented a flag with "The Union Forever" worked into its fabric.

• • •

The Gazette couldn't resist pointing out that Early's Maryland raiders successfully requisitioned money from Hagerstown and Frederick.

David Small and his newspaper reminded its readers that the people of those towns criticized York when residents answered the requisition the previous summer.

"The people of those places were destined to experience the same humiliation," The Gazette stated, "and are now doubtless more reasonable in their opinions."

With an eye to the fall presidential election, The York Gazette made a horribly prophetic editorial point in pushing for a unified America.

"We hope every good citizen and christian will join in the effort for peace and forgiveness," the newspaper stated. "The answer to such prayers must be the removal of Abraham 'to kingdom come' — the cause must cease before we can hope to be relieved of the effect."

• • •

Such political sentiments moved to the background when the Confederates again threatened the North in late July. A large Confederate cavalry detachment, headed by Gen. John McCausland acting under Early's orders, entered Chambersburg and issued a threat:

"That in retaliation of the depredations committed by Major-General Hunter, of the U.S. forces, during his recent raid, it is ordered that the citizens of Chambersburg pay to the Confederate States by General McCausland the sum of $100,000 in gold; or in lieu thereof $500,000 in greenbacks or national currency was required to ransom the town, otherwise the town would be laid in ashes within three hours."

Chambersburg's fathers chose not to raise the money.

McCausland's men applied the torch to Chambersburg in 50 places.

About 550 buildings burned, York residents soon learned. A full two-thirds of Chambersburg was gone.

• • •

Rumors of the most recent Confederate thrust northward had been floating for days, but an early Saturday morning telegram confirmed the occupation of Chambersburg.

This began a day of escalating concerns in York. Later that day, a dispatch told of the burning of Chambersburg. Then hundreds of refugees reached York County.

York merchants packed again. Some did not have much to box. They had not yet fetched their valuables since Jubal Early had moved on Washington.

On Sunday morning, good news reached York. The Confederates had evacuated Chambersburg and were moving away from them.

By Monday, life was returning to normal.

"At the present writing…a calm has succeeded the storm," The Gazette reported, "and the farmers are again returning with their horses and other effects."

'You have nobly performed your duty'

Their three-year commitment up, many soldiers from the 87th Pennsylvania headed home from their Union camps via the Northern Central Railway.

Telegraph messages moved faster than the train, alerting York that a homecoming would take place in two hours — at 1 p.m. on Sept. 27, 1864.

Citizens met at the courthouse to plan a hastily arranged Centre Square reception, a proper banquet deferred until the soldiers gained their formal discharge several days later.

The train's whistle alerted the town that their heroes approached. Stores and offices closed. A crowd assembled at the train station. Bells pealed, and thousands cheered.

The crowd waved handkerchiefs, and the soldiers stepped off the train to warm handshakes and greetings from friends and relatives.

The procession moved toward Centre Square, to the cheers of the townspeople. The 87th's torn and shredded banner carried in so many battles moved with the procession.

Henry L. Fisher, a York lawyer, welcomed the soldiers in the town square.

"We watched your career in the army, and sympathized with those whose friends have fallen in battle," he said. "Although we have not yet seen the end of the

Sgt. Daniel Reigle of the 87th Pennsylvania won a Medal of Honor for his heroics at the Battle of Cedar Creek. He defended his regiment's flag and captured a rebel banner.

Rebellion, you have nobly performed your duty, and your services will be recorded on the bright pages of history, which shall chronicle the martial deeds of this era."

Col. John R. Schall, regiment commander for the past 16 months, responded on behalf of the soldiers.

The regiment, he noted, had performed their duty as true soldiers — in camp, on the march and on the field of battle.

• • •

Some York County veterans re-enlisted in the 87th, and recruits swelled its ranks. The regiment became part of Gen. Philip Sheridan's Shenandoah Valley campaign. One of Sheridan's objectives was to push Jubal Early's troops from the valley. He met that goal.

Sheridan routed Early's men, many of whom had been in York. The Battle of Cedar Creek in October broke the back of the rebels in the valley.

York County troops, battling against Early's men, sustained heavy losses at Cedar Creek.

The fighting sent several of the 87th regiment's officers out of action.

Capt. Edgar M. Ruhl sustained a mortal wound, Lt. Robert K. Slagle, a severe hip wound, and a bullet caught Lt. Ramsey Hannegan's arm. A spent ball put Lt. George J. Chalfant out of action.

Ruhl's troops recovered their commander's body, and Maj. N.G. Ruhl arrived in camp to recover his son's remains.

Capt. Ruhl was buried in Shrewsbury, in southern York County, with military honors.

• • •

Sgt. Daniel P. Reigle of the 87th became a hero at Cedar Creek.

He was near Edgar Ruhl, carrying a banner, when a bullet struck the captain.

"Boys, it's all up with me," Ruhl cried.

Reigle stuck the flag into the ground and carried his fallen commander to the rear. He then rushed forward to retrieve the banner with the enemy only 10 yards away.

Reigle later fought to capture and hold a battery, finally helping to pull the cannons to the rear because the artillery horses were dead.

When the rebels made a final charge, Reigle captured their flag.

Flags were important to men in uniform, serving as as a beacon for troop movement and forming the heart of the regiment. To defend the flag was an honor; to lose the banner, a disgrace.

Not only had Reigle defended his flag, but the banner he captured would have demoralized the rebel unit. Sheridan recognized Reigle's bravery by sending him to Washington to present the flag to the War Department.

For his bravery, he received the Medal of Honor.

• • •

While many in the 87th were gaining their discharge from service and others fighting on, James Barton answered roll call at Camp William Penn near Philadelphia.

The 19-year-old Wrightsville man was ready to train as part of the 127th Regiment, United States Colored Troops. Enrollment in the USCT unit was a route open for Negro soldiers who wanted to fight for the Union.

A life-threatening case of the measles soon brought his training to a halt.

His head and faced swelled, closing his eyes to the point of blindness. His skin paled and became blotchy.

After two months in the hospital, the Army sent Barton home so his family could care for him.

"(H)e was home for more than a week... ," neighbor Josephine Elizabeth Brown said, "his face was swollen."

• • •

Soldiers from the 87th walked into an officer's tent in November to vote in the presidential race between Abraham Lincoln and George McClellan, the former Union general and now the Democrat candidate.

They were about to exercise their rights under a newly enacted law giving the vote to soldiers in the field. After five hours, the tallies from the 87th were in. Lincoln won by a 74-11 score. Soldiers from all York County units backed Lincoln by a 680-389 vote.

Sheridan's success in the Shenandoah Valley and William T. Sherman's victories in Georgia propelled Lincoln to a second term.

Still, The Gazette attributed the Lincoln margin in military voting to pressure from commanding officers loyal to their commander in chief as well as the denial of ballots to some fighting units that leaned toward the Democrat Party.

Their civic work done, the men of the 87th went on the march again.

• • •

Back home, York County voters backed McClellan over Abraham Lincoln, whose platform emphasized prosecuting the war to the end.

As in the 1860 election, county voters cast tallies out of step with Pennsylvania and the voting states.

McClellan outpaced Lincoln in York County by a 3,225-vote margin, an even larger deficit for the president than in 1860.

The Republican-leaning borough of York had backed Lincoln in 1860 but turned to McClellan, 977-792.

Lincoln won Pennsylvania by better than 20,000 votes and dominated the electoral vote, 212-21.

"Had the Democracy (Democratic Party) elsewhere done as we have done," David Small's Gazette opined, "M'Clellan and Pendleton would have been elected and the country restored to Peace and Union."

The Republican would have none of that.

"... Copperheadism is no where," The Republican said, "though that 'pink of decency,' the loppy of the York Gazette, is trying to whistle, like a frightened boy in a grave yard at night, over the desperate fortunes of his traitorous faction."

Such acute partisanship was echoed out in the county.

"Well, we did whip the Copperheads in Hopewell (Township) this time at the polls and whipped them with

James Barton, Wrightsville, made his mark, above, on this enlistment form. Another part of the form is at left. Barton traveled to Camp William Penn near Philadelphia, where he contracted a severe case of measles that impaired his health for the rest of his life. He recovered sufficiently to serve in the United States Colored Troops.

our fists and sent them home with bloody noses," a resident wrote John Harvey Anderson, a Union soldier fighting far from home in the South.

• • •

In December, James Barton caught up with the rest of 127th regiment at Fort Harrison, Va. There, his regiment manned trenches in the siege of Petersburg.

The soldiers later trailed what was left of Robert E. Lee's Army as it fled Petersburg before giving up at Appomattox Courthouse.

Barton continued to suffer from the aftermath of the measles.

"... (H)e was not put on duty," John Jamison, a fellow soldier and one of several men from Wrightsville to serve in the 127th, "... his face and head did not seem right then."

• • •

Abraham Lighty, a York County soldier in the South, huddled against a "Hericain." He laid behind a stump and could barely catch his breath.

Later, he and "Zach," another county soldier, fought the elements by finding a grassy spot and tucking up together in a gum blanket.

The upcoming campaign will be a hard one, he wrote his wife, Ann.

"... (B)ut I hope God will Spare me to Come Safe through and to get Safe home to see you and the Children for Absenst makes the Hart grow fonder ... ."

He would never see his loved ones again.

Lighty died of fever as a prisoner in South Carolina in February 1865, less than two months before the end of

Goodridge's
Shaving and Hair Cutting Saloon!!
No. 49, North Duke Street, about 10 Doors from
the Railroad Station.

Razors, Scissors, Knives and all kinds of Surgical In-
struments put in order. Good prices paid for human
hair. Wigs, Braids, Frizzetts, Curls and all kinds of
Hair Work made and repaired. Hair, Whiskers and
Moustaches Dyed. Grease, Tar, Paint, &c., removed from
Clothing without injury to the same. my7:65

An advertisement for a barbershop operated by William C. Goodridge appears in a May 1865 edition of The Cartridge Box, above, suggesting that the former slave's business survived the Civil War. This is one of the last evidences of this noted former slave's residence in York. He joined family members in Saginaw, Mich., and Minneapolis later that year.

the war.

• • •

Other county residents served until the war's end, or almost so.

Lt. Samuel W. Keasey of the 87th Pennsylvania led his men in a charge against the Confederate works at Petersburg.

Keasey had been part of countless charges against enemy positions since his Sept. 25, 1861, enlistment.

This time, he was killed instantly, perhaps the last member of the 87th to die in action.

Seven days later, Robert E. Lee surrendered to Ulysses S. Grant at Appomattox Courthouse.

'No man stands higher amongst us'

Glenalvin J. Goodridge, oldest son of the former slave and York merchant, William C. Goodridge, became a free man in time for Christmas 1864.

His release marked a rare moment when the York community set aside its political differences.

In 1862, a York jury had found the photographer guilty and had sentenced him for five years in prison for raping a young woman in his studio.

The conviction had come despite mitigating facts: The woman waited three months to report the attack. Goodridge presented a credible alibi. The jury took 20 hours to reach a verdict.

Many in town questioned the conviction, and 107 prominent Republicans and Democrats petitioned Gov. Curtin for Goodridge's release from Eastern Penitentiary near Philadelphia. The Gazette's David Small and the True Democrat's Hiram Young signed their names as part of a bipartisan group who claimed the jury lacked evidence to

Dr. Charles H. Bressler's letter to Gov. Andrew Curtin helped gain Glenalvin J. Goodridge's pardon.

convict. The True Democrat was a new Republican weekly newspaper in town.

The petition did not quite pry Goodridge loose. Months passed, but William Goodridge, fighting for his son's life, did not give up. He relentlessly sought support for his son's release.

Dr. Charles H. Bressler, a prominent county physician and ardent Republican, was convinced of the unjust conviction.

"There is not a man in our party, but is satisfied that he never would have been convicted if he had been a white man and if he had been a Democrat," he wrote Curtin, his friend and political ally.

Further, many of the "hardest Democrats" in York found the conviction unfair, he argued.

This support helped convince Curtin to pardon Goodridge in December.

He left the penitentiary burdened with disease — the beginning stages of tuberculosis.

• • •

A squad of patients at the U.S. Army Hospital paraded the streets of York on Christmas Day, 1864. They dressed in grotesque costumes, attracting a large crowd and creating immense excitement.

They were following a custom in York of people

By the time the large chapel at the U.S. Army General Hospital, above, opened in early 1865, the complex had been consolidating for months. At one time, the hospital had moved patients into the second and third stories of the four-story Washington Hall, a popular York meeting and entertainment place. In early 1864, hospital officials consolidated the sick and wounded into buildings at Penn Common.

masquerading in the Christmas season. War-time conditions reduced the number of those dressing up that Christmas.

Churches opened as usual on Christmas Day, and congregants at the Catholic and Episcopal churches, in particular, attractively decorated with evergreens.

York residents did not forget the exchange of presents either.

"Notwithstanding the hard times, the custom of giving presents was not neglected, as far as we can learn a whit more than usual," The Gazette observed, "and the amount of money expended for such purposes must have been considerable."

• • •

With the new year, the Yankees had pinned Lee's Army of Northern Virginia in its trenches around Petersburg.

Gen. Philip Sheridan's cavalry controlled the once-fruitful Shenandoah Valley in Virginia, and Gen. William Sherman's men were cutting a swath across Georgia to the sea.

Still, improvements went on to the military hospital in York, suggesting that the Union Army anticipated massive casualties and many more months of fighting in 1865.

In January, seven wards stood, each measuring 200 feet long and 18 feet wide.

A new chapel, measuring 200 feet long, 28 feet wide and 14 feet in height, was dedicated.

"We have now ... a building in which all those in the Hospital can hear the Word of Life preached ... ," The Cartridge Box stated.

The chapel would be used as a school during the week, and Drs. Alexander Blair, George Byers and E.F. Spaulding drew assignments to educate patients so they could be self-supporting upon their release.

Drs. H.F. Bowden, James W. Kerr and H.L. Smyser

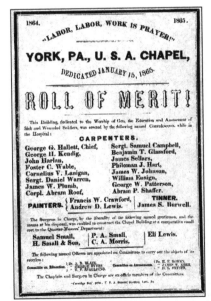

This handbill celebrates completion of a chapel at York's military hospital in January 1865. Soldiers worshipped in the chapel for only a few months. The war ended in April, and the military hospital closed later that year.

drew assignments to provide evening entertainment and instructional activities for patients in the chapel. The chapel was valued at $6,000. Strict economy by a carpenter's corps, led by George G. Hallett, meant the cost to the U.S. government was no more than $200.

The York Gazette sought to bestow proper credit. In an editor's note with its republication of The Cartridge Box's story, The Gazette added, "This is owing, we understand, to the management and liberality of the Building Committee, consisting of Messrs. Samuel Small, Eli Lewis, P.A. Small, C.A. Morris, and H. Small & Son, of this borough."

• • •

The York Gazette criticized Abraham Lincoln's speech inaugurating the start of his second term in

March 1865.

Reflect upon four weary years of war, extravagance and corruption, The Gazette urged. And remember the change of a once-happy country from prosperity and glory such as the world has never witnessed to the gloomy present.

Lincoln's short speech lacked focus and suggested its author could not clearly see or define his own policy, the newspaper stated. He sees the difficulties. The president fears to look at them.

"Four years more of such rule! Can the country survive it?" The Gazette asked. "Is there any hope?"

• • •

The chief executive's speech impressed Charles E. Gotwalt, the York soldier who had entered the service at 15. Gotwalt had just gained a second parole, this time after surviving Andersonville. He recuperated from his five months of confinement at Annapolis, Md., and received his discharge paper in February.

He traveled to the nation's capital to collect back pay for his prison time. There, he heard Lincoln's second inaugural speech with the words: "With malice toward none; with charity toward all."

One evening, he shook the commander in chief's hand. He stood in a long line that moved slowly toward the president. At last, he reached the chief executive, who gave the 19-year-old a pump-handle shake and the greeting, "How do you do?"

Gotwalt kept in line and walked to a White House window where a plank led the line to the ground.

• • •

The True Democrat informed York County residents on March 7, that Philip Sheridan had routed Jubal Early's command and had taken the much-despised general captive.

"Gen. Sheridan at Work, Grand Success of His Movement, The Capture of Charlottesville — Total Defeat of Gen. Early — Early and Most of His Command Captured — Lee Moving Forces to Lynchburg," the newspaper reported under the headline "Latest War News!"

Hiram Young's Republican weekly had quickly positioned itself in opposition to the Democrat Party and its loudest voice, The York Gazette.

County residents wishing for Early's comeuppance soon learned that word of his capture at Waynesboro, Va., was greatly exaggerated. He escaped with 20 others. Federal figures indicate that they captured 1,600 of Early's men, 17 flags, 11 cannons and all of the general's supplies.

Robert E. Lee relieved the Virginian of what was left of his command, and a disguised Early headed west to Texas with plans to meet up with the Trans-Miss. Department, headed by Gen. Kirby Smith.

• • •

A handbill circulated around York on the eve of the borough's spring 1865 election.

"What effort has been made by the Democratic Borough Council and Chief Burgess to obtain repayment of the amount demanded of the Borough at the point of Gen. Early's bayonets?" the handbill asked and then provided an answer, "None that the public know of."

The Democrats had no standing to ask the Republican-led federal or state governments for repayment of an amount now counted at $40,000 in cash and

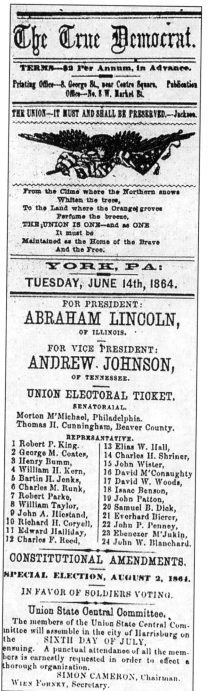

The True Democrat.

TERMS—$2 Per Annum, in Advance.

Printing Office—8. George St., near Centre Square. Publication Office—No. 8 W. Market St.

THE UNION—IT MUST AND SHALL BE PRESERVED.—Jackson.

From the Clime where the Northern snows
Whiten the trees,
To the Land where the Orange groves
Perfume the breeze,
THE UNION IS ONE—and as ONE
It must be
Maintained as the Home of the Brave
And the Free.

YORK, PA:
TUESDAY, JUNE 14th, 1864.

FOR PRESIDENT:
ABRAHAM LINCOLN,
OF ILLINOIS.

FOR VICE PRESIDENT:
ANDREW JOHNSON,
OF TENNESSEE.

UNION ELECTORAL TICKET.
SENATORIAL.
Morton M'Michael, Philadelphia.
Thomas H. Cunningham, Beaver County.

REPRESENTATIVE.

1 Robert P. King.	13 Elias W. Hall.
2 George M. Coates.	14 Charles H. Shriner.
3 Henry Bumm.	15 John Wister.
4 William H. Kern.	16 David M'Conaughty
5 Bartin H. Jenks.	17 David W. Woods.
6 Charles M. Runk.	18 Isaac Benson.
7 Robert Parke.	19 John Patton.
8 William Taylor.	20 Samuel B. Dick.
9 John A. Hiestand.	21 Everhard Bierer.
10 Richard H. Coryell.	22 John P. Penney.
11 Edward Halliday.	23 Ebenezer M'Jukin.
12 Charles F. Reed.	24 John W. Blanchard.

CONSTITUTIONAL AMENDMENTS.
SPECIAL ELECTION, AUGUST 2, 1864.
IN FAVOR OF SOLDIERS VOTING.

Union State Central Committee.
The members of the Union State Central Committee will assemble in the city of Harrisburg on the SIXTH DAY OF JULY, ensuing. A punctual attendance of all the members is earnestly requested in order to effect a thorough organization.
SIMON CAMERON, Chairman.
WIEN FORNEY, Secretary.

By the summer of 1864, Hiram Young's True Democrat joined The York Republican as Republican voices against Democratic Party organs, The York Gazette and The Democratic Press. Young's newspaper suggested its Republican principles reflected the historical voice of the Democrats and thus called it 'True Democrat.' Before the war, Republicans produced three newspapers in York. Before the True Democrat began publishing, the number of newspapers considered to be oriented toward Republicans was down to one, and the Democratic majority had grown substantially in York County. Thus, Young started his newspaper to help balance the scales. Young later converted his weekly into a daily, The York Dispatch.

supplies.

"No, not when it is known that that party sympathises with the rebels in arms, in their efforts to overthrow the government," the handbill contended.

The politicking did not help the Republican candidate for chief burgess, even a man as respected as Charles H. Bressler. David Small captured another term — his fourth — by a majority of 235. Since first elected by a 59-vote margin in 1862, Small had quadrupled his margin.

The Gazette conjectured the Republican-generated handbill backfired, causing a crossover vote in Small's favor.

As for Small's lack of success in gaining

reimbursement for the "Early debt," even influential Republican Franklin County representative A.K. McClure could not push a payment measure through the state Legislature just the previous week.

The borough would eventually assume the debt and then tax property owners, the benefactors of the requisitions that allayed Early's wrath. The property taxes, in turn, paid off the debt.

Seven hundred and twenty-three county residents would put forth $124,728 in claims for damages caused primarily by the rebels.

The True Democrat discounted a Republican misfire as the reason for Small's victory.

"We have always respected Mr. Small as a man and a gentleman," The True Democrat stated.

"No one doubts his personal respectability, or can be ignorant of his standing and influence in society. Apart from his copperhead proclivities, no man stands higher amongst us, or is more popular with the masses of people."

But Small needed to throw aside politics, the Republican newspaper lectured. If he persisted in his former system of appointing men for political purposes, his administration would be a failure.

"He is precisely the man," the newspaper said, "who is calculated to do much harm or much good, in the position he occupies."

'The boys had a gay time in York'

Mary C. Cox, a telegraph operator for the Northern Central Railway in York County, was accustomed to receiving and keying sensitive military messages traveling up and down the telegraphic corridor.

One message, dated Monday, April 3, 1865, was particularly significant.

Cox snatched a report off the telegraph wire from Union Gen. Godfrey Weitzel.

Richmond had fallen.

Weitzel's message said Union troops took the Confederate capital at 8:15 a.m., capturing many big guns. The enemy left them behind, departing in great haste. Union forces in Richmond worked to put out part of the city that was on fire.

"The people received us with enthusiastic expressions of joy," the telegraph said, "Genl. Grant started early this morning with his army . . . to cut of Lee's retreating army if possible. President Lincoln has gone to the front."

• • •

York set a celebration for Thursday, April 6, but rainy weather postponed the event until Saturday. The need for Union loyalists to celebrate boiled over in York. An inaccurate report on Friday that Robert E. Lee had surrendered to Union Gen. U.S. Grant gave them a reason. It also nearly caused a riot.

A crowd of convalescents from the military hospital and other Yankees walked through town, ensuring that American flags were duly displayed as a sign of loyalty.

In most cases, they did not have to work hard. Residents threw flags to the breeze, and bells rang continuously. People crowded the streets, extending their hands in congratulations.

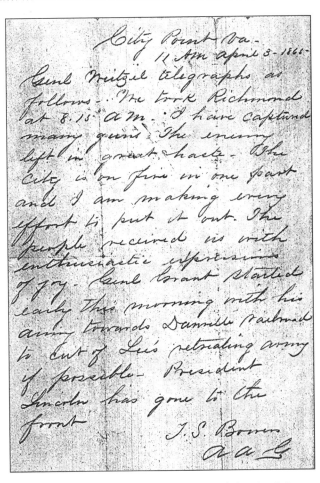

Telegraph operator Mary C. Cox received this April 3, 1865, message indicating that Richmond had fallen. Gen. Ulysses S. Grant, general in chief of all Union armies, directed the Union pursuit of the fleeing Army of Northern Virginia. Six days later, Robert E. Lee surrendered his Army to Grant at Appomattox Courthouse, Va.

Robert J. Fisher, judge of York and Adams counties, refused to be muscled by a crowd celebrating a premature report that Robert E. Lee had surrendered his Army. The crowd pressed Fisher to display an American flag, but the judge contended that an unruly bunch should not dictate a judge's actions. Here, Lewis Miller shows Fisher, left, with his predecessor Daniel Durkee. Fisher served three 10-year terms as judge.

The celebrators gave special attention to Democrats and passed by houses of Republicans who did not display flags, according to The Gazette.

"In several cases, when those on whom they waited refused at the dictation of the mob to put out flags, protesting that they are as good Unionists as any, the windows were broken and other riotous demonstrations made," The Gazette stated.

Judge Robert J. Fisher was one recipient of the crowd's visit. The Gazette particularly criticized the crowd's visit to homes occupied by only women and children, where it caused great consternation. Many of those residing in the targeted homes had provided aid and comfort for Union soldiers.

"It is gratifying to know that many of these parties are known and marked, and will at some day receive their just deserts," The Gazette stated. "Now at a time when at the end of four years of bloody war, and common sacrifices, when peace appears to be dawning, and all should be rejoiced in the hope at a return of peace and Union, every good citizen, of all parties, should endeavor to foster charity and friendship."

The Democratic Press said the judge was ill and resting. He did not have a flag and intended to get one the following day. But after a visit from such a mob, he would not show any flag to satisfy its whims. Such action would be improper for the chief judicial officer in York and Adams counties.

It was then that a rock went through one of the windowpanes of the Fisher house.

At another point, the mob entered Peter McIntyre's house through a window, went upstairs and hung a flag out the window.

The outrage of the attacks, The Press stated, was that many of the victims had taken an interest in the sick and wounded at the military hospital.

"And in one instance, before there were any hospital accommodations here," The Press noted, "Judge Fisher had a sick soldier, who was an entire stranger, taken to his house and carefully nursed for six weeks."

• • •

In the True Democrat, the Republican newspaper, that same day, the convalescents had their say: When word came in about the Union victories, every soldier in the hospital gave an exuberant cheer. Even the cripples, those who had trouble getting around, flew their flags.

Some soldiers spent their last cent, and others paid $10 to buy flags for those in York who didn't have any. Dr. S.J.W. Mintzer, who had replaced Henry Palmer as chief surgeon, also supplied 50 small flags, and the convalescents started around town, accompanied by celebrating York residents.

"The gate was opened and the boys had a gay time in York ... ," one patient stated.

They suspended Jefferson Davis's effigy over George Street. A card on his back stated, "Jeff in the Last Ditch." A marking on its front said, "The Traitor's Doom."

When they came to Judge Fisher's house on East Market Street, their only request was that he display his flag. He said he had none.

"He was then asked to wave a flag, which was extended toward him," the convalescents wrote, "but he refused to do so, and let it fall to the ground, as though to touch it was pollution."

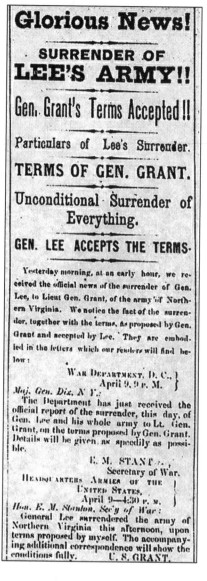

Glorious News!

SURRENDER OF LEE'S ARMY!!

Gen. Grant's Terms Accepted!!

Particulars of Lee's Surrender.

TERMS OF GEN. GRANT.

Unconditional Surrender of Everything.

GEN. LEE ACCEPTS THE TERMS.

Yesterday morning, at an early hour, we received the official news of the surrender of Gen. Lee, to Lieut Gen. Grant, of the army of Northern Virginia. We notice the fact of the surrender, together with the terms, as proposed by Gen. Grant and accepted by Lee. They are embodied in the letters which our readers will find below:

WAR DEPARTMENT, D. C., April 9, 9 P. M.
Maj. Gen. Dix, N. Y.:
The Department has just received the official report of the surrender, this day, of Gen. Lee and his whole army to Lt. Gen. Grant, on the terms proposed by Gen. Grant. Details will be given, as speedily as possible.
E. M. STANTON, Secretary of War.

HEADQUARTERS ARMIES OF THE UNITED STATES, April 9—4:30 P. M.
Hon. E. M. Stanton, Sec'y of War:
General Lee surrendered the army of Northern Virginia this afternoon, upon terms proposed by myself. The accompanying additional correspondence will show the conditions fully.
U. S. GRANT.

U.S. Grant

The True Democrat alerts readers in its April 11, 1865, edition of Robert E. Lee's surrender of The Army of Northern Virginia to U.S. Grant's Army of the Potomac. Word of the surrender reached York early the day before. The news caused celebrations throughout York County. 'News came that Lee surrendered his whole army to Grant,' Wrightsville diarist George Stoner Beidler wrote on April 10. 'Bells ringing all around this morning.' In the Copperhead stronghold of Peach Bottom, people in the village lighted candles, fired guns and heard an inspirational speech from North Carolinian D.P. Once. Rob Dunn announced he had only done one thing in his 60 years to hurt the Union — vote for 'Jim Buchanan' for president. Dr. Hugh Burk said he had always voted Democrat and hoped the people would forgive such past crimes, which he would not repeat. 'We think a little more good news,' a newspaper reported, 'a few more illuminations, and a few more meetings of this kind in Peach Bottom, will totally and forever demoralize the Democratic party of this section.'

Fisher called the crowd a mob, talked about his power to enforce the civil law and claimed they were soused. If they were drunk, the convalescents countered, it with joy of the Union victory. Further, drinking houses closed with the reception of the good news and not a glass of liquor could be purchased in the borough.

"His language and demeanor was such, throughout the entire colloquy, as to provoke and court assault," the

Select Miscellany.

WHAT WILL BE DONE WITH OUR HOSPITAL.

An order issued from the Surgeon General's office, in the city of Washington, on the 5th day of May inst., to the effect that the "Medical Directors will, as rapidly as possible, reduce the number and accommodations of General Hospitals within their Departments, retaining such buildings as are owned by the United States, or occupied without rental and substituting, with permanent commands, posts for General Hospitals."

This order will doubtless have the effect of closing up many of the military hospitals in the country, and the question has been put to us, "What will be done with ours?" Of course this question is difficult to answer. We do not know whether it will be closed or kept on. The Surgeon in Charge has not, to our knowledge, any positive orders upon the subject. Our own opinion, heretofore expressed, and founded upon our own personal knowledge of the hospital, is, that it would be of infinite advantage to the government to retain it as long as the sick and wounded men of our army require care and attention. There is no rent paid by the government for the ground upon which the buildings are erected. It is an open common and has been known as such since the first organization of the commonwealth. This, of course, brings it within the meaning of those expressed in the order, which are to be retained. But whether retention will be permanent, or otherwise, of course will finally be determined by the authorities which have the matter in charge. What their duty will be, under the circumstances, we do not claim the liberty to suggest.

An editorial in this May 1865 issue of The Cartridge Box, the newspaper published at the U.S. Army General Hospital, ponders whether the military medical facility would remain at Penn Common, an area of historical importance to York residents or face demolition after the last patient left. The latter option won the day.

Lewis Miller captures the joyous spirit of the North after hearing about the Confederate surrender. 'Changes their tune,' Miller wrote under the drawing. He added, 'Our gun is pois'd, our aim is Sure, Our wish is good, our End is pure; To virtue we are Sworn allies, And Shoot at folly as it flies.'

flag, the judge clearly replied, "I will do nothing at the demand of a rioutious assembly and command that you disperse."

An ugly incident was avoided in a manner not recorded in the newspapers.

Mary C. Fisher, the judge's wife, appeared in a second-story window with a flag. At the same time, Union officers approached the crowd.

"The crowd cheered good naturedly and moved on," Niles wrote.

• • •

The day after the convalescents' rowdy exhibition, York held its official celebration of the fall of Richmond. The town of York celebrated in a fashion practiced often in its past — by planning a grand procession and illuminating houses. A makeshift parade wound through York's streets for two hours.

Able-bodied hospital residents marched in the procession, joined by two horse-drawn ambulances with disabled soldiers. A wagon pulled the hospital's press, which printed circulars given to the crowd. David Small and other borough leaders rode in the procession. The Vigilant Fire Company's Gallery Engine, pulled by four white horses, moved near the end of the marchers, bearing the 87th Pennsylvania's flag.

After two hours, marchers disbanded, and residents went home to eat their supper. The whole town awaited April's darkness to set in. As soon as residents lit candles, crowds gathered to view the shining homes in such numbers that they spilled from the paved sidewalks into the dirt streets.

"... (O)ur town shone with such a brightness as to eclipse the light of the moon, even though she sailed through a cloudless sky," The Gazette stated.

Music from the local Philby Cornet Band and a brass band from Baltimore combined with the pleasant sound of mingling multitudes to create a long-remembered evening.

"The lights were kept burning long after the appointed hours," The Gazette stated, "and as they were gradually distinguished, the crowd again sought their homes well pleased with the ceremonies of the day."

• • •

The next day — Sunday, April 9 — Lee surrendered to Grant at Appomattox Courthouse, Va.

Artillerist Abraham Rudisill celebrated the surrender with his artillery unit at City Point, The Army of the Potomac's base of supplies in its Richmond and

convalescents wrote.

At that moment, Mintzer arrived and ordered the men to retire. The convalescents obeyed, but the judge continued his indiscreet comments. Up to that point, the convalescents had been onlookers, but they stepped forward and called the judge a Copperhead and traitor to his country.

• • •

Six-year-old Henry C. Niles, son of York's new Presbyterian minister, viewed the crowd's dispute with the judge from a half block away. He provided details from what he saw and later heard:

Indeed, the cheering band of soldiers from the hospital paraded the streets demanding that flags be flown from all houses.

Sarah Small and Isabel Small, whose houses sat across the East Market and North Duke Street intersection from each other, appeared in the windows of their residences with large flags. The crowd greeted this show of support from the wives of Philip and Samuel Small, respectively, with cheers.

But the band seemed particularly drawn to the homes of prominent citizens known to hold Copperhead views.

One rumor stated that the crowd threw stones and a brickbat at the Fisher residence or perhaps a round from a pistol passed through a front parlor window. That aroused the judge, who appeared at the door with his glasses perched atop his head of white hair. Fisher was fearless. Two years before, he stood unfazed in dissuading Jubal Early from burning the courthouse records.

So, when the crowd demanded that he put out his

Petersburg campaign. The Union men cheered, fired their guns and lighted bonfires.

The next day, Rudisill wrote in his diary, "Praise the Lord for victory."

Early that Monday, word of the surrender reached York.

• • •

Differences cut through the York community even as it came together to observe the war's end.

The U.S. surgeon general was deciding which military hospitals to keep open for permanent use. The rest would be closed as soon as the wounded recovered.

A writer in The Cartridge Box believed that prisoners should not be moved from the hospital on Penn Common.

The York County location commended itself for a permanent hospital.

It was located in the finest agricultural area in the land. Water was pure and abundant, food inexpensive and plentiful, and rail connections ran in all directions.

But some in town opposed the long-term use of the Common as a military hospital.

"But those who are opposed, are principally of the class of politicians whose personal comfort is greatly interfered with by the appearance among them of the blue coat and brass button," the hospital's newspaper stated, "who have been, through this whole war, notorious sympathizers with the rebellion, and have never had any special love or affection for Union soldiers."

These opponents would much prefer "a legion of the offscourings of the graybacked chivalry" than men of "iron heart and patriotic impulse" who have just won the war.

"The authorities in determining the question whether the York Hospital shall be continued, of course, will attach no importance to their opinion," the newspaper said.

• • •

The Gazette was one of those opponents. At war's end, the newspaper noted the closure of the hospital ward at Washington Hall. Only 674 patients remained at the Penn Common hospital.

"Now that the war is over," the newspaper observed, "there will probably be no occasion for the continuance of this hospital for any great length of time."

As it turned out, military authorities sided with The Gazette.

• • •

The war's end came at a time when a series of conflicting events evoked mixed emotions in York County.

The military hospital, indeed, was winding down, but the Children's Home to accommodate orphans of those soldiers killed in the war opened at a former dwelling on East Market Street. It would soon have a new home of its own on East Philadelphia Street. The Ladies Aid Society was shifting its attention from the hospital to the Children's Home.

The fighting was over, but word still filtered into the county about deaths on Southern battlefields.

William Decker, son of Samuel Decker of York, was killed near Richmond in the last days of the war. The body of the youth, listed at about 18 years old, had not yet been recovered.

Decker counted among the 6,200 men to serve in the Union Army from York County. He was among the last to die. Those with service records in these years came to

Lawrence August Gobright, a Hanover native and longtime Associated Press correspondent in Washington, D.C., covered the assassination of Abraham Lincoln. 'I carefully wrote my dispatch, though with trembling and nervous fingers,' his memoirs stated.

As a youngster, John Wilkes Booth spent a few weeks in a private boys school in York. 'Jack had a yellow streak in him,' classmate Clarence F. Cobb said years later.

Edman 'Ned' Spangler, a York County native, was implicated in the Lincoln assassination conspiracy. He was convicted and imprisoned on charges that he cared for John Wilkes Booth's horse when the actor went inside to perform his deadly act. Spangler served four years of his prison sentence. After his release on a pardon, the York native lived out the remaining six years of his life in the Maryland home of Dr. Samuel Mudd. Mudd, also implicated in the conspiracy for treating Booth, met Spangler in prison. Nettie Mudd, Samuel's wife, described Spangler: 'His greatest pleasure seemed to be found in extended kindness to others and particularly children, of whom he was very fond.' As for Spangler's involvement in Lincoln's death, a newspaper conjectured years later: 'Booth had failed to mention to him that he intended to shoot President Abraham Lincoln, a fact Spangler found difficult to prove to a jury.'

about half of the approximately 13,000 county men between the ages of 18 and 45 years.

Soldiers by the hundreds traveled northward through York County on the Northern Central to be mustered out of service in Harrisburg. But three or four soldiers who escaped death on the field or from disease in camp met an untimely end on the railroad. They made the mistake of standing on moving railcars, not seeing approaching low-clearance bridges.

In one case, Fred Denkert, called "Dutch Fred," had recovered well enough to gain release from York's mili-

The York Gazette, no friend to President Lincoln, published an account of the president's assassination complete with heavy score lines between columns to flag the seriousness of the news. The Gazette expressed dismay over the assassination of the man who the newspaper had so long opposed. The crime was unparalleled in the history of America and designed to paralyze the people and fill the land with sorrow. 'The Chief Magistrate of the Country, the chosen servant of the people struck down in the prime of life... ,' the newspaper lamented, 'just at this critical period when all lovers of their country were looking to President Lincoln for restoration of an honorable peace and the Union... '

tary hospital.

On his way home, he fell under the wheels of the train on which he was riding. The wheels severed his head and mangled his body. His broken body was taken back to the hospital for a coroner's inquest.

Denkert was believed to have been under the influence of alcohol.

"Another warning and example to our brave men to be careful how they indulge in the use of intoxicating drinks," The Gazette admonished.

It was only early spring, but county schools had closed early. Many teachers shouldered muskets, rather

The telegraph lines from Washington via Hanover Junction to York sparked with the news of the assassination of President Abraham Lincoln. Chief Burgess David Small immediately issued a handbill calling for all businesses to close for the rest of the day.

than the responsibility of teaching the young. But school officials established the next term for November when the soldier/teachers were home from the field.

Philip Small and others asked the Northern Central Railway for an appropriation toward paying the expenses of about $40,000 incurred by the borough in protecting the town and railroad property during the Confederate occupancy two years before. But the railroad came through with only a fraction of the amount, contributing $2,500.

An immense harvest of wheat, rye, oats and other grass crops were expected. The prospects for peaches, pears, cherries and plums looked good. These bounties were important to help feed a county and nation recovering from war. But judging by the few blossoms evident on apple trees, it would not be a bearing year.

At least men would be home to help with the harvest. In past harvests, reports came in from the country that valuable crops rotted in the field because of lack of hands to bring them in.

• • •

Despite such happenings of import, community life struggled for normality. Residents looked forward to a visit by Thayer & Noyes Celebrated Circus with Van Amburgh's far-famed Menagerie.

The star of the circus would be the war elephant, Hannibal. York residents caught a glimpse of the 7,000-pound animal, reportedly insured for $10,000, when it passed through on its way to another stop.

With the bridge still out, Hannibal crossed the Susquehanna on the ferry without incident, feeling his way aboard the craft and standing firm and erect until his landing at Wrightsville.

The Gazette touted the elephant as the largest passenger ever carried on the ferry.

'This is an occasion without parallel'

Lawrence August Gobright, veteran Washington cor-

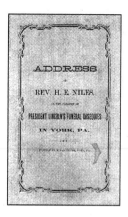

Although new in town, the Rev. Henry E. Niles, minister of the Presbyterian Church, had the honor of giving one of two addresses at a community funeral service for Abraham Lincoln in York. 'Fellow citizens!' Niles preached, 'It is impossible adequately to express our proper abhorrence of this deed of blood!' The sermon was later printed, left, for wide distribution.

respondent for The Associated Press, had seen the blood.

He had examined the gun used in the shooting.

Now the Hanover native, with shaking hands and trembling fingers, was ready to write his dispatch, the most important story he would ever write.

"The President was shot in a theatre to-night," he wrote from Washington, D.C., "and is perhaps mortally wounded."

• • •

S.I. Koontz, a former York County resident, sat 15 feet from Abraham Lincoln in Ford's Theatre when John Wilkes Booth fired his deadly shot on Friday, April 14. The U.S. Treasury Department worker wrote to a Dillsburg friend to look out for the gunman, who went to school in York County as a youth.

"Booth is just as likely to be in York County as anywhere else," Koontz informed blacksmith William Weaver, "and if you see a suspicious character about five feet, eight inches tall, with black hair and eyes, good looking, have him arrested."

Booth was not in York County, but in Virginia, where he was tracked down and shot 12 days later.

• • •

Booth had asked Ned Spangler, an acquaintance and stagehand at Ford's Theatre, to hold his horse for a few minutes, according to the story later recounted in court.

Booth went inside the theater where he shot Lincoln.

Spangler, a York native, prossibly met Booth in 1853 during the actor's short stint in York.

The prosecution's net pulled Spangler into the assassination conspiracy. Spangler unsuccessfully argued that he arranged for another person to hold Booth's horse because his duties as a scene changer required his attention inside.

The court sentenced him to spend hard time in Florida's Fort Jefferson.

• • •

The people of York awoke early Saturday morning to news of Abraham Lincoln's death. At first, the barest of details came through the telegraph office. Lincoln and Secretary of State William H. Seward had been shot. Lincoln's wounds were fatal beyond all hope.

"Many entirely disbelieved it," David Small wrote in his Gazette, "and all hoped it was not true."

Soon, the wire flashed words that proved to the shocked people that the earlier message was no canard, as some contended. The president was dead.

"Within the memory of the writer of this," Small reported, "York never experienced a day of such universal

PROCLAMATION!

An Address issued to the People of the United States by W. Hunter, Acting Secretary of State, dated Washington, April 17th, announces "that the Funeral ceremonies of the late lamented Chief Magistrate will take place at 12 o'clock, noon, on Wednesday, the 19th instant," and invites all religious denominations to meet "at that hour for the purpose of solemnizing the occasion with appropriate ceremonies," therefore, in accordance with the above recommendation as well as with a Resolution of the Town Council of the Borough of York, adopted at a meeting held on Monday Evening last, the Citizens are requested

1. To close all places of business between the hours of 11 o'clock A. M. and 3 P. M.

2. To attend Religious Services at the Lutheran Church on George Street, (Rev. Dr. Lochman's,) commencing at 12 o'clock, noon.

3. To toll the bells between the hours of two and three o'clock in the afternoon.

DAVID SMALL, Chief Burgess.

York, April 18, 1865.

PROGRAMME of the Funeral Exercises agreed upon by the Clergy on the occasion of the Burial of President Lincoln.

Rev. A. W. LILLY, TO CONDUCT EXERCISES.

Hymn, Rev. A. W. Lilly.——Prayer, Rev. J. H. C. Dosh.——Scriptures, Rev. C. W. Thomson.——Address, Rev. H. E. Niles.——Hymn, Rev. W. W. Evans.——Address; Rev. G. M. Slaysman.——Prayer, Rev. J. O. Miller.
Doxology 760.

This handbill invites York residents to attend religious services at Christ Lutheran Church in York, concurrent with services for assassinated President Abraham Lincoln in Washington, D.C. Ministers from several York churches conducted the service. Americans across the land attended church services at the same time as Abraham Lincoln's funeral in Washington, D.C., at noon April 19, 1865.

gloom... ."

If the day had been bright, it would have taken on a melancholy hue. But the day was cloudy. Rain fell. The news of Lincoln's death took on an even more terrible tone. The gloom was profound. The gloom was irrepressible.

Those were the tearful thoughts of David Small, the newspaper man and longtime Lincoln opponent. But as in so many other times of public crisis, Small had work to do as chief burgess.

He put forth a proclamation of how those in town

should conduct themselves that day.

"In consequence of the death of President Lincoln ... the citizens of the borough of York are hereby enjoined to observe the following order as an expression of their deep regret at the great and sudden calamity which has befallen the country at this critical juncture of its affairs ... ."

The proclamation suspended business in York after noon. Bells should toll from 1-2 p.m.

Flags should flay at half staff or draped in mourning.

The order about how to portray flags was not needed.

The people of York had already responded. Flags appeared draped in windows throughout the borough.

• • •

On Sunday, congregations worshiped in the midst of the black of mourning instead of Easter palms and lilies. Clergymen remembered the president's death in prayers on this "Black Easter."

The installation of the Rev. Henry E. Niles, who had replaced Thomas Street in the Presbyterian church's pulpit, took place on Sunday night rather than in the morning service.

The Rev. John H.C. Dosh, pastor of the Methodist church, conducted a well-attended Sunday night service. The minister's solemn sermon brought many to tears.

"The town wore a sad and solemn aspect," The True Democrat reported, "the bells in all our churches were tolled, and everyone felt as though a great and terrible calamity had befallen the country."

Below that report, a notice informed readers that portraits of the martyred president could be purchased at True Democrat owner Hiram Young's bookstore on West Market Street.

• • •

Lincoln's assassination stirred emotions throughout York County.

In Stewartstown, John Gemmill was driven out of town for an ill-advised comment.

He reportedly said, "It served Lincoln right. He should have been shot long ago."

To which, some boys pelted him with rotten eggs.

"The aim of young America on that occasion was straight and true," a resident wrote John Harvey Anderson, the Union soldier serving in the South. "One of the foul eggs struck him in the mouth, and he beat a hasty retreat."

Gemmill had not been seen in town since.

In Wellsville, members of John Walker's family lay on the floor as rocks shattered the windows of their house.

This treatment came after they boldly stated their loyalty to the Democratic Party.

In contrast, The Hanover Spectator told of scattered incidents of rejoicing in Jefferson and other more partisan parts of the county.

• • •

The day before the Lincoln's assassination, the people of Wrightsville had celebrated the war's end with illuminations in nearly every house, a large torchlight procession and a visit from a delegation from Columbia.

That joy disappeared the next morning. First, the news came that Lincoln was shot. With the confirmation of Lincoln's death, businesses closed. People were downcast, and tears were seen throughout town.

"Copperheads are as silent as the grave," Wrightsville business John Stoner Beidler wrote in his diary. "They dare not open their mouths."

To the Citizens of Hanover!

"The funeral ceremonies of the late lamented Chief Magistrate, Abraham Lincoln, will take place on Wednesday, the 19th inst., at 12 o'clock. The various religious denominations throughout the country are invited to meet in their respective places of worship at that hour for the purpose of solemnizing the occasion with appropriate ceremonies."

In consequence with the above request from the Acting Secretary of State, the citizens of Hanover are respectfully requested to suspend all business on said occasion from 11 to 2 o'clock.

At a meeting of the Burgess & Town Council of Hanover, held last evening, the following programme was agreed upon:

Bells to commence tolling at 11 o'clock---continue tolling one hour. Citizens to meet on the Public Square at half-past eleven o'clock, form into procession and proceed to German Reformed Church, where services appropriate to the occasion are to be held.

The Soldiers all who have been in service, will lead the procession, with Martial Music.

Ministers of different denominations.

Borough Authorities.

Citizens.

It is expected that the citizens generally will join in the procession. A Great, a Good Man has been taken away from us---and as Americans, as Patriots, it becomes us to honor the Upright Magistrate, the Honest Man, the Faithful Servant.

By Order of the Council.

DAVID S. TANGER,
CHIEF BURGESS.

L. P. MELSHEIMER, Secretary.

Hanover, April 18, 1865.

Chief Burgess David S. Tanger orders the suspension of business in Hanover between 11 a.m. and 2 p.m. on Wednesday, April 19. Ministers from different denominations led a service at the German Reformed Church in Hanover. In Wrightsville, stores suspended business for five hours. 'The funeral of Abraham Lincoln was today,' John Stoner Beidler wrote in his diary, 'The largest funeral ever known in America, perhaps in the known world.'

A day later, Beidler wrote, "Everybody except Copperheads are downhearted... ."

• • •

Word of the attack on Lincoln reached Abraham Rudisill's camp in Virginia on Saturday.

The president was alive, but the vice president was dead, he learned.

"Oh, I wept for joy and thankfulness that our President was not assassinated — not dead," he wrote in his diary.

Two days later, he corrected himself, "Our Chief is indeed dead.

He then wrote a passage from his Bible, Psalm 46: "Be still and know that I am God."

• • •

Lincoln's death brought York's religious community together at high noon, Wednesday, April 19.

An overflow crowd at Christ Lutheran Church began a special worship service to coincide with the funeral of the fallen president in Washington, D.C. The Rev. A.W.

The show went on in York, despite the devastating news of Abraham Lincoln's death. In the same edition that The True Democrat carried news about Lincoln's death, it ran advertisements touting upcoming circuses to perform in York. The Thayer & Noyes circus boasted a menagerie of animals, including Hannibal, a 66-year-old elephant. The elephant died shortly after its visit to York in Centreville, Pa.

Lilly conducted the service, and the Rev. Dosh and J.O. Miller delivered the prayers. C.W. Thompson read from the Bible before Henry E. Niles mounted the pulpit to begin the first of two addresses that day:

"This is an occasion without parallel. For the first time, the business of our whole people is suspended on a bright, sunny vernal day, and badges of mourning are everywhere displayed, and the great heart of a mighty nation weeps because of its murdered head!

"True, Death has often been in our high places, and wide-spread sorrow has been felt when we learned that his skeleton foot had stalked the President's floor. But, never before was the hand of violence raised against the man whom our American people delighted most to honor. Never before did the assassin's bullet accomplish such a far-reaching, irrevocable, dreadful result."

The Rev. Niles continued on, calling for people to come together because the crime against Lincoln was an offense against all civilization. But America's government would move on with harmony and power.

"This day shall be forever sacred in the calendar of our nation," he said near the end of his address. "It is, as though there was 'not a house in the land, where is not one dead.' This day, when a mighty nation is bowed as by one common impulse of sorrow and shame, shall be remembered as the beginning of increased Union and Loyalty and Fidelity to the truth... .

"Today, shall they pledge themselves anew, amid the music of funeral hymns, to stand by and uphold by their influence, their prayer, their property, and if need be, their lives, the government of these United States by whomsoever administered; trusting in the President of the Universe, our fathers' God, to guide us safely through this whirlwind of confusion and over this sea of blood, into the fair haven of an honorable, a lasting and a glorious Peace."

Methodist, Baptist and German Reformed ministers led other parts of the service before the Rev. J.A. Gere,

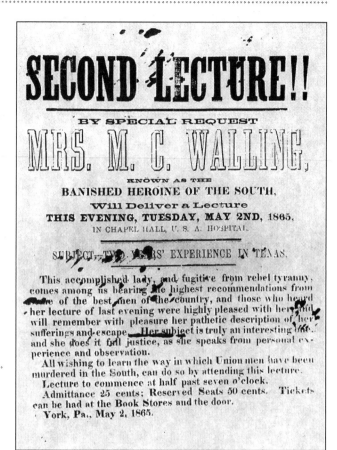

The U.S. Army General Hospital at Penn Common in York added a diversion to a community in mourning. This handbill touts a speaker, Mrs. M.C. Walling, held over for a second address. Mrs. Walling was busy on the lecture circuit. One year earlier, the U.S. Senate had authorized her to deliver a post-Civil War reconstruction lecture in its 600-seat chamber in the Capitol with the understanding that use of the chamber thereafter 'shall not be granted for any purpose other than for the use of the Senate.'

chaplain of the military hospital, closed with the Doxology and benediction.

York would now await the arrival of Abraham Lincoln's body aboard a special train traveling along the Northern Central — a procession that would make its final stop in Springfield, Ill., where the president called home.

• • •

David Small prepared the people of York to pay homage to the fallen president when the funeral procession stopped two days later.

Much was threatening to distract the minds of York residents. The Stone & Rosston Circus would soon be in town. The circus featured a trapeze performer, Signor Ferdinand, who would fly in the air and demonstrate feats of acrobatic "oscillation."

George Miller caught a 15-inch trout in the Codorus Creek, unusual considering its polluted condition. A decline in gold prices caused clothier Lehmeyer & Bro. to lower its prices.

Twenty-seven-year-old Jacob Doebler, of the 87th Pennsylvania, was laid to rest with military honors at

Soldiers lounge outside a U.S. Army General Hospital building, draped in black after word of President Abraham Lincoln's assassination reached York.

Prospect Hill Cemetery near York. The True Democrat noted that Doebler, a freed prisoner of war, "was starved to death in one of their miserable, filthy dens, in which so many of our brave men were sacrificed."

Likewise, 26-year-old Rudolph S. Folkemer, 54th Pennsylvania, died at home from chronic diarrhea, contracted during eight months in Southern prisons.

Another soldier, Lawrence Griffin, was not expected to recover after four people beat him and two other soldiers in a York drinking establishment. Two women, Cecelia Smith and Ann Lehr, and a man, Robert Smith, were arrested and jailed in the assault.

The chief burgess sought to focus the town by issuing an order calling for all businesses to close after 4 p.m. Friday, April 21, and remain closed as long as the president's body was in Pennsylvania. Military men and civilians would assemble in York's Centre Square with the procession to march to the railroad station on North Duke Street. Chief Marshal James A. Stahle would lead the procession.

A line would form at the station extending toward Baltimore.

"During the passing of the train, the line will remain uncovered (with hats off)," the order stated.

Citizens should take their flags and "drapery of mourning" to Water Street, later Pershing Avenue, for suspension on buildings along the railroad line. Bells would toll while the body was within the borough limits.

The York County commissioners did not equal Small's show of respect. They either neglected or refused to hang emblems of mourning on the courthouse, according to The York Republican.

The commissioners would have preferred to hang out black trappings upon receipt of the news of Lee's surrender, the newspaper asserted.

Patients and guards of the hospital took up the matter.

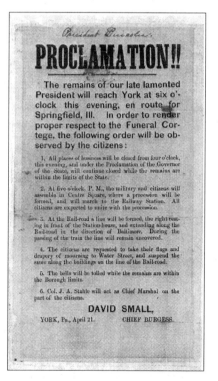

Chief Burgess David Small prepared this handbill establishing how York residents should receive the train bearing the body of Abraham Lincoln. The train traveled northward through York County on the Northern Central Railway. When it chugged into town a few minutes late, a group of women from York dressed in black awaited with a large floral arrangement. The crowd parted for the women, who approached the car. '… General McCollum broke over his rules, and allowed them to enter the sacred car,' a Philadelphia Inquirer reporter stated. 'They carried it (the flowers) to the coffin, and as the tears chased one another down their fair cheeks, they left it upon the cold bier. Not a word was spoken. There were half a dozen present who had gone in with them, but no dry eyes came out.'

They hung black drapery on the building's six columns and a shield-shaped funeral arrangement over the front entrance, surrounding a likeness of Abraham Lincoln.

• • •

The train bearing the president's body left the Northern Central Railway station in Baltimore at 3 p.m. Friday and stopped near the Mason-Dixon Line to pick up Andrew Curtin and other dignitaries. Gov. Curtin joined Maryland's Gov. Augustus W. Bradford, who had boarded the train in Baltimore.

As the train passed northward, crowds strained to catch a glimpse. Men took off their hats, and men and women shed tears. Behind schedule, the train steamed into York to the ringing of bells, the sound of guns and the strains of a dirge played by the military hospital's band.

Soldiers restrained the crowd, but some observers believed the train "plowed" its way through the horde of mourners for a 10-minute water stop.

Young Henry C. Niles provided this recollection from a prime perch on the shoulders of his friend, John Joice, a Negro waiter at the Washington House hotel:

"The silent crowd made a way for York's floral expression of patriotism and grief, borne by Aquilla Howard, the tall negro butler of the Philip A. Small family. From John Joice's shoulder, I saw my mother, following Mrs. Samuel Small, pass into one car door and out the other."

• • •

Jeannie E. Niles, Isabel Small, Mary Ann Small, Jane Latimer, Louisa Durkee, Jane Fulton and others helped deliver the wreath, three feet around, made up of white roses and camellias. Inside, a national shield was arranged with a blue background made of violets, stars of myrtle and bars of red and white verbena.

That wreath would remain with the flag-draped coffin. Viewers in Philadelphia would soon read its inscription: "Presented by the ladies of York, Pennsylvania, to be laid on the body of our lamented President if possible."

A Philadelphia Inquirer reporter on the train remembered the smell of the flowers.

"The fragrance of those violets seemed like incense from heaven," he wrote.

He would remember the scene, too.

"Old men, tottering to their graves with the rain pattering upon their bald heads; wounded soldiers hobbling to the roadside to show their love for him who sleeps before them; old women sobbing as though they had lost their first born; fair maidens brush away the tears, and men hold up their little ones to see the car that contains the remains of the people's friend," he wrote.

Within earshot of The Inquirer reporter, an elderly Negro man proclaimed, "He was crucified for us."

The train's whistle blew, and it rolled north to its next stop in Harrisburg.

In contrast to that disappointing day four years earlier, the slowly dispersing crowd in York wished Abraham Lincoln was not in that train.

They yearned for him to be sitting in Washington instead, taking care of important business.

American disunion now must progress toward Union.

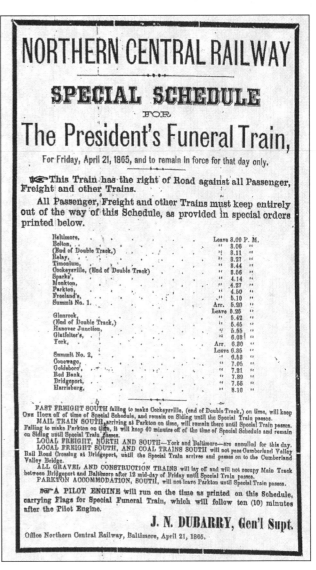

J.N. Dubarry, Northern Central Railway superintendent, issued this special one-day schedule detailing how President Lincoln's funeral train would move on the line between Baltimore and Harrisburg. The schedule included two stops: One in New Freedom to pick up Gov. Andrew G. Curtin and his entourage to accompany the train on its stops in Pennsylvania and the other in York for the steam-powered train to take on water.

Epilogue

'We are no longer unprotected.'
— York Mayor William Althaus, on the
125th anniversary of the Confederate occupation of York

'We felt kind of lost'

The officers

Jubal Early never faced prosecution for his role in the rebellion.

Fearing arrest after Appomattox, Early fled to Texas, then traveled to Mexico, Cuba and eventually Canada.

When the federal government pardoned former Confederates, Early returned to Lynchburg, Va., where he took up the defense of the Lost Cause and subsisted on earnings from a Louisiana State Lottery endorsement.

Early's mistress married after the war, and Early remained a bachelor living in Lynchburg.

Twenty years after leaving York, Jubal Early was still fighting.

York owed him money, he told the Boston Globe.

The passage of time had clouded his recollection and inflated the success of his requisition. York had raised only $72,000 of the $100,000 demanded, Early contended, and the town still owed him $28,000.

To this, The Gazette countered that the amount of money and goods provided to Early actually was $48,000.

Folks in York were eager to have the general settle his debt.

An often-told but unlikely tale illustrates that Early kept his profane ways until his death. After a fire damaged his Lynchburg office, Early entered the upstairs room and sat at his desk. The building fell, and Early disappeared.

People worked frantically to dig him out of the rubble and found him several hours later still seated at his desk. The general immediately ordered the mayor to get him a julep. He sipped on the drink, lowered in a basket, before emerging with the comment, "I didn't know there were that many bricks between me and hell."

• • •

John B. Gordon ranked as one of Robert E. Lee's top generals at war's end. When the time came for Gordon's men to surrender their arms at Appomattox, Joshua Lawrence Chamberlain, one of U.S. Grant's ranking officers, and his men saluted the bedraggled rebels.

Gordon and his men returned the compliment with a salute.

After the war, Gordon embarked on a political career, gaining seats as Georgia's governor and U.S. senator.

During the Reconstruction period, he developed deep beliefs about maintaining white social order. He reportedly became involved with the Ku Klux Klan and served as the Grand Dragon of the Klan in Georgia.

His success on the national lecture circuit highlighted his post-war life. In a visit to York, he met an old man in the parlor of the Colonial Hotel on Centre Square.

It was the Rev. John Roth, still a Mennonite minister. Roth's comments brought tears to Gordon's eyes. The minister expressed thanks that Gordon had returned the family horse taken by the general's men.

"I wanted to grasp your hand and pay tribute to you for your noble manhood toward me in the days of the past," Roth said.

Jubal Early posed as a farmer during his exile in Mexico, awaiting a post-war pardon afforded to Confederate officers.

John B. Gordon became a popular post-war speaker on the lecture circuit.

AMUSEMENTS.

YORK OPERA HOUSE
B. C. PENTZ, Manager.

TUESDAY, MARCH 6th.

LECTURE BY

GEN. JOHN B. GORDON,

U. S. Senator from Georgia. Subject,

Last Days of the Confederacy,

Delivered to crowded houses in New York, Brooklyn, Philadelphia, Baltimore and Washington.

Prices - - - 25, 50 and 75c.

Seats at Link & Hamme's.

John B. Gordon received a hero's welcome on his return to York in 1894. He spoke before a full house at the finest venue in town, the York Opera House.

Gordon's travels also caused him to cross paths with two former acquaintances.

The ball from a Confederate gun at Gettysburg had not claimed Francis Barlow's life. Later in the war, Barlow learned that Gen. J.B. Gordon from North Carolina had been killed. This was a kinsman of the Gordon from Georgia, who came to Barlow's aid at Gettysburg.

Meanwhile, Gordon thought it impossible that Barlow would survive his wounds. After the war in Washington, Gordon dined with a former Union general named Barlow. He had heard another Barlow fought with the Union Army so Gordon asked the soldier at dinner: "General, are you related to the Barlow who was killed at Gettysburg?"

"Why I am the man, sir. Are you related to the Gordon who killed me?" Barlow replied.

"I am the man, sir," Gordon responded.

"Nothing short of an actual resurrection from the dead," Gordon wrote, "could have amazed either of us more."

The Confederates had left Barlow behind, thinking his wounds were mortal. Arabella Barlow helped nurse her husband back to health. Despite the severity of his wounds, Barlow survived the war, dying in 1896 at the age of 61. His wife, still nursing Union soldiers, died of typhus contracted in a military hospital in July 1864.

Gordon often spoke of the boldness of Wrightsville's Mary Jane Rewalt, the "Heroine of the Susquehanna," as he called her in his speeches.

In Madison, Wis., 30 years after the war, a minister accompanied Rewalt to a hotel where Gordon was staying. He met with Gordon and asked the general's thoughts on the heroine.

"I would cross the continent to see the hostess of that day," Gordon said.

The minister replied, "If you will but step across the hall, General, you can meet her."

The general and heroine had a joyful meeting.

• • •

Early (1816-1894) and Gordon (1832-1904) lived long lives, developed a refined taste for controversy and wrote detailed memoirs justifying their actions and defending the cause of the South.

They became two leading spokesmen for the post-war movement "Lost Cause of the Confederacy," seeking explanations for the South's defeat, promoting the heroism of its soldiers and vindicating its honor.

Gordon promoted the Lost Cause on the lecture circuit. Early, who apparently never returned to York, organized the Southern Historical Society that published works on the Lost Cause.

Gordon spoke in York just days after Early's death in 1894 on the "Last Days of the Confederacy."

Survivors of the 87th Pennsylvania escorted him to the Opera House as the band played "The Star-Spangled Banner" and "Yankee Doodle." On stage, he gave a stirring address to a large audience.

"The cannon was silent and the sword was fast in its scabbard," The Gazette reported. "No requisition came for '165 barrels of flour or 28,000 pounds of baked bread... .' "

Men and time change, The Gazette observed.

"Thus have died the old rancor," the newspaper stated, "and the old differences."

• • •

William "Extra Billy" Smith (1796-1887) fought at Gettysburg and then served as governor of Virginia until the war's end.

When Richmond was evacuated in advance of the Union occupation in April 1865, Smith took the Confederate government elsewhere in Virginia — to Lynchburg and then Danville.

After the war, he farmed and served in Virginia's Legislature until his death in 1887.

• • •

Harry T. Hays (1820-1876), leader of the unrestrained Louisiana Tigers, sustained a severe wound at Spotsylvania in 1864 that laid him up until virtually the end of the war.

He returned to a more sedate occupation — the practice of law — in Louisiana after the war, on record as leader of one of the most lawless brigades of the war.

• • •

James Ewell Brown Stuart (1833-1864), flamboyant Confederate cavalry commander, died from a gunshot wound sustained in a clash at Yellow Tavern outside Richmond.

Jeb Stuart's late arrival at Gettysburg made him a ready target for finger-pointing by those who looked for reasons for the Confederate loss.

Post-war journals from the North and South waged a war of words over Stuart's ride around the Union Army, passing through the western half of York County, that resulted in his tardy arrival to Lee's side.

Several cavalry officers who marched across York County's soil lived long lives.

Rebel Gen. Wade Hampton (1818-1902) served as South Carolina's governor and a U.S. senator. Fellow rebel Fitz Lee (1835-1905) lived long enough to serve as a corps commander in the Spanish-American War. Union Gen. David M. Gregg (1833-1916) lived in Reading, Pa., serving for a time as a diplomat in Prague.

Other prominent cavalry generals died as young men. Elon John Farnsworth (1837-1863) was killed on the third day in the Battle of Gettysburg, sustaining five severe wounds in a charge ordered by Judson Kilpatrick. Post-war Indian fighter George Armstrong Custer (1839-1876) was massacred with his men at Little Big Horn.

John R. Chambliss (1833-1864), who led the initial rebel charge at Hanover, was killed in action in Virginia. Gregg, the opposing general in that action, was Chambliss' West Point classmate.

Judson Kilpatrick (1836-1881) died while serving as U.S. minister to Chile.

Elijah White refused to surrender with Lee's troops at Appomattox. His Comanches rode away and disbanded.

• • •

William Buel Franklin (1823-1903) retired from the Army and used his organizational genius as the successful general manager of Colt's Firearms in Hartford, Conn.

He became active in civic life in Hartford and took on national-level duties. He held the post of chief commissioner to the Paris Exposition, an opportunity for the United States and other countries to show off agricultural, industrial and cultural accomplishments.

He also served as president of the National Home for Disabled Volunteer Soldiers, a system of homes for veterans, later absorbed into the Veterans Administration.

He and his wife, the former Anna Louisa Clarke, are buried in Prospect Hill Cemetery, North York.

• • •

The Army of the Potomac discharged Granville Haller (1819-1897) for disloyal conduct and making disloyal statements in late July 1863.

The dismissal did not result from the York native's performance in defending York and Adams counties. The charge came after his statement months before while sharing a toddy in his tent with other Union officers: "Here's to a Northern and Southern Confederacy during the administration of Lincoln."

Haller, a Democrat, admitted that he was upset that

his admired commander in chief, George McClellan, had been relieved of command. But he testified his statement was, "Here's to the constitution as it is, the Union as it was."

About 15 years after the war's end, a court of inquiry exonerated Haller. After the war, he lived in Washington state.

• • •

Dr. Henry Palmer (1827-1895) resigned as surgeon in charge of York's U.S. Army General Hospital in July 1864.

By war's end, Palmer was breveted lieutenant colonel and returned to his lucrative private practice in Janesville, Wis.

The surgeon and other physicians at the military hospital treated more than 14,000 patients. One hundred and ninety-three died, a death rate of 2 percent.

After the last patient was discharged sometime in 1865, remaining supplies went to the Children's Home of York. The home was founded to accommodate children orphaned because of the war. The institution's goal was to educate and board "poor white orphans and half orphans" and other "poor, friendless, destitute or vagrant white children under the age of 12."

The Ladies Aid Society started its volunteer work feeding soldiers at Camp Scott and caring for them at the camp's hospital, transferred its attention to the military hospital on Penn Common and then supported the Children's Home when the hospital closed.

The soldiers

Fighting men returning to York County soil had seen a different world — a land without German-speakers and lacking the familiarity of their rural communities.

Their world would never again be so small.

Many had no jobs at first. Fortunately, the war helped fuel the Industrial Revolution. The former soldiers started leaving their rural communities to work with people they did not know in factories in larger York County towns — York, Wrightsville and Hanover.

Their war experience helped in this adjustment. Their time on the march and on the field was spent with people they just met.

Nostalgia about Army life set in and grew deeper with age.

"Settling down to routine daily employment in slow shop and store was not favorable to our habits of life; we felt kind of lost," Ephraim M. Myers of the 45th Pennsylvania wrote years later. "Our world of thought and action was breaking up; our accustomed ways in four years of singular existence seemed forsaking us ... ."

Myers recalled how he and others felt the loss of camp life and a happy-go-lucky army.

They picked up habits considered peculiar by some.

He wrote about a York County mother who was glad to have her three sons return alive.

To make certain the boys were comfortable upon returning to their York County home, she would open their door and take a look at them. She soon discovered that they had forsaken their feather ticks for the hard floor. One morning, the distressed mother awoke them.

"Web! Dave! Jack! What are you doing there on that

P.H. Glatfelter's Spring Grove Paper Mills stood among the many York County industries that blossomed after the war. Glatfelter purchased the mill in 1863, and by 1874, his business had become a major manufacturer of printing paper. The drawings, above, show the Spring Grove mill a decade after its founding.

Upon returning home after the war, some of York County's estimated 6,200 Union soldiers picked up where they left off. Others came back maimed or diseased and unable to work. John W. Hoffacker and scores of others paid the ultimate price. Hoffacker was killed in the Battle of Hanover, just a few miles from his West Manheim Township home. He was buried in Hanover's Mount Olivet Cemetery.

When Col. George Hay's health prevented him from heading the 87th Pennsylvania in the spring of 1863, he turned to other wartime leadership roles. Hay, right, was one of the five Committee of Safety members who met with Gen. John B. Gordon to surrender York the day before the rebels entered town.

In the early months of the war, Col. James A. Stahle led the Ellsworth Zouaves, a York County unit that later became part of the 87th Pennsylvania. After the war, Stahle served as a U.S. congressman from York County.

Members of the 87th Pennsylvania's band started playing together in a carpenter shop in Freystown, East York, in 1855. William Frey, first cornet player, was an early leader of the band. The band went off to war with the regiment in September 1861, and the U.S. Department of War discharged the band in August 1862. The band reformed after the war and later became known as the Spring Garden Band.

hard floor?" she asked.

"We can't sleep in no darn bed, mother," came their reply.

• • •

After the war, some former Union soldiers returned to Hanover.

They didn't stay, just spent enough time to search for buried treasure.

At the time of the Battle of Hanover, some under Judson Kilpatrick's command reportedly buried $20,000 to $30,000 secured by some unknown means. Years passed, dimming the recollections of the burial site.

After several weeks of searching, the former soldiers departed empty-handed. Townspeople then took up the search, covering the countryside for miles around, also without success.

• • •

As years passed, reminders of the war trickled into the county.

A former soldier, walking the battlefield at Gettysburg picked up a medal bearing the name of George Dosh, 87th Pennsylvania.

He returned the decoration to Dosh, who had lost it in fighting at Winchester, Va., in 1863.

How the medal ended up in Gettysburg was not known. Some speculated that a Confederate soldier found the emblem in Dosh's deserted knapsack and kept it as a souvenir. The rebel probably died in the Gettysburg conflict.

"Mr. Dosh greatly prizes the relic," The York

Dispatch reported, "and no amount of money would induce him to give up his treasure."

• • •

The 87th Pennsylvania held several reunions and witnessed publication of a book detailing its war adventures and sufferings.

The fighting unit had a lot to talk about, and its stories grew in width and depth as the years passed. The regiment formed in August 1861, and some soldiers from the unit served through the war's end in April 1865. The volunteers fought in more than 25 skirmishes and battles.

After his discharge because of bad health, George Hay, respected leader of the York Rifles and 87th, went back to his furniture making and undertaking business until his death in 1879.

Abraham Rudisill, the 50-year-old who could not successfully enlist in the 87th or any other infantry unit,

Two aging Civil War veterans flank a Lincoln impersonator. The black veteran is thought to be John Aquilla Wilson, known as 'Quil,' of Fawn Township in southeastern York County. He enlisted in the United States Colored Troops, 32nd Regiment, in 1864. Wilson died at the age of 101.

Camp William Penn in LaMott, near Philadelphia, served as a collection and training point for black recruits in Pennsylvania, Delaware and New Jersey to enter the United States Colored Troops. One hundred and seventy-nine thousand black soldiers and 10,000 black sailors served in the Union forces. Many still were enslaved only months, or days, before enlisting. Thirty-eight thousand black soldiers and sailors lost their lives in uniform — many from disease — and 22 won the Medal of Honor, America's top award.

served until war's end as an artillerist.

He returned to York County, where he became the founding minister of Harmony Grove United Brethren Church.

• • •

Despite ill health, James Barton traveled with his regiment to Texas after the peace at Appomattox, where the Negro troop unit was assigned to guard the Rio Grande against a suspected incursion by French troops.

He remained there until Sept. 8, when the Army honorably discharged him in New Orleans.

He received discharge pay of $100 and owed the government $24.24 for his clothing.

His health broken by the war, Barton later fought a harsh battle for a full pension for his Army service. Barton, one of seven members of his family to fight for Negro units, eventually received a monthly check of $6.

• • •

Some of the scores of the county's Negro soldiers fighting in the war lived about fourscore years after the conflict ended.

Joseph J. Howard, whose obituary said he was the last of the black Civil War veterans in the city of York, died at the age of 90 in 1933.

Howard served in the Fifth Regiment, Massachusetts Cavalry.

John Aquilla Wilson enlisted as a 15-year-old in the 32nd Regiment, Volunteer Infantry. Born in 1841, he lived to be 101 and was buried in the Fawn AME Cemetery in southeastern York County.

Levi Taylor of Wrightsville, a 12-year-old band boy, died in the 1940s.

Four black soldiers from York County served in the 54th Massachusetts Regiment, highlighted in the late 20th-century film 'Glory.'

George Ellender was wounded in the assault on Fort Wagner, S.C., that took the life of regiment commander Col. Robert Gould Shaw and was wounded a second time in Olustee, Fla. Aaron Cummings was also wounded in Olustee, Fla. George Batson, a Peach Bottom farmer, and William Freeman, a Lower Chanceford farmer, also served in the regiment.

Other soldiers who served in Negro troops and are buried in southeastern York County or lived there for many years include: J. T. Young, George Barton, John H. Barton, James Jefferson, Stephen Barton, Nathaniel Bones, William E. Bones, Charles Davis, John T. Stephenson and Richard Lee.

• • •

Soldiers and families continued to live with the effects of the war for years after it ended.

From just one community — the southeastern York County village of Airville — George McCauley, Thomas Collins, D. Wilson Grove, Samuel Wambaugh, Henry Burns and Charles Markel received pensions for sustaining gunshot wounds in the war.

Margaret Stokes, Rebecca Crymer, Annie Davidson, Margaret Grey, Judy Gable and Mary Bupp, all from southeastern York County, received widow pensions.

The invading Confederates did not trample the Airville area and other parts of southeastern York County,

Letterhead from A.B. Farquhar's *Pennsylvania Agricultural Works* shows the immensity of his company 25 years after the Civil War's end. The presence of a New York office points to the international scope of the company's business. The office in Macon, Ga., indicated that the company remained a major distributor of farm machinery in the South. Soldiers back from the war found employment in such burgeoning industries. Between 1880 and 1930, York's population quadrupled and the county's census doubled, drawn by the plentiful jobs in York industries. Many freedmen and their descendants from the South traveled the rail lines to York County to work in its growing factories.

the only section of the county to be spared.

But that section provided scores of men and supported these native sons. For example, the Session of the Hopewell Presbyterian Church voted on April 2, 1863, to allocate $6.50 in church funds to purchase books for soldiers.

• • •

Artifacts sometimes served as reminders of the war's fury.

Unexploded shells from Confederate cannon in Wrightsville had a deadly impact months after the rebel assault.

One shell killed two children of John Schenberger in the East Prospect area, south of Wrightsville.

Some boys exploded a shell on the riverbank north of Wrightsville. A shell fragment severely wounded Ashbel Lane, one of the boys, but he recovered.

• • •

Sometime after the battle, workers disinterred the bodies of Union soldiers killed in the Battle of Hanover and moved them to the National Cemetery at Gettysburg.

Townspeople initially moved the bodies to a makeshift morgue in the Flickinger Foundry on York Street. Henry Wirt, a prominent Hanover resident, directed the making of caskets, and the Rev. William K. Zieber officiated at the service.

The body of the Union artillerist, killed when the caisson exploded on the countermarch to Hanover, was interred in the Lutheran cemetery in Abbottstown. His comrades later collected money for reburial of his body in

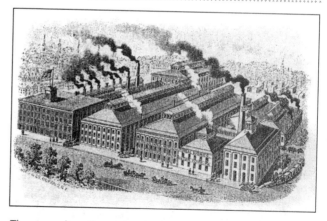

The sprawling Pennsylvania Agricultural Works faces York's North George Street. Less than three decades after Farquhar's death in 1925, the company passed into corporate hands when Oliver, another maker of farm equipment, purchased it. The local plant was later closed and the dilapidated buildings razed as part of urban renewal efforts.

the Paradise Catholic Church cemetery.

The people

York County residents had seen the world, too, as

men of the South and elsewhere in the North marched across their soil. Freed Negroes started coming north for jobs as York County participated fully in the Industrial Revolution.

Some county residents moved elsewhere, to places unknown before the war. To take their place, people who had never seen the county before the war moved north and made it their home.

Former Confederate soldiers added to York County's population. Some stayed after the battles of Hanover and Gettysburg.

Harry Sinner, a lad of 14 serving as a water boy for railroad workers, recalled one such soldier who left the rebel army and lived in York and Adams counties.

Allen Tiel worked with Sinner in laying the Western Maryland Railroad from Porter's Sideling, in southern York County, to York in 1892. On one occasion, Tiel complimented Sinner, bringing tears to the boy's eyes.

Another deserter settled in Warrington Township. He was a Connecticut man, who was drafted into the Confederate Army during a visit to Virginia early in the war.

When the rebels invaded York County, he left the ranks and took up farming.

He became known as "the Rebel."

• • •

At the age of 35 in 1864, letter writer Cassandra Morris Small married Dr. Alexander Blair.

Blair, a York physician, served as a surgeon at the military hospital in York.

Small was respected in the community and honored particularly by the teachers and students at York's Westminster Presbyterian Church, where she worked many years in the Sunday school. Her letters to cousin Lissie Latimer were later published. She died in 1891 at the age of 62.

James Latimer (1836-1899), another noted writer of letters about the rebel occupation, became one of York's most successful lawyers.

After the war, he married Judge Robert Fisher's daughter, Helen, and gained a York County judgeship in 1885.

• • •

Even 20 years after the war, Mary Sophia Cadwell Fisher (1827-1913) gained encouragement from letters penned by soldiers she served in those days after Gettysburg.

Her reputation grew after details of her acts of mercy at the battlefield appeared in The Philadelphia Times in 1882.

Judge Robert Fisher's (1806-1888) reticence to fly an American banner at war's end did not affect him at the polls. His stubbornness that day was balanced by his equally stout opposition to Jubal Early's demand for the courthouse keys.

He was re-elected judge in 1871 and retired in 1881, after spending 30 years on the bench. He died 60 years after gaining admittance to the county bar.

After Mary and Robert Fisher's deaths, the family kept alive stories about the great days that the Fishers witnessed the rebel occupation.

Daughter Mary, a youngster at the time, later recalled how a rebel officer picked her up as he rode through York and said, "I have a little daughter at home with eyes just

This mural shows William C. Goodridge's growth from slavery in Maryland to his barber business in York after he gained his freedom. He went on to own a five-story building on York's Centre Square and is believed to have transported fugitive slaves traveling the Underground Railroad on his railroad line before the outbreak of the Civil War.

By 1885, attorney James W. Latimer represented many of York's leading businesses. He topped off his career by earning a seat that year as York County judge. He joined lawyer and historian John Gibson on the bench, a seat vacated earlier that decade by his father-in-law, Robert J. Fisher.

as blue as yours."

• • •

Philip Albright Small (1797-1875) and Samuel Small (1799-1885) remained community stalwarts after the war.

Samuel Small was instrumental in founding York Hospital, Children's Home of York, York Benevolent Association and York Collegiate Institute, a forerunner of York College of Pennsylvania.

After their deaths, P.A. Small's children continued to expand the family's vast business interests.

• • •

Mary Jane Magee Rewalt's support of the Union in a room full of Confederate officers earned her a glowing tribute in John B. Gordon's popular post-war lectures.

She convinced Gordon that day in late June 1863 that she was not the writer of the note among the flowers handed to the general in York. The writer has never been identified.

Her husband, a military surgeon, practiced medicine in Wrightsville after the war.

The couple, who were married just two months before the rebel invasion, had five children. She was the great-grandmother of writer Gore Vidal.

Lewis Miller shows the execution of the conspirators behind the assassination of Abraham Lincoln. The U.S. government executed Mary E. Surratt, Lewis Payne, David Herold and George Atzerodt on July 7, 1865, in Washington, D.C. By this time, assassin John Wilkes Booth had been tracked down and shot.

Strangely, Gordon, writing years after the war, remembered Rewalt as older than a woman in her 20s.

The passing of Gordon's own mother came to Gordon's mind as he parted the Magee house.

"Nothing short of death's hand can ever obliterate from my heart the impression of that parting," he wrote. "Holding me in her arms, her heart almost bursting with anguish, and the tears running down her cheeks, she asked God to take care of me, and then said: 'Go, my son; I shall perhaps never see you again, but I commit you freely to the service of your country.' "

• • •

A.B. Farquhar's (1838-1925) role in York's surrender did not cost him long-term respect in the county.

He lived his dream of success, establishing a farm machinery manufacturing company of international scope. He became York County's leading industrialist by 1900 and died a wealthy man in 1925.

This post-war success came despite his living out a fear.

He lost his factory to a fire and had to rebuild from scratch.

Mechanization made him wealthy, but it also hastened his death. Injuries sustained after an automobile struck him weakened the octogenarian shortly before his death.

• • •

William C. Goodridge (1806-1873), the former slave who became a successful York businessman, died in Minneapolis.

His son, Glenalvin, who found widespread support from the York community after his imprisonment, had died of tuberculosis in Minneapolis six years before.

But William C. Goodridge's other sons, Wallace L. and William O., moved their York photo studio to East Saginaw, Mich. The business operated until 1922, earning the Goodridge enterprise recognition as the most significant and long-lasting black photography business of its time.

The stories

The Confederate invasion of York County spawned countless rich and sometimes imaginative stories, some told from the moment the rebels left town and passed on for generations. Historians have uncovered others over the years.

One story tells of the Confederates crossing the Codorus Creek because of the burning of Black Bridge, north of York.

The rebels waded across the Codorus, thinking it was the Susquehanna River. The squad laughed at the federals for thinking that a missing bridge would prevent them from fording such an insignificant waterway.

Union soldiers dug trenches in the hillside to protect the bridge, but the Union soldiers had departed without making use of them.

• • •

Near Kralltown, in northern York County, a youth named Gross rode on a wagon, taking in hay with three others.

Two mounted rebels rode up and one laid claim to a workhorse, "I'll take this one."

David Myers, owner of the farm, replied, "You will like h—."

The rebels, amused at the farmer's high squeaky voice, observed the four pitchforks in the workers' hands.

One said, "I guess we won't."

Soon, more men in gray joined the original pair.

At that point, Myers squeaked, "I guess you will now."

• • •

The John Walker family from Wellsville, not far from Kralltown, also weathered a visit.

The leader of the pack tried to calm the family: "Don't be scared, we didn't come to do you any harm, we're hungry."

"Then get off your horses," Mrs. Walker stated, "and stay for dinner."

Their stomachs full, one of the horsemen said, "Now Mr. Walker, we want to trade horses with you."

The horses had been taken across the river, John

Walker fibbed. He showed the soldiers a mare with a new-born colt.

Actually, the Walkers had hidden the family's horses nearby.

• • •

The Confederates demanded Henry King's horse, but the North George Street resident tried to avoid losing his mount by claiming his Southern sympathies.

The rebels gave King a gun and tried to recruit him.

He changed his position and refused to fight.

The graycoats produced a noose and prepared to hang King.

King produced his horse and avoided the noose.

• • •

Some residents used a trick to make their horses appear lame.

They tied a tight string around the lower leg of the animals and covered the string with hair.

The trick probably did not fool the savvy Southern farmboys.

• • •

Four horses pulled David Hursh's hay-filled wagon across the bridge at Wrightsville, and Hursh and his brother headed on to Lititz in Lancaster County.

When it was safe to come back, Hursh faced a problem confronting hundreds of other people: how to get the horses and wagon back across.

They eventually deployed a flatboat, an experience the horses did not relish.

• • •

David Landis stood along a road watching the rebels walk by.

One soldier liked Landis' hat and removed it from the 17-year-old's head.

"You can get another one," the rebel said. "I need this."

"I didn't say a word," the boy later said.

• • •

Some Confederate officers asked Joseph Kauffman, who lived between York and Wrightsville, about his horses.

They had been sent away, he said.

The rebels informed him that such actions could cost him his life.

"You can take my life, my land, my home and my possessions, but you can't take my politics," Kauffman replied.

The rebels honored his forthrightness with a note ordering other invaders to not disturb Kauffman.

• • •

An enduring story tells of a Confederate soldier buried on the west shore of the Susquehanna River, near Wildcat Falls north of the Accomac area.

Area residents have long maintained the grave site, where tradition holds that a rebel soldier was laid to rest. The tradition persists even though the site has been marked with Stars and Stripes and a Union marker.

The stories vary, but a common version tells of three soldiers detached from Gen. John B. Gordon's rebel brigade, who tried to cross the river on a raft. Perhaps the soldiers were testing the river's depth to find a ford where the brigade could cross.

The raft struck a rock, and one of the soldiers, who couldn't swim, drowned. His comrades dragged his body

Mary Shaw Leader helped her family publish The Hanover Spectator during the Civil War. Her burial site in Hanover's Mount Olivet Cemetery is marked with a monument commemorating her accomplishments as a pioneering woman journalist.

ashore and buried him, the resting place of a lonely soldier.

• • •

Mary Shaw Leader wrote for her mother's newspaper, The Hanover Spectator, during the Civil War.

Leader's father, Senary, died soon after the start of the conflict leaving a heavy obligation for the newspaper's success to his family, including his wife, Maria, and daughter. Maria Leader ran the Republican Party-oriented newspaper until her death in 1875.

Her newspaper ran a story on Lincoln's Gettysburg Address on Nov. 27, 1863, with the credit: "From the Inquirer."

An oft-repeated story tells of Mary Shaw Leader walking to Gettysburg to cover the dedication of the National Cemetery. There, the young woman was one of only a few reporters who wrote down Lincoln's address and the only one to recognize its greatness.

Leader was a pioneer newspaperwoman, as her tombstone claims, but researchers still look for evidence that she contributed to the long memories of the remarkable event.

• • •

Lizzie Sweitzer worked as a domestic for Rev. M. J. Alleman of Hanover's St. Matthew Lutheran Church.

She was helping to feed the Union troopers when the Confederates surprised and shattered the 18th Pennsylvania's column, pushing the disorganized unit through the crowded Hanover streets.

Before the young woman could find cover, a rifle or pistol ball struck her in the ankle.

After the war, she married and lived in South Dakota. But she visited Hanover in 1898 on a trip east, seeking a military pension for her wound.

She walked with a crutch during her visit.

• • •

During a lull in the Hanover fighting, Judson Kilpatrick called for a conference with his two brigade commanders, Elon Farnsworth and George Custer.

Custer rode up to the Central Hotel, Kilpatrick's headquarters, and tied his horse to a tree in front of the nearby Gitt home. He directed his Negro servant to watch the horse while he conferred with his commander.

George D. Gitt remembered the servant feeding the horse oats and hay as the mount stood by the tree.

This is the third bridge Lewis Miller (1796-1882) saw span the Susquehanna River at Wrightsville. This covered bridge replaced the similar wooden structure burned by Union troops to stop the Confederate advance. Columbia Bank, owner of the bridge, sold the piers, abutments, toll houses and ferry rights to the Pennsylvania Railroad Co. in 1864. Workers constructed two iron spans in the middle of the new bridge so a fire would not claim the entire structure. Miller did not live to see a fourth bridge connecting York and Lancaster counties. A cyclone blew down the 1869 bridge in 1896.

Over time, the maple became known as "The Custer Tree," a reminder to Gitt and the town of the proud days in which blue troopers blocked Jeb Stuart's men from joining up with Robert E. Lee.

After six decades, the tree began to die, and workers rendered it into firewood.

Gitt was out of town when the tree was cut down. What he said when he discovered it missing was not recorded.

• • •

When Jeb Stuart's men headed up Panther Hill between Jefferson and York New Salem during their night march, the column passed Ziegler's Church.

The Rev. Constantine Deininger conducted a burial service for one of his congregants, when the gray vanguard came in sight.

One account suggests that Deininger held the service at that late hour because the burial involved the body of a soldier, which was deteriorating in the heat.

Those at the burial, seeing the rebels, quickly dispersed so they could protect their homes and property.

The flag

Residents of York regularly debated the fate of York's Centre Square flag after the rebels left town.

Cassandra Small, for instance, informed her cousin, Lissie Latimer, that the rebels handed the flag to Chief Burgess David Small. In a later letter, she corrected that, stating that the rebels tore it into strips, and others rendered the strips into smaller pieces while singing "We'll Plant Our Colors on a Northern Hill."

Attorney James Latimer wrote to his brother, Bartow, that the rebels took down the borough flag, probably the Centre Square banner, and one at Pearce's bookstore. The Confederates trailed one of them down East Market Street. York resident Kirk White, Latimer contended, helped to take down one of them.

Col. Clement A. Evans, commander of an advance rebel regiment securing the town, wrote in his diary that he pulled down the large stand of colors waving above Centre Square. In his battle report, John B. Gordon confirmed that his men lowered the flag. George Prowell, a county historian, wrote that Gordon recalled after the war that the banner was placed on one of the brigade's ambulance wagons.

A North Carolinian named Wilson told Prowell in 1898 that as far as he recalled, the story told by General Gordon was correct. Wilson thought it was torn into shreds as bandages for Confederate soldiers who had become sick or wounded.

Historian John Gibson, who was in York during the occupation, reported that the rebels took down the flag and carried it away.

Mrs. L. M. Hartman, who witnessed the rebel entry into town, adds a wrinkle to the story. After the rebels lowered the flag, a young girl with the last name of Cornwell, rushed into the square, seized the banner and waved it defiantly.

At least two other accounts have come forth.

Adam Wisner, residing in Marietta in 1888, claimed John Bupp, a pump maker, skinnied up the pole about 20 feet to untie the rope to lower the flag. Wisner with several other residents caught the flag and folded it into a tight bundle.

Wisner asked permission to keep the flag, and it was granted.

"I know the flag was taken out of York, but not in an ambulance," he said.

W.S. King later marched with Gordon's brigade but did not accompany the Georgia brigade to York. In the winter of 1863-64, some of Gordon's men conducted a minstrel show. One part called for a soldier to dress up as a Negro woman. They cut up a flag that they had brought back from Pennsylvania to make a dress for the show.

The flagpole stood for a considerable time after the war. When it was taken down, H.C. Adams, a bookseller on North George Street, bought the pole and the rope and took them to the residence of the Adams family on South George Street, Prowell wrote.

For several years, the rope was used as a swing by the Sunday school of York's St. John the Baptist Episcopal Church, when the congregation held annual picnics. Many times, it was tied to a tree limb at the Springwood picnic ground, along the Maryland and Pennsylvania Railroad, south of York. Adams was not certain what became of the rope.

Interesting stories also surround Hanover's flags.

People in Hanover stretched a flag across Frederick Street connecting two residences. The rebels raced under the flag during their charges, but it was too high to pull down.

Likewise, a flag in Pennville, site of the initial rebel charge, floated above the battle. The fighting so occupied Stuart's men that they could not pause to lower the banner.

• • •

Interesting stories surround the fate of the flag at the Pierce bookstore in York and the banner at the the military hospital in York.

A large wooden book supported the flag at Pierce's. The rope along the pole had been cut, but a lame York resident loyal to the South urged a soldier to take his cane and stand on his horse to snag the rope. This strategy worked, and the flag came down. The soldier rode off with the flag trailing in the dust.

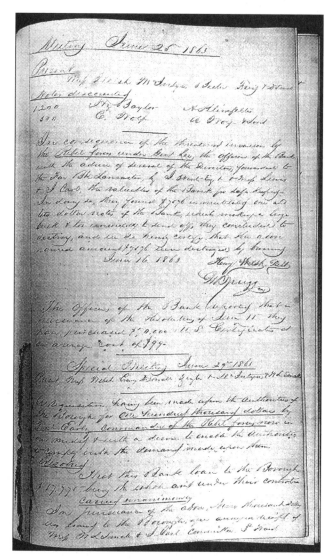

Henry Welsh, brother-in-law and mentor to Chief Burgess/Gazette owner David Small, served as president of York Bank during the Confederate occupation. The county's oldest depository operated through the war and participated in the county's post-war growth. This page from the bank's minute book tells of two meetings in June 1863. The June 25 action directed the bank's assets to be shipped to a Lancaster bank before the rebels reached town. The June 29 meeting, held during the occupation, showed ongoing behind-the-scenes efforts to raise money to allay Jubal Early's threats to burn the town. The bank approved a $17,775 loan toward satisfying the requisition and actually put forth $9,000. Early prepared to leave town that day so the money probably never reached his hands.

Farther out East Market Street, a resident named Mary Spangler grabbed at the flag but came away with only a few shreds.

Women at the hospital conceived the idea of wrapping the hospital's flag around Mammy Ruggles' body and between the folds of her petticoats.

The hospital matron walked down George Street with

her long skirts flapping until she reached her son's home near the Codorus Creek.

With each step, she said a prayer to save her flag from the Confederates who surrounded her.

The bridge

By 1869, another covered bridge spanned the Susquehanna River at Wrightsville, on the same piers that supported its predecessor. This bridge lasted less than 30 years.

A cyclone blew it down in 1896. Its iron replacement, again built on the same stone piers, lasted until 1964, when it was dismantled for scrap.

The first four bridges across the river met their ends by ice, fire, wind and the hand of man, respectively. The piers stand today.

By the early 1970s, two other bridges crossed the river between Wrightsville and Columbia.

The mayors

David Small (1812-1885) remained an involved newspaperman to his last days, despite paralysis in his lower limbs. With the aid of a conveyance, he still made it to the office until days before his death.

He served nine, one-year terms as chief burgess and died as one of York's most honored citizens. On the day of his burial, businesses closed for one-half hour, and the borough flag waved at half staff. His obituary suggests that controversy surrounding his actions as newspaper owner and chief burgess during the Confederate occupation continued to the end of his life:

"In June 1863, Mr. Small ... and several prominent citizens ... incurred the displeasure of a number of people, by visiting the invading forces of General Early ... in the interest of the weaker portion of the population, whose fears had well-nigh created a panic, but as a result was to leave us without a scar to disfigure our beautiful town, or without an ache to our fear-stricken hearts, that indiscretion (?) the creature of an impulse to preserve intact the fruits of our labors and the inheritances of our fathers, has, apparently, been softened by time and laid away as a sweet morsel in the storehouse of our memories, only to be resurrected when truth and justice shall require vindication."

• • •

From the earliest days after the Battle of Gettysburg, the Committee of Safety and others involved in the decision to surrender York drew criticism from both inside and outside the county.

Not only had the town's leaders initiated the decision to surrender, but the honor combat brings to a town did not come York's way. Fighting occurred in Hanover and Wrightsville. Carlisle initially filled a requisition, but later fought off Jeb Stuart's demand for supplies.

After the war ended, York haltingly celebrated anniversaries of the occupation. In 1963, The York Dispatch, successor to The True Democrat, did not cover the 100th anniversary of occupation, not that the City of York celebrated the event. The Gazette and Daily, as David Small's former newspaper was then called, reprinted the article from The York Gazette of June 30, 1863.

Hanover and Wrightsville, meanwhile, have celebrated the invasion with parades, statues and museums.

The freeze thawed a bit in York on the 125th anniversary of the occupation, and the topic has increasingly captured interest since. A re-creation of the surrender and occupation was part of the anniversary program in 1988. Re-enactors portrayed Jubal Early and other Confederates.

William Althaus, mayor of the City of York, played both himself and re-enacted his predecessor, David Small. Rather than re-enactors playing A.B. Farquhar and Robert Stiles, newspaper reporters from the York Daily Record and The York Dispatch were there to report on the event:

A small crowd gathered at the York County Courthouse on East Market Street to observe several gray-clad officers meet with York's fathers.

The occasion was a ceremony marking the Confederate occupation.

One of the speakers, David Bupp, York County Bar Association president, summed up York's participation in the Civil War:

"York did what York does best — York treated the Civil War as a commercial enterprise. York did not want the city burned so the city's business leaders asked, 'what can we do to avoid that?' and came up with this transaction.

"The founding fathers," the York lawyer said, "had the good sense to surrender."

The moment came for Mayor William Althaus to surrender the city to a re-enactor in the role of Confederate Gen. Jubal Early.

Althaus recalled that the city met Early's demands on those days in late June 1863.

Times had changed, the mayor said, and so had York.

"We are no longer unprotected," Althaus told Early, "having the finest police department in the country."

That said, Althaus declined Early's demand to surrender.

"With all due respect, General Early," the mayor proclaimed. "Hell no."

The crowd approved this revision of history with a spirited round of applause.

During the ceremony, Althaus said he did not quite agree with the decisions of York's fathers in those days before Gettysburg, particularly why the Civil War was fought.

"The Civil War was a struggle for equality and justice," the mayor said. "A great deal has occurred during the last 125 years, but that struggle is not finished. We still have a long way to go."

Appendix

'Aunt Bella … thought it a pity someone
shouldn't make an account of all these funny things,
that they would make an interesting book.'
— Cassandra M. Small

5

years of

wartime

events

THE BATTLE OF GETTYSBURG—GENERAL CRAWFORD'S CHARGE ON THE REBEL LINES.—[See Page 86.]

Harper's Weekly , one of America's leading illustrated newspapers during the Civil War, published numerous engravings of battle scenes on its pages. This scene shows Union soldiers — Gen. Samuel Crawford in the lead — charging rebel lines in fighting at Little Round Top. Crawford, a Pennsylvanian, and his men marched through southwestern York County with Gen. George Sykes' corps on their way to battle in Gettysburg.

1860

Nov. 6 — Abraham Lincoln is elected U.S. president, gaining 180 of 303 electoral votes and 40 percent of the popular vote.

Dec. 20 — South Carolina secedes from the Union. Mississippi, Florida, Alabama, Georgia, Louisiana and Texas follow South Carolina in secession.

1861

Feb. 9 — The Confederate States of America forms with Jefferson Davis as president.

March 4 — Lincoln is sworn in as 16th president of the United States.

April 12 — Confederates open fire upon Fort Sumter in Charleston, S.C. The Civil War begins.

April 15 — Lincoln calls for 75,000 militiamen. Robert E. Lee, a 25-year veteran of the U.S. Army and former superintendent of the U.S. Military Academy at West Point, N.Y., is offered command of the

Union Army. Lee declines.

April 17 — Virginia secedes from the Union, followed within weeks by Arkansas, Tennessee and North Carolina. An eleven-state Confederacy forms.

April 19 — Lincoln calls for blockades against Southern ports, limiting the ability of the rural South to stay well supplied in its war against the industrialized North.

April 20 — Lee resigns from the U.S. Army, and then goes to the Confederate capital of Richmond, Va., accepting command of military and naval forces there.

July 4 — Congress authorizes a call for 500,000 men.

July 21 — The Union Army suffers a defeat at Bull Run. Confederate Gen. Thomas J. Jackson earns the nickname "Stonewall" as his brigade resists Union attacks. Union troops retreat in disorder to Washington.

July 27 — Lincoln appoints George B. McClellan as commander of The Army of the Potomac.

Sept. 11 — Lincoln revokes Gen. John C. Fremont's unauthorized military proclamation of emancipation in Missouri. Later, the president relieves Gen. Fremont of command and replaces him with Gen. David Hunter.

Nov. 1 — Lincoln appoints McClellan as general-in-chief of all Union forces.

Nov. 8 — The U.S. Navy seizes two Confederate officials sailing to England. England demands their release, threatening war. Lincoln eventually orders their release.

1862

Jan. 31 — Lincoln issues General War Order No. 1, calling for all United States naval and land forces to begin a general advance by Feb 22.

Feb. 6 — Gen. Ulysses S. Grant achieves victory in Tennessee, capturing Fort Henry and Fort Donelson 10 days later.

March 8-9 — The Confederate Ironclad "Virginia" ("Merrimac") sinks two wooden Union ships and battles the Union ironclad "Monitor" to a draw off Norfolk, Va.

March — The Peninsular Campaign begins as McClellan's Army advances from Washington, D.C., to the peninsula south of Richmond, then begins an advance toward the Confederate capital.

April 6-7 — Confederate surprise attack on Grant's troops at Shiloh on the Tennessee River results in a bitter struggle with 13,000 Union soldiers killed and wounded. The Confederates sustain 10,000 casualties.

April 24 — Seventeen Union ships under the command of David Farragut take New Orleans, a key Southern seaport. York County native Johnson Kelly Duncan was a key Confederate commander in the battle.

May 31 — At the Battle of Seven Pines, Confederate Gen. Joseph E. Johnston's Army attacks McClellan's troops in front of Richmond and nearly defeats them.

June 1 — Lee assumes Confederate command, replacing the wounded Johnston. Lee then renames his force The Army of Northern Virginia.

June 25-July 1 — The Seven Days Battle begins as Lee attacks McClellan near Richmond, resulting in heavy losses for both armies. McClellan withdraws toward Washington.

July 11 — After four months as his own general-in-chief, Lincoln hands over the task to Gen. Henry W. Halleck.

Aug. 29-30 — Seventy-five thousand Union troops under Gen. John Pope are defeated by Confederates under Gen. Stonewall Jackson and Gen. James Longstreet at the Second Battle of Bull Run. The Union Army again retreats to Washington. The president relieves Pope.

Sept. 4-9 — Lee invades the North, heading for Harpers Ferry in western Virginia, 50 miles northwest of Washington.

Sept. 17 — Fighting results in the bloodiest day in U.S. military history as Lee's Army is stopped at Antietam Creek in Maryland by McClellan's Union forces, resulting in 26,000 casualties sustained by both sides. Lee withdraws to Virginia.

Sept. 22 — Lincoln issues a Preliminary Emancipation Proclamation freeing all slaves in territories held by Confederates.

Nov. 7 — Lincoln replaces McClellan with Gen. Ambrose E. Burnside as the commander of The Army of the Potomac.

Dec. 13 — Burnside's Army suffers a costly defeat at Fredericksburg in Virginia with a loss of 12,653 men after 14 assaults on well-entrenched rebels on Marye's Heights.

GENERAL VIEW OF GETTYSBURG, FROM THE WEST.—Photographed by Brady.—[See Page 384.]

This view, from Harper's Weekly, shows the crossroads community of Gettysburg, from the west. It is based on a photograph taken by famed Civil War photographer Mathew Brady.

1863

Jan. 1 — Lincoln issues the final Emancipation Proclamation and emphasizes enlistment of black soldiers in the Union Army.

Jan. 25 — The president appoints Gen. Joseph (Fighting Joe) Hooker as commander of The Army of the Potomac, replacing Burnside.

Jan. 29 — Grant is placed in command of the Army of the West, with orders to capture Vicksburg, Miss.

March 3 — The U.S. Congress enacts a draft, covering male citizens aged 20 to 45, but also exempts those who pay $300 or provide a substitute.

May 1-4 — The Union Army under Gen. Hooker is decisively defeated by Lee's much smaller force at the Battle of Chancellorsville in Virginia. Confederate Gen. Stonewall Jackson is mortally wounded by his own soldiers.

May 10 — The South suffers a huge blow as Jackson dies from his wounds; his last words, "Let us cross over the river and rest under the shade of the trees."

June 3 — Lee launches his second invasion of the North, heading into Pennsylvania in a campaign that will soon lead to Gettysburg.

June 28 — Lincoln appoints Gen. George G. Meade as commander of The Army of the Potomac, replacing Hooker. Gen. Jubal Early's division invades York. The Union Army burns the Wrightsville bridge to keep John B. Gordon's brigade from crossing the Susquehanna River.

June 30 — Lee recalls Early's division from York County as part of a concentration of rebel forces in Adams County. In Hanover, Union forces stop Jeb Stuart's horsemen from rejoining Lee's Army in a major cavalry battle on the streets of Hanover.

July 1-3 — The tide of war turns against the South as the Confederates are defeated at the Battle of Gettysburg in Pennsylvania.

July 4 — Vicksburg, the last Confederate stronghold on the Mississippi River, surrenders to Grant and the Army of the West after a six-week siege, splitting the Confederacy in two.

July 13-16 — Anti-draft riots in New York City include arson and the murder of blacks by poor immigrant whites. At least 120 people are killed, and the riots cause $2 million in damage.

July 18 — Negro troops of the 54th Massachusetts Infantry Regiment under Col. Robert G. Shaw assault rebels at Fort Wagner, S.C. Shaw and half of the 600 men in the regiment are killed.

Aug. 10 — Lincoln meets with abolitionist Frederick

This view shows Confederate Gen. Fitz Lee's horse artillery, cannons that accompanied cavalry units, commanding the streets of Carlisle on the evening of July 1, 1863. Lee's men bombarded Carlisle, after the town refused the Confederate demands for food and supplies.

Douglass, who pushes for full equality for Union Negro troops.

Sept. 19-20 — A Confederate victory by Gen. Braxton Bragg's Army of Tennessee at Chickamauga leaves Gen. William S. Rosecrans' Union Army trapped in Chattanooga, Tenn.

Oct. 16 — Lincoln appoints Grant to command all operations in the western theater.

Nov. 19 — Lincoln delivers a two-minute Gettysburg Address at a ceremony dedicating the battlefield as a National Cemetery.

Nov. 23-25 — The Rebel siege of Chattanooga ends as Union forces under Grant defeat Bragg's Army.

1864

March 9 — Lincoln appoints Grant to command all of the armies of the United States. Gen. William T. Sherman succeeds Grant as commander in the west.

May 4 — A massive, coordinated campaign involving all the Union armies begins. In Virginia, Grant advances toward Richmond to engage Lee's Army of Northern Virginia. In the west, Sherman advances toward Atlanta to engage Joseph E. Johnston's Army of Tennessee.

June 3 — A costly mistake by Grant results in 7,000 Union casualties in 20 minutes during an offensive at Cold Harbor in Virginia.

June 15 — Union forces miss an opportunity to capture Petersburg, south of Richmond, and cut off the Confederate rail lines. As a result, Grant's forces begin a nine-month siege of Petersburg.

THE INVASION OF THE NORTH—HARRISBURG, PENNSYLVANIA.—From a Sketch by Mr. Fearen.—(See Page 459.)

A Confederate scouting party reached a position overlooking Harrisburg on Monday, June 29, 1863, but Gen. Richard Ewell's men received orders to concentrate near Gettysburg before they could move on Pennsylvania's capital.

July 20 — At Atlanta, Sherman's forces battle the rebels now under the command of Gen. John B. Hood, who replaced Johnston.

Aug. 29 — Democrats nominate McClellan for president to run against Lincoln.

Sept. 2 — Sherman's Army captures Atlanta. The victory helps Lincoln's bid for re-election.

Oct. 19 — Union cavalry Gen. Philip H. Sheridan scores a decisive victory in the Shenandoah Valley over Jubal Early's troops.

Nov. 8 — Lincoln is re-elected president, carrying all but three states with 55 percent of the popular vote and 212 of 233 electoral votes. The Southern states did not participate.

Nov. 15 — After destroying Atlanta's warehouses and railroad facilities, Sherman, with 62,000 men, begins his "March to the Sea."

Dec. 15-16 — Hood's rebel force of 23,000 is crushed at Nashville by 55,000 Federals, including Negro troops under Gen. George H. Thomas.

Dec. 21 — Sherman reaches Savannah, Ga., leaving behind a path of destruction 300 miles long, all the way from Atlanta.

1865

Jan. 31 — Congress approves the Thirteenth Amendment to the U.S. Constitution, to abolish slavery.

Feb. 3 — A peace conference occurs as Lincoln meets with Confederate Vice President Alexander Stephens at Hampton Roads, Va., but the meeting ends in failure.

March 4 — Lincoln participates in inauguration ceremonies in Washington.

March 25 — The last offensive for Lee's Army of Northern Virginia begins with a doomed attack on the center of Grant's forces at Petersburg.

April 2 — Grant's forces break through Lee's lines at Petersburg. Richmond is evacuated.

April 4 — Lincoln tours Richmond where he enters the Confederate White House.

April 9 — Lee surrenders his Confederate Army to Gen. Ulysses S. Grant at Appomattox Court House in Virginia.

April 10 — Celebrations break out in Washington.

April 14 — The Stars and Stripes is raised with ceremony over Fort Sumter. Lincoln and his wife, Mary, see a play at Ford's Theater. During the play, John Wilkes Booth shoots the president in the head.

April 15 — Lincoln dies in the morning. Vice President Andrew Johnson assumes the presidency.

April 18 — Johnston surrenders to Sherman near Durham in North Carolina.

April 26 — Booth is shot and killed in a tobacco barn in Virginia.

May — Remaining Confederate forces surrender. The nation reunites as the Civil War ends. More than 620,000 Americans died in the war.

May 4 — Lincoln is laid to rest in Oak Ridge Cemetery, outside Springfield, Ill.

Dec. 6 — The Thirteenth Amendment, passed by Congress on Jan. 31, 1865, is ratified. Slavery is abolished.

4

rebel infantry brigades occupy York

These particular gray and blue units — infantry, cavalry and artillery — rank among those overrunning York County in late June and early July, 1863.

Official roster

The Army of Northern Virginia, 2nd Army Corps June-July 1863
Commanding officer: Lt. Gen. Richard S. Ewell *

• • •

Confederate Infantry
Early's Division *(Occupied York County, Pa., June 28-30)*
Commanding officer: Major Gen. Jubal A. Early

Hay's Brigade
Commanding officer: Gen. Harry T. Hays
5th Louisiana
6th Louisiana
7th Louisiana
8th Louisiana
9th Louisiana

Hoke's Brigade
Commanding officer: Col. Isaac E. Avery
Col. A.C. Godwin
6th North Carolina
21st North Carolina
57th North Carolina

Smith's Brigade
Commanding officer: Brig. Gen. William Smith
31st Virginia
49th Virginia
52nd Virginia

Gordon's Brigade
Commanding officer: Brig. Gen. John B. Gordon
13th Georgia
26th Georgia
31st Georgia
38th Georgia
60th Georgia
61st Georgia

Artillery
Commanding officer: Lt. Col. H.P. Jones
Charlottesville (Virginia) Artillery
Courtney (Virginia) Artillery
Louisiana Guard Artillery
Staunton (Virginia) Artillery

• • •

Confederate Cavalry
Stuart's Division *(Fought in Hanover, Pa., June 30. Rode through York County, July 1.)*
Commanding officer: Maj. Gen. J.E.B. Stuart

Hampton's Brigade
Commanding officer: Brig. Gen. Wade Hampton
Col. L.S. Baker
1st North Carolina

1st South Carolina
2nd South Carolina
Cobb's (Georgia) Legion
Jeff. Davis Legion
Phillips (Georgia) Legion

Fitzhugh Lee's Brigade
Commanding officer: Brig. Gen. Fitz Lee
1st Maryland Battalion
1st Virginia
2nd Virginia
3rd Virginia
4th Virginia
5th Virginia

W.H.F. Lee's Brigade
Commanding officer: Col. J.R. Chambliss Jr.
2nd North Carolina
9th Virginia
10th Virginia
13th Virginia

Stuart Horse Artillery
Commanding officer: Maj. R.F. Beckham
Breathed's (Virginia) Battery
Chew's (Virginia) Battery
Griffin's (Maryland) Battery
Hart's (South Carolina) Battery
McGregor's (Virginia) Battery
Moorman's (Virginia) Battery

Jenkins' Brigade *(Detached to Robert E. Rodes Division, 2nd Corps, occupying Cumberland County, Pa. Detachments raided towns in northern York County.)*
Commanding officer: Brig. Gen. A.G. Jenkins
Col. M.J. Ferguson
14th Virginia
16th Virginia
17th Virginia
34th Virginia Battalion
36th Virginia Battalion
Jackson's (Virginia) Battery

*An infantryman could be classified by the following system using a soldier in a company, a unit of up to 100 soldiers, of the 13th Georgia as an example: He would be in the 13th Georgia Regiment, Gordon's Brigade, Early's Division, 2nd Corps, The Army of Northern Virginia, Confederate States of America.

Jubal A. Early, seventh from left, background; John B. Gordon, 11th from left, foreground; and Jeb Stuart, fourth from right, background, led the Confederate invasion of York County. They stand among the top generals who served under Robert E. Lee, foreground, center.

Official roster
The Army of the Potomac
Cavalry, June-July 1863
Commanding officer: Alfred Pleasonton

• • •

2nd Division (*Passed through southern York County, July 1-2.*)
Brig. Gen. David Gregg

First Brigade
Col. John B. McIntosh
1st Maryland (eleven companies)
Purnell (Maryland) Legion, Company
1st Massachusetts
1st New Jersey
1st Pennsylvania
3rd Pennsylvania
3rd Pennsylvania Artillery, Section Battery H

3rd Brigade
Col. J. Irvin Gregg
1st Maine
10th New York
4th Pennsylvania
16th Pennsylvania

3rd Division (*Fought in Hanover, Pa., June 30.*)
Brig. Gen. Judson Kilpatrick

Headquarters Guard
1st Ohio, Company C

1st Brigade
Brig. Gen. Elon J. Farnsworth
Col. Nathaniel P. Richmond
5th New York

18th Pennsylvania
1st Vermont
1st West Virginia

2nd Brigade
Brig. Gen. George A. Custer
1st Michigan
5th Michigan
6th Michigan
7th Michigan

Horse Artillery

1st Brigade
Capt. James M. Robertson
9th Michigan Battery
6th New York Battery
2nd United States, Batteries B and L
2nd United States, Battery M
4th United States, Battery E

2nd Brigade
Capt. John C. Tidball
1st United States, Batteries E and G
1st United States, Battery K
2nd United States, Battery A

• • •

5th Army Corps (*Passed through southwestern York County, July 1-2*)
Commanding officer: Maj. Gen. George Sykes

1st Division
Brig. Gen James Barnes

1st Brigade
Col. William S. Tilton
18th Massachusetts

Medical workers converted Hanover's Pleasant Hill Hotel into a hospital — one of several buildings around Hanover used to treat scores of wounded cavalrymen after the Battle of Hanover. A week after the June 30, 1863, battle, 150 wounded Yankee horsemen remained in makeshift hospitals in the borough. 'The inhabitants had furnished them with bunks, bedding, utensils, and food in sufficient quantity,' a U.S. medical inspector wrote, 'the people in each street furnishing food, delicacies, nurses ... two days at a time.'

22nd Massachusetts
1st Michigan
118th Pennsylvania

2nd Brigade
Col. Jacob B. Sweitzer
9th Massachusetts
32nd Masschusetts
4th Michigan
62nd Pennsylvania

3rd Brigade
Col. Strong Vincent
Col. James C. Rice
20th Maine (Joshua Lawrence Chamberlain)
16th Michigan
44th New York
83rd Pennsylvania

2nd Division
Brig. Gen. Romeyn B. Ayres

1st Brigade
Col. Hannibal Day
3rd United States (six companies)
4th United States (four companies)
6th United States (five companies)
12th United States (eight companies)
14th United States (eight companies)

2nd Brigade
Col. Sidney Burbank
2nd United States (six companies)
7th United States (four companies)
10th United States (three companies)
11th United States (six companies)
17th United States (seven companies)

3rd Brigade
Brig. Gen. Stephen H. Weed
Col. Kenner Garrard
140th New York
146th New York
91st Pennsylvania
155th Pennsylvania

3rd Division
Brig. Gen. Samuel W. Crawford

1st Brigade
Col. William McCandless
1st Pennsylvania Reserves (nine companies)
2nd Pennsylvania Reserves
6th Pennsylvania Reserves
13th Pennsylvania Reserves

3rd Brigade
Col. Joseph W. Fisher
5th Pennsylvania Reserves
9th Pennsylvania Reserves
10th Pennsylvania Reserves
11th Pennsylvania Reserves
12th Pennsylvania Reserves (nine companies)

Artillery Brigade
Capt. Augustus P. Martin
Massachusetts Light, 3rd Battery (C)
1st New York Light, Battery C
1st Ohio Light, Battery L
5th United States, Battery D
5th United States, Battery I

25

major battles of the Civil War

Lewis Miller captures the nation and its capital celebrating the end of the Civil War. On May 23-24, 1865, more then 200,000 Yankees marched in the Grand Review, applauded by thousands of onlookers. Spectators sat on bleachers along Pennsylvania Avenue from the Capitol to the reviewing stand in front of the White House. Gen. George Meade led The Army of the Potomac as it passed the reviewing stand occupied by President Andrew Johnson, Gen. U.S. Grant and other dignitaries.

Bull Run/Manassas (Virginia)
First
July 21, 1861
Confederate rout forces the North to realize the gravity — and prospective length — of the war.

Fort Henry (Tennessee)
Feb. 6, 1862
Union victory spurs Gen. U.S. Grant's campaign in the West.

Fort Donelson (Tennessee)
Feb. 13-16, 1862
Yankees achieve first significant victory.

Shiloh (Tennessee)
April 6-7, 1862

Rebels forced back by Grant.

Fair Oaks (Virginia)
May 31-June 1, 1862
Union Gen. George B. McClellan pushes the Confederates back.

Siege of Seven Days (Virginia)
June 25-July 1, 1862
Union fails to capture Richmond.

Bull Run/Manassas (Virginia)
Second
Aug. 27-30, 1862
Confederate victory enables the rebels to retake most of Virginia.

Antietam/Sharpsburg (Maryland)
Sept. 17, 1862
After more than 25,000 casualties and a Confederate retreat, President Abraham Lincoln delivers the Emancipation Proclamation.

Perryville (Kentucky)
Oct. 8, 1862
Union pushes Confederates out of Kentucky.

Fredericksburg (Virginia)
Dec. 13, 1862
North suffers a devastating defeat, sustaining twice as many losses as the Confederates. York native Gen. William B. Franklin, commander of the Union left, blamed for debacle.

Chancellorsville (Virginia)
May 1-4, 1863
Decisive Confederate victory marred by the death of Gen. Stonewall Jackson.

Gettysburg (Pennsylvania)
July 1-3, 1863
Union victory marks the turning point of the war. This campaign brought rebel troops to York County.

Vicksburg (Mississippi)
May 19-July 4, 1863
While the Union emerges victorious at Gettysburg in the East, Grant wins important Yankee victory in the West.

Chickamauga (Georgia)
Sept. 19-20, 1863
Confederacy scores its last significant victory.

Chattanooga (Tennessee)
Nov. 23-25, 1863
Victorious Union forces gain most of Tennessee.

Stones River (Tennessee)
Dec. 31-Jan. 2, 1863
Union Army prevails after initial setbacks.

Wilderness (Virginia)
May 5-6, 1864
Relentless Union forces drive southward.

Spotsylvania Court House (Virginia)
May 8-19, 1864
Grant pummels the rebels.

Cold Harbor (Virginia)
June 1-3, 1864
Heavy losses earns Grant the nickname "Butcher Grant."

Kennesaw Mountain (Georgia)
June 27, 1864
Gen. John B. Hood replaces Gen. Joseph Johnston despite a solid rebel victory.

Mobile Bay (Alabama)
Aug. 5, 1864
Union victory closes off major Confederate port.

Both armies destroyed bridges to impede movement of the enemy. This drawing from the 87th Pennsylvania's regimental history shows a crossing alternative that fighting units deployed to move around the well-watered Eastern Theater, site of many major battles: Engineers built pontoon bridges — temporary structures made by placing boards across anchored boats. The scene is from the spring of 1864 at the Rapidan River in Virginia.

Franklin (Tennessee)
Nov. 30, 1864
Confederate campaign fails to pull Union Gen. William T. Sherman from his destructive path in Georgia.

Nashville (Tennessee)
Dec. 15-16, 1864
Victory gives Union control of the West.

Petersburg (Virginia)
June 20, 1864-April 2, 1865
Confederate Commander Robert E. Lee forced to stay on the defensive during nine months of trench warfare.

Flight to Appomattox
April 1-April 9, 1865
Confederacy dissolves as rebels flee from Richmond and Petersburg, ending in surrender of Lee's Army of Northern Virginia at Appomattox Courthouse, Va.

3

letters tell

story of

rebel

invasion

These letters original-
ly appeared in a
booklet "Letters of
'63," printed by Stair-
Jordan-Baker Inc., of
Detroit. That publica-
tion included a quote
after its foreword:
"Dreaming dreams of
dawning splendor
when the curse of war
shall cease." That
foreword precedes
the first letter.

Letters of '63

The York Gazette of Tuesday, June
30, 1863, devoted its editorial page to an
account of the coming of the rebels to
York. Under the heading, "The Invasion-
Occupation of York by the Enemy," these
facts were set forth: "On Sunday morning
about 10 o'clock the vanguard of the
enemy approached in three columns, the
center through Main Street...General Early
next arrived with another brigade of his
division, and after an interview with the
Chief Burgess, took possession of the Fair
Grounds and Government Hospital.
Thither the forces were stationed with
their artillery."

Also on the morning of June 30th,
another account, not only of the facts, but
of the thoughts and feelings of the inhabitants of the town was being hurriedly written. Shocked by the experience, yet
breathless with the excitement of it,
Cassandra Morris Small (later Blair) wrote
to her cousin and intimate friend, Lissie
Latimer, of Wilmington, Delaware, relat-
ing with unusual vividness the events that
had transpired during those days.

Some sixty-five years later these three
letters in an old faded envelope were
found in the Latimer attic by another
Cassandra Morris Small (Franklin). In a
small wooden box they had lain unseen
and untouched through the years, yet time
had not dimmed their imagery, nor faded
their freshness.

• • •

Tuesday Morning
June 30, 1863

Oh my dear Lissie:

How shall I begin to write you and
what shall I say! We hope soon to have
communication again with some of our
friends, so I write this to have it ready to
go by the first mail, knowing how anxious
you must all feel to know the true state of
the case — but how far short of the reality
any description of mine will fall. Can it be
true that our quiet town has been in possession of the Rebels, and that for the last
two days we have all been prisoners of
war! Oh, Lissie, you can't form any idea
of our situation, but thanks be to our
Heavenly Father, they have all left us this
morning. When to return — who can tell,
for the impression is that General P........is
coming to meet them and there will be a
bloody battle somewhere near. In case they
are defeated, all will come rushing back
pell-mell on us. Oh, how fearful we are
still, but I will begin at the beginning and
tell you all — as I can.

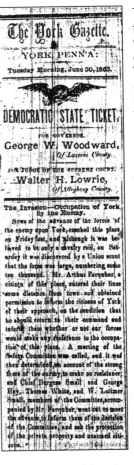

This is part of
the account of
the Confederate
occupation of
York that
appeared in
David Small's
The York
Gazette, the
first story to be
published on
Jubal Early's
visit to York. The
account tells
how and why
the town's
fathers, includ-
ing Chief
Burgess David
Small, surren-
dered York.
Researchers
often have
relied on this
eyewitness
account in their
work on the
Confederate
occupation.

For several days last week, all persons
were expecting fearfully to hear of the
enemy's approach. Saturday the news
came that they were certainly within ten
miles of us with an immense force. One
young man, a Mr. Farquhar (who married
an intimate friend of ours), started off on
his own responsibility without telling anybody — went twenty miles before he met
them — rode into their lines at the risk of
his life, and asked to see the Commanding
General. He was told that that was impossible, but insisted, and presently met an
old college mate who introduced him to
General Gordon and left. The General
demanded his business. Mr. F. said he
came in behalf of the women and children
of York who were dreadfully terrified and
wished to know what his intentions were
— that they might have time to escape.
The General replied that if they were
allowed to come in unresisted, nobody
would be harmed, and all private property
would be respected. When Mr. F. was
asked what force we had, and a number of
other questions, he replied as best he
could, but the General said he knew all
about it, and told Mr. F. a great deal —
how many men we had — by whom commanded — how many troops at Harrisburg
— where many persons lived — their poli-

Cassandra Small, left, penned three letters to her cousin, Lissie Latimer, in the days before, during and after the Confederate invasion of York. She married Dr. Alexander Blair, right, a Lancaster native, who quickly became involved in York affairs before the war and served as a surgeon at the U.S. Army General Hospital at Penn Common.

tics — all about the roads — and then took a little map of York County out of his pocket which had everything on it. Mr. F. then said he wished to return to York; the General said he couldn't, that he must remain with them, but Mr. F. plead with him and then gave his word of honor not to reveal anything, not to tell their numbers, and in case we should decide to make a resistance, promised to return to them and be hung as a spy.

Mr. F. rode back furiously — went first to Major H......(who had command of our little force), but he was a stranger to him. The Major said Mr. F. must go with him to some reliable person, so they came to P.A. and S. Small, who had unbounded confidence in all that Mr. F. said. Their numbers were immense but Mr. F. said he could say nothing more. Then it was decided to withdraw all our little force (about 130 men in all) to the river and have several of our citizens go out to meet the advancing army.

The first we knew of it was at tea time, when we were all sitting quietly at the table. Pappa knew nothing of all this as he was in the country until we sat down, and Lat hadn't come up — Lat and Mary have been staying here as all their servants fled. Suddenly we heard music, ran out, and here was our little force retreating — all whom we knew — some of the "87th" who came home after the late fight, and many of our pass men from the hospital. Oh, how do you think we felt — and they, too, for they were leaving us to the mercy of the Rebels, but of course it was all right.

About 6 o'clock our beautiful flag was raised in the Square; many objected, but others said, "let them come in seeing our colors flying," and Lat helped to raise it. Oh, Lissie, imagine the whole excitement. Then Lat, Mr. Farquhar and two others — one our Chief Burgess — started out with a flag of truce, rode into their lines, and had a long, satisfactory conversation with the General. He told them the same thing he had told Mr. F. — said they didn't intend pursuing the same system of warfare that our soldiers had, though they might retaliate, but they respected private property, and had spared some railroad stations and mills, because by burning them private residences would go too. General Gordon said he knew all about the Smalls, and their mills shouldn't be touched. We can only suppose Ewell and Trimble must have spoken about them. When our citizens wished to leave, the General told them they couldn't, but after some little talk, he allowed them to come back. They got home at 1:30 o'clock, saying an immense army was coming in on Sunday, but said any resistance would be madness and our town laid in ashes. We felt so relieved that all was settled.

Sunday morning Mother, Mary and I, dressed for church; all the rest expected to stay at home. Just as the bells rang, the cry was heard, "They are coming!" Oh, Lissy, what did we feel like? Humiliated! disgraced! Men who don't often weep, wept then. They came with loud music, flags flying. First we saw a picket in front of our door. Where he came from or how he got there, no one knew, he came so suddenly and quietly (other pickets were all along the street). When we spoke to him, he said they were only to keep the men in line.

Then came General Gordon's Division; they halted in the Square and took down our flag, but gave it to the Chief Burgess and didn't put one of their own up. Mr. F. begged them not to. The General said they wouldn't at first, and would see, afterwards. (We didn't have it up at all.) He also persuaded them to make our hospital buildings a camping place (they were so near residences they couldn't be burnt). They actually took them. (We thought they would tear the buildings down, but we don't know yet what they did, for it is raining so hard no one is out.) Then they came up the street; General Gordon stopped his horse at our door, came up to the pavement and said, "Ladies, I have a word to say. I suppose you think me a pretty rough looking man, but when I am shaved and dressed, my wife considers me a very good looking fellow. I want to say to you we have not come among you to pursue the same warfare your men did in our country. You need not have any fear of us, whilst we are in your midst.

The families of Philip and Samuel Small lived on the corners of East Market and North Duke streets in York. Samuel Small's house, above, was later demolished. Right, P.A. Small's house later became the Lafayette Club.

You are just as safe as though we were a thousand miles away. That is all I have to say." He bowed and turning his horse rode away.

They continued to pass until dinner time, and after dinner came another Division. Between 25,000 and 30,000 men were in and around our town. George Latimer was with General Gordon's Division; happily we didn't see him, as we should not have spoken to him. Some of his Copperhead friends shook hands with him, and he begged them not to tell us, but they couldn't keep it to themselves. We all respect him a great deal more than we do them. There will now be a dividing line drawn here. Some ladies received them with waving handkerchiefs and red streamers, and some stopped them and got their buttons — they will never be recognized again. Such order and strict discipline as they were under; they all passed perfectly quiet — no noise at all — though they were not insulted or fired upon from the windows and had no flags waved in their faces, as our poor fellows had wherever they went.

General Gordon's Division passed right through to Wrightsville. General Early took possession of our Court House; General Smith ("Extra Billie") with the Louisiana Tigers was a little out of town. No liquor was allowed them; guards were stationed at every drinking house and bar. Almost at once they handed in their requisitions. (They told the gentlemen who went out to meet them that if they were not given what they demanded it would be taken.) The requisitions were filled with the exception of the money, which they saw was an impossibility, but they were given sufficient to satisfy them.

Some men fled on Saturday, among them Mary's Husband, and his two brothers and father. All thought their property would be destroyed, but our people bought it off. Isn't it disgraceful? They destroyed some property but nothing like what was expected. Our miller, at Codorus, left. His house was ransacked, but the General put a guard around the mill. It is uninjured. A report came once that it was being torn down, but the General told Pappa after sending two orders down, that the men would be executed at once. Fortunately it was a mistake. They said, "Insult or injury offered to a female was punished with death and every man knew it." Of course our people emptied their

mills and opened their stores, but no soldier was allowed to go into the stores without a pass from General Early. They had plenty of confederate money and greenbacks, too — paid sometimes in one and sometimes in another. All stores were opened. Stockings were demanded. Such a looking set! Some were barefoot! Some had soles of shoes strapped on, no two dressed alike. All — officers and men the same. Mary Wilson recognized a number of her Baltimore beaux, but she turned her back upon all.

Yesterday afternoon, to our horror they came back from Wrightsville. The burning of the bridge entirely thwarted their plans. We dreaded the night, and directly after tea closed all of our shutters and bolted the doors. But all was quiet — no disturbance at all; and this morning the first word we heard was when Mother came into our room (we slept down next to her) and said that all had gone. Oh, what a happy people! How thankful we should be that our lives and property are spared. We are so thankful, too, we all stayed at home. Pappa and Uncle S., Lat, and Sam, were absolutely necessary here. Lat has now gone to Wrightsville to see the extent of the damage there. A considerable part of the town is destroyed.

It would take quires of paper to tell all — the state we were in — the terror — the different conversations the Generals had with our people — how our people acted — but you must be tired reading. Oh, how much I could tell! Well, they have gone — I hope never to return. May the Lord preserve us from such distress again. They came to our houses for something to eat; and fed their horses in the stable. I will stop, now, until I can send this off. Perhaps then something else will have transpired.

(After dinner.) Pappa has just told me that he is sending some letters and will forward this one. A great many stragglers and deserters are still here. We hear nothing of the outside world. I hope you can read this. I have written it very hurriedly.

Your attached
Cass

• • •

Wednesday Morning
July 8, 1863

As owners of vast business enterprises, Samuel Small, left, and Philip Small had a say about most of what was done in York. They, thus, attracted extensive criticism about the decision to surrender York to the Confederates as well as praise for preserving the city. The 'I' after Samuel's name differentiates him in this family photo from Philip and Sarah Small's son, also named Samuel. Samuel and Isabel Small had no children. P.A. and Sarah Small named their third son Samuel.

Cassandra Small Morris, sister of Philip and Samuel Small, was also active in philanthropy and community service. She served as an early leader in the Ladies Aid Society and helped found the Children's Home. Her marriage to Charles A. Morris, proprietor of the Morris Drug Co., represented another link between prominent York County families.

I received your letter last evening, just before Tea, my dear Lissie. First I read it to the girls upstairs, and after Tea, again to Mother, Pappa, and Lat, who all pronounced it the most sympathizing one we have received. I will reply at once as you wished me to, and then if you write again on Sunday, it will bring our correspondence into its regular channel again. I felt so badly after I sent my letter off that I had not kept it and looked over it a little, but I had not time to look at even the first line, and couldn't remember one thing I had written, it was done in such a hurry, and before my mind was at all settled. Sally said many times while I was at it, "How can you collect your thoughts sufficiently to write a letter?" It seemed to me I had better try while everything was so fresh in my memory, though every act of the atrocious villains is indelibly impressed.

But Lissie, I made some mistakes. I thought they gave our flag to the Chief Burgess, but they did not. And as they were leaving the town on Tuesday morning, going through the main street, they tore it into strips, then others took the strips and tore them into little pieces, all singing, "We'll Plant Our Colors on a Northern Hill." A good many houses were ransacked all through the country, cleared of horses and mules, cattle, etc. Our beautiful hospital! I would be ashamed to tell you all they did there, and to think, Lissie, there are some who call themselves ladies, who went out to see them there, and entertained them, but they are sorry already, I guess — no one will visit them any more, they must form a party among themselves — a distinct line is drawn. The Rebels, themselves, spoke of them to some of our townsmen and said had they dared they would have put bullets through the hearts of those persons who welcomed and waved to them — that "friends in an enemy's country are worse than traitors." They said they held them in supreme contempt.

You may imagine our horror on the Monday afternoon when looking out of the window, we saw Sam riding along on a Rebel's horse, between two soldiers on horseback at the head of a wagon train. Well! We could only try to be patient until it was explained. He had been sent to show them the way to our mills to take out the flour. Before very long all the wagons returned loaded. Oh, my! oh, my! Who would think we could have lived through it. Mother doesn't think she could again. Only think how Sam talked to them! — he said he was a black Republican, the strongest kind of a Union man, and in favor of a most vigorous prosecution of the war, and that he hoped our army would fight until every man of them was either taken or had laid down his arms. They looked at him with surprise, said they were astonished to hear him speak so plain, that they honored him for it, that they despised these friendly traitors.

Only think, Lissie, it is the Copperheads that have suffered all through the country. In many cases Union men living beside them were untouched, and now, these poor ignorant people come into town in crowds to some smart people here, bringing their tickets of the Knights of the

William Latimer Small, brother of Cassandra Small, was involved in the family business and a leader in the community. He was among the contingent that approached Gen. John B. Gordon before the Confederates entered town to negotiate terms of the surrender.

These photos from a Small family album are believed to show Isabel Cassat Small, left, and Sarah Latimer Small, both born into distinguished York families who married into the Small family. Sarah Small and her husband, Philip, had 10 children, including Cassandra Morris Small. Three of her sons, George, William Latimer and Samuel became prominent in the York business community. Isabel Small married Samuel Small. Like her husband, she was deeply involved in community affairs, helping to organize the Ladies Aid Society and the Children's Home of York during the Civil War.

Golden Circle and saying: "Here, we want our dollar back, we showed the ticket, and made the signs, but it did no good. They struck it out of our hands, and said we don't care for that now, and made us give whatever they wanted." In many cases, when they were told that the horses had been sent away, they made them pay as much as the horses were valued at.

No, Lissie, we shouldn't think it the least disgrace, if our town had been surrendered; but it was not; no surrender was asked for; it was taken possession of without anything; the only thing that took the Committee of Safety out was on behalf of the women and children — so as to give us all time to fly, and the only question of business was, "How do you come?" The Rebels' reply was, "Peacefully if unresisted, but if resisted, your town shall be laid in ashes." Oh, how well it was that we had such thoughtful men — what a panic we would have been in! The first we would have known of their approach would have been shells in our midst. We found they had already planted a number of cannon on our hills, pointed and ready if they were retarded. It makes us shiver to think of it now! We might have been situated as the Carlisle people were, and only think — Fitz Hugh Lee was at a small town (the same time the Rebels were here) — about six miles from

us — and told them that their whole force was coming here to York, and they were going to bring desolation to Pennsylvania! People outside and inside of our town — may talk as they please about what was done — it was right, and it is only those who ran off, and others who don't know, that talk so. All the Rebels say it was their intention to have the battle here, and then we would have been in the situation of Gettysburg.

They were so filthy looking! Only think! Our market house, where some slept, was literally alive. A man had to be largely paid to clean it; had to turn the hose all over it. Oh, you can form no idea of their appearance.

You ask about Aunt Lissie. Henry Harris came over last Wednesday evening; he and another young man. They were the first over the road. They came in hand cars whenever they could; then they would have to leave the car and walk until they could get another one. He said his mother was not in the least frightened, that there was not the faintest probability of their getting Harrisburg, for the city had 40,000 effective men. Lissie, I blame the authorities, too, for not sending a force to protect Pennsylvania; but Pappa looks upon it in an entirely different light — says it was one of the plans to catch them, that we have been trying for two years to subdue that army and couldn't do it — no prospect of it until this plan. He says, "What are a few counties in Pennsylvania to all the other expenditures?" He thinks it right, and I begin to agree with him; for what a glorious defeat we gave them, and we do believe they will all be caught.

Lat has been twice to the battlefield — while they were fighting on Thursday and Friday; his descriptions were awful! He drew the whole plan of the battle and explained it fully. He returned on Friday evening and went back again Saturday with five of our ladies as nurses, and an immense wagon filled with provisions for the wounded. Since then hundreds of wagons have gone with all sorts of things, as the Gettysburg people are nearly starving. Lat said many poor fellows were dying from want of something to eat. Lat and his party returned at midnight Sunday; said it was no place for ladies then. But yesterday the ladies went again; said they could prepare niceties for the wounded. They took a large supply of things, including shirts and drawers. Sam came home yesterday. He gave, too, an awful description of the unburied, and half buried, and the awful smell! I hope we can go after a while.

Only think, this is the first day for nearly two weeks that we have heard the whistle of an engine! When the engine came in we began to feel as though we belonged to the rest of the world again. Oh, Lissie, if you only knew how we felt last week one day, when we heard a cry that 130 of our men — paroled prisoners, were coming, and that all persons should send provisions for them to the market house. Before you could scarcely speak it was loaded with things, and up went our beautiful flag; out of windows and doors it was thrown, and one shout went up. We were out of the hands of the enemy then! It was the first certainty we had had of it. Oh, what a happy people!

Since then we have had constant excitement — cavalry passing, farmers returning, people in crowds going to the battlefield. Our hospital has been cleaned as well as possible; some of our men have returned, but we are to have 1,110 wounded as soon as they can be brought. Lat is all the time at work sending up provisions, etc.

Well, dear Lissie, I believe I have told you all. We have certainly been mercifully spared, and we pray earnestly that we may never have such trouble again. Be sure to write me the beginning of the week.

Your attached,
Cass

We would rather give the rascals twice over what we did than have them back! Oh, I could fill sheet after sheet with all their audacious villainies. It is a matter never to be forgotten.

• • •

July 20, 1863

I do have to laugh at you, my dear Lissie. Your great anxiety to hear all about the Rebel invasion. Think I have told you all the principal things. Now we hear all sorts of little incidents and funny experiences. Aunt Bella said the other evening, she thought it a pity someone shouldn't make an account of all of these funny things, that they would make an interesting book. We can begin to laugh now at it all; a week ago it was certainly too serious.

Only think, Lissie, some of the country people are so ignorant that they say, "Well, the Smalls made the war, and now they can pay for it." And they believe it, too! Another one came to Uncle S. on Saturday and said, "Well, Sam, all the people around us say you and Philip saved the town so they are going to raise a monument to you as high as the Lutheran steeple." Then it is currently reported that we entertained many of the officers, and that Uncle S. had General Early and others there. Such dreadful stories! We wouldn't look at them even, let alone invite them in. I couldn't begin to tell you all, but I don't think you need wish that you had been here. Oh, it was too humiliating — almost more than human nature could bear, to see such a ragged horde marching up our street and know that they were our enemies — panting to revenge themselves. I don't think I told you that the first ones to appear — an immense number with shovels, spades, pickaxes, hoes and all sorts of tools — carried them like guns.

One lady told us she thought that she would see first officers on prancing horses with handsome uniforms, but when she saw these frightful creatures, she raised her hands and exclaimed: "Oh, my Heavenly Father, protect us; they are coming to dig our graves."

It is as plain as daylight that an Almighty Power saved us and that our Safety Committee was the instrument in his hands. Why didn't we suffer as they did at Carlisle? They attempted to act just as we did, but their town was shelled, which was the first that they knew of the Rebels' approach. Women and children had to fly from the town. Alex Cathcart and Sue had to leave their home, and got shelter with a number of others under a tree. Soon the shells came so near them that they had to go farther to another tree where they stayed all night and until 10 the next day.

Now we know why we were spared; they told themselves they expected to make this their headquarters. The battle was to be here and that was the reason they guarded our warehouses and mills so well. They inquired whether there was anything in them and when told, "Full of Grain and Flour," they said at once, "A guard shall be placed there." They intended it for their own use, but they hurried off too unexpectedly. Were they to return again, nothing would be spared, so we would all leave.

Colonel Ewell, in the West, is Mary Mc.'s brother-in-law, and General Ewell, who was at Carlisle, is the Colonel's brother. Mary was at home when General Early called to see Mrs. Ewell. He had done so at the Colonel's request, or rather at his daughter's request. A very short visit! Mary Mc. ran out for fear she would have to speak to him, and after he left washed the chair he sat on with soap and water.

Pappa says that we didn't lose much — the flour will be paid for. One of his horses was taken; all the rest were sent away. Our ponies, too, are safe. The wounded are coming in now and several hundred are here, but Doctor Palmer (the Surgeon in charge) is ready for a thousand. They were very anxious to fill our hospital with Rebels, but Doctor P. positively refused to have them, saying he would resign.

On Saturday evening, a carload of wounded were detained at our depot all night, a bridge was down again, and they could not go on — but they were more comfortable than at Gettysburg. They had five surgeons with them and drew their rations from our hospital. Three of them died and were buried here. Oh, but I did pity them! I went out to our hospital last week, the first time since those wretches were in it. It seemed to me I had never seen it look sweeter or cleaner, but it did require labor and toil. So much damage was done. The pictures which hung all around the room were all destroyed, and they haven't all been replaced yet. I talked with a number who had made their way down from Gettysburg. I guess we all will be as busy as possible again. There is to be a meeting at the Ladies' Room this morning to arrange matters once more.

Members of his family surround Philip Small in a visit to Niagara Falls in this post-Civil War photo.

We haven't been to the battlefield yet. Everybody who has been, says it is no place for ladies. Several who went up (strong, hearty women) have been sick in bed since their return. We think it is caused by the terrible smell! Only to think of seeing a head sticking out of the ground, feet, arms, etc. Many, many such scenes our boys tell us of.

You asked about Aunt Cassy. She was terrified beyond all. Didn't take her clothes off at night for more than a week; sat up in a large chair; couldn't sleep at all; looked miserably, and never smiled.

Our next neighbor has proved himself a Secessionist! We all liked him and his family so much before. We couldn't believe it — but then he proved himself one. He entertained the officers all the time. His sister (Mary Campbell's friend) waved her handkerchief to them, until our clergyman rushed to her and stopped her, saying, "If you have no respect for yourself, have some for the people you live among." Now we have nothing to do with them; but only think that after his numerous entertainments, an officer deliberately walked through his office and through the yard to the stable and took his horse. Oh, we have many such persons, but nobody speaks to them.

Don't I wish I could sit down and talk to you. How many things I could tell. This was the day Mary George expected to come up, but we don't expect her now as everybody who leaves Baltimore must take the oath of allegiance, which we know she wouldn't do. And we would rather she wouldn't come for fear she would feel slighted by the people. Many would not call — (we think) — though real Southerners are more bearable than these traitors. Lat and Mary went down this morning to Baltimore; both will have to take the oath when leaving and have a pass. Anybody — the strongest Union person, must, too.

Annie Weiser is miserable — thinks all the excitement injured her very much. If the bridge is up she will start today for New York and the Catskills for a while.

I had to laugh at the way you talked about my letter — it was such an awful looking document, but at such a time all was excusable, I know. Your letters come by Columbia. We have a regular mail by carriage that way.

My love to all at your house and in the country, and write just such a long letter again, to your attached
Cass

5

counties in state bear brunt of invasion

York County by the numbers

York's founding date: 1741

County separated from Lancaster County: 1749

Rank among state's oldest counties: 5th

Rank west of the Susquehanna: 1st

Mason and Dixon surveyed Pennsylvania-Maryland boundary line: 1763-1767

Dates of Continental Congress' American Revolution visit: 1777 (Sept. 30) - 1778 (June 27)

Approximate county size before 1800: More than 1,400 square miles

Adams County, with Gettysburg as county seat, separated from York County: 1800

Approximate size of York County after 1800: About 905 square miles

Eastern boundary along Susquehanna River: 48 miles

Southern boundary, Mason-Dixon Line: 40 miles

Latitude, Mason-Dixon Line: 39 degrees 44 minutes

Longitude, Susquehanna River: 76 degrees 15 minutes west

Lowest county elevation: 109 feet (Susquehanna River near Peach Bottom)

York's elevation (above sea level): 392.975 feet

Highest county elevation: 1,384 feet (Stone Head, near Dillsburg)

Average July temperature: 75

Average January temperature: 30.4 degrees

Average annual rainfall: 42 inches

1790 ranking in state, slaves: 2nd

1790 ranking in state, freedmen: 2nd

Reported date last slave died: 1841

Northern Central Railway reached York: 1838

Telegraph reached York: 1847

First bridge at Wrightsville: 1814

Number of subsequent bridges crossing river at Wrightsville: 5

Incorporation of York as a borough: 1787

Incorporation of York as a city: 1887

Estimated number of Union soldiers from county: 6,200

Approximate percentage of men between 18 and 45 years in age to serve Civil War: 50

Thousands of Americans die in major wars

War	Numbers engaged	Battle deaths	Other deaths	Total deaths	Non-mortal wounds
Revolutionary War	Not available	4,435	Not available	Not available	6,188
War of 1812	286,730	2,260	Not available	Not available	4,505
Mexican War	78,718	1,733	Not available	Not available	4,152
Civil War	3,867,500	184,594	373,458	558,052	412,175
Union	2,803,300	110,070	249,458	359,528	275,175
Confederate	1,064,200	74,524	124,000	198,524	137,000
Spanish-American War	306,760	385	2,061	2,446	1,662
World War I	4,734,991	53,402	63,114	116,516	204,002
World War II	16,112,566	291,557	113,842	405,399	670,846
Korean War	5,720,000	33,652	3,262	36,914	103,284
War in Southeast Asia	8,744,000	47,366	10,801	58,167	153,303

Note: Numbers should be considered estimates

Confederates invade Pennsylvania: June – July 1863

*Primary counties touched by invasion.

York County presidential voting patterns

County winners, all in Democratic lineage, in bold

1812 - **Madison**/Clinton
1816 - **Monroe**/King
1824 - **Jackson**/Adams
1828 - **Jackson**/Adams
1832 - **Jackson**/Wirt
1836 - **Van Buren**/Harrison
1840 - **Van Buren**/Harrison
1844 - **Polk**/Clay
1848 - **Cass**/Taylor
1852 - **Pierce**/Scott
1856 - **Buchanan**/Fillmore
1860 - **Reading Ticket-Douglas-Bell**/Lincoln
1864 - **McClellan**/Lincoln
1868 - **Seymour**/Grant
1872 - **Greeley**/Grant
1876 - **Tilden**/Hayes
1880 - **Hancock**/Garfield
1884 - **Cleveland**/Blaine
1888 - **Cleveland**/Harrison
1892 - **Cleveland**/Harrison
1896 - **Bryan**/McKinley
1900 - **Bryan**/McKinley
1904 - **Parker**/Roosevelt
1908 - **Bryan**/Taft
1912 - **Wilson**/Taft-Roosevelt
1916 - **Wilson**/Hughes

York County's population

The county's census in 1860 stood at 68,200, comparable to the combined population of York, Springettsbury, Spring Garden and Manchester townships in 2000. York's population totaled 8,600 in 1860, slightly lower than the combined census of Red Lion and Dallastown boroughs in 2000.

York County head count

Year	City	County
1750	York Town: About 100	County: 6,000
1777	York Town: About 1,700	
1783	York Town: 1,779	County: 27,000
1790	York: 2,076	County: 37,747
1800	York: 2,503	County: 25,643
1850	York: 6,963	County: 57,450
1860	York: 8, 605	County: 68,200
1870	York: 11,003	County: 76,134
1880	York: 13,979	County: 87,841
1890	York: 20,793	County: 99,489
1900	York: 33,708	County: 116,413
1910	York: 44,750	County: 136,405
1920	York: 47,512	County: 144,521
1930	York: 55,254	County: 167,135
1940	York: 56,712	County: 178,022
1950	York: 59,704	County: 202,737
2000	York: 40,862	County: 381,751

5 days in York County

Saturday, June 27 / Confederate troops invade York County

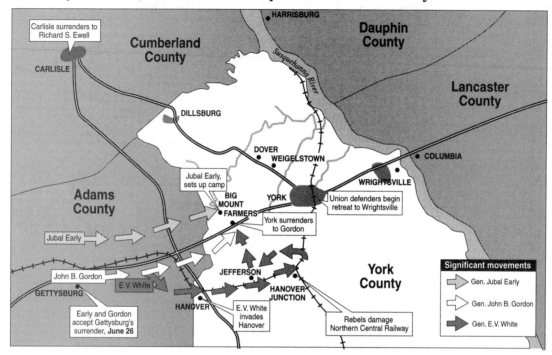

Sunday, June 28 / Confederates enter York

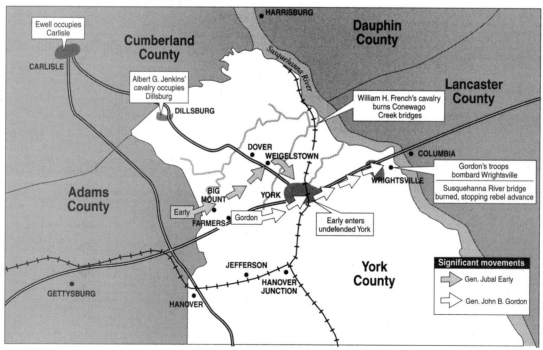

Monday, June 29 / Robert E. Lee orders rebels to concentrate for pending battle

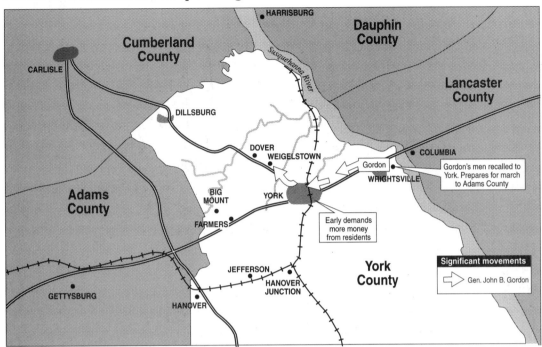

Tuesday, June 30-Wednesday, July 1 / Early's division heads west; Blue and gray clash at Hanover

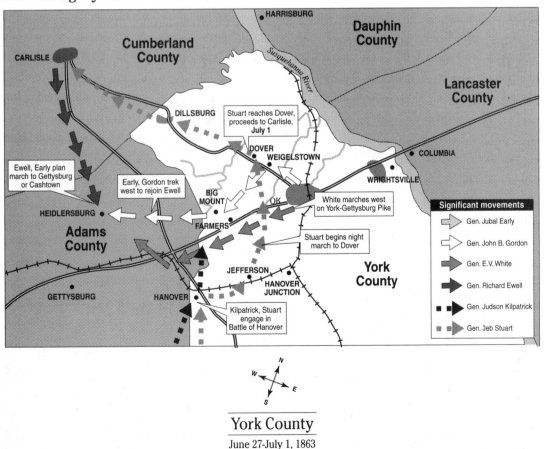

York County
June 27-July 1, 1863

Works
consulted

Writers of history must ride on the shoulders of others who have provided scholarship in specific areas. The work is indebted to the following writers, whose material was used directly or indirectly. Many of these works are available at the York County Heritage Trust's Historical Society Library.

York County in the Civil War

Anthony, William, ed. "Anthony's History of the Battle of Hanover." Hanover, Pa.: Anthony Printing Company, 1945.

Coddington, Edwin B. "The Gettysburg Campaign: A Study in Command." New York: Charles Scribner's Sons, 1968. Official rosters on Pages 166-168 were adapted from this work.

Early, Jubal A. "Autobiographical Sketch and Narrative of the War Between the States." Philadelphia: J.B. Lippincott Company, 1912. Available online through University of North Carolina at Chapel Hill Libraries, docsouth.unc.edu/early/menu.html

Farquhar, Arthur B. in collaboration with Samuel Crowther. "An Autobiography of A. B. Farquhar." Garden City, N.Y.: Doubleday, Page and Company, 1922.

Gordon, John B. "Reminiscences of the Civil War." New York: Charles Scribner's Sons, 1903. Online through University of North Carolina at Chapel Hill Libraries, docsouth.unc.edu/gordon/gordon.html

Haller, Granville O. "The Dismissal of Major Granville O. Haller of the Regular Army of the United States." Paterson, N.J.: Daily Guardian Press, 1863.

"Lewis Miller, Sketches and Chronicles." York, Pa.: The Historical Society of York County, 1966.

McClure, James. "No Small Matter: Politics and a Small-Town Editor." Master's thesis. Penn State University, 1994.

Nye, Wilbur Sturtevant. "Here Come the Rebels." Baton Rouge, La.: Louisiana State University Press, 1965.
— Nye, W. S. and John G. Redman. "Farthest East, Wrightsville, Pa." No publisher, 1963.

Prowell, George R. "Prelude to Gettysburg, Encounter at Hanover." Hanover, Pa.: Hanover Chamber of Commerce, 1962.

As the war years passed, the York Ladies Aid Society grew concerned about the children who had lost fathers in the war. In February 1865, the state Legislature approved the Children's Home of York. Two years later, the home moved from temporary quarters to this building on East Philadelphia Street in York. It was demolished in 1973.

Robison, Gerald Austin Jr. "Confederate Operations in York County." Master's thesis. Millersville State College, 1964.

Rudisill, James Jefferson. "The Days of our Abraham." York, Pa.: The York Printing Company, 1936.

Rummel, George A. III. "Cavalry on the Roads to Gettysburg, Kilpatrick at Hanover and Hunterstown." Shippensburg, Pa.: White Mane Books, 1999.

Schaefer, Thomas L. "A matter never to be forgotten," York Sunday News, June 5-July 17, 1988.

Small, Cassandra M. "Letters of '63." Detroit: Stair-Jordan-Baker Inc., undated.

Snell, Mark A. "From First to Last, The Life of Major General William B. Franklin." New York: Fordham University Press, 2002.
—"A Northern County Goes to War: Recruiting, the Draft, and Social Response in York County, Pa., 1861-1865." Master's thesis, Rutgers University, 1987.

Other York County history

"A History of Dover Township, York County, Pennsylvania, 1740s-1990s." Dover, Pa.: Dover Township Board of Supervisors, 1994.

"Borough of New Salem, Pennsylvania, 1876-1976." York, Pa.:

Mehl Ad-Associates, 1976.

Crist, Robert Grant. "Confederate Invasion of the West Shore — 1863." Lemoyne, Pa.: Lemoyne Trust Company, 1963.

Denig, John. "The York Gazetteer and Business Directory for 1856." York, Pa.: The Eagle Press, 1856.

Drawbaugh, Charles C., ed. "A History of Dover Township, York County Pennsylvania, 1740s-1990s." Dover, Pa.: Dover Township Board of Supervisors, 1994.

Frey, Edward S. "A Little Booklet Depicting the 100 Years of Life in St. Paul's English Evangelical Lutheran Church." York, Pa.: Dispatch Printers, 1936.

Garrett, Elizabeth S., ed. "Greater Dover Bicentennial Celebration, 1764-1964." Dover, Pa.: No publisher, 1964.

Gibson, John. "History of York County." Chicago: F.A. Battey Pub. Co., 1886.

Glatfelter, Charles. "The Story of Jefferson Codorus, Pennsylvania." Codorus, Pa.: Jefferson Community Centennial, Inc., 1966.

"Gopsill's Directory of Lancaster, Harrisburg, Lebanon and York." Jersey City, N.J.: John H. Lyon, pub., 1863.

Grove, June R. and Richard K. Konkel. "A History of Chanceford Township, York County, Pennsylvania, 1747-1997." Brogue, Pa.: Brogue Community Lions Club, 1997.

Hershner, Ronald L. "Crossroads, A History and Reminiscences." York, Pa.: Ronald L. Hershner, 1999.

Jezierski, John V. "Enterprising Images, The Goodridge Brothers, African American Photographers, 1847-1922." Detroit: Wayne State University Press, 2000.

Lehman, Donald I., general chairman. "Wrightsville, 1736-1976, Gateway to the West." Wrightsville, Pa.: Historic Wrightsville, 1976.

Lloyd, June Burk. "Faith and Family, Pennsylvania German Heritage in York County Area Fraktur." York, Pa.: York County Heritage Trust, 2001.

McClure, James. "Almost Forgotten, A Glimpse at Black History in York County, Pa." York, Pa.: York Daily Record, 2002.
— "Never to be Forgotten," York, Pa.: York Daily Record, 1999.
— 200th Anniversary Edition, York Daily Record, November 1996.

Mellander, G.A. and Carl E. Hatch. "York County's Presidential Elections." York, Pa.: Strine Publishing, undated. Election numbers on Page 179 were adapted from this work.

In the middle of a summer night in 1887, residents used mule power to pull down market sheds in York's Centre Square. The post-Civil War industrial growth caused congestion in the heart of York, and the sheds had become controversial. No legal challenge could be mounted that time of day to stop demolition. The pole that bore the American flag that greeted Confederates upon their entry to York 24 years earlier continued to stand tall.

Mouat, Malcolm Palmer. "Dr. Henry Palmer, 'The Fighting Surgeon, 1827-1895." Detroit: Harlo, undated.

Prowell, George R. "History of York County, Pa.," Chicago: J. H. Beers and Co., 1907.
— "History of the 87th Regiment, Pennsylvania Volunteers." York, Pa.: York Daily, 1903.

Rentzel, Bradley. "A History of Mount Wolf." Mount Wolf, Pa.: Mount Wolf Borough Council, 1978.

Sheets, Georg R. "To the Setting of the Sun: The Story of York." U.S.A.: Windsor Publications, 1981.
— "Children of the Circuit Riders, The Story of Asbury United Methodist Church." York, Pa.: Asbury United Methodist Church, 1985.
— "Made in York, A Survey of the Agricultural & Industrial Heritage of York County, Pennsylvania." York, Pa.: Agricultural & Industrial Museum of York County, 1991. York County census figures on Page 179 were adapted from this work.

Smallwood, Wm. Lee. "York's 250th Celebration, 1741-1991, African-Americans of Note." No publisher, 1991.

Smith, Malcolm O. "Annals of Hanover." Hanover Herald, July 6, 1872-May 24, 1873.

Centre Hall, William C. Goodridge's building, continues to rank among York's tallest buildings in this stereograph scene of York's Centre Square sometime before 1900. Goodridge is believed to have hidden slaves, moving along the Underground Railroad, in this building and at his East Philadelphia Street residence. Goodridge's building, sitting on a prime downtown location, was later razed.

Spangler, Edward W. "My Little War Experience." York, Pa.: York Daily Publishing Company, 1904.

Strong, Michael J. "Keystone Confederate, The Life and Times of General Johnson Kelly Duncan, CSA." York, Pa.: Historical Society of York County, 1994.

Trustees of York County Academy and Historical Society of York County. "A History of The York County Academy." York, Pa.: York County Academy, 1953.

General Civil War history

Bates, Samuel P. "History of Pa. Volunteers, 1861-65." Harrisburg, Pa.: B. Singerly State Printer, 1870.

Blockson, Charles L. "The Underground Railroad in Pennsylvania." Jacksonville, N.C.: Flame International, 1981.

Burgess, Milton V. "David Gregg, Pennsylvania Cavalryman." State College, Pa.: Nittany Valley Offset, 1984.

Davis, Burke. "Jeb Stuart, The Last Cavalier." Short Hills, N.J.: Burford Books, 1957.

Daughtry, Mary Brady. "Gray Cavalier, The Life and Wars of General W.H.F. 'Rooney' Lee." Cambridge, Mass.: Da Capa Press, 2002.

Eckert, Ralph Lowell. "John Brown Gordon, Soldier, Southerner, American." Baton Rouge, La.: Louisiana State University Press, 1989.

Egle, William H. "History of Pennsylvania." Harrisburg, Pa.: DeWitt C. Goodrich & Co., 1876.

Freeman, Douglas Southall. "Lee's Lieutenants: A Study in Command." New York: Charles Scribner's Sons, 1943.

Gottfried, Bradley M. "Brigades of Gettysburg, The Union and Confederate Brigades at the Battle of Gettysburg." Cambridge, Mass.: Da Capo Press, 2002.

Hatch, Thom. "Clashes of Cavalry, The Civil War Careers of George Armstrong Custer and Jeb Stuart." Mechanicsburg, Pa.: Stackpole Books, 2001.

Heidler, David S. and Jeanne T. Heidler, eds. "Encyclopedia of the American Civil War, A Political, Social and Military History." New York: W.W. Norton and Company, 2000.

Hoch, Bradley R. "The Lincoln Trail in Pennsylvania, a History and Guide." University Park, Pa.: Pennsylvania State University Press, 2001.

Jones, Terry L. "Lee's Tigers, The Louisiana Infantry in the Army of Northern Virginia." Baton Rouge, La.: Louisiana State University Press, 1987.

Longacre, Edward G. "Lee's Cavalrymen, A History of the Mounted Force of the Army of Northern Virginia." Mechanicsburg, Pa.: Stackpole Books, 2002.
— "Lee's Cavalrymen, A History of the Mounted Force of the Army of the Potomac." Mechanicsburg, Pa.: Stackpole Books, 2000.
— "Custer and His Wolverines, The Michigan Brigade, 1861-1865." Conshohocken, Pa.: Combined Publishing, 1997.

Martin, Samuel J. "Kill-Cavalry, The Life of Union General Hugh Judson Kilpatrick." Mechanicsburg, Pa.: Stackpole Books, 2000.

"Massachusetts Soldiers, Sailors, and Marines in the

Civil War," Vol. IV. Norwood, Mass.: Norwood Press, 1932.

McCarthy, Carlton. "Detailed Minutiae of Soldier Life in the Army of Northern Virginia, 1861-1865." Lincoln, Neb.: University of Nebraska Press, 1993.

McPherson, James M. "Drawn With The Sword." New York: Oxford University Press, 1996.

Moore, Frank, ed. "The Rebellion Record: A Diary of American Events, with Documents, Narratives, Illustrative Incidents, Poetry, Etc." New York: D. Van Nostrand, 1865.

Nesbitt, Mark. "Saber and Scapegoat, J.E.B. Stuart and the Gettysburg Controversy." Mechanicsburg, Pa.: Stackpole Books, 2002.

Osborne, Charles C. "Jubal, The Life and Times of General Jubal A. Early, CSA, Defender of the Lost Cause." Baton Rouge, La.: Louisiana State University Press, 1992.

Patterson, Gerard. "Debris of Battle, The Wounded of Gettysburg." Mechanicsburg, Pa.: Stackpole Books, 2003.

Pullen, John J. "The Twentieth Maine, A Volunteer Regiment in the Civil War." Philadelphia: J.P. Lippincott Company, 1957.

Stiles, Robert. "Four Years Under Marse Robert." New York: The Neale Publishling Company, 1903.

Still, William. "Underground Railroad Records." Hartford, Conn.: Betts & Company, 1886.

Tankersley, Allen B. "John B. Gordon." Atlanta: The White Hall Press, 1955.

"The War of the Rebellion: A Compilation of the Official Records of the Union and Confederate Armies." (Washington: 1880-1901), 73 volumes in 128 parts. Available on searchable CD-ROM from Guild Press of Indiana Inc., Carmel, Ind. The CD also contains: "A Compendium of the War of the Rebellion," Frederick H. Dyer; "Regimental Losses in the American Civil War (1861-1865), William F. Fox; "A User's Guide to the Official Records of the American Civil War," Alan and Barbara Aimone; "Military Operations of the Union and Confederate Armies."

Thomason, John W. Jr. "Jeb Stuart." New York: Charles Scribner's Sons, 1929-1930.

Wallace, Willard M. "Soul of the Lion, a Biography of General Joshua L. Chamberlain." New York: Thomas Nelson & Sons, 1960.

Newspapers

Hanover Evening Sun
The Baltimore Sun
The Gazette and Daily, 1918-1970
The Philadelphia Inquirer

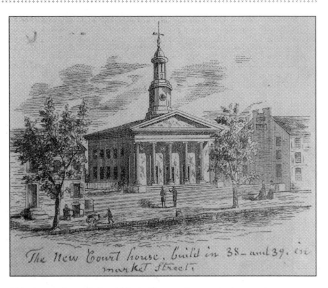

Workers demolished York County's second courthouse, where Jubal Early held court, in 1898 to make way for a new courthouse. The six columns that marked the entrance to this courthouse were salvaged and reinstalled as part of the new courthouse's facade.

The Philadelphia Times
The True Democrat, 1864-1876
The York Dispatch, 1876-
The York Gazette, 1796-1918
The York Republican
York County Star and Wrightsville Advertiser
York Daily Record, 1970-
York Democratic Press

Publications, pamphlets

Billet, Glenn E. "The Department of the Susquehanna." Journal of the Lancaster County Historical Society. Volume 66, 1962.

Ent, Uzal. "Rebels in Pennsylvania." "Civil War Times Illustrated," August 1998.

Epperson, James F. "Lee's Slave-Makers." "Civil War Times Illustrated," August 2002.

Haller, Theodore N. "Life and Public Services of Colonel Granville O. Haller, Soldier, Citizen, Pioneer." "The Washington Historian." Washington State Historical Society: Vol. 1, No. 3, April 1900.

"Maryland Historical Magazine," The Museum and Library of Maryland History, The Maryland Historical Society, Spring 1981.

Swisher, James K. "Unrecontructed Rebel, Jubal Early." "Military History," February 2001.

"The Billmeyer House in York, Pennsylvania." No publisher, undated.

This scene appears to show the gazebo still standing in 1866 near demolished buildings that made up the U.S. Army General Hospital in York. Physicians and nurses treated more than 14,000 wounded Civil War soldiers in the three years the hospital operated. About 200 patients died, and many of the dead are buried in Soldier's Circle, Prospect Hill Cemetery, North York, where a memorial commemorates their names.

Van Baman, M. L. "Confederate Invasion of York Just Fifty Years Ago Today." York Gazette, June 28, 1913.

Vosburg, Brent L., "Cavalry Clash at Hanover." "America's Civil War," January 1998.

Wilkinson, Norma B. Historic Pennsylvania Leaflets. "Thaddeus Stevens: Champion of Freedom." Harrisburg, Pa.: Pennsylvania Historical and Museum Commission, 1957.

Unpublished works

Bair, Robert C. "Address at Dedication of Tablet at Dover, November 23, 1907." File 737, York County Heritage Trust, York, Pa.

Carter, Leroy, Jr. "The Bartons: Black Civil War Soldiers." Prepared for Family Reunion, 1996.

Gotwalt, Charles E. "Adventures of a Private in the Civil War." No date.

James Latimer Papers. File 12801, York County Heritage Trust, York, Pa.

Ketterman, Marie Webb. "U.S. Army General Hospital, York." Manuscript, File 904, York County Heritage Trust.

LaFleur, Harold A. Jr. "Amos Rupert in the Civil War," 1989.

George Miller papers. File 12629, York County Heritage Trust, York, Pa.

Miscellaneous Civil War Papers. File 737, York County Heritage Trust, York, Pa.

Myers, Ephraim E. "A True Story of a Civil War Veteran." 1910.

Rohrbaugh, Carroll G., Jr. "Operation Underground in York County." History 21 paper, Gettysburg College, 1953.

Russell, David. "A History of the First Baptist Church of York, Pa. (1850-1969)."

Wilcox, Charles Douglas. "John Stoner Beidler." Transcription of diary, 1996.

World Wide Web

"American Battlefield Protection Program," www2.cr.nps.gov/abpp.

"A Nation Divided, The U.S. Civil War, 1861-1865," www.historyplace.com. This chronology and descriptions in World Book, Inc., 1991, were adapted for Pages 162-165 and 169-170.

"Camp William Penn," www.usct.org/CampWilliamPenn.

"Medicine in the Civil War," University of Toledo Libraries, www.utoledo.edu.

"Statistical Summary, America's Major Wars," U.S. Civil War Center, www.cwc.lsu.edu. Casualty numbers on Page 178 adapted from this work.

"William D. Lyon Papers, 1863," Pearce Civil War Collection, Navarro College, Corsicana, Texas, www.nav.cc.tx.us.

Index

The Big Mount house where Confederate Gen. Jubal Early stayed on the night before the Confederates entered York stands today at the intersection of Canal and Big Mount roads in Paradise Township. Early wrote that a widow, Mrs. Zinn, and her daughter played host during his overnight visit.

The night before he entered York, Confederate Gen. John B. Gordon stayed at Jacob Altland's house at Farmers along the York-Gettyburg Pike. Here, he met the delegation from York and accepted the town's surrender. The house, still standing today in Jackson Township, is shown as it looked in 1963, the 100th anniversary of the occupation of York and the Battle of Gettysburg.

I

J

K

Wrightsville Mayor James Magee's house served as headquarters for Gen. John B. Gordon during the rebel occupation of the borough. The mayor's daughter, Mary Jane Rewalt, played host to Gordon and some of his staff at breakfast on Monday, June 29, 1863. The house, shown in this undated photo, remains standing today.

L

M

In 1905, the state of Pennsylvania erected The Picket in the middle of Hanover's Center Square, where fighting occurred in the Battle of Hanover. The battle monument — a bronze mounted cavalryman placed on a pedestal of granite — later was moved to a corner of the square.

N

O

P

The statue of Victory, standing atop the 65-foot-tall Soldiers and Sailors Monument, was erected in York's Penn Park in the late 1800s. Noted York architects J.A. and Rhinehart Dempwolf designed the monument, made of Vermont marble.

JAMES McCLURE

James McClure is managing editor of the York Daily Record. He earned a master's degree in American studies from Penn State Harrisburg. He has taught local history at Penn State York and journalism at Penn State Harrisburg. He is past president of the Pennsylvania Associated Press Managing Editors and the Pennsylvania Society of Newspaper Editors. His previous historical publications include three books: "Never to be Forgotten, A year-by-year look at York County's past" "Nine Months in York Town, America's revolutionaries labor on Pennsylvania's frontier" and "Almost Forgotten, A glimpse at black history in York County, Pa." He served as general editor of the three-volume "250th Chronicles," published during York County's bisesquicentennial in 1999.

Editors

KIM STRONG
Kim Strong, Daily Record editorial page editor and writing coach, served as the primary content editor of this work. She earned a bachelor of arts degree from Penn State University and later served as adviser to the Daily Collegian at Penn State. She is a frequent presenter at regional and national newspaper writing workshops.

DEBORAH L. HUMMEL
Deborah L. Hummel, Daily Record copy editor, edited this work. She earned a bachelor of arts degree in English from Millersville University, a master's of education degree in reading and the language arts from the same university, and holds elementary education and reading specialist certifications.

Designers

TED SICKLER
Ted Sickler, photo/graphics editor for the Daily Record, coordinated photographs and served as principal designer

for this work. He is a doctoral candidate in American history at the University of Delaware. He earned a master's degree in American studies from Penn State Harrisburg and serves as an adjunct instructor in American studies at Lebanon Valley College.

JOANNE ALTHOFF
Joanne Althoff, Daily Record photo technician, prepared photographs and designed pages. She earned a bachelor of fine arts degree from Virginia Commonwealth University.

TRACEY BISHER CULLEN
Tracey Bisher Cullen, Daily Record graphic artist, designed the cover and other pages. She earned a bachelor of fine arts degree from Kutztown University.

SAMANTHA K. HARROLD
Samantha Harrold, Daily Record graphic artist, designed the maps and other pages. She earned an associate's degree in graphic design at the Pennsylvania School of Art and Design.

Artist Henry Barratt drew a flag flapping in York's Centre Square during America's centennial in 1876 — the same scene that greeted rebel soldiers marching into York on June 30, 1863. Residents cleared the market sheds from York's square 11 years after the centennial, and the flagpole was removed sometime thereafter. Gone were the days, a newspaper wrote, that the York area could 'still devote its very commercial centre to a retail trade in squalling hens, slobbering calves and squealing pigs.' Post-Civil War industrial growth was beginning to win the day against the agricultural base that had dominated York County since its founding in 1749.

The 87th Pennsylvania fords the Potomac River in the summer of 1864. A year earlier — on June 24, 1863 — Jubal Early's rebel division confidently waded across the wide river on its way to Pennsylvania. After about two days in York and bitter fighting on Cemetery Hill in the Battle of Gettysburg, Early's battered men re-crossed to the safety of the river's south bank in mid-July. Thus ended that summer's invasion of the North and York County. Cassandra Small called the event, 'It is a matter never to be forgotten.'